EARLY MODERN EUROPEAN SOCIETY

Early Modern European Society surveys the sweeping changes affecting Europe from the end of the fifteenth century to the early decades of the eighteenth century. More than simply a factual survey, this book conveys an imaginative understanding of the salient characteristics of society throughout pre-industrial Europe, from Italy and Spain to Poland and Russia.

Drawing on the great success of his earlier works, *The Iron Century* and *European Society 1500–1700*, and the large amount of recent and important research opening up new areas of historical debate, Henry Kamen includes discussion of:

- European identities, frontiers and language
- leisure, work and migration
- population change
- religion, ritual and witchcraft
- the aristocracy, the bourgeoisie and the poor
- gender roles
- social discipline and absolutism

Early Modern European Society is the only comprehensive study of early modern European society, and remains essential reading for all those interested in this fascinating period.

Henry Kamen is Professor of the Higher Council for Scientific Research, Barcelona, Spain. His many books include *Philip of Spain* (Yale, 1997) and *The Spanish Inquisition: An Historical Revision* (Weidenfeld & Nicolson/Yale, 1998).

EARLY MODERN EUROPEAN SOCIETY

Henry Kamen

LONDON AND NEW YORK

First published 2000
by Routledge
2 Park Square, Milton Park, Abingdon, Oxon OX14 4RN

Simultaneously published in the USA and Canada
by Routledge
270 Madison Avenue, New York, NY 10016

Reprinted 2006 (twice), 2007 (three times)

Routledge is an imprint of the Taylor & Francis Group, an informa business

Typeset in Baskerville by Taylor & Francis Books Ltd
Printed and bound in Great Britain by MPG Books Ltd, Bodmin

British Library Cataloguing in Publication Data
A catalogue record for this book is available from the British Library

Library of Congress Cataloging in Publication Data
Kamen, Henry Arthur Francis.
Early modern European society/Henry Kamen.
Includes bibliographical references and index.
1. Europe–Social conditions–16th century. 2. Europe–Social conditions–
17th century. 3. Europe–Social conditions–18th century.
I. Title HN373.K293 1999
306'.094–dc21   99-37008
CIP

ISBN 10: 0–415–15864–8 (hbk)
ISBN 10: 0–415–15865–6 (pbk)
ISBN 13: 978–0–415–15864–0 (hbk)
ISBN 13: 978–0–415–15865–7 (pbk)

CONTENTS

PREFACE

The central theme of this book is the study of changes within European society over a period of well over two centuries, from the end of the fifteenth to the early decades of the eighteenth century. There was of course no such thing as an autonomous 'European society'; my survey considers, rather, some common features observed from a range of different contexts within the European area, and offers signposts to understanding how some linkages functioned in traditional society. Two main perspectives are considered: basic social structures of Europe over the period, and aspects of change in social attitudes. At the same time two simple themes have been pursued, within a broad political context: the significance of broad community-based norms, and the development of social discipline at all levels. The substantial differences between northwest, south and eastern Europe are respected, but integrated into a general view. The coverage, inevitably, is both selective and simplified, but what this book offers is a broad-based perspective of one of the most formative epochs of European history.

An early and very different version of the study, centred mainly on economic history, was published in 1971 as *The Iron Century*. Its success led, just over ten years later, to the issue of a revised version under the title *European Society*. In the quarter-century since the book first appeared, an enormous amount of first-rate research has opened up perspectives in all branches of historical scholarship. To assimilate this new work adequately would have called for an entirely different type of volume. Though I have preserved the general approach of the previous study, it should be emphasised that this is a completely revised and substantially new book, in which economic history has been restricted to a secondary role. Some endnotes have been given in order to indicate controversial or recent sources of information; but the very large amount of references in the text has made it impractical to include notes for all sources or quotations.

No single volume like this can do justice to the many stimulating perspectives of early modern civilisation, or to the many excellent books that have been produced recently by scholars of many countries. Nor has it been possible from my outpost in the Mediterranean to gain access to all the studies that I would have wished to consult. For what appears here, I express my lifelong debt to teachers, colleagues and students in all the places where I have been privileged to learn and to teach, not least the Oxford of my early academic career and the Paris of my research years.

H. K., Barcelona, 1999

1

IDENTITIES AND HORIZONS

'My dear Raphael, do not attempt to be brief, but explain in order the fields, rivers, cities, people, customs, institutions, laws and everything you think we should know.'

'There is nothing I would rather do,' he said, 'however it will require some time.'

'Let us dine first and then afterwards we can arrange a time.'

(Thomas More, *Utopia*, Book I, 1516)

Europe: an insecure identity

The fall of Constantinople to the Turks in 1453 focussed the attention of western states on the menace of Islam, creating for the first time a consciousness of their common interest against the enemy. The humanist Aeneas Sylvius Piccolomini, writing the year after its fall, appealed to the west to rally to the concept of 'Europe', which he identified with the Christian cause and whose leadership he assigned to the states of 'Germania'. Subsequent writers tended to agree that the continent of Europe included all those countries that had been Catholic in faith and Latin in culture. Exceptionally, the French humanist Montaigne included 'Muscovy' in the continent, since the Russians also were a line of defence against Islam. But in the *Cosmographia* (1588) of Sebastian Münster, Muscovy and the Balkan states were portrayed as the mere skirt-trails of a queenly Europe whose heart was in central Europe and whose crowned head was in Spain.

'Europe' remained a nebulous idea, seldom encountered even in print. Though delineated carefully in the pioneering maps of Münster, it formed no part of the mental baggage of westerners. During the Renaissance, propagandists identified the idea either with the religious extension of papal Christendom or with the temporal power of the Holy Roman Emperor. Those, like the humanist Valla, who rejected both these identifications, preferred to believe in a Europe unified rather by the uplifting value of a common Latin culture. The attempt to define the continent became increasingly difficult at its edges. Most westerners were unhappy about admitting non-Catholic Slav culture. And what was one to make of multi-cultural Spain? Valla accepted that the Muslims of Spain might be termed Europeans, but a Bohemian traveller to the peninsula in the 1460s, Leo von Rozmital, could not disguise his unease at the mixture of Jewish and Islamic culture he encountered.[1]

The discovery of the New World in 1492 initiated another phase in the process of the definition of Europe. America became a mirror to the Old World, the 'other' against which Europeans could contrast themselves. Because they were made aware of the clear differences of inhabitants of other continents, and in the process became more aware of their own attributes, capacities and culture, Europeans were slowly initiated into a consciousness of their special identity. 'Europe' as a cosmographic entity took on shape in maps and travel accounts, even while its inhabitants remained in general unaware that any such development was taking place. Contact with other civilisations, notably with the highly developed ones in Asia, gave further solidity to the perception of Europe viewed on a global scale.

Dimensions of European space

By the early sixteenth century the traders, adventurers and explorers of the Atlantic seaboard had immeasurably extended the horizons of Europeans. The brief and fragmentary medieval contacts between Europe and Asia were replaced in the Renaissance epoch by direct and profitable exchanges between the traders of Europe and the Asian monarchies. 'What on earth have you come seeking so far away in India?', Vasco da Gama was asked in Malabar. 'Christians and spices', was his prompt reply. Spices, particularly pepper and ginger, became the chief source of wealth of the Portuguese crown, which in the first half of the sixteenth century pioneered the European discovery of the East Indian territories and China and Japan. The Portuguese Magellan, who had spent seven years in the Indies, eventually passed over into the service of Spain and helped to give the latter a definitive role in the struggle for overseas possessions. Between them these two small nations, some nine million in population, opened up the globe.

The riches harvested by Portugal – between 1500 and 1520 some 10,500 tonnes of spices from the east, some 410 kilograms of gold a year from west Africa – stimulated rivalry. The Portuguese exercised strict control over information about their trade, but the Spaniards were never so secretive and allowed the free exchange of ideas, for otherwise, as the historian Antonio de Herrera argued, 'the reputation of Spain would fall rapidly, for foreign and enemy nations would say that small credence could be placed in the word of her rulers since their subjects were not allowed to speak freely'. After mid-century the great collections of travel literature, notably the Venetian Ramusio's *Delle Navigazioni* (1550) and Hakluyt's *Principall Navigations* (1589), began to dispel old myths about the overseas territories and presented the literate public with realities far removed from the tales of bisexual monsters and dog-headed men with which their fathers had been regaled.

Trade and exploration were the first stage, largely limited to the early century, of Europe's discovery of the outside world. In that early period the sense of wonder was still paramount: many realised with a shock that Asia and America frequently outdid any marvels that Europe might offer. Antonio Pigafetta, who sailed with Magellan in 1519 on the first European circumnavigation of the globe, claimed to have heard that the Emperor of China was 'the greatest in all the world'. Cortés, writing to his own emperor after entering Tenochtitlan in 1521, claimed of Moctezuma's palaces that 'there is not their like in all Spain'. The great temple, he said, was one 'whose size and magnificence no human tongue could describe', and the city itself he called 'the most beautiful thing in the world'. Recalling in his old age the splendours of Mexico, Bernal Díaz said that even the market-place was such that 'some of our soldiers who had been in many parts of the world, in Constantinople, in Rome, and all over Italy, said that they had never seen a market so well laid out, so large, so orderly, and so full of people'.

In the course of the century this awareness of Europe's modest part in world civilisation was superseded by a more aggressive attitude. Confident in his own superiority, the European moved forward into the colonial epoch. Gama's epic voyage of 1497–8 initiated the process.[2] The aggressiveness was in part fed by the conviction that Christianity must be taken to the heathen. The most remarkable achievements in this respect were of men like St Francis Xavier (d. 1552), whose global vision took him to Goa, Malabar, Malacca, Japan and the Chinese coast; and of Fray Toribio de Motolinía, who in 1524 landed in Mexico with eleven other Franciscans to begin the first large-scale conversion ever undertaken by Christians outside Europe. In part, however, the attitude sprang from an assumption of inherent racial superiority. 'How can we doubt', wrote the Spanish humanist Sepúlveda in 1547, 'that these people – so uncivilised, so barbaric, contaminated with so many impieties and obscenities – have been justly conquered by a nation so humane and excelling in every virtue?' This may be compared with the words of Jan Pieterz Coen, seventeenth-century creator of the Dutch East Indies. 'May not a man in Europe', he asked a critic of his policies, 'do what he likes with his cattle? Even so does the master here do with his men, for these with all that belongs to them are as much the property of the master as are brute beasts in the Netherlands.' European perception of the outside world was thus rooted in a supreme confidence. 'All has now been traversed and all is known', proclaimed the historian López de Gómara in 1552. And in tune with this confidence came the growing urge to dominate, as stated firmly in 1590 by the Jesuit José de Acosta when, applauding the possession by Spain of America, he affirmed that this was entirely 'in accord with the desire of Providence that certain kingdoms rule others'.

Not the least amazing feature of the expansion of Europe was the conquest of distance. A look at the distances covered by the ships trading to Asia round the Cape, the voyages made by the English settlers to north America, the territory traversed by Francis Xavier or Pizarro, might lead to the suspicion that technological progress had made it possible. Yet, for all the improvements in nautical science, time was barely attacked, and the endurance of man alone was a decisive factor in the conquest of distance. From the mid-sixteenth century European travellers undertook a determined advance to all points of the compass. Some seventy accounts survive of travels to Russia during the period 1550–99, where there were only a dozen for the first half of the century.

Water, horse or coach were the three means of transport, and their efficiency varied.[3] Over long distances the sea was beyond all doubt the quickest method of communication, but over smaller overland areas the horse was faster and more reliable, making it the obvious basis for the nascent postal services of Europe. Governments took a special interest in improving the quality of the postal service, which remained very expensive and therefore used less by private individuals than by the state and by merchants. In any case, there was no significant increase in speed during the early modern period. Uncertainty of conditions meant that in the sixteenth century the post from Antwerp to Amsterdam normally took from three to nine days, and to Gdańsk from twenty-four to thirty-five days. An English regulation of 1637 specified that mail was to travel in summer at seven miles an hour and in winter at six. A generation later, in 1666, the average speed of letters was not more than four miles an hour. Compare this with the New World, where the Inca postal system attained speeds unequalled until the invention of the internal combustion engine. The distance from Lima to Cuzco by mail-runner took three days, whereas a post-horse in the seventeenth century doing the same distance took twelve. So efficient was the delivery that the Inca used to have fresh fish run up from the coast, a distance of some 350 miles, in two days.

Outside Europe the vastness of distance required measurement in terms of endurance rather than time. The heroes were those like Columbus, who informed Queen Isabella in 1503 that 'the world is small: I mean that it is not as large as people say it is'. Few would have agreed. The expedition of Magellan and Sebastian del Cano, which set out from Seville with five ships in 1519 and returned in 1522 with only one vessel containing eighteen men, after having sailed round the world, was proof of the high cost of any attempt to make the globe smaller. When Francis Drake made the same voyage fifty-five years later the difficulties were still prohibitive: he had five ships when he set sail from Plymouth in 1577 and only one when he returned in 1580. The long absence is deceptive, for in most voyages far longer periods were spent in harbour than at sea. The ships of the American passage, the *carrera de Indias*, took on average seventy-five days to cross from Seville to Vera Cruz and 130 days to cross back. The entire journey, including long waits in Vera Cruz and Havana, might mean that a ship leaving Seville in July one year did not normally return before October of the subsequent year. The fortitude of the explorers was acclaimed by the historian Cieza de León, who asked what other race but the Spaniards could have penetrated 'through such rugged lands, such dense forests, such great mountains and deserts, and over such broad rivers?'. We can reply that the

Russians in Siberia, the Puritans in New England, the Dutch and Portuguese in Africa and Asia, and the French in Canada, were each in their own way, and often with methods that few would approve, bringing the outside world closer to Europe and thereby conquering the great gulf imposed by time and space.

The government of a world empire was made peculiarly difficult for Philip II by the inability to communicate speedily with his administrators. 'I have not heard anything from the king about the affairs of the Netherlands since 20 November last', complained the governor of that region, Requeséns, from Antwerp on 24 February 1575. Businessmen no less than politicians had an investment in overcoming distance and time. In any case it was less the delay in letters than the unpredictability of their arrival that came to be the biggest problem.[4] Of thirty-two letters received by Philip from his ambassador in Paris in 1578, the fastest took only seven days and the slowest forty-nine. Any delay in the payment of bills of exchange, the arrival of the galleons, the shipment of perishable cargo, might spell ruin. Yet when all the evidence for the urgent demands of these men of the world is considered, there can be little doubt that they were only a minority group. Time was not yet a universal pacemaker, and the age appears to move at a casual pace regulated only by the movements of the sun, the cycle of the seasons, and an occasional clock.

Identities and frontiers

The notion of 'Europe' remained little more than a perceived ideal. Erasmus in the 1520s centred upon Christendom (he seldom used the word 'Europe') his yearnings for a united, peaceful and cultured civilisation without frontiers. Though proud to be Dutch, he asserted that 'I want to be a citizen of the world, not just of one town'. Yearning for a universal polity was also the dream over a century later of Tommaso Campanella. As men of culture, these and others looked beyond the conflict of governments and faiths, to a system where there were no frontiers.

In the real world, however, there were frontiers, to which map-makers tended to give a visible reality but which were difficult to define. In administrative terms, a frontier was not territorial but described rather the limits of a jurisdiction (noble, ecclesiastical, urban). Even then, the overlapping of different types of jurisdiction made it impossible to arrive at geographic precision in peace treaties, and frontiers did not necessarily mean that there were any firm differences of politics and culture between independent political units. The simplest frontiers (and always the most desired, for commercial reasons) were represented by water. The division of land was frequently determined by the division of waters: nations tried to define their frontiers according to the seas and rivers that fed them. Communities fought for the right to include streams (precious for both food and irrigation) within their domains. States fighting to establish their identity made every effort to obtain a sea-coast or at least a seaport: seventeenth-century Muscovy successfully ceased to be a landlocked country and obtained an extensive coastline, whereas a poorer region like Aragon failed to break through to the sea, remaining as the only landlocked kingdom in Spain.

The nation, the 'state'

For historians the most fascinating aspect of European evolution has been the emergence of the 'state', at one time identified principally with the concept of a 'nation state' but more concretely studied over recent decades in terms of 'power', that is, in terms of territorial size, population, wealth, military potential and administrative systems. A central feature of western civilisation, the state operated from above and imposed its authority.[5] It did not represent a primary identity for most Europeans, who identified themselves rather with the town or community into which they were born. Thereafter any sense of 'belonging' came into existence through a series of linkages that operated upwards, through allegiance to lords and to institutions. Until the eighteenth century the European landscape was divided up among these various allegiances, which reflected the feudal pattern of authority. Those who ruled, whether lords or kings, were in control of jurisdictions that frequently overlapped, did not coincide with political divisions, and often changed according to the mischance of war or of marriage alliances. The growth of the state has been explained in multiple ways, depending on the perspective adopted.[6] The explanations tend to coincide in pointing to the primary role of war and coercion in bringing about the organised state,[7] a view that confirms traditional thinking (including that of Hobbes) and has the virtue of coinciding with much of the historical evidence. The view also makes it clear that the state was an entity quite alien to the interests and identities of its subjects, and became acceptable only when it took on the guise of being a 'nation'.

If 'nation' signifies an autonomous political entity, then around 1500 there were possibly over 500 nations in Europe, each with its own history, traditional rulers and institutions. By around 1750, however, 'nation' had come to mean something different. The general rule was for large entities to swallow up small ones, reserving the description of nation only for the large unit. The absorption of the principality of Béarn (which claimed to be a 'sovereign entity, separate from any other sovereignty and realm') into the kingdom of France in 1620 illustrated the trend.[8] The king of both territories happened to be the same person, Louis XIII of France, who favoured the merger for administrative convenience. Most modern nations have achieved their condition simply by conquest or the fusion of smaller units. Muscovy absorbed the Ukraine in the seventeenth century in order to further the growth of the Russian state; Castile absorbed the crown of Aragon in the early eighteenth century in order to further the unity of Spain; and England and Scotland, after sharing a common ruler since 1603, fused together in 1706 to form a state with its seat in London.

Though the formation of modern nations appears, at first sight, to have been a process imposed from above, the reality was more complex. Absorption and conquest added to the territories of a 'state', but did not help to create a 'nation'. Throughout Europe, absorbed regions continued to operate for a century or more as autonomous nations, conserving their own administration, laws and language. With time, however, the regional elites began to identify themselves with the interests of the central government and might even participate in it. When that happened, integration into a 'nation' began to take place. Centralisation, in short, repeatedly took place from below rather than from above.[9] When provinces began to identify their interests with that of the central state, and when members of the provincial elite took power at the centre, a broad community of interest came into existence.[10] In the same way, it might happen that the population in frontier areas, where identity was always fuzzy, began to accept a relationship with the centre, thereby allowing some feeling of nationality to take place. On France's southern frontier of Roussillon, acquired definitively from Spain in 1659, the people began by the eighteenth century to identify themselves with France as a reaction against their previous identity as subjects of the Spanish crown.[11]

Nations, in short, created themselves by accepting a series of shared linkages. It is possible that some of the linkages were 'imagined', for they defined perceptions or objectives rather than concrete links. It is certain that the end product, the nation state, was also 'imagined',[12] for much effort would be spent over subsequent generations in trying to endow its existence with some reality. Historically, only the smaller peoples in Europe – such as Bohemia or Catalonia or Wales – had a coherent identity in early modern times. There was no national problem, because strictly speaking there were no nation states and the political reality was one of semi-autonomous regional entities. At the same time, however, there were extensive shared experiences that brought the entities together and gave them the outlines of a 'nation';[13] neither unity of administration nor unity of language were prerequisites for national identity. As the sociologist Van Gennep has observed, a nation can be a complex of collective units that are constantly changing and constantly varying their relationship to each other.[14]

Language

Central to a certain concept of national territory is the idea that its members should share common aspirations, expressed in a common language. The problem was that few political states in early modern Europe had their own language. Since most states were composite entities, they possessed many languages rather than one alone.[15] In Spain in 1600 one quarter of the population did not use Spanish as its daily tongue. In an area with several distinctive dialects, such as Germany, the linguae francae used by the elite in practice were Latin for scholars and (often) French for the princely court. In Hungary, a state of many cultures and languages, the standard speech used in the Diet was Latin, which remained the official administrative tongue until 1844.[16] This made communication easier but prejudiced the growth of a native literary culture.

Language furnished an identity only within smaller nations, and even then might suffer serious disabilities. There was some doubt in the sixteenth century about what constituted standard spoken English. Thomas Wilson in his *Art of Rhetorique* (1553) distinguished between 'learned Englishe and rude Englishe...courte talke and countrey speache'.[17] If the local spoken language were not also privileged by the support of the local elite and the mechanisms of state, it might end up by being categorised as a mere 'dialect'; worse, books would not be published in it and it would end up as a medium of speech but not of literature.

For reasons of administration and communication, the evolving state began to favour use of a 'common tongue'. When England and Wales were united by law in 1536, only the English tongue was sanctioned for official use. The French crown in 1539 made a similar rule, that only northern French (known as *langue d'oeil*) be used in its law courts. The Spanish Inquisition from around 1560 conducted all its proceedings in Castilian, even in areas (such as Catalonia) where few spoke the language. Absorption of smaller territories supplied a strong motive for using the language of the bigger unit. 'It hath ever been the use of the conqueror', the poet Edmund Spenser commented in the sixteenth century, with reference to the English occupation of Ireland, 'to despise the language of the conquered and to force him by all means to learn his'.

The diversity of tongues ensured the persistence of two major trends in Europe down to the nineteenth century. On the one hand, multiplicity of tongues preserved multiple cultural identities, without in any way impeding the growth of broader perspectives. Within the same frontiers people might continue to speak different languages without thereby losing their sense of belonging to a shared society. The best example of this is the Netherlands, which encompassed several tongues and dialects, but managed all the same to cultivate a sense of national feeling, thanks in good measure to the struggle for independence from Spain. In the same way the inhabitants of the Grey Leagues in Switzerland were conscious of a common political destiny, despite the use of three quite distinct tongues in the area.

On the other hand, the trend towards an imposition of a 'common tongue' was irreversible, and had significant consequences. France under Louis XIV and Spain under Philip V began a policy of administrative change in the provinces that involved obligatory use of the official language in public affairs. The changes, pursued by all states with a concern to improve government, took over a century to mature. For the most part, they were poorly applied. State intervention, undertaken with the aim of facilitating the paperwork of the state (and of the Church), implied an emphasis on the written word. One consequence was the marginalisation of oral culture. A parish priest in Bohemia or Catalonia in the 1720s might preach to his flock in Czech or Catalan, but then have to carry out his correspondence with the authorities in German or in Spanish respectively. In Russia the government of Peter the Great took steps to reform the Russian language, but made little practical use of it other than to print government decrees, which made up 90 per cent of printed matter (the other printed language was unreformed Church Slavonic).[18] In such cases Czech or Catalan or Russian failed to develop adequately, with negative consequences for creative literature. Though the first Russian grammar appeared in 1696 (published in Oxford by a Dutchman), it was not until the nineteenth century that a sophisticated creative literature developed. In Scotland the union with England from 1603 onwards led to the dominance of the English language in both administration and public worship, with serious effects on the country's literary culture. By the end of the seventeenth century, Scots tended to publish their books in English, and in London.[19]

A common language, then, was the preserve of small nations but took a very long time to get established in large nations. In France a report made in 1794, shortly after the Revolution, affirmed that the majority of people in France did not speak French, which was the main spoken language in only fifteen of the country's eighty-nine departments.[20] The situation a century earlier is reflected in Racine's despairing complaint from the Mediterranean coast that 'I can't understand their French in this country and they can't understand mine'.[21] In eighteenth-century Languedoc, the people spoke French only when they were drunk, or swearing, or speaking to outsiders.[22] The lack of a single national language was a common phenomenon in all territories aspiring to be nation states. In 1861 not more than 3 per cent of the Italian population understood Italian.[23] Throughout the early modern period, Europeans accepted an environment where language tended to divide rather than unite. This was unacceptable to both intellectuals and statesmen, and by the early eighteenth century there were serious moves to make language conform to the realities of political unity. J. C. Gottsched's *Deutsche Sprachkunst* (1748) proposed a solution that became common: to make one dialect, in this case German as spoken in Upper Saxony, serve as the norm for both a written and a spoken tongue.

Basic identities: the rural community

Early modern Europe was a predominantly rural society. In western and central Europe in about 1600, less than 5 per cent of the people lived in some hundred 'cities' of over 20,000 inhabitants each. A further fifth of the population lived in small country towns; all the rest lived in rural communities. The great developments of early modern society – the elements of economic, social and domestic change – occurred less in the great metropolises and seats of government than away in oft-forgotten corners of the European countryside. It was in the local communities that the social life and solidarities of a European were concentrated: 'state' and 'nation' were abstracts with which they seldom came into contact.

The units of organisation in provincial society varied according to region. At the most elementary level, in most of Christian Europe the village community coincided with the parish unit, so that the Church played a leading role in defining the character of the community. In more feudalised areas, the authority of a seigneur might be more decisive, particularly if he controlled most of the land. The community proper, however, was definable not in terms of outside influences such as Church and lord, but solely by the bonds between its members. Some villages, as in England where the peasantry were free and land distribution equitable, gave the appearance of being happy, self-sufficient units, with a full spectrum of social classes. By contrast, over much of eastern and Mediterranean Europe the villages could be depressed one-class communities, unable to survive out of their own resources. Few villages existed as viable independent units: all had to have close links with other nearby settlements for such basic needs as marriage partners and commercial exchange. In a very real sense, then, the village was not a complete community, which could be identified more exactly in the broader cultural area that included the village: within this area people grew the same crops, experienced the same environment of soil and weather, did the same types of labour, dressed similarly and spoke the same language. In England one might think of a village and its district for ten miles around as a community, but in the Pyrenees or in Norway one could apply the term to several villages encompassed within the broad sweep of a mountain valley.

Though the basic unit within each village was the household or family, the importance of kinship as a social bond was not always paramount. In smaller communities, and in areas from which people seldom moved, endogamy might be high and the links of parentage strong. But in those many villages of northern Europe from which there was constant movement, family bonds were weaker and people were held together more by relationships of neighbourliness. Whatever the nature of the bond, the sense of 'belonging', the feeling of 'solidarity', was always intense and profound. Community feeling, of a sort seldom experienced today in our more individualistic world, was indeed perhaps the most powerful social force in early modern Europe.[24] All human activity was judged by norms created by the community: disapproved marriages were mocked by the 'charivari', 'witches' were driven out by hostile neighbours, unfair taxes were resisted with revolt.

The focus of loyalties in the community in turn created intense conflicts. Very small quarrels might lead to the growth of factions, some based on kinship, some on status. It was possible for such low-level conflict to last from generation to generation, particularly in the Mediterranean where the notion of 'honour' (or one's 'reputation' in the community) was always deeply cherished. Others might spill out beyond the local level, as in the Sussex village of Cuckfield in the 1570s, when a quarrel between the vicar and the squire split first the community then the county, and was carried to national level, ending when Sir Francis Walsingham intervened in 1582 to secure the vicar's deprivation.[25] Communities were naturally jealous of each other. In France and Spain the youths of one village would show their resentment at any of their girls being married to a man from another village, by creating a riot, extorting money or even resorting to violence. In times of distress, however, the village could unite remarkably well;

and popular revolt, particularly against the local seigneur, often reinforced local loyalties.

Communities always had an historical origin; if they had not been able to prove their original privileges they would have been ill equipped to defend themselves against outside authorities. Small settlements of medieval origin might retain a document or deed. The Grey Leagues in Switzerland, a fascinating case, evolved among the Alpine valleys during the late fifteenth century through local agreements made in the face of threats from outside.[26] In the German lands the communities became weaker during the sixteenth century and tended to get submerged into princely states. Over much of Europe, however, even where clerical and lay lords dominated, ancient forms of communal government still survived in the sixteenth and seventeenth centuries. A village might be governed by its 'assembly of inhabitants' (France) or its 'general council' (Spain), consisting in theory of all adult inhabitants but in practice of the propertied male heads of households; even these did not all attend, and decisions fell more and more into the hands of an elite. Assemblies could coexist with seigneurial authority: in eastern Europe the lord sanctioned assembly meetings, and in England a jury of villagers might help to dispense seigneurial justice. Meetings were called only for exceptional business, sometimes as infrequently as once a year. In Spain bells were rung and the council met after mass on a Sunday, in a traditional or symbolic location (the Basque national assembly met under the famous tree at Gernika). In Swedish and Savoyard villages the vote at meetings had to be unanimous.

The community and the village assembly played a crucial role in all aspects of economic and social life.[27] The economy was the basic reality on which the community was based. The assembly set times for ploughing, decided what crops should be planted and what cattle should be kept. Exploitation of the soil would sometimes be on a communalist basis: ploughland and pasture were periodically redistributed among households, since they belonged in some areas to the community as a whole and not to each family. A village with communal holdings – such as arable land, pasture, woods, a mill – might be economically strong; though a dominant feature of early modern Europe was the steady alienation of these assets to pay taxes and debts. In France the process of alienation became so great a threat to economic viability that Colbert forbade sales, and ordered intendants to try and recover property alienated since 1620. Law and order was often communally enforced, even when the court was technically within the jurisdiction of a seigneur.[28] In Valencia the community Tribunal of the Waters, composed of village elders, still meets weekly outside the cathedral to deal verbally with disputes between peasants of the region. The community also watched over honour and morality, and by extension intruded into family life: in Russia village elders had a say in the arrangement of marriages.[29] Well into the eighteenth century, in the Black Forest countryside of Württemberg, the community supervised marriages, work, crop-rotation, market arrangements, land transactions and poor relief; and local family and marital conflicts were settled by a Church court presided over by the pastor and community officials.[30]

By the end of the seventeenth century the autonomous village community was decaying through much of Europe. The single most important cause was the polarisation of wealth within the village, creating on one hand a propertied and often tax-exempt elite, and on the other a growing number of landless families. In a group of communities in seventeenth-century Languedoc, over three quarters of the soil was owned by 15 per cent of the residents, among them the local nobles, who effectively held the power in the countryside.[31] Control of the assembly fell into the hands of the minority. At the same time capitalisation of the soil by outside interests (the lord, the city) and the growing demands of the state (for taxes and military service) helped to undermine the fragile economic supports of the community. There may have been, all the same, significant exceptions to this trend. It has been suggested that in Burgundy, for instance, the state gave its support to communal structures because they offered a useful basis for taxation purposes. Communal lands produced good taxable income, so that from about 1683 the government of Louis XIV blocked alienation of communal property in the province.[32] Even in parts of eastern Europe, where changes in the manorial economy threatened peasant autonomy, it appears that the state authorities adapted the structures of the community (as in Prussia)[33] rather than suppressing them. Rural peasant units survived, but with considerable changes.

The intense localism of community feeling survived long after the disappearance of political autonomy, and penetrated upwards into all levels of the state. The loyalty of a man to his hearth was basic: solidarities were with family, kin, lord and village, and throughout the early modern period there was little sign that they had been shaken. Local loyalties preceded those to the distant 'state'. A telling example is the series of traditional peace-agreements (*patzeries*) made in the early sixteenth century by villages on the French and Spanish sides of the Pyrenees, agreeing to keep the peace between themselves and not participate in the wars between their respective countries.[34] From one political level to the next, regional loyalties threatened the emerging centralised state. Throughout the early sixteenth century the self-governing city states of northern Italy remained the political ideal of Europeans, being proposed by many during the Comunidades in Spain in 1520 as the model for government. Even within themselves, the cities broke down into constituent communities, as with the 'communes' in Paris in the revolutionary years 1588 and 1648, and in Bordeaux during the Ormée in 1650. Persistent particularism everywhere – in Spain, in the Netherlands – delayed the formation of national identities. For most people, the village community of one's birth was one's 'country' (*pays*, *país*), not the nation state of which it formed a tiny part. So fluid were loyalties that Marseille in 1591 and again in 1660 proclaimed itself independent of the nation: when Henry IV recaptured the city in 1596 he exclaimed, 'Only now am I king of France!' In the French Pyrenees as late as 1688 the valley of Aspe claimed that it was an independent republic not subject to the laws of France.[35]

The sense of identity of local communities did not of course exclude external realities: most were integrated at some point into the wider world. The link was often provided by the nobility and gentry, who were equally at home in their local countryside and in the capital city, and indeed frequently acted as agents for central government in the provinces, helping to collect taxes and recruit troops. A great many other activities also helped to create linkages, among them the need for inter-regional trade, and also the effects of the constant movement of population. Moreover, for reasons of defence or political common sense, many communities felt it necessary to collaborate with each other. When communes managed to combine their interests, as among the several communes of the Grey Leagues in seventeenth-century Switzerland, they were capable of acting virtually as sovereign states.

Basic identities: the urban community

Town communities were the fundamental political unit of civilised Europe. In the most densely populated areas – northern Italy and the Netherlands – they were the only political presence, superseding the existence of either nation or state. Problems of size may give rise to confusion over what a 'town' was. In many regions the proliferation of very small settlements makes it difficult to distinguish them from 'villages'. In practice, small towns were five times more numerous than all other types of urban community in Europe.[36] Very many of them were strictly part of the rural landscape: they were centres of the agrarian economy, and providers of services to the countryside. Though the majority of the population lived in the rural areas, therefore, their economic activity was closely bound up with local urban centres.

Our perspective here is centred on those towns, both small and large, that had a special identity based on political and civic privileges (in England, for example, the privileges were sometimes created by royal charter). They were often distinguished by possession of walls and roads, special fiscal rights, and an autonomous constitution. The ideal type perhaps was the German free imperial city, but in reality such towns – which developed in the thirteenth century and continued unchanged to the eighteenth – could be found everywhere in the great 'urban belt' that stretched from the Netherlands through western Germany and Switzerland to the cities of northern Italy.[37] Each town or city consisted of communal units that together composed the political community. Historians agree that the urban communities possessed distinctive identities that made their citizens feel both a sense of belonging and a sense of pride. One view is that in the German lands the small entities – with an upper population limit of around 10,000 people – can be seen as 'home towns', where there was strong social cohesion between the governing oligarchy, the guilds and the citizen body.[38] Enjoying continuous internal stability, such towns represented the backbone of the nation and helped to influence the direction of national politics without necessarily participating in the government of the state.

Even in the large and complex urban structure of a 'city', the sense of belonging and of community was fundamental. In Paris, the primary loyalty of the people was to their neighbourhood, their parish and the local community.[39] Neighbourhood values predominated, and local concerns took precedence over more distant ones. The scale of values extended to religion, with each parish fiercely jealous of its own church, saints and traditional customs. Though immigration into large towns was always very substantial, it seems not to have altered the primacy of neighbourhood values among the population. There was, it appears, sufficient continuity of residents in an area to maintain a continuity also of social values. In the London borough of Southwark in the early seventeenth century, nearly half the householders were still in residence over a ten year period,[40] a proportion paralleled in other towns. The population turnover would clearly diminish some aspects of community feeling, but would also guarantee the survival of enough residents to maintain a certain continuity in the neighbourhood. Despite the complexity of a city such as London, residents participated in local concerns of the parish, the guild and the administration, with sufficient dedication to help maintain social stability.[41]

Within towns the fundamental value was 'peace', understood in the sense of the 'common good' that citizens shared with each other, and their common purpose to accept norms that regulated their institutions and kept order.[42] In many towns, citizens had to take an oath to observe the conventions that maintained the peace. On this basis, a town might build up a tradition of loyalty that made its government stable and ensured both survival and the creation of self-interest and identity among citizens. The way these rules functioned can be seen most clearly in the constitution of Italian and German city states. Florence was an outstanding example of a city that evolved an elaborate civic ritual, combining both secular and religious emblems, to affirm the common interest that all citizens had in their *patria*, while the Germans enjoyed a more modest pride in the dignity of their 'home town' or *Vaterland*.

The primacy of the 'home town' or the neighbourhood did not exclude perception of larger identities. Economic links between local markets made the growth of some sort of consumer society inevitable, and improved communications (stagecoach and postal services) brought the provinces into contact with large towns. There was, moreover, a shared culture[43] among all communities, based in some measure on local schools and what was taught in them, on the spread of news, and on the theatre. This allowed territories with a notorious complexity of autonomous towns, such as Germany, the Netherlands and northern Italy, still to feel capable of sharing a broader outlook in times of crisis.

A core identity: the family

In its most traditional sense a family was a kinship group based on lineage. This concept was particularly important among the upper classes, who traced their descent, and assured the survival of their property, from father to son; it was less common among classes that had little property to transmit. A family was also a household, a group of people living together on the basis of marriage. Until recently it was held that the traditional west European household was a multiple or stem family, comprising more than one generation and including servants as well. An influential book by Ariès[44] argued that this multiple household gradually gave way by about the sixteenth century to the emergent nuclear family, consisting only of parents and children. The evolution from multiple to nuclear family was accompanied, it was argued, by a major change in emotional attitudes. Unlike the large household, in which relationships were very impersonal and children received little affection, the nuclear family brought with it what has been called 'sentiment', 'affective individualism', or more simply 'love': the parents esteemed and respected each other and also their children. This conclusion has been successfully refuted by English demographic historians, whose research shows that in pre-industrial England the normal structure of households was the conjugal family: husband, wife and children; with extended or multiple families numerically quite insignificant.

It is currently agreed, then, that 'in the European peasant family day-to-day life was centred round the conjugal pair', and that kinship was nowhere in western Europe the dominant basis for social organisation.[45] The conclusion can be illustrated from northern France: in Brueil-en-Vexin in 1625, 85 per cent of households were nuclear and only 7 per cent extended. In northwest Europe at least there was no measurable transition from one type of family to another; even in medieval times the conjugal family may have been predominant, and the changes in affective sentiment within the family have been frequently exaggerated. The function of the conjugal pair, however, must be placed within context. In practice, husband and wife existed as realities not solely because of a sentiment that bound them together, but because other obligations connected them: family, children, household, work. By contrast, in Europe east of the Elbe, for which our knowledge in this period is extremely fragmentary, the large multiple family (known as the *zadruga* in Serb areas) was more common.

Though core loyalties centred on the household family, kinship continued in some ways to be of crucial importance throughout early modern times.[46] The nature and extent of kinship links varied from society to society, and have provoked firm differences of opinion among historians.[47] But there is agreement on some aspects. The rules of consanguinity, laid down by canon law, prohibited marriage with any relatives within four or more degrees of relationship. In small societies, normal in the Europe of that time, this could make the choice of a partner difficult. Not everyone knew how to calculate the degrees. The problem was made more acute by the general practice of counting even spiritual relationships, such as being godfather at a baptism, as kinship. Kinship was also important because it affected the laws of inheritance of property; in an age when titles to land were often complex and imprecise, it was useful to be able to identify prospective heirs. In addition to these two practical considerations, kinship also continued to be a sort of bond that created cohesion among elite families and linked families together in their provinces. The links were usually fragile, but they contributed to a feeling that the nuclear family was not alone.

Our detailed knowledge of household structure is based on the technique of 'family reconstitution', which involves the arduous collation from parish records of data on baptisms, marriages and burials, to give a full profile of life and death in the community. The demographic data, however, do not by themselves explain the size and evolution of the family. In practice, household size was dependent closely on economic and social conditions. In northern France and in England, where the size of landholdings was small, it was logical that small family units would be required. But in southern France, over a large arc stretching from Béarn and Gascony to Provence, and in other parts of the Mediterranean, farms were larger and family life often tended to concentrate around the large house: here multiple units were more common. In Montplaisant in Périgord in 1644 simple families were 50.8 per cent, multiple or extended families 36.5 per cent of the population. In Altopascio in rural Tuscany in 1684, 58 per cent were simple, 36 per cent were multiple. In Provence, and in Franche Comté, multiple families were between one- and two fifths of the population. Thus the larger estates of southern Europe helped the survival of communal forms of exploitation, and encouraged branches of the same family to live together.[48] But as property division proceeded and as laws of inheritance changed, the multiple tended to be replaced by the nuclear family. It is likely, moreover, that in many parts of Europe (judging by research on eighteenth-century Austria)[49] the very same household could vary between multiple and nuclear characteristics, depending on which members of the family were in residence and which had died. Austria supplies a further example of possible confusions over the size of the household. Records for Innsbruck in 1603 indicate that each household had around four members but each house had around twelve inhabitants, so that in such a case a house was evidently not the same thing as a household.[50]

Marriage was a major step, nowhere more than among the upper classes where it tied up property. Gentry who married beneath their station, contracting *mésalliances* and so putting the family fortune in danger as well as causing inter-family conflicts, prompted the state to take an early interest in the question. In France the king by edict in 1556 banned marriages that did not have the consent of parents, and in 1639 Louis XIII formulated the view that marriage was the cement of the state. These attempts to protect the social order, however, were counterbalanced in two respects. The Church (even after Trent, when the rules were tightened up considerably with the decree *Tametsi* of 1563, forbidding 'clandestine' marriages) recognised all marriages validly agreed between the two contracting parties; and social custom for most people outside the aristocracy allowed a surprising degree of freedom in courtship. In traditional society, courtship and sexual practice were often freer than has been thought (see Chapter 8). The allegedly cold English were not so in 1499 when Erasmus commented delightedly that 'wherever you move, there is nothing but kisses'; while a native said in 1620 that 'for us to salute strangers with a kiss is counted but civility, but with foreign nations immodesty'.

A powerful argument against the theory that love, and the corresponding freedom to choose one's mate, was a late phenomenon identifiable with the evolution of the nuclear family, is that most young people in western Europe did have some freedom of choice. Parental consent would continue to be a fundamental feature of marriage, but even when in the upper classes property considerations were uppermost, 'there was a widespread belief among would-be marriage partners that freedom of choice was their right'.[51] In Spain the consent of parents for those marrying under the age of twenty-five was not made obligatory until 1776. In the seventeenth century in Spain, a young man with legitimate claims on a girl could ask the vicar-general of the diocese to send an official to remove a girl from parental custody in order to wed her. In any case, in Spain, England, France and elsewhere the fact that young men of the lower classes were usually independently employed, had probably left the family home and had possibly lost at least one parent through early mortality, freed them in practice from dependence on parents in the choice of a partner. Many, moreover, had to go out of their own villages in search of a husband or wife, thanks to the high level of consanguinity in some country parishes. These elements of freedom must, of course, be balanced against strong traditional controls exercised by the head of the family, by the local community, and even by the feudal seigneur. At every level, both in the village and in the town, marriage was normally less a private affair based on personal affection, than a considered contract involving other elements in kinship and in the neighbourhood. Love, however, was never wholly absent. 'If you can be contented to marry for love', an understanding sixteenth-century English father told his daughter, 'I am contented and do grant you my good will'.[52]

Once a choice of partner was made, the young couple could proceed to 'betrothal', which in traditional Europe was the same as marriage. Catholic practice, as seen in Renaissance Italy,[53] pre-Reformation Hohenlohe, and post-Reformation Catalonia, was that all the essentials of marriage were completed outside church.[54] The exchange of promises (*verba de futuro*) was viewed as a firm contract, sealed later by the exchange of vows (*verba de presenti*); agreement on the financial conditions confirmed the contract, and copulation completed the marriage. The completely secular aspect of this procedure disturbed religious leaders. The Lutherans made it a firm rule that marriages required a church ceremony, and the Catholics subsequently refused to recognise contracts that did not include a blessing in church before a priest.

At the same time Protestants emphasised (as the Catholic state in France also began to do after 1556) that the consent of parents was essential for marriage. In rural Hohenlohe in Germany, the Lutheran authorities over the period 1550–1680 terminated all marriage agreements that did not have the express permission of the parents involved.[55] The Catholic Church after the Council of Trent (1563), however, reaffirmed the complete liberty of young people to marry if need be without consent, though at the same time emphasising the authority of parents and the obligations of children. In practice, the rules laid down by Church and state varied widely in their application. In England, not until the early eighteenth century was some order put into the rules validating marriage, with Lord Hardwicke's Act of 1753.[56]

In many parts of France, Switzerland and Spain it was accepted that a betrothed couple could, with parental consent, sleep together under the family roof until they were financially ready to marry and set up their own home: the custom helps to explain high prenuptial pregnancy in some villages. The Counter-Reformation Church denounced the practice strenuously, but failed to alter it. In England, where the custom was almost unknown, it was nonetheless often deemed acceptable for a contracted couple to progress to full intercourse.[57] In Spain young couples might live in this condition for years, bringing up their children but still not proceeding to formal marriage. The Calvinist authorities in north Holland were informed in 1598 that 'many persons remain for some months or even years in unlawful households, with their children, and afterwards leave each other in a scandalous manner'.[58]

The informal approach to marriage and sex in many European peasant households arose largely from economic causes: the lack of enough space to afford privacy. Communal beds, in which both family and servants slept, were traditional. A French noble, Noël du Fail, commented in the late sixteenth century:

> Do you not remember those big beds in which everyone slept together without difficulty? All the people, married or unmarried, slept together in a big bed made for the purpose, three fathoms long and nine feet wide, without fear or danger or any unseemly thought or serious consequence; for in those days men did not become aroused at the sight of naked women. However, ever since the world has become badly behaved, each has his own separate bed, and with good reason.[59]

Birth, youth, marriage

Early modern European society was overshadowed by death. Life expectancy at birth was, by our standards, alarmingly low. In the English peerage in 1575–1674 the average male expectation at birth was 32 years, the female 34.8 (in the early twentieth century, by contrast, a male peer could expect to live to 60, a female to 70).[60] In thirteen English parishes in the seventeenth and eighteenth centuries the male life expectancy at birth was 36 years. The lot of the poorer people was inevitably worse. A study covering 3,700 children of all classes born in Paris at the end of the seventeenth century arrives at an overall life expectancy of 23 years. A baby born into the elite of Geneva in the seventeenth century might expect to live 36 years, but the child of a skilled worker there had an expectancy of only 18.3 years.

These figures are statistical abstracts, but are reflected in the real data for infant mortality. In the demographic system of early modern Europe it was a rule that one out of every four or five children born failed to survive the first year of life: in England the average was a fifth of all children, in France a quarter. Survival beyond infancy continued to be extremely hazardous. In the Castilian villages of Simancas, Cabezón and Cigales in the sixteenth century, up to 50 per cent of children died before their seventh year; in the nearby city of Palencia the figure was 68 per cent.[61] In England less than two thirds of all children born survived the age of ten, in northern France barely a half. Almost one child in two in early modern Europe failed to live to the age of ten, and two live births were required to produce one human adult. The example of the Capdebosc family in the Condomois (France) is instructive. Jean Dudrot de Capdebosc married Margaride de Mouille in 1560. They had ten children, of whom five died before their tenth year. Odet, the eldest son, married Marie de la Cromp in 1595: of their eight children five did not reach their tenth year. Jean, the eldest, married twice. Jeanne, his first wife, had two children, one of whom died at nine years, the other at five weeks. Marie, the second wife, had thirteen children in twenty-one years: six of them died in infancy, one was killed in war, two became nuns. Of the thirty-three children born to this prolific family during the century, only six founded a family. The principal reason: infant mortality.[62]

The process of birth did not spare the mother either. The risk of death when giving birth was high; in England it accounted for a maximum of one fifth of all deaths among women aged between twenty-five and thirty-four. Since the risk was seen as normal, it did not provoke comment.

Because life was short, the Europe of around 1600 was predominantly youthful. Children and young people must have been everywhere more in evidence than the aged. Sebastian Franck claimed (1538) that 'the whole of Germany is teeming with children'. In four parishes of Cologne in 1574, 35 per cent of the population were aged under fifteen; in six districts of Jena in 1640 the proportion was about 38 per cent. Leiden in 1622 had around 47 per cent in the same age group. Gregory King in 1695 estimated that over 45 per cent of the people of England and Wales were children. In Table 1.1 below, seventeenth-century data are set beside those of twentieth-century England.

In public life the young played a role that is rare today. Charles V was twenty when he faced the challenge of Luther at the Diet of Worms, Don Juan of Austria was twenty-three when appointed to lead the Mediterranean fleets of Spain. The predominance of youth in the population had important cultural effects that extended into the smallest rural communities (see Chapter 2).

Despite the large numbers of young people they did not, as was once thought, marry young. Scholars are generally agreed on the existence of a 'northwest European' marriage pattern distinguished by a late age of marriage with a small age difference between partners, a high rate of celibacy, and a relatively low birth rate.[63] The pattern is normally viewed as a contrast to that of eastern Europe, where conditions were markedly different, and of the Mediterranean,

Table 1.1 Population age groups expressed as percentages; seventeenth-century Europe and twentieth-century England

Age group	*Venice 1610–20*	*England and Wales 1695 (King)*	*Elbogen circle (Bohemia) late 17th C*	*England and Wales 1958*
0–9	*18.5*	*27.6*	*26*	*14.8*
10–19	*18.2*	*20.2*	*20*	*14.2*
20–29	*15.4*	*15.5*	*18*	*13.8*
30–39	*15.7*	*11.7*	*14*	*14.1*
40–49	*11.0*	*8.4*	*9*	*13.9*
50–59	*8.3*	*5.8*	} *13*	*13.2*
60+	*12.9*	*10.7*		*16.9*

where there were variations. Evidence for Spain tends to suggest that in the sixteenth and early seventeenth centuries girls married at the age of twenty, men at about twenty-five. In Altopascio (Tuscany) in the seventeenth century girls married when just over twenty-one, though after 1700 the age was over twenty-four.[64] By contrast, over most of western Europe women's first marriage occurred between the ages of 24.5 and 26.5; the men were usually two to three years older. In all cases, there were firm economic reasons that played a part in deciding when marriages occurred. Among the elite, the age at marriage tended to be lower, since an early and profitable wedding helped to secure property: in the sixteenth century daughters of the Genevan bourgeoisie wed at about twenty-two years, English noblewomen at just over twenty. The lower orders, on the other hand, probably delayed marriage until they could afford to set up their own family unit; though some couples, as we have seen, were allowed to live together after betrothal.

The relatively long wait for marriage raises interesting questions about how young persons who remained unmarried until the age of twenty-nine spent their sexual energy. Sexual dalliance short of intercourse appears to have been tolerated quite freely (Chapter 2) among the common people of western Europe. None the less, illegitimacy rates were modest: in England in twenty-four parishes studied, the rate was 2.6 per cent of live births; in Spain the level at Talavera de la Reina was 3 per cent; in Germany in Mainz in the century and a half to 1780 it did not rise above 3 per cent.[65] Communal prejudice against mothers of illegitimate children was strong enough to restrict levels. Nearly all births occurred within marriage.

On the other hand, the rate of premarital conception was everywhere quite high, and more in the cities than in the countryside. In the seventeenth century the rate in Amiens was nearly 6 per cent of first births, in Lyon up to 10 per cent; in one village in Galicia (Spain) 7.5 per cent of children were born within seven months of marriage. German towns appear to have had a high level, up to 21 per cent for Oldenburg in 1606–1700. England provides the most startling evidence: one fifth of all first births in the sixteenth and seventeenth centuries were conceived before marriage, and in some villages as many as one third. The figures leave no doubt that courtship customs in pre-industrial Europe often did not conform to the official Christian ideal of chastity before marriage.

Marriage was seldom for life. Thanks to the high mortality rate, the average couple could look forward to a shorter married life than is usual today. In the Barcelona area in early modern times, the average length of marriage before the death of a partner was not much over thirteen years, though in the interior of Catalonia it rose to around twenty years.[66] At Basel in the 1660s the mean length of marriage was just over twenty years. In Colyton (Devon) between 1550 and 1699 it was around twenty years. A nuclear family would thus be thrown adrift by the untimely death not only of half the children but also of one parent. Early death (rather than, as now, divorce) contributed to the early breakup of marriages. It consequently became the rule rather than the exception to remarry, within the limits of available wealth and ease of access to new marriage partners. In the rich Genevan elite in 1550–99, 26 per cent of marriages by men were remarriages.[67] In Crulai (Normandy) a fifth of all male and a tenth of all female marriages were remarriages; one widower out of two, and one widow out of six, married again. In one French peasant parish in the seventeenth century, we are told by a contemporary,

> when a husband loses his wife or a wife her husband, the surviving spouse at once invites everyone to a meal: this sometimes takes place in the house where the corpse is lying, and the guests laugh, drink, sing and make arrangements for remarrying their host or hostess. The widower or widow receives proposals, and gives reasons for acceptance or rejection: it is only rarely that the party comes to an end before the arrangement has been concluded.[68]

The relative brevity of married life, and the very high infant mortality, meant that the balance of birth over death was very precariously maintained. Enormous importance must therefore be attached to the fertility rate at this period. In almost every town deaths normally exceeded births, and population levels could only be maintained by continuous immigration. In Norwich there were 10,000 more deaths than births between 1582 and 1646, yet the town's population rose by at least 5,000, because of constant repletion by newcomers. It may have been that the newer immigrants in fact brought with them lower rates of survival; and that towns left to themselves would have had a healthy demographic balance with a need for only modest help from newcomers.[69] But the observation is largely an academic one, since in practice all large towns of early modern Europe experienced very considerable immigration. Though the birth rate among immigrants may have been lower, they often contributed solidly in numbers to urban expansion.

Female fertility was radically affected by late marriage, which meant that girls started reproducing some ten years after they were able to do so. Pierre Chaunu has referred to this as pre-industrial Europe's natural system of birth control. When we bear in mind that most women had borne their last child by about forty (the evidence for this across several countries is quite clear), it can be seen that the average reproductive period of women at the time was fifteen years, less than half the span of a woman's normal fertility. The inevitable result was few children. Age-specific fertility rates show that women marrying in the age group 25–29 years tended to produce about four children; in older age groups the rate declined. In Spain mothers conceived immediately after marriage; in England and France on the other hand they tended not to give birth until fourteen and sixteen months respectively after marriage. The interval between births grew longer with subsequent children: English averages suggest an interval of twenty-eight months between the births of the first and second child, where in France the interval was about twenty-three months.

This fairly low reproductive rate, in a society where a high proportion of women never married, created a distinctive family pattern. In twentieth-century Europe the economically privileged classes and nations tend to have small families, the poorer communities tend to have large ones. In pre-industrial Europe precisely the opposite held good: the poor had fewer children, the rich could afford to have more. In the sixteenth-century village of Villabáñez (Old Castile) families seldom had more than four children; in Córdoba in 1683, 58 per cent of families had no more than two children, 32 per cent had no more than four. In France the average number of children was just over four per family. In late sixteenth-century Norwich the poor had 2.3 children per family, the richer burgesses had 4.2. Europe was thus far from having the large families usually associated with pre-industrial communities. The gentry and nobles, however, often exceeded the norm. The Genevan bourgeoisie, where girls habitually married younger, were capable of producing eleven and even fifteen children per family. The English aristocracy modestly limited themselves to five per family, though the record was occasionally upset by the heroic few, such as the first Earl Ferrers (d. 1717), who had thirty bastards and twenty-seven legitimate children to his credit.

The absolute dependence of fertility on the age of the mother is solid proof that artificial birth control was not widely practised. At the same time, however, there were mechanisms in existence that controlled fertility. It has been argued, as we have seen, that late marriage in itself was a conscious method of control; though against this thesis one might cite the evidence of Spain, where a lower marriage age did not result in a different pattern of fertility. Breast-feeding, which delays a mother's possibility of conceiving, remained normal practice; but the evidence at least from French towns shows that a fair proportion of mothers from the elite and artisan classes gave their infants out to be wet-nursed, and this increased their ability to conceive while reducing that of the wet-nurses. The most commonly practised method of controlling unwanted children was exposure after birth; illegitimate infants were the chief victims, but several babies were also left by parents too poor to care for them. The practice of leaving infants on the steps of churches and hospitals grew regularly throughout the early modern period and led to the establishment of foundling hospitals in the major European cities. By the end of the seventeenth century the number of foundlings had attained alarming proportions: the hospital in Madrid had 1,400 infants in its care in 1698, and in the same decade the hospital in Paris was taking in over 2,000 a year.

The best documented cases of birth control refer not to the rural but to the urban population and elites. Henri Estienne referred in 1566 to women who utilised 'preservatives that prevent them becoming pregnant'; and another French writer, Bourdeille, quoted the case of a servant-maid who, on being scolded by her master for becoming pregnant, claimed that it would not have happened 'if I had been as well instructed as most of my friends'.[70] By the next century, according to a confessor's manual published in Paris in 1671, priests were instructed to inquire in the confessional whether the faithful had 'employed means to prevent generation', and whether 'women during their pregnancy had taken a drink or some other concoction to prevent conception'. At the same period contraceptive and abortive practices were known in Spain, to judge by confessors' manuals and the prosecutions undertaken by the Inquisition. A more scientific, though necessarily indirect, guide to contraceptive practices is the study of birth intervals: lengthy intervals, such as those of forty-nine months or more found in all social classes in early eighteenth-century Geneva, are clear testimony that controls were practised; but it is less certain that the practices involved anything more than careful abstention. Very gradually, the unspeakable came to be spoken, and birth control was recognised to exist. In England in 1695 a book called *Populaidias, or a Discourse concerning the having many children, in which the prejudices against having a numerous offspring are removed*, defended the older values and attacked those 'who look upon the fruitfulness of wives to be less eligible than their barrenness; and had rather their families should be none, than large'.

Population trends

Although information about population can be found in tax and military censuses of the period, it is to parish records that we turn for reliable details. Fragmentary data on births, marriages and burials were kept in several countries prior to the Reformation. But even after such registrations became compulsory – in England after 1538 (not fully effective until 1653), in Catholic countries after the Council of Trent (1563) – it was rare for a parish priest to keep his records up to date.

From about 1450 Europe's population began to increase, but unevenly, given the considerable differences in demographic structure between various countries. The highest rate of increase was in the north, where the Scandinavian countries by 1600 registered an advance of two thirds on their 1500 levels, and Britain and the Netherlands over one half. Central Europe, Spain and Italy increased by up to one third, France by perhaps only one eighth. The most notable increase was in the great cities: Antwerp and Seville, under the impetus of trade, doubled in size in the first two thirds of the sixteenth century. Lyon quadrupled its population from 1450 to 1550, while Rouen tripled in size during the early sixteenth century. Where in 1500 there had been few towns of over 100,000 inhabitants (only Paris, Naples, Venice and Milan), by 1600 there were at least nine (Antwerp, Seville, Rome, Lisbon, Palermo, Messina, Milan, Venice, Amsterdam), and three of over 200,000 (Naples, Paris, London). By 1700 these last three had half a million each, and Madrid, Vienna and Moscow had joined the ranks of those with over 100,000.

Both on a small and a large scale, both in town and country, the growth in population levels was unmistakable. In the village of La Chapelle-des-Fougerets (Ile-et-Vilaine) the records show an increase of 50 per cent between 1520 and 1610; in the Valladolid region, the village of Tudela de Duero increased by 81.7 per cent between 1530 and 1593. In Provence the demographic level of 1540 was three times that of 1470, in Luxembourg population increased by 39 per cent between 1501 and 1554, in Leicestershire by 58 per cent between 1563 and 1603. The territory of Zürich (excluding the city) increased in population by 45 per cent between 1529 and 1585; Norway's population grew 46 per cent between 1520 and 1590.

The causes of the demographic increase are not clear, though it is possible to point – for the early sixteenth century at least – to a relative absence of destructive wars and a lull in the frequent attacks of epidemics. The consequences of the increase were momentous: a restless movement of migratory populations, settlement of overseas territories, growing pressure on land use, a rise in prices stimulated in part by higher demand, a crisis in the exploitation of labour and the level of wages. There was a disproportionate increase in the town population, which probably doubled in England during the sixteenth century. In the province of Holland the rural population between 1514 and 1622 grew by 58 per cent, the urban by 471 per cent. Urbanisation was thus a notable feature of the period.[71] Towns grew principally, as we have seen above, through immigration from the rural areas. As cities grew they generated demand and stimulated the economy. On the negative side, however, urbanisation pushed up property and rent values, and worsened the material condition of the lower classes. In the rural areas population growth was an undeniable stimulus to higher output in agriculture.

The period of expansion that began in about 1450 came to an end after the 1580s. Throughout Mediterranean Europe the decades after this were marked by reverses, associated particularly with epidemics. In France and the Netherlands the major negative factor was war. By the early seventeenth century, much of Europe was entering a phase of demographic stagnation and, in some cases, decline. In southern Europe the population levels of the early sixteenth century were not recovered for 200 years.

Mortality: epidemics

In both the sixteenth and seventeenth centuries, there were powerful negative influences on demography. The one great reality of life was death, readily accepted because always unavoidable. It was reflected in the whole cultural environment: in the teaching and imagery of religion; in art, poetry and drama; in popular entertainment and public celebrations. Of the three scourges bewailed by the litany – *a peste, fame et bello, libera nos Domine* – the first two could be considered as natural, though already there were suggestions that public policy could remedy their worst effects. In practice, for most people the environment in which they lived was a permanent source of mortality,[72] but they were seldom conscious of it.

Fears were focussed rather on the sudden mortality brought on by epidemic disease. Though plague was the most virulent of all epidemics, the regular toll of other diseases such as influenza, typhus, typhoid and smallpox may have in reality been responsible for more deaths.[73] Influenza, for example, may have been responsible for the English report of 1558 that 'in the beginning of this year died many of the wealthiest men all England through, of a strange fever': it was a severe crisis (1557–9) during which possibly a tenth of the English population died. 'Fevers' were a regular phenomenon, whereas plague could be more easily identified by its savage impact.

The proportion of people who succumbed to plague, especially in the cities, could be staggering. Possibly a quarter of the population of London perished in the plague of 1563, when the death rate was seven times higher than in normal years. Although 1665 became known as the year of the Great Plague, in fact proportionately more people died in the outbreaks of 1603 and 1625; together the epidemics of these three years caused the death in London of up to 200,000 people. Measuring the impact of plague over a run of years offers a somewhat different perspective (just 15 per cent of deaths in London from 1580 to 1650) but hides the gravity of the periodic outbreak. The outbreaks in Amsterdam in 1624, 1636, 1655 and 1664 are estimated to have removed, respectively, one ninth, one seventh, one eighth and one sixth of the population. In Uelzen (Lower Saxony) the plague of 1597 carried off 33 per cent of the population, whereas a dysentery epidemic in 1599 killed only 14 per cent.[74] Santander in Spain was virtually wiped off the map in 1599, losing 83 per cent of its 3,000 inhabitants. The great 'Atlantic plague' of 1596–1603, which gnawed at the coasts of western Europe, possibly cost one million lives, two thirds of them in Spain alone. In France between 1600 and 1670 plague carried off between 2.2 and 3.3 millions. Mantua in 1630 lost nearly 70 per cent of its population, Naples and Genoa in 1656 nearly half theirs. Barcelona lost 28.8 per cent of its population in the plague of 1589 and about 45 per cent in that of 1651. Marseille lost half its people in 1720.[75]

Epidemics were spread by contact, probably the most mortal of contacts being the passage of troops in wartime.[76] Isolation was the commonest remedy adopted: during the 1563 epidemic in England the court moved to Windsor and (reports the annalist Stow) 'a gallows was set up in the market-place to hang all such as should come there from London'. The flea-infected rat was eventually recognised to be the principal carrier of the disease, though some recent studies suggest that human fleas were equally responsible, since the rapidity with which plague spread is more explicable by the mobility of humans than by the movements of the less mobile black rat. It was significant that plague followed trade routes, and was also spread by armies on the march. Isolation was fairly effective. In seventeenth-century Spain, for example, double military cordons were put around infected communities and commerce was cut; but it was always difficult to control inland epidemics. A ban on commerce by sea was, on the other hand, invariably successful: it saved the Netherlands from the English plague of 1563 (but not from its indirect impact through Germany in 1566, after being taken to the Baltic in English ships), and Spain from the Marseille plague of 1720. The latter was the last outbreak known in mainland Europe. The epidemic at Messina in 1743 ended the reign of plague in the west.

The social effects of plague have been imperfectly studied, but there can be no doubt that it discriminated among its victims. Thriving on filthy conditions, it struck first and foremost at the lower classes in the towns. In London, the Mortality Bills show epidemics having their origin in the poorest suburbs. When an epidemic struck Lyon in 1628, a contemporary comforted himself with the thought that 'only seven or eight persons of quality died, and five or six hundred of lower condition'. We find a bourgeois of Toulouse observing in his journal in 1561: 'The contagion only ever hits the poor people....God by his grace will have it so. The rich protect themselves against it.' The surest protection was in flight. When the plague hit Bilbao in the early autumn of 1598 'only the totally impoverished remained' in the city. The bourgeoisie moved to other towns, the nobility to their country estates. Those rich who remained were aware that the plague discriminated in their favour. The banker Fabio Nelli, writing from Valladolid in July 1599 in a week when nearly a thousand people had died, commented that 'I don't intend to move from here...almost nobody of consideration has died.' Social tensions were aggravated. With the evidence plain before their eyes, the upper classes felt that the plague had been spread by the poor. The poor in their turn resented the fact that those who had never lacked material comforts should also be spared the vengeance of the scourge.

Poverty and poor nutrition were the two main features of epidemic victims. In Sepúlveda (Spain) in April 1599 'all those who have died in this town and its region were very poor and lacked all sustenance'. The connection between poverty and epidemics encouraged public authorities to improve conditions of hygiene in the towns, but it is doubtful if any of the measures taken by municipalities was really effective. The lack of defence against disease highlights what was certainly the biggest failure of early modern European civilisation: its inability to achieve advances in medicine.

Mortality: famine

'This year', a Spanish correspondent wrote home from Naples in 1606, 'God has seen fit to visit this realm and Sicily and other parts of Italy with a ruinous harvest, and the one here is said to be the worst for forty years'. The report was an exaggeration, for there had been an even more severe famine only ten years previously, but inevitably each crisis seemed to be worse than its predecessor, and bad years were regular enough to have an adverse cumulative effect. In early modern England one harvest in four was poor. Between 1549 and 1556 there was not a single good harvest, and the Privy Council banned corn exports every year between 1546 and 1550; in 1549 grain prices were 84 per cent higher than in the preceding year, and in 1556 they were 240 per cent higher than the year before.[77] The incidence of such crises must be put in perspective. Famines, in the sense of great natural disasters, were infrequent; far more significant was the threat from the common, daily inability to obtain enough food.

The availability of food was affected primarily by the weather, but it depended also on human factors such as adequate agricultural methods, the volume of demand from the population, good communication and transport, and the presence of war. In an era when in some countries customs barriers even separated one province from another, it was possible for one of two contiguous regions to starve while the other fed adequately. The significance of the 'subsistence crisis' for mortality has been much debated. Some scholars have argued that subsistence crises could have a devastating effect, and that people could die in big numbers in famine conditions. Others have maintained that few ever died from starvation or malnutrition in early modern Europe; and that though undernourishment may have weakened health the real killer in most cases was disease. The latter argument has been based principally on a study of price data: because in many cases high mortality has not coincided with high grain prices, it has been argued that lack of food could not have caused death.

The evidence for a link between dearth and death prior to the eighteenth century seems to be firm, judging by the crises of the 1590s, of 1661 and of the 1690s. The years 1594–7 over most of Europe were ones of excessive rain and bad harvests, resulting in a steep rise in grain prices.[78] In Spain, Italy and Germany in particular the disaster coincided with heavy mortality brought on by epidemics of plague. Discontent and unrest led to large-scale peasant revolts all over the continent (see Chapter 6). In England there were unsuccessful attempts at armed uprisings. The English government drew up a new Poor Law in 1597 to deal with widespread poverty and distress. The authorities at Bristol undertook relief measures whereby, they claimed with satisfaction, 'the poor of our city were all relieved and kept from starving or rising'. Newcastle was not so fortunate. An entry in the town accounts reads: 'October 1597. Paid for the charge of buringe 16 poore folks who died for wante in the strettes 6s. 8d.' In Aix-en-Provence in 1597 when 'the clergy of the church of Saint-Esprit were giving bread to succour the poor, of whom there were over twelve hundred, six or seven of them died, including little girls and a woman'. At Senlis in 1595 an observer saw 'men and women, young and old, shivering in the streets, skin hanging and stomachs swollen, others stretched out breathing their last sighs, the grass sticking out of their mouths'.

The crisis of 1659–62 created conditions that in many countries eased the way to absolute monarchy. The harvest failure of 1661 in north and eastern France helped to present the young Louis XIV to his people as a beneficent ruler. Colbert reported that the king 'not only distributed grain to individuals and communities in Paris and around, but even ordered thirty and forty thousand pounds of bread to be given out daily'. As in most subsistence crises, children were the most vulnerable: in the parish of Athis, south of Paris, 62 per cent of those who died in 1660–2 were aged under ten. In the countryside, reported an eyewitness, 'the pasturage of wolves has become the food of Christians, for when they find horses, asses and other dead animals they feed off the rotting flesh'. 'In the thirty-two years that I have practised medicine in this province', reported a doctor in Blois, 'I have seen nothing to approach the desolation throughout the countryside. The famine is so great that the peasants go without bread and throw themselves on to carrion. As soon as a horse or other animal dies, they eat it.'

The years 1692–4 produced poor harvests in western Europe. In November 1693 the city of Alicante reported that 'there has been virtually no harvest because it has not rained for fourteen months'. In Galicia the city of Santiago reported that 'most of the people have died of hunger and most homes have been depopulated'. The exaggeration was not unfounded. In the district of Xallas in Galicia, most of the conceptions of 1693–4 disappeared in the infant mortality of 1694–5; in 1691 there had been thirty-eight marriages in the parishes, in 1695 there were only twelve. For France 1693 was possibly the worst year of the century: at Meulan, northeast of Paris, the price of grain tripled and burials were nearly two and a half times those of a normal year. With associated attacks of epidemic, the mortality in France in 1693–4 may have exceeded two millions. Three years later, in 1696, Finland suffered a disastrous harvest failure which swept away possibly one quarter of the country's population in the course of 1696–7.

Not all the people starved. 'Nothing new here', reported a Rome newsletter in February 1558, 'except that people are dying of hunger'. The same newsletter then went on to describe a great banquet given by the Pope at which the chief wonders were 'statues made of sugar carrying real torches'. The rich were sometimes touched by the plague, but almost never by hunger. In Dijon in the great famine of 1694 the number of deaths in the wealthy parish of Nôtre Dame was ninety-nine, in the poor parish of St Philibert 266. Even in normal times the mortality rate was tipped heavily against the undernourished poor: in seventeenth-century Geneva, 38 per cent of children born to the upper bourgeoisie died before the age of ten, but 62.8 per cent of those born to working-class parents.

Among the lower classes, mortality was as a rule higher among the rural proletariat than in the towns, for while the townspeople could beg for relief the peasants had to find sustenance from their own inhospitable environment. When the soil had no grain to offer them they turned to carrion, roots, bark, straw and vermin. Of the famine in 1637 in Franche Comté, a contemporary recorded that 'posterity will not believe it: people lived off the plants in gardens and fields; they even sought out the carcasses of dead animals. The roads were strewn with people.…Finally it came to cannibalism.'

It remains possible to maintain that death from hunger was rare in normal conditions, but it is not easy to define what 'normal conditions' were in a society that suffered frequently from crises of one sort or another. The common people were under no illusion about their susceptibility to starvation, and the regularity of bread riots in towns illustrates their refusal to accept their fate with resignation. In 1628 one of the pastors in Geneva explained to his congregation that the current food crisis (which was to last until 1631) was brought upon them by their sins:

> The people, who had been suffering for a very long time on a meagre diet were outraged by this and left the church in great dissatisfaction, saying that they were more in need of consolation than of accusations…that they were very well aware of the true state of things; and that the pastor had no idea of the misery of the great number who passed whole days and weeks in their homes without a few loaves of bread; and that they had to go without that which others fattened themselves upon.[79]

Undernourishment was common in Geneva in both normal and abnormal times. In January 1630, during the subsistence crisis, silk workers were earning only two *sols* a day, whereas the cost of bread was five *sols* a pound and two pounds was the minimum required for a reasonable daily diet. In these circumstances the city council had to order the payment of supplementary wages.

Whole provinces and nations in early modern Europe lived at a parlous level of subsistence, and even in normal harvest years relied on food imports. The wheat fields of Sicily and of eastern Europe became the great suppliers. Spain in the sixteenth century was notoriously unable to meet its own needs, and became a regular importer from the Baltic, Sicily and north Africa. In early modern times, two crops imported from America (maize, and the potato) helped to solve the food problem in certain areas. In northwest Spain (Galicia) maize, already in use by 1600, formed by 1700 two thirds of all cereals grown, and by 1750 nearly 90 per cent.[80] With a yield ratio of 40:1, maize saved the peasantry of Spain's northern coast. In the Netherlands there was not enough land available to feed the high density of population, and import of grain was always necessary: it was logical that Amsterdam should become the great clearing house for Baltic wheat.

On a smaller scale, rural communities and individual peasants constantly lived close to subsistence level, since the land they possessed did not suffice for their needs. In some areas, fragmentation of peasant estates further destroyed self-sufficiency. The village of Lespignan in Languedoc is evidence of this process. In 1492 the great majority of peasant proprietors here were able to produce a surplus which they sold in order to buy goods, so putting themselves above the minimum level of independence. By 1607 the majority were having to buy grain in order to feed themselves, and had to support their families by finding work elsewhere. In Beauvaisis the fragmentation of peasant holdings led to a situation where as many as nine tenths of the peasant population were not economically independent and could not guarantee to feed their families adequately. The peasant who aspired to economic independence had to farm at least 12 hectares (30 acres) in years of plenty, 27 hectares (65 acres) in years of dearth; yet in the seventeenth century less than one tenth of the peasants here owned 27 or more hectares.

Assessment of health at this period has sometimes been made on the basis of the calorie content of food.[81] This has led to a number of disparate calculations. In modern diets 3,000 calories a day is assumed to give a minimum level of adequate nourishment. A study of the food of building workers in Antwerp around the year 1600, with bread, vegetables, butter, cheese and meat in the diet, suggests a value of some 2,000 calories a day.[82] The average citizen of Valladolid in the same period apparently had a daily diet of some 1,580 calories. Both these food levels have been assumed to be adequate for the time. On the other hand, a study of peasant diets on the Polish royal estates in the late sixteenth century arrives at a daily average of 3,500 calories; Spanish seamen are supposed to have consumed up to 4,000 calories a day in the period; and the Collegio Borromeo in Pavia supplied its indigent inmates with about 6,000 calories a day. Since in all cases most (perhaps three quarters) of these calories came from cereals, the bare figures may be misleading; an analysis of food and vitamin content would give a truer picture of health values. On the grounds that among the peasants of the Beauvaisis meat was almost unknown, fruit rare, vegetables poor and the staple was normally bread, soup, gruel, peas and beans, it has been argued that undernourishment here was constant. The same might convincingly be said of many other peasantries, and it has been shown that armies of the time – notorious spreaders of epidemics – were also grossly underfed, meat and vegetables being largely absent from their diet. By the mid-eighteenth century, however, it appears that the link between dearth and death had all but disappeared. An improvement in diet would have been a prerequisite for the population recovery that took place from that period.

Mortality: war

In post-Renaissance Europe the increase in collective violence was seen by many commentators as a new and deplorable phenomenon. It showed itself not simply in acts of 'war' but in all levels of group conflict. Men of culture who had previously categorised as barbarians only those who lived beyond the confines of western Christendom, now recognised that Europeans also were capable of barbarism. It was against this background that Montaigne employed his irony to argue that the 'savages' of the New World were perhaps less so than those of the Old. Frenchmen in the late sixteenth century, for whom 'barbarism' had previously been a virtually unknown concept, began during the violence of the civil wars to realise that the state of nature of American Indians was one of innocence rather than of savagery. 'Nous les surpassons en toute sorte de barbarie', Montaigne wrote.

At a time when armies were fairly small, deaths in battle were the lesser part of the impact of war. It has been estimated[83] that in the English Civil War deaths in battle totalled 85,000 but that war-related mortality was much higher, possibly 100,000 people or 3.7 per cent of the English population. When armies increased in size, the battlefield casualties rose alarmingly. At Blenheim (1704), perhaps the most notorious case, 30,000 men died. Yes, the Poet Laureate Southey commented with sharp irony, but 'it was a famous victory'. Other factors, such as a long siege, tended to raise the death rate, especially among the civilian population. There were also exceptional events, such as the disaster of the Armada in 1588, which cost the Spaniards 15,000 men. It can be argued that military campaigns did not cause extensive mortality. Even so, their impact cannot be minimised: the soldiery spread epidemics, aggravated famine, and sometimes committed horrifying atrocities. In general, it was the civilian population that suffered most. 'It has been impossible to collect any taxes', runs a report from Lorraine in the 1630s, 'because of the wars that have hit most of the villages, which are deserted through the flight of some of the inhabitants and the death of others from disease or from sickness arising out of starvation'. Summarising the consequences of the great Cromwellian repression of Ireland, Sir William Petty, who had full access to state papers, estimated that 'about 504,000 of the Irish perished, and were wasted by the sword, plague, famine, hardship and banishment, between the 23 of October 1641 and the same day 1652'.

The early sixteenth century was relatively free from wars within Christian Europe, only Italy suffering to any extent (the sack of Rome in 1527 was a notorious example). By the late century war had become universal on both land and sea, whether in civil and religious conflicts or against the Turk; and armies began to grow in size: Philip II's army in Flanders rose to 85,000 men, in 1630 Wallenstein in Germany commanded about 100,000. By 1659 the French state had 125,000 under arms, the number doubling and tripling under Louis XIV. The following paragraphs touch on five areas where the army, as in most wars of the time, ruined the cornfields, drove civilians from their homes, spread infection, and in the process aggravated mortality and retarded fertility.

The French civil wars (1562–98) were costly in terms of lives: the massacre of St Bartholomew's Eve, for example, exterminated over 3,000 Protestants in Paris and 20,000 throughout France. Many localities suffered an overall loss of population: Rouen lost one quarter of its inhabitants between 1562 and 1594. There was a brighter side to the picture. A survey of parish registers reveals that the earlier period, up to the 1580s, coincided with the general expansion of population in Europe. In Burgundy births and marriages increased regularly during the wars, decreasing only in the 1590s, when famines rather than war were responsible for falling birth rates. There is little doubt that the civil wars were a principal reason why the total increase of population in France was smaller than in any other western European country, but the mortality was not so great as to reverse the period of positive growth up to the 1580s.

In the same years the Netherlands were going through a civil war. The Eighty Years War (1568–1648) split the country into a northern section (the United Provinces) and a southern (under Spanish rule). In the early years the north suffered substantially, but from the end of the sixteenth century it was the south that took the brunt of the war. Not until the 1630s, when the Dunkirk privateers successfully attacked northern shipping, did the United Provinces suffer serious reverses. A number of factors combined to produce disastrous effects on the south. The collapse of the country was to some extent a consequence of the collapse of Antwerp, which suffered from the blockade of the Scheldt after 1572 and from the rebellion of Spanish troops – the 'Spanish fury' – in 1576. From 1580 onwards a severe crisis developed in Belgian territory as the economy ground to a halt. In 1581 the linen industries of Courtrai and Oudenarde collapsed, and nothing could be sown in the fields round Brussels because of the war. In 1582 the Duke of Anjou's troops sacked several industrial towns. Mercenaries murdered farmers, farms were destroyed, fields were left untilled. In 1585 the Scheldt was firmly closed by the Dutch. Around Ghent for a while the area of cultivation fell by 92 per cent. In most villages of Brabant the population by 1586 had dropped to between 25 and 50 per cent of 1575 levels. 'Trade has almost totally ceased', reported the Duke of Saxony when he visited Antwerp in 1613. The outbreak of war in 1621, after the expiry of the Twelve Years Truce between Spain and the United Provinces, brought further problems. 'I have come to Amsterdam where I now am', reported a priest in 1627, 'and find all the towns as full of people as those held by Spain are empty'. Fortunately, in many areas the survival of good land and other resources helped the people to recover rapidly from the war. The earlier phase of the Dutch wars coincided with demographic expansion, so that there was only a moderate check to fertility. The wars of the seventeenth century, however, came at a time of demographic stagnation or decline, and had a more marked effect.

In France the most serious reverses were associated with the Fronde (1648–53), which took place mainly in the north, around Paris. Angélique Arnauld in 1649 lamented 'the frightful state of this poor countryside; all is pillaged, ploughing has ceased, there are no horses, everything is stolen, the peasants are driven to sleeping in the woods'.[84] A report of 1652 on the area speaks of

> villages and hamlets deserted, streets infected by stinking carrion and dead bodies lying exposed, everything reduced to cesspools and stables, and above all the sick and dying, with no bread, meat, medicine, heating, beds, linen or covering, and no priest, doctor or anyone to comfort them.

Harvests collapsed in the affected region. Though war was the cause of misery in these years, in fact the highest mortality was caused by epidemic disease spread by the soldiers. The population loss around Paris was about a fifth. In the summer of 1652, the year of highest mortality in the whole century in the south of Paris, the death rate was fifteen times higher than in the previous four crisis years.[85]

The Thirty Years War (1618–48) is the most famous of the scourges of this period. Though literary accounts, notably Grimmelshausen's famous anti-war tract *Simplicissimus* (1668), have helped to exaggerate some of the effects of the war, detailed research has supported the traditional picture. At the same time there can be little doubt that epidemic disease, particularly the extensive plague of 1634–6, was the single most lethal killer. Nördlingen, for example, lost one third of its population of 9,000 in the plague of 1634. The human misery caused by military occupation that same year nevertheless caused a diarist to write that 'it was considered a blessing in these times to die of the plague'. The Rhineland, fought for by the troops of every nation in Europe, was reduced to ruins. 'From Cologne hither' (to Frankfurt), reported an English ambassador in 1635, 'all the towns, villages and castles be battered, pillaged and burnt'. 'I am leading my men', claimed the Bavarian general von Werth when crossing the Rhineland in 1637, 'through a country where many thousands of men have died of hunger and not a living soul can be seen for many miles along the way'. In the county of Lippe, a region only moderately hit by the war, the population fell by 35 per cent between 1618 and 1648. In the district of Lautern in the Rhineland, a more severely devastated region, of a total of sixty-two towns thirty were still deserted in 1656, and a population of 4,200 (excluding the chief town Kaiserslautern) had sunk to about 500. Augsburg lost half its population and three quarters of its wealth during the war; its richest taxpayers fell in number from 142 to eighteen. Over the German lands as a whole the urban centres lost one third of their inhabitants, the rural areas about 40 per cent.[86] The losses varied from under 10 per cent in Lower Saxony in the northwest to over 50 per cent in Württemberg in the south and Pomerania in the north. These figures must be treated with caution; there was an enormous refugee population, of whom many returned eventually to their homes, so that 'loss' may not necessarily mean death so much as displacement. Not only the German lands, but other adjacent countries, suffered badly: Franche Comté, devastated between 1635 and 1644, lost between a half and three quarters of its population.

A long-forgotten war whose consequences persist down to today was that of 1640–68 between Spain and Portugal, which ended with Spain recognising the latter's independence. Years of skirmishes and raids across the frontier turned every major town into a garrison town, periodically ruined both livestock and agriculture, aggravated emigration and led to the collapse of both dwellings and population. The already poor province of Extremadura may have lost half its population in the quarter century that the war lasted; its capital, Badajoz, declined by 43 per cent between 1640 and 1691, at a time when most major cities in Spain were increasing in size.[87]

Although some areas took as much as a generation to recover pre-crisis levels, many managed to do so with surprising speed. The virtual cessation of marriages and births in some communities was only temporary. As the crisis neared its end, households which had lost one parent would look around for a replacement, and the stock of unmarried women would become available for men seeking wives. Marriages and remarriages would increase steeply. In Nördlingen[88] during the four months of the plague and military crisis at the end of 1634, only three marriages took place. When the plague died away in December, a massive increase in weddings occurred: 121 were celebrated in the first four months of 1635. This wave of crisis marriages would then produce a big upsurge in births, as duly happened in Nördlingen. Helped additionally by an increase in immigration, the cities and eventually the countryside would recover steadily from the disastrous years of war.

2

LEISURE, WORK AND MOVEMENT

> Twelfth of February at Lille in the Low Country; here I break off until morning, and I in gloom and grief; and during my life's length unless only that I might have one look at Ireland.
>
> (the exiled priest Fergal O'Gara, 1565)

The countryside, with some 85 per cent of the total population, dominated Europe: its woods and plains, punctuated here and there by villages and small towns, gave the traveller a feeling of immense loneliness. But there were significant differences in the density of settlement. The most highly populated territories were northern Italy and the Netherlands. By contrast, Russia and the Ukraine were vast emptinesses: as one went farther east the towns disappeared and the spaces opened up.

The primacy of the rural economy was simply one perspective of a dual reality. Town and country were closely interlinked at every level of activity. Rural areas were primary producers (food, wool, wine) but relied heavily on the local town-market to be able to sell their wares. Towns, in their turn, relied entirely on the local producers for their sustenance. The weekly market, still to be seen throughout much of rural Europe, was a social event of the first importance.[1] Market day determined economic life through prices and levels of profits (and taxes); kept rural and urban populations in contact for social intercourse and business (the inn was a common meeting place); and facilitated personal transactions (such as marriages). Villages might have several market towns within easy access, thereby allowing them to sell produce not simply on one day but on several days a week.[2]

In political terms, moreover, the distinction between urban and rural was often unreal.[3] A city might be physically defined by the limits of its walls, but in Italy, Germany and Spain all the surrounding territory, including its villages, was normally attached to the city in terms of jurisdiction and fiscal obligation. A very great part of the countryside consequently functioned intimately in step with urban life and cannot be dissociated from it.

Time, work and leisure

Within their native communities, Europeans were not tied down, as in post-industrial society, to a clear distinction between work time and leisure time. Labour hours and leisure hours intermingled; in practice, leisure tended to predominate at all social levels. The imprecision of labour obligations was, in part, a consequence of the imprecise measurement of time.

Clocks were a relative novelty in the early sixteenth century. The population still took its division of the hours and minutes from the Church: the day was measured by liturgical hours; church bells tolled their passing and called the faithful to prayer. Protestantism helped to liberate time from its clerical dress, and clocks completed the process of secularisation. By the end of the sixteenth century the clock industry was booming, particularly when the clockmakers from Catholic countries fled as refugees to Protestant states. In 1515 there were no clockmakers in Geneva; after 1550 they came as refugees from France, and by 1600 the city had twenty-five to thirty master clockmakers and an unknown number of apprentices. In the mathematical universe of early seventeenth-century intellectuals, clocks played an essential part. In contrast to the genial pace of earlier decades, in contrast to Gargantua's protest, 'I never rule myself by time!', the seventeenth century began the subjection of humanity to the clock. It was the astronomer Kepler who looked upon the universe and pronounced it 'similar to a clock', and it was Boyle who considered it 'a great piece of clock-work'. The ordering of time seems to have been part of a general attempt by Europeans to organise the environment in which they worked.[4] This could be seen already in commerce and navigation, which stimulated the development of mapping; in philosophy and technology, where the science of mathematics became more precise; and in art and engineering, where the study of physics promoted new advances.

Clocks and watches remained the preserve of a minority. There were, however, objections when attempts were made to change the calendar. In France, the king in 1563 decreed that the year should start in January instead of at Easter; the Parlement of Paris refused to register the edict until January 1567, a refusal which made the year 1566 in France only eight months long. A definitive international reform of the old calendar (called 'Julian' after its sponsor Julius Caesar) did not come until 1582, when Pope Gregory XIII abolished ten days from the year. The change was accepted by different countries at different times, Philip II of Spain decreeing it for his territories in the autumn of 1582. Most Protestant countries refused to accept the change, which led to the operation of a dual calendar in Europe. The Orthodox Church in Russia continued with its own separate calendar until the twentieth century.

Industrial time was measured by daylight hours, a winter working day being shorter than a summer one by about two hours, with wages consequently lower. In sixteenth-century Antwerp, building workers had a seven-hour day in winter but a twelve-hour day in summer; winter wages were one fifth lower. Concepts like 'from sunrise to sunset' were written into work regulations, but were inevitably imprecise. Only a few trades had their hours of work laid down by the clock rather than by daylight: in 1571 the printers of Lyon complained because their working day was timed to begin at 2 a.m. and ended only at 8 p.m. For most workers, especially on the land, imprecision of time took strict discipline out of work. Rest from labours was both recognised and encouraged. La Fontaine commented at the time that 'on nous ruine en fêtes', but the system was not necessarily as harmful as might appear.

Despite the measuring of time, it was difficult to separate leisure time from work time, for 'work' might be onerous but was not yet a rigorous discipline. Working for a wage did not, as in post-industrial society, dominate daily life. This was even more true in those extensive areas of Europe where there was little coin in circulation and where as a result money did not regulate labour relationships. In the Baltic, central and eastern Europe and large areas of the west, a money economy was still in the process of formation. Peasants paid their tax dues in the form of labour services, and received their wages in kind rather than in cash.

At the same time, work was seldom a personal, individualised burden. Individuals tended to contribute to the work output of groups, rather than having to labour for themselves alone. Thus in a peasant family the various members had their allotted tasks, which might involve only a small proportion of the hours in a day. Many younger members could be spared to go and work elsewhere, in order to learn a trade; their employment as apprentices or as labour in the towns formed for them a fundamental phase in their life cycle. For adults, work was a partial occupation of time, and only for the few was it a full-time obligation. Those who lived outside supportive group structures could, obviously, face economic difficulties. Normally in the villages of Europe family and community structures served to maintain those who were in need because they could not even find work, and in the towns poor-relief systems were beginning to cater for vagrants.

Unpleasant work was also invariably communal. The labour obligations imposed by feudal authorities in western Europe, and by serfdom in the east, derived from the system within which peasants lived and they accepted the burden even while resenting it.

Though not rigidly defined by obligations, work had its disciplines. All agrarian activity was determined by very clear signposts, normally decided by the local community. The days and seasons for sowing, shearing, harvesting, threshing and other duties were fixed according to the local climate and the local economy. There is no formal way of calculating what proportion of time was set aside for 'work'. In village communities, the norm appears to have been that enough hours were worked to maintain the means of subsistence (crops, herds, fishing). The attention given to leisure commitments and the absence of work discipline were to create problems for employers of a later period, who complained in particular that workers did not respect the working week, and treated Monday ('Saint Monday' in England) as an extension of Sunday, the

Lord's day of rest. Labourers for their part were aware of their work obligations, but preferred to choose the days or hours when those obligations could be met. The situation therefore was one of 'alternate bouts of intense labour and of idleness wherever men were in control of their own working lives'.[5] In early modern Europe, work was not an oppressive regime. 'The labouring man will take his rest long in the morning', an English bishop complained, 'then must he have his breakfast...at noon he must have his sleeping time'.[6] In the hot Mediterranean summer the hours spent in avoiding the direct rays of the sun were even longer, causing northern travellers to comment on the apparent 'idleness' of southern peasants.

The Church authorities, for their part, had problems trying to persuade the people to distinguish labour time from religious time. It was normal in much of Catholic Europe for over a third of the days in the year to be officially days of rest. In the diocese of Paris at the beginning of the seventeenth century there were fifty-nine obligatory religious holidays, which together with the Sundays made up well over 100 days a year. In pre-industrial Spain between one third and one half of the days in the year were holidays.[7] Obligatory religious holidays were, of course, only a proportion of these; the rest were periods of celebration laid down by local communities. With such a proliferation of rest days, it was normal in traditional society to work indiscriminately during any days of the year, even when they coincided with religious festivals. The Counter-Reformation Church from the later sixteenth century onwards made firm attempts to restrict this practice, by decreeing that feast days were days of total rest. The intention was to distinguish the sacred from the profane, what belonged to God from what belonged to man. The disciplining of time – part of a general policy of disciplining religion (Chapter 3) – was difficult to achieve. In 1641 the bishops of Catalonia complained that in the rural areas 'the feasts ordered by the Church are not observed', and in Andalusia in 1673 a Jesuit missionary observed that farm workers worked straight through feast days, and only went to mass once a fortnight. There was, in the popular mind, no clear difference between the sacred and the secular, or between work and leisure. All formed part of the same daily reality, and each part was given due attention, but only when it was convenient.

By the same token, leisure in pre-industrial Europe was not a distinct concept.[8] There were many occasional activities, available particularly to the upper classes, that allowed people to indulge in recreations, sports and pastimes. For most of the population, however, 'leisure' was less a specific period of rest that alternated with work, than a traditional time of neighbourly concerns and of attention to matters not immediately connected with productivity. If seen as a sum of all activities that did not represent 'work', it included fulfilment of obligations to the family, to the community, to the Church and (for the unmarried) to courtship. Leisure was not, as it is now, a privilege of the individual, but a commitment of all members of the community. It was an essential dimension of good relationships, whether expressed in festivities, sports or quite simply drinking at the inn. When it functioned properly, it strengthened social bonds and helped to bring about understanding between people who might otherwise have provoked conflict within local society. A ball game on the village green had the appearance of being leisure, but it was also a fulfilment of neighbourly obligations. Village football was, for the Elizabethan Philip Stubbes, 'rather a friendly kind of fight, than a play or recreation'. Sometimes the fighting was real, as in the football match in Berkshire in 1598 when two men were murdered.[9] Within the annual cycle of days of rest, there were also days (such as Carnival) which by custom allowed the communal expression of conflict and protest, [10] usually through the activities of the young. Once again, the conflict regularly produced violence. Leisure, in short, was not divorced from work nor a refuge from it. It complemented the work activities of members of the community.

Since young people formed the most substantial cohort in the population, they played a leading role in the ordering of leisure, notably in communal activities at harvest time, in festivities and at weddings. Organised youth groups – called 'abbeys' in southern France, 'cencerradas' in southern Spain – were often to be found in both villages and big cities (Lyon in the sixteenth century had some twenty 'abbeys'), and had recognised duties that included watching over the correct performance of obligations in the community. Though the groups tended to be limited normally to men, women sometimes had a role: in Roussillon girls played a leading part in them, organised popular ceremonies, and were in charge of charity.[11]

A substantial portion of the leisure of the young was spent in courtship. The late age at which young people married (Chapter 1) has raised the question of how they spent their sexual energies in the preceding years.[12] There is little doubt that a considerable part of leisure time was spent simply in getting to know the other sex; courtship would come at a later stage. Meetings took place within the restraints imposed by the family and the community, and were usually carefully regulated. Domestic and communal work might bring people together, as in the spinning group (*Spinnstube*) of rural Germany, where 'young persons of both sexes run together and much wanton frivolousness creeps in' (a complaint of 1587 from Württemberg).[13] Despite controls imposed on the *Spinnstube*, such as the frequent exclusion of males, it was a normal recreative aspect of rural society, and served also to promote marriages. Young people as a rule, therefore, made use of their social institutions to develop sexual awareness. At a popular level courting might involve 'bundling', or petting. Evidence from France and Germany shows a considerable range of tolerated sexual practices, usually stopping short of intercourse. The intention was primarily entertainment to fill in the years before marriage, as we learn from a young man in Barcelona who stated (1625) that 'it is common and habitual practice among young men and young women to court only for pleasure and in order to pass the time, with no intention of getting married'.[14] Contacts for courtship were made also with other local communities, notably on market and festival days, thereby in some measure promoting social solidarity.

In perspective, perhaps the most crucial aspect of leisure in pre-industrial society was that it enjoyed freedom from discipline. Though there were things to be done, they could be done when it seemed fit. The duration of community festivals is a case in point. One of the high points of the year's festivities was Carnival, normally celebrated in the few days before the coming of Lent on Ash Wednesday. In the Mediterranean things were different. In the Catalan lands, Carnival began the day after Christmas and ended over six weeks later, on Ash Wednesday. Leisure took its most active form in feasts, which may be seen as rites of communication that celebrated a traditional event and expressed themselves through symbolic or real means such as dancing, drinking, ceremonial, satire and sexuality.[15] Feasts celebrated not only release from work but also release from society's norms. They encouraged an atmosphere of merriment that contrasted vividly with the orderly world of conventional relationships. The disorder of feasts was, by a process paralleled in all pre-industrial societies,[16] transmuted into a series of rituals of mockery, laughter and social inversion that varied in form from community to community.[17] At one level, inversion represented the community at play, indulging the freedom to jest and criticise. At another level, role reversal, inversion and mockery can be regarded as alternative rituals offering a differing symbolism for the crucial stages of a person's role in the community. From this point of view, they were possibly subversive.

During the role reversal practised during the Feast of Innocents in early December, Catholic clergy all over western Europe gave up their role, allowed laymen to say mass, disguised themselves as women and danced in the streets. Town councils surrendered their authority for a day, appointed women as mayors, or conceded government to the youth confraternity. The festivities, we should note, were not merely 'popular' but integral to the culture of society as a whole. Nobility and ecclesiastics took part equally in the masques, celebrations and role reversals. As a young man, Philip II of Spain habitually took part in the Carnival festivities. In addition to the street celebrations, however, nobles might have their own festivities, of which perhaps the most interesting were the rites of chivalry, practised actively in the aristocratic circles of many countries throughout early modern times.

A population on the move

Early modern Europe was, like the late medieval world, predominantly a stable society in which little appeared to be changing. Most people's experience was limited to their own region. Food, tools and clothing were all normally produced within the home area. There had always been elements of movement: traders, pilgrims and artisans had ranged over the continent; a few explorers had looked to Africa and Asia in search of riches. In the course of the sixteenth century, however, men began to be aware of new and profound changes in the quality of life. William Harrison, in his *Description of England* (1577), commented that the elders in his village 'have noted...things to be marvellously altered in England within their sound remembrance'. A generation later Thomas Wilson, in his *The State of England* (1600), said that 'I find great alterations almost every year, so mutable are worldly things and worldly men's affairs'. One of the most widely noted aspects of change was population increase.

The demographic expansion of the early sixteenth century seems to have led commentators to exaggerate its impact. As early as 1518, Ulrich von Hutten claimed that 'there is a dearth of provisions and Germany is overcrowded'; while in the same year a commission of Jeronimite friars in Spain suggested that 'the surplus population of these realms go and colonise' America. In Germany in 1538, Sebastian Franck described the country as being 'full of people'. So great was the pressure on space in Swabia, according to a chronicler of 1550, that 'there was not a corner, even in the wildest woods and the highest mountains, that was not occupied'.[18] 'France is full of people', reported the Venetian ambassador there in 1561, 'every spot is occupied to capacity'. Bodin in 1568 believed that 'an infinite number of people has multiplied in this realm'. Sir John Hawkins could speak of 'England, where no room remains, her dwellers to bestow'. 'The people are increased and ground for ploughs doth want', complained an English writer in 1576.

The exaggerations reflect a basic reality that people were on the move. Most peasant societies of course remained structurally immobile. Where adult labourers had their own property, or where they were tied down by feudal obligation and seigneurial control, they were very unlikely to move away. There were fundamental structures, such as the pattern of political control and the distribution of the land, that changed very little over generations. Geography – isolation in mountain areas or quite simply a fertile environment that gave self-sufficiency – sometimes froze communities into relative immobility.

But there is ample evidence that elements within the rural societies of early modern Europe were more on the move than has been thought. For England, a study of the tax-rolls in Northamptonshire shows that in some areas up to 60 per cent of the non-freeholders disappeared between 1597 and 1628, and about 27 per cent of the freeholders.[19] About half the population of the village of Cogenhoe was replaced between 1618 and 1628.[20] In eighteen villages in Nottinghamshire, only 16 per cent of the family names present in 1544 could be found in 1641. Evidence from Germany points the same way. A study of three towns in Brandenburg shows that in Beeskow only 15 per cent of the family names present in 1518 were still there in 1652; in Freienwalde between 1652 and 1704 only four family names survived; in Driesen between 1591 and 1718 only 9 per cent of names did so. A century and a half of rural emigration is illustrated by the villages around the town of Ratzeburg (near Hamburg), where between 1444 and 1618 about 90 per cent of peasant households changed their place of residence, a fifth of them as many as seven or eight times.

Most people did not move very far. In seventeenth-century Sussex they tended not to move farther than twenty miles away. In south and central England between 1660 and 1730, an analysis of over 7,000 cases shows that more than half of those who changed their domicile did so within a range of ten miles; only 3 per cent had moved more than 100 miles. By their nature, big urban centres encouraged a rapid turnover. A London clergyman at the end of the sixteenth century claimed that every twelve years or so 'the most part of the parish changeth, as I by experience know, some going and some coming' . In east London between 1580 and 1639 only 26 per cent of studied cases were born within the locality. In Cologne one sixth of the population changed domicile between 1568 and 1574.

While many small towns and rural areas in Europe continued to experience stability of population, therefore, there is ample evidence that for other communities a high degree of movement was quite normal. Three main reasons for mobility are apparent: marriage, employment and distress. In an average small community blood relationships could present a problem. Marriages within the fourth degree of kinship were forbidden by canon law, and since a high proportion of the village's population might be interrelated it became necessary to seek outside the community for a partner. Consanguinity therefore became a barrier, but not always so in practice: in the seventeenth-century Spanish village of Pedralba (Valencia) about one tenth of marriages were within the forbidden degrees. As a rule young people in smaller settlements went, from choice or because of kinship restrictions, to neighbouring villages where they would be likely to meet prospective partners at local religious and harvest festivities.

The search for partners would occasionally provoke inter-village strife, as young men tried to defend their women against outsiders and put pressure on the girls and their families or sought dispensations from consanguinity. Community pressures of this sort might result in a high level of endogamous marriages, though in general it can be concluded that the degree of endogamy was directly related to the size of the village. In the small village of Rouvray (216 inhabitants) in seventeenth-century Champagne, 31 per cent of marriages were endogamous, while in Mussey (511 inhabitants) in the same area the figure was 68 per cent, presumably because of the larger choice available. Exogamy was always higher in the countryside than in the towns. In Altopascio (rural Tuscany) in the late seventeenth century, about 60 per cent of marriages were with a partner from outside the parish; in the community of Mediona (Catalonia) a quarter of partners came from outside. In most cases the external partner was male, suggesting that mobility for marriage was generally masculine except where there was positive discrimination against men. In exceptional circumstances, when the availability of partners was for instance made difficult by war conditions, cities might also have a high proportion of marriage with outsiders. In the course of the seventeenth century, the majority of Amsterdam bridegrooms were born outside the city; in the early century they came from the southern Netherlands, in the late century from Germany.[21]

Movement in the short distance between communities, and between communities and the city, accounted for the bulk of migration. The city was at all times the greatest magnet, offering all the prospects – freedom, fortune, marriage, work – not readily available in other communities: the increase in urban population in this period has already been noted. All classes moved cityward. In Dorset, reports that 'some of our welthie men and merchauntes be gone from us' suggest a move to the commercial attractions of London. London too was the setting of the play *The History of Richard Whittington* (1605), which showed how a penniless youth came to the big city, rose to the top of the social ladder and became thrice Lord Mayor of London. For the rural underprivileged, all cities had their streets paved with gold. In times of distress the drift to towns became a flood. In 1667, the residents of the villages of Palencia (Spain) claimed to have lost nine tenths of their population in the preceding forty years, 'households and residents moving to the large towns such as Valladolid, Rioseco, Palencia and other nearby cities, deserting their houses and property through lack of capital'.

Mobility over longer distances was occasioned primarily by the search for employment. In most rural societies migration began when children left home to enter into service, a spell as servant being part of the life cycle of a large part of the population, both male and female.[22] The years of absence from home were also directly related to the northwest European pattern of late marriage. In Ealing (England) in 1599, all the children aged under fourteen still lived at home; but 80 per cent of the boys and 30 per cent of the girls aged from fifteen to nineteen lived away from home, working with other families.[23] This young mobile labour force possibly made up one fifth of London's population in the 1690s.[24] In the city of Bern in the 1760s service personnel represented a quarter of the population. In France apprentices were encouraged to train in different towns. Jean de la Mothe, a sixteenth-century cordwainer, left his home town of Tours at the age of sixteen and ended up in Dijon four years later, after having trained in thirteen different localities. In sixteenth-century Würzburg, 93 per cent of apprentices were immigrants; in this city the group showing the highest mobility were males aged from fifteen to twenty-four years.[25] As a rule, migrants of good standing and with skills that were in ready demand did not need to move very far; whereas the lower and less skilled levels of the working population had to move farther and in greater numbers in order to find employment. The differences can be seen in Frankfurt: in the fifteenth century three quarters of immigrants who were granted the privilege of citizenship came from less than seventy-five kilometres away, whereas of the locksmiths who came to train and work, 56 per cent came from over 150 kilometres away. Figures for the city of Zürich in 1637 are similar: only 4 per cent of new citizens came from distant foreign parts (mainly Germany) but one third of apprentices did. In Oxford in 1538–57 some 45 per cent of apprentices came from distant areas of Wales and northwestern England.

Seasonal employment accounted for very large numbers of migrants, but only in specific areas of Europe, where the available data – for the seventeenth century – coincide with a period of agrarian crisis that may exaggerate its extent. Northwest Germany tended to send its workers to help with summer labour in neighbouring Holland; in the eighteenth century some districts sent half their male population.[26] Very many stayed to become part of the resident workforce, both on the land and on the ships. A village in Extremadura reported in 1575 that 'most of the people are poor, and they go to Andalusia to earn enough to eat and are gone most of the year'.[27] The best known example of Spanish seasonal emigration is that of the peasants of Galicia, who because of their inadequate landholdings emigrated regularly to Castile and Andalusia to find supplementary work, returning usually to help with their own harvest. In the same way, thousands of French rural labourers crossed the Pyrenees each summer to help gather the Spanish harvest. Seasonal workers seem not to have been dissuaded by distance: the records of the hospital at Montpellier in 1696–9 show that hundreds of labourers came from as far as northern France in search of a wage.

Distress was a regular precipitant of migration between countries. Thousands of young men left the depressed countryside and went abroad to serve in the wars: 8,000 Scots are estimated to have left their country to fight in the Thirty Years War; from Castile in the sixteenth century some 9,000 men a year went overseas to fight. Inflation, enclosures and rising rents drove rural labourers from the villages; heavy taxation and the depredations of war forced many to leave and look for a new life elsewhere. The available lands of central and eastern Europe were a magnet for emigrant groups from within the Holy Roman Empire:[28] Flemish workers who went to Gdańsk, German artisans who went to Poland, Hutterite sectarians who went to Moravia. The distress of refugees was, finally, one of the most decisive phenomena of early modern Europe.

Apart from the three reasons for movement that have been noted, it should be remembered that inheritance systems often made it necessary for young people to leave home. In areas where primogeniture (property going to the eldest alone) or impartible inheritance prevailed, such as southern France or Britain, the younger sons were obliged to leave if they wished to be their own masters. Likewise, where nuclear families predominated – in effect, northern Europe – the limited size of the property might oblige children to leave the village in order to marry or to set up home.

Emigration and refugees

From the sixteenth century attempts were made to expand the European frontier into the still unexplored reaches of the globe. The Russians had no difficulty in crossing the Urals, but their penetration of Siberia did not involve any significant movement of population: even as late as 1650 the outposts in Siberia were manned by no more than 10,000, and these were not settlers so much as mercenaries and Cossacks employed by the tsar. The hero and pioneer of the eastern frontier was Yermak, the famous brigand turned mercenary soldier, who went to Siberia in 1582. The decades after him saw no heroes, only the remorseless push forward of troop detachments and fur merchants.[29] The south of Europe was even less promising a frontier, since the whole of the eastern and southern Mediterranean lay in the hands of the Muslim powers. Parallel with and contemporary to Yermak was Sebastian, king of Portugal, who like the Russian perished in an attempt to extend the frontier. Marching out to Morocco in 1578 at the head of his army, the young king was overwhelmed by Moorish forces at the battle of Alcazar-al-Kebir. The dream, initiated by Cardinal Cisneros' conquest of Oran in 1509 and continued by Charles V after him, of extending Christian rule into Africa, was subsequently abandoned. There was no significant emigration eastward: the distances were too hazardous, and the advanced civilisations of the Arabs and the rulers of India and east Asia were too formidable a barrier.

Westward, on the other hand, there were new and apparently empty lands. 'Why then should we stand striving here for places of habitation', argued John Winthrop in 1629, 'and in the mean time suffer a whole continent [America] to be waste without any improvement?'.

The sixteenth century opened with Spain's gradual advance into America. After the discoveries of 1492, settlement was restricted largely to the West Indies and in particular to the island of Hispaniola, where the New World's first city, Santo Domingo, was founded. Thanks to the dangers and the high death rate the number of settlers was at first fairly small, some thousand in 1499. In the first decade of the sixteenth century the principal islands and the early mainland settlements were colonised. The whole enterprise was conducted extremely slowly: nearly thirty years – a whole generation – elapsed between Columbus' landfall and the conquest of Mexico City by Cortés. At the end of that timespan, however, Spain had carried out two epoch-making feats: the circumnavigation of the globe (1519–22) and the overthrow of the Aztecs (1519–21).

Great rewards were seen to await even the humblest settler. Most of the conquistadors were social nonentities: Cortés was the son of a 'poor and humble' captain of infantry; Francisco Pizarro had been a swineherd; Valdivia and Alvarado did not even know where they were born. Yet many of them achieved an apotheosis. Cortés became a marquis in 1529, with the grant of an immense territory in Mexico comprising over twenty large towns and villages and some 23,000 Indian vassals. His case also illustrates the point that the Spanish frontier in America, for all its apparent initial freedom, rapidly began to reproduce the restrictive social patterns of Spain. The earliest settlers had never wanted this: they consisted of small traders – shoemakers, blacksmiths, swordsmiths, cooks, plasterers, masons – who sought new opportunity in freedom. In Paraguay the governor asked that no lawyers be permitted, 'because in newly settled countries they encourage dissension and litigation among the people'. In Mexico, according to Bernal Díaz, the Spaniards asked 'that His Majesty be pleased not to suffer any scholars or men of letters to come into this country, to throw us in confusion with their learning, quibbling and books'.

The ease in attaining wealth, however, helped bar the way to a democratic society. Wealth can be a spur to social mobility, but in America it made the white colonists into a leisured class exploiting the native population. As new reports of fabled riches trickled through, the settlers moved into the mainland. 'Being men fond of adventure, those who go to the Indies are for the most part unmarried', observed the historian Fernández de Oviedo, 'and therefore do not feel obliged to reside in any one place. Since new lands are being discovered every day, those men believe that they will swell their purses more quickly in new territory.' A highly mobile settler class needed a secure source of labour to exploit the land and feed the population: this came from the Indians and later the blacks. 'In the Indies', reported a magistrate of Hispaniola in 1550, 'Spaniards do not work. All who go there immediately become gentlemen.' Spanish America certainly offered the underprivileged of the mother country a new perspective in life, but it did so at the cost of reproducing the inegalitarian structure of European society. The attempt to break away from the European pattern and create a new Utopian society (see Chapter 9) collapsed by the mid-sixteenth century.

English emigration westward began with Ireland. The plunder of the island by English soldiers and settlers precipitated the extensive depopulation observed by Sir William Petty. Approximately 170,000 English and 30,000 Scots had migrated to Ireland by 1672, with further substantial Scots – maybe 60,000 more – arriving before 1700.[30] When the English went to America, they began to construct a society quite distinct from the colonialist regimes in Ireland and Spanish America. In New England the relevant social feature of emigrants was their economic status rather than their religion. Consisting for the most part of small yeoman farmers and lesser traders, they were – unlike the Spaniards, and in default of a readily available labour force – content to till their own soil and trade their own produce. As a self-sufficient community they were from the beginning very close to being a one-class society, without any landlord or noble stratum above them or any depressed labour force below. There were several exceptions to this in the early days, notably in Virginia and the crown colonies, but the dominant trend, even in the proprietary colonies, was socially democratic and politically oligarchic. The attraction, then, was not so much the winning of great wealth which could be got only through farming or energetic trading, as the winning of freedom from the social barriers in Old England.

The liberty sought by emigrants was complete. One could 'live freely there', a playwright informed his London audience in 1605, 'without sergeants or courtiers or lawyers or intelligencers'. Land was free, rents rare, opportunities unlimited. Sir Edwin Sandys naively hoped that this environment would produce in Virginia 'a form of government as may be to the greatest benefit and comfort of the people, and whereby all injustice, grievances and oppression may be prevented'. Some went to the land of promise involuntarily. It became the practice (not, however, of the Spaniards) to transport penal offenders to the new lands, though less than 180 were sent to America prior to 1640. Among others forcibly transported were orphans, vagabonds, loose women and unemployed men; thereby, it was claimed with some truth, 'many men of excellent wits and of divers singular gifts...that are not able to live in England, may be raised again'. Not without reason did Captain John Smith in 1624 call America 'the poor man's best country in the world'. Much of the optimism was misplaced, and not all the colonies were as comfortable as seventeenth-century Massachusetts, where poverty was almost unknown. The positive aspects of the American experience were, however, undoubted. Liberation from the feudal structure of Europe, its class conventions, its economic disabilities and religious oppression, opened up new horizons and helped to provoke change in Europe. 'I have lived in a country', the preacher Hugh Peter, recently back from America, told the Long Parliament in 1645, 'where in seven years I never saw beggar, nor heard an oath, nor looked upon a drunkard. Why should there be beggars in your Israel when there is so much work to do?'

Though movements of population out of Europe were impressive, few can be measured with any accuracy. From Portugal about 2,400 people a year are believed to have emigrated to India in the first quarter of the sixteenth century. In mid-century the emigration to Brazil and the Atlantic took over 3,000 people a year. Since Portugal had a population of only just over a million, the drain was serious. Totals for the number of Spaniards emigrating to America are problematic. The official documentation is deficient, and there was considerable unauthorised emigration. In the half century between the discovery of America and 1550, some 150,000 Spaniards probably crossed the Atlantic; in the entire sixteenth century the total was possibly around 250,000.[31] The northern European nations did not begin to lose emigrants on any considerable scale until the seventeenth century, when perhaps 200,000 emigrated to north America and the Caribbean. Between 1620 and 1640, about 80,000 English emigrated to north America and the West Indies. By around 1800 English north America (including Canada) had around 4.5 million whites, and Spanish America around four million.

Europe was not an immobile continent. Long after the Reformation, pilgrimages caused large movements of people. The famous pilgrim route from France to Santiago de Compostela in Spain regularly brought thousands of visitors every year, even in the late seventeenth century. All the towns on the pilgrimage route profited economically from the enterprise, a lesson that has not been lost on the government of that region today. Holy Year 1575 brought 400,000 visitors to papal Rome; in 1600 the number was 536,000, and this to a city whose resident population that year was only 100,000.[32] Major cities elsewhere housed permanent foreign communities: Antwerp in 1568 had over 16 per cent of its inhabitants listed as 'foreigners', Zürich in 1637 had 14.7 per cent, London in 1587 had 4.5 per cent. To emigrate knowing that one could return home was one thing; to know that return was impossible was quite another. For hundreds of thousands, their native land became no more than a memory.

Both the Reformation and the Counter-Reformation created permanent refugees, who formed part of what has been termed 'confessional migration'.[33] Their motives were often complex, for many moved not simply to escape repression but also to continue their lives in a better environment.[34] Some Catholics could be found, for example, among the European refugees in sixteenth-century London. Fugitives from the Catholic states first became numerous in the 1540s with the creation of the Chambre Ardente in France in 1547 and the establishment of the Roman Inquisition in Italy in 1542. The Italian Protestants fled principally to Switzerland. In 1555 emigration from England began, as a result of the Catholic restoration there. Of the 800 or so English refugees who fled to the continent, most went to the Rhineland. Emigration from France was numerically the most important. Originating in the repression of the 1540s, it reached its peak after the massacre of St Bartholomew's.[35] The chief centre of refuge was Switzerland and Geneva. From 1549 to 1587 Geneva probably received as many as 12,000 French refugees, most of them in 1572. Plans were also made at this period for Protestants to emigrate to America. Admiral Coligny made efforts to set up a Huguenot colony in Brazil, and some emigrants did leave France for the New World. In the seventeenth century these efforts continued: in 1627, 600 Huguenots went to colonise the island of Saint-Christophe.

The expansion of resources devoted to warfare had a direct impact on population, through the emigration of mercenaries. Tens of thousands of Irish, for example, found a living abroad in the armies of France, Spain and Germany. The most typical case, however, was Switzerland. The cantons' population in early modern times possibly did not exceed 1.75 million, yet it has been estimated that between the sixteenth and the seventeenth centuries a total of perhaps one million Swiss men left their country to serve in foreign armies. The greater part returned, for without them the cantons would have faced a demographic crisis.

The combination of war, persecution and distress did not limit its impact to the lower classes.[36] Very many members of the elite also found it in their interest to emigrate. Italian emigrants from the sixteenth century onwards began to play a prominent part in the life of neighbouring states. They went principally to German-speaking Switzerland, from the northern cities of Vicenza, Locarno and Lucca, and their chief contribution was in textiles. Zürich's economic success came to be founded on the work of the Locarno entrepreneur Evangelista Zanino (d. 1603), who established the first large-scale industry there. The most important of the Lucca refugees, Francesco Turrettini (d. 1628), went to Geneva in 1575 and in 1593 founded the Grande Boutique, the biggest Genevan silk company of its time.[37] Those who went to France sought economic and social opportunity, brought their skills with them, and settled principally in the cities of Lyon, Paris, Nantes and Marseille.[38] Several became bankers, rose into the elite, and helped to nurture popular attitudes about the parasitic nature of Italian immigrants, an attitude that played a prominent role in later political events.

The elite were also an important component of the refugees who, during the long years of military conflict with Spain, fled from the southern Netherlands to the north. To Middelburg alone in 1584–5 over 1,900 southern families came. Southern immigration to Leiden was so heavy that it came to be looked on as a Flemish city, though the Flemings (most came from Bruges) in fact amounted to only 10 per cent of the population. From 1500 to 1574 only 7.2 per cent of the citizens (bourgeois) had come from the south; from 1575 to 1619 the figure rose to 38.4 per cent. In Amsterdam from 1575 to 1606 southerners made up 31 per cent, in Middelburg from 1580 to 1591 three quarters, of all new citizens.[39] In total, perhaps around 100,000 people moved from the southern Netherlands to the north. Netherlanders also went abroad in large numbers. In London up to the end of the sixteenth century they always formed about five sixths of the foreign population. In western Europe they lived chiefly in west Germany and notably in Frankfurt, where from 1554 to 1561 over 38 per cent of those obtaining citizenship were Netherlanders.[40] By the late 1580s the Netherlands refugees made up nearly a third of Frankfurt's population. It took a long time for so many immigrants, most of whom were poor, to become accepted by the host communities. Even noted Dutch liberals could not conceal their attitude; Grotius referred to the immigrants as 'foreigners, impatient for change' and Brandt called the southerners 'restless troublemakers'. 'People exclude us everywhere', complained the Antwerper Willem Usselincx, who in fact went on to become one of the great citizens of the Dutch Republic.

Emigration from the Celtic nations of Britain was in some measure provoked by English hegemony. Scots went to the Baltic countries and, according to an estimate of 1620, there were about 30,000 of them in Poland alone. Between 1600 and 1700 possibly 240,000 Scots emigrated from their homeland, mainly to Ireland and the Baltic countries.[41] The Irish were, of course, the most direct victims of English rule. Writing in 1596, the poet Edmund Spenser described the province of Munster as 'a most populous and plentiful country suddenly made void of man and beast'. Irish nobles, soldiers, clergy and scholars all felt obliged to emigrate. Every Catholic university on the continent had its contingent of Irishmen. Typical of these wandering scholars was young Christopher Roche of Wexford, who in 1583 at the age of twenty-two took passage to Bordeaux, worked and taught for his living there, then went on to study in Toulouse, Paris, Lorraine (for three years), Antwerp, Brussels, Douai and St Ouen, a long tour of eight years, during which he both worked for his food and studied when his circumstances allowed.[42] Sir William Petty, as we have seen, estimated Irish population losses in mid-century alone as over half a million. This total included deportees, of whom 'there were transported into Spain, Flanders, France, 34,000 soldiers; and of boys, women, priests etc no less than 6,000 more, where not half are returned'; and those transported to the Barbados and elsewhere as slaves (estimated at about 10,000).

The largest mass deportation in early modern history was that of the Moriscos from Spain. In 1569, as the result of a rebellion, Moriscos had been expelled from Granada and exiled to Castile. Attempts to Christianise these Moriscos, as well as those in the communities of Valencia and Aragon, were unsuccessful. When the expulsion was eventually decided upon, it was in the conviction that the Moriscos were an alien minority; yet many informed Spaniards including nobles, clergy, intellectuals and government ministers were opposed in principle to the measure. The expulsions began in April 1609 and, with various intervals, continued up to 1614. In all, some 300,000 Moriscos were deported, representing a third of the population of Valencia and a fifth of that of Aragon, with smaller proportions from other parts of Spain. The great majority went to north Africa: in some towns, such as Algiers, they were well received; in others, they were hated as foreigners. Perhaps as many as 50,000 were received in France, but most decided to travel on to the Levant because of hostility from the French government.

The Thirty Years War was responsible for another great migration, from the Czech nation. The battle of the White Mountain (1620) marked the end of Czech independence. The first refugees were the elite who had served the Winter King, Frederick of the Palatinate. Early in 1621 the arrests and expulsions began. Fifty of the Czech leaders were arrested and their estates confiscated: in June twenty-five of them, both Catholic and Protestant, were executed. Religious persecution began somewhat later, and not until 1624 were the last Protestant clergy ordered out of the country. In 1627 alone about 36,000 families fled Bohemia.[43] Inevitably there were others who came in to take their place: over the years 1618–53, outsiders made up 87 per cent of those who obtained citizenship in Prague.[44] Voluntary and involuntary evacuation reduced the population of some towns by as much as a third. By the end of the Thirty Years War the population of Bohemia had sunk by 45 per cent, that of Moravia by a quarter.

The peak of Huguenot emigration from France was reached with the persecution before and after Louis XIV's revocation of the Edict of Nantes. Some two million people, or one tenth of France's population, were Huguenots, living principally in the southwest of the country. As religious persecution gathered momentum in the 1680s, many resolved to emigrate, though the bulk of refugees left only after the Edict of Nantes (which had theoretically granted toleration since 1598) was officially revoked in October 1685. The Calvinist clergy were expelled, but Huguenots in general were discouraged from leaving. Despite this, some 200,000 French people fled their country between about 1680 and 1720. The largest numbers (70,000) went to the United Provinces, the rest to England, Brandenburg, and other Protestant countries. The refugees were mainly from the professional and artisan classes, who could rebuild their careers in a strange land; but even members of the highest elite chose to go abroad, among them two of France's most prominent generals, Schomberg and Ruvigny. The revocation and emigration were inevitably condemned by Protestant nations, and many Frenchmen both then and later doubted the wisdom of the measure. In 1716 the council of Commerce claimed that of the many reasons for France's declining trade position, 'the first is the flight of our Religionists who have transplanted our industry to foreign soil'. In fact, the revocation varied in its impact, and was not uniformly disastrous. Business and industrial centres like Paris and Lyon, where there had been few Huguenots, were barely affected. France's problems at the end of the century were due to a number of factors, among which the revocation was not always the most important.

Refugees helped to transfer technical skills from one country to another.[45] Although some social tension was caused in host communities, the newcomers contributed handsomely to their new economic environment.[46] The growth of commerce in Leipzig was sustained almost entirely, over two centuries, by the efforts of immigrant traders and financiers.[47] Emigration also extended national culture. In Alsace-Lorraine, the frontier of the German language was extended several kilometres as a result of emigration after the Thirty Years War. The same happened to a significant extent in both Switzerland and Bohemia. Culture was likewise transplanted, but usually to the detriment of the country of origin: of some 10,000 Czech exiles in Saxony in the mid-seventeenth century, as many as 22 per cent were nobles or intellectuals, a proportion that must have helped to impoverish intellectual life in Bohemia after the White Mountain.

Rich and poor suffered dispossession equally. Like the Moriscos, few saw their native homes again. 'If I forget thee, Jerusalem, let my tongue cleave to the roof of my mouth….How shall we sing the Lord's song in a strange land?'

3

COMMUNITIES OF BELIEF

> Often when on a winter's night we youngsters were seated round the hearth, [my aunt] would set her wheel aside, take a pinch of snuff, and excite our curiosity and wonder by strange and fearful tales of witches, spirits and apparitions, whilst we listened in silence and awe, and scarcely breathing, contemplated in imagination the visions of an unseen world which her narratives conjured up before us.
>
> (Samuel Bamford, *Early Days*, 1549)

The ritual year

There was an evident social distinction in pre-industrial society between the diversions of the elite, based on property and privilege, and the diversions of the people, based on communal tradition. But both formed part of a common culture. Both occupied a crucial role in daily life, and were intimately tied to the everyday framework of religious belief, which seemed to govern most aspects of existence. Religion in pre-industrial society was less a matter of strict creeds than of social rituals and symbols. Christianity was not simply the list of beliefs and practices laid down by the Church; it was also the sum of inherited attitudes and rituals relating both to the invisible and to the visible world.[1] All sections of society, in both town and country, participated in these rituals, which on one hand determined leisure and work activity, and on the other hand assigned people roles and status within the community. On this view, there was no separate entity that we might refer to as 'popular' culture; traditional culture was shared in, to a greater or lesser degree, by all sections of the community. Moreover, there was no formal separation between the sacred and the secular in early modern Europe; the sacred was always part of the profane world, on which it drew for its symbols and functioning. Religious leaders, both Protestant and Catholic, subsequently spent much effort in claiming a special and privileged place for the 'sacred', but were less successful than they might have hoped.[2]

The interaction of ritual and religion can still be seen today in parts of Europe that have managed to retain their old traditions. Through the surviving documentation, scholars have attempted to penetrate this disappearing world, in order to understand more about the way in which the great revolutions known as the Reformation and the Counter-Reformation came about. Considered at one time as two great theological systems locked in struggle for the soul of European man, the movements are now seen to have had much in common. Both were heirs to the same reforming, humanist tradition; both shared a wish to extirpate superstition and inculcate a new morality. While Luther was preaching change in Germany, the Franciscans inveighed in America against superstition, animism, idolatry and other ineradicable obstacles to the faith. In the same decade the theologian Alfonso de Castro pointed out that these defects existed also in Spain: in the Basque mountains, he had heard, they even worshipped a goat. The Protestants realised that it was not enough to persuade the people to give up popery, but the Jesuits also in their correspondence recognised that Europe remained to be converted: there were 'Indies' at home no less than in the New World. The fact that there was a common drive against irreligion should not, however, obscure an elementary distinction between the Catholics and the Protestants: the former were fighting against traditional unbelief, the latter considered that Catholicism itself was the great unbelief.[3]

The environment into which zealots of Reform and Counter-Reform thrust their dogmatic certainties was overwhelmingly rural. It was a largely unlettered world, often isolated from the culture of the great cities; the dominant realities were the precariousness of harvests and the insecurity of life. Food and survival, as in primitive rural communities today, dictated social, moral and religious attitudes. Poor diet, frequent crop failures and a high mortality rate were all, as we have seen, not mere hazards but part of the very fabric of existence. They were therefore accepted as inevitable: the response to them was not necessarily one of fear or of profound anxiety, as is sometimes suggested, but of determination to overcome the obstacles to survival. Then as now, people took out insurance against what they could not foresee or control. Religion was a major protective force, and where official religion seemed inadequate other rites were used. Life was not, for all that, a pessimistic attempt to ward off disaster. Given that some things were inevitable, there was every reason to abandon oneself to joy and celebration. In a rural Europe, there could never be the full-time labour of post-industrial society, and the Christian Church obliged by turning at least one third of the days in the year into obligatory feasts.

Ritual festivities – plays, carnivals, processions – were not incidental but a major, integral and regular aspect of life.[4] They were essential to the life of the community, which normally dictated their form and content; and they were pleasing to the Church, with whose great festivals (Christmas, pre-Lenten Carnival) they coincided. The mixture of communal and religious elements in popular festivities had always caused problems and friction, but long use tended to hallow the ceremonies. In a pre-industrial economy, virtually all rituals were related to the agrarian life of the community; some might be wholly agrarian in nature but were normally permitted within the ambit of a church service.

A division may be made between rituals of joy, which welcomed in the seasons of the year, and rituals of protection; all coincided with the liturgical cycle of the Christian churches. The annual calendar began at Christmas, succeeded very quickly by an outburst of celebration for Carnival, which was the prelude to Lent, the season of waiting and reflection. After the spring equinox, the month of May arrived with its symbols of life and fertility. Work resumed in the fields, and the productive season was crowned by the midsummer fire rituals of St John's Eve, when in London there were 'bonfires in the streets, every man's door with garlands of flowers, lamps burning all night', as the annalist John Stow remembered.[5] From July the harvest was gathered in, with further celebrations in the community.

One feature of community festivities was the deliberate inversion of authority roles – referred to in the last chapter – at a time of celebration. Wise men and fools, princes and beggars, old age and youth, were exchanged, reversed and stood upside down, in a brief mockery of the world and its ways. At carnivals, similarly, there was an informal licence to gluttonise (as a prelude to Lent, when no meat could be eaten), be lascivious, and misbehave. Role reversal occurred in the English custom of the 'lords of misrule', and in the west European custom of the 'boy bishop' (who was placed in the bishop's chair at some Christmas celebrations). Partly as a role reversal, partly also as a gesture to sexual fecundity, young people were given a leading part in carnivals, festivities and harvest ceremonies; in some areas the young were organised (as we have seen in Chapter 2) into 'abbeys of misrule' headed by an 'abbot' (in Provence) or other symbolic personage. They also directed 'charivaris', a curious custom of making a noise at second weddings (Chapter 8). During the great religious feasts, such as Corpus Christi was in southern Europe, all the ingenuity of the community was directed to organising processions, with giant statues, dances and music. Some of the celebration might be incorporated into the church service, as in Artois where sheep were brought into midnight mass, or in Besançon where the labourers did a dance in the church to mark the end of the wine harvest.

There were also rituals of protection, which predominated among the types of ritual used by the community.[6] In the Mediterranean, which suffered from frequent droughts, virtually all religious processions were made in order to intercede for rain. Of thirty-four identified processions in eighteenth-century Barcelona, thirty-three were pleas for rain and one was for protection against epidemic.[7]

Death in pre-industrial society was never greeted passively. Wholly uncontrollable scourges, such as an epidemic, were accepted with resignation, but no effort was spared to identify the origins, control the outbreak and punish those deemed culpable of bringing it in. Violent death was always looked on as an outrage. In spite of this, it is true that mortality was a close companion of all Europeans. As a result, there grew up an extensive series of rituals connected with death, both now and in the afterlife. Death was an individual, personal experience, but it took place within one's family or community and involved passing into another.

For many Christians the late medieval doctrine of purgatory, a halfway stage between heaven and hell, offered some hope to the dead sinner. The soul in purgatory could be fully cleansed of its sins by the prayers of the living, and so pass into paradise. But the doctrine never adequately penetrated all corners of Christendom, and was being formally reaffirmed (for example, in Spain) only as late as the seventeenth century.[8] By then, half of Europe – the Protestant half – had turned its back on the doctrine.

Repeated use over centuries of the term 'Christendom' has tended to make us think of pre-Reformation Catholic Europe as a monolith, and of 'belief' as participation in a great universal creed. More recently, scholars have preferred to place emphasis on what 'belief' really meant in the day to day experience of ordinary Christians. The picture that emerges, at the popular level of villages and towns, is of a Christian body made up of an infinite multiplicity of local communities that could easily, under pressure, split apart from the official structure of the Church and cause it to disintegrate. The peasants who took part in the great revolts (1525) in the German lands demanded that their beliefs should be rooted only in the community.[9] It was not a demand for something new, but a reaffirmation of what already existed. If beliefs were to be scaled down everywhere to the local level, the universal Church became superfluous. This was the threat that seemed to be directed against Catholic Christendom, but that in time every Church organisation, both Catholic and Protestant, had to contend with.

Disciplining belief: confessionalisation

In pre-industrial Europe, 'religion' was a social system that pervaded all aspects of life, and 'belief' implied a firm assent to its principles. One influential view[10] has suggested that the late medieval system offered men a broad range of spiritual and psychological alternatives (summarised in the concept of 'magic') that later became unavailable in the reformed system offered by the Reformation. The view should be modified in one important respect: the alternatives were seldom part of the official 'belief' of the Church, and flourished rather within the society in which the Church functioned. In a very real sense, the old Church could even be criticised for its lack of 'magic' and lack of answers to the spiritual and moral problems posed by post-Renaissance society. Both before and after the Reformation, believing Catholics went *outside* the Church for folk remedies and practices, or for exotic knowledge, or for spiritual and mystical solutions to their anxieties. Both Catholics and Protestants were in this way heirs to a tradition of unofficial religion that had always coexisted with official 'belief' and was not considered contradictory to it. Many in authority were sceptical of the ideas of Paracelsus or the prognostications of Nostradamus, but the two thinkers were representative of an extensive area of free intellectual speculation. In the same way, at a more popular level the prophetic tradition, expressed most famously by Savonarola but continued throughout Europe by various religious men and women, such as Muggleton in seventeenth-century England, was not always considered alien to official belief. Within the heart of post-Tridentine Spain, the highest nobility of the court of Philip II became supporters of prophetic cranks.[11]

The generation of religious reformers in the sixteenth century perceived the problem as essentially one of ignorance. Well before the Reformation, critics had pointed to the low cultural level of the country areas and the superficial Christianity of those who participated in the festivals but who otherwise came seldom to church or communion and sought remedies for their daily ills in superstitious practices. Many of these ignorant simple folk were in later years singled out as witches. The Protestant reformers were faced with a dual problem: the survival of Catholic practice and the continuation of popular rites. The former survived for a remarkably long time: 'three parts at least of the people', it was claimed of England with some exaggeration in 1584, 'are wedded to their old superstition still'. As late as 1604 the people of Lancashire were said to be in the habit of crossing themselves 'in all their actions'. In seventeenth-century Languedoc the sign of the cross was still used among Calvinists, and the cult of the saints continued for a long time in the Lutheran Rhineland. More ineradicable than Catholic practice, however, were the popular customs: the agrarian festivals, maypoles and Morris dances in England; the 'maypole garlands, carnal songs and choruses' condemned by Dutch Calvinists in 1591. After persistent legislation and prohibition, it proved possible to do away with most Catholic as well as popular rites; but that was no guarantee that the people were being Christianised. Lutherans could complain in Wolfenbüttel in the 1570s that 'people do not go to church on Sundays....Even if one finds a man or woman who remembers the words, ask him who Christ is, or what sin is, and he won't be able to give you an answer.' From Wiesbaden in 1594 it was reported that 'all the people hereabout engage in superstitious practices with familiar and unfamiliar words, names and rhymes...they also make strange signs, they do things with herbs, roots, branches'. Criticisms of this sort were invariably made by men with high and exacting theological standards, and may not fully reflect the real situation.

The evidence does suggest, however, that Protestant reformers were up against more than mere survival of Catholic or community rituals: in a real sense, they were beginning to penetrate into regions where Christianity had never shown its face. This situation was worst in isolated and mountainous areas, but there were also large patches of ignorance close to civilisation. In Essex as late as 1656 there were apparently people as ignorant of Christianity as the Red Indians, and Hampshire was said to have 'ignorant heathenish people'. In many parts of Europe, then, the Protestants were attempting to convert people not just from Catholicism but in effect from paganism. In the process, they were trying to change generations of culture at all levels and replace it with a new disciplined outlook.[12]

The Catholics started from the same point: Erasmus, for example, condemned a carnival he had witnessed in Siena in 1509 as 'unchristian'.

Church legislators were trying to stamp out disorder, licentiousness and superstition long before the Reformation commenced. The Protestant movement gave a timely stimulus to ineffective and half-hearted Catholic efforts, which picked up energy only from the mid-sixteenth century and after the closure of the Council of Trent (1563). Although the Counter-Reformation may appear to have had a simpler task, that of defending what existed and purifying it, in reality the obstacles were no less daunting, because the Catholic reformers were committed to changes as revolutionary as those proposed by the Protestants. Their early missionaries quickly concluded that much of Catholic Europe was still pagan. 'Near Bordeaux', reported an appalled Jesuit in 1553, 'stretch about thirty leagues of forest whose inhabitants live like rude beasts, without any concern for heavenly things. You can find persons fifty years old who have never heard a mass or learnt one word of religion.' There were similar reports from Spain[13] and Italy. Another Jesuit in Brittany in 1610 was horrified to see women beating and drowning images of saints who had not answered prayers.

In the course of the later sixteenth century, both in Catholic and in Protestant Europe, the authorities took the initiative of imposing order on their people. The impact was more decisive in Protestant areas, where changes in the power structure, often accompanied by military conflict, had broken down political relationships and undermined the autonomy of community religion. It became imperative in these areas to impose stability. Some German historians have identified for these years, roughly from about 1560 to the outbreak of the Thirty Years War, the beginning of an effort by German territorial rulers to impose a social and theological framework that would strengthen their states. This development, which has been termed 'confessionalisation', suffers like all labels from imprecision, from the considerable evidence of exceptions, and from its inapplicability to other regions of Europe. For some scholars it provides a useful way of explaining the move, at least within the Germanic lands, to creating a state-wide context rather than simply a regional one for the development of religion.[14] On this showing, the stabilisation of religious structures aided the development of the territorial state.

Disciplining of religion was undertaken at two levels: at the top, through a spate of legislation both from the state and from the religious authorities; and at the popular level, through missionary activity. Coercive legislation became a typical feature of Protestant states: penalties were threatened against those who did not attend the new services, or continued with old practices, or observed customs that the new faith deemed licentious. Calvinist Geneva became famous for its stringent application of the new regulations. The evidence suggests that coercion may have worked more in small communities, such as Geneva, than in larger ones. A report on the northwest counties, made to the English Privy Council in 1591, stated that 'small reformation has been made there, as may appear by the emptiness of churches on Sundays and holidays and the multitude of bastards and drunkards'.[15] In Brandenburg strict ordinances were passed in 1566 and 1572, with little practical result. The officials there reported in 1572 that 'the former disorder and gross disobedience continues unabated'; all attempts to control prenuptial sex failed; and in 1586 'although the ringing of bells has been abolished it still persists'.[16]

Where effective change occurred, it came from within the community itself. In England, more reformation was achieved at local level by the religious practices of influential members of the elite than by all the repression decreed by bishops.[17] This explains why a creed organised on the basis of fully autonomous religious communities, like Calvinism, scored successes in imposing moral control. Within their small communities, presided over by pastors, the Calvinists paid attention to all types of divergence from the approved norm; they discussed and controlled matters dealing with belief, personal behaviour, family life, sexuality and dress.[18] The discipline was internal and voluntary, not external or imposed from above.

'Confessionalisation' had various shapes and forms; in many areas, such as the Palatinate, it appears to have provoked resistance rather than conformity. Protestant 'confessionalisation' was set in motion by structural changes at the top.[19] The tendency since the end of the Reformation period had been for state units and their rulers to adhere to one official creed only. This insistence on uniformity provoked disastrous and negative consequences in the last real religious conflict of European history, the Thirty Years War. After the war, the attempt to identify religious allegiance with state allegiance seems to have decayed. From the end of the seventeenth century, confessional solidarity was certainly being reinforced, but mainly at the traditional community level. For example, in Augsburg the two dominant faiths, Lutheran and Catholic, asserted their identities and separateness without attempting to achieve exclusive control of state power.[20] In some cities and states, this retreat from full confessionalisation came to produce, by the eighteenth century, a measure of civil toleration. A notable case is Brandenburg-Prussia, where different regions of the state allowed a practical toleration to all faiths, without the state itself attempting to impose an overall conformity. In Lutheran Hamburg toleration was slowly introduced.[21]

Like the newly formed Protestant faiths, the Catholics also had to struggle to impose their forms of control. The problem arose in part out of the enormous inroads that other authorities had made into Church jurisdiction. In Tarbes in the French Pyrenees, the bishop could nominate to only half the benefices in his diocese; in Mallorca in 1590 the bishop controlled only 7 per cent of benefices. In the same way, many other spheres of Church activity were effectively out of its control. The church building itself was frequently the property not of the Church but of nobles or the community; the religious services held in it were governed by traditional usage rather than by ecclesiastical custom; the public processions held in the name of religion were invariably regulated and led by laymen. In eighteenth-century Pamplona, virtually all the parish priests were appointed by the community rather than by the bishop. With support from the state, Church authorities therefore began a systematic attempt to impose order on the disordered Catholic body.

But the evidence for Catholic Europe outside Germany suggests that religious change was not utilised, as it was by German authorities, for the purpose of state-building; the role of 'confessionalisation' in the Mediterranean, for example, was negligible. Though substantial novelties were introduced into the faith and practice of European Catholics, the continuity of Catholic political systems, and the fact that the ruling classes had not altered their confessional allegiances, minimised visible change.

The Counter-Reformation produced new religious orders, new religious services (including a new mass), new prayers and practices, and reinforced the role of both clergy and bishops. It also inspired impressive new music, art and architecture. The changes introduced from above took a long time, perhaps more than a century, to filter through into the daily practice of Catholics. Through the period of most intense reform, the Catholic communities of the countryside, as shown clearly from the experience of the villages in the bishopric of Speyer[22] and the bishopric of Barcelona, maintained their autonomy in religious belief and in church administration. Reaffirmation of religion took place within the old parameters of a community faith.

Though changes at the level of the state system were limited in Catholic countries, important developments took place at the level of societal structure. A substantial shift in power took place within society, even at village level, giving thereby to the Church a primacy that it had not possessed in late medieval times. Three forms of discipline were affected.[23] Public order was reformed, allowing the Church to control feast days (formerly secularised), carnivals, morality and all public matters affecting religion. Celebrations such as Corpus Christi were allowed to pass under Church control, and public processions were now headed by priests. Second, the Church reaffirmed control over its clergy and over their unique capacity to celebrate matrimony and the sacraments and administer other parish matters. The bishop was affirmed as the competent authority, and all clergy at the fringes of the episcopal structure were marginalised. Uncontrollable countryside religion, in the form of itinerant clergy and pious hermits,[24] was frowned upon and sometimes prosecuted. Formerly the parish had been under the control of the community, and lay power was expressed by institutions which were independent of the hierarchy. Now the village church came to be seen as an outpost of episcopal authority. Finally, religion became universalised, with universal piety (and universal saints) taking precedence over local and community religion. Italian practices (such as use of the confessional), rituals and saints no longer remained Italian but were exported to other Catholic countries. The form of the mass became standardised and imposed, despite much opposition, on all Catholics everywhere. A traveller from Poland would now find himself in an identical Catholic environment whether he went to church in Warsaw, Paris or Palermo.

One consequence of greater Church activity was the use of pressure against non-Catholics, a policy that provoked religious persecution and many decades of military conflict. Pressure continued long after the end of the epoch of so-called 'religious' wars. The outstanding example was the long persecution to which French Protestants were subjected in the seventeenth century, culminating in the expulsion of a fifth of their number from France in 1685 (the famous Revocation of the Edict of Nantes). In Germany a similar persecution took place, with the expulsion from Salzburg territory in 1731–2 of 20,000 of its Protestant population.[25] The important changes in the structure of religion, accompanied by a sharpening of ideological conflict, did not, however, always lead to confrontation. Coexistence of communities with different faiths was still a continuing reality in the confessional age. Across the whole of northern Europe, in both town and country, Catholics and Protestants lived together peaceably even while their political systems practised discrimination. They remained rivals for power, and followed distinct professional and economic lives; but they evolved towards mutual acceptance rather than towards conflict. In the period after the peace of Westphalia (1648), Germans of all faiths coexisted. In Augsburg Catholics and Lutherans shared office; in Osnabrück Catholic and Lutheran rulers alternated; in one northern German village (Goldenstedt) officials even attended each other's religious services.[26]

Disciplining belief: the missions

The Protestant and Catholic reform movements were directed towards the rural frontiers of Europe. It was some time before religious leaders turned their efforts to the core of unbelief, or ignorance of belief, in the urban centres. In 1595, when the police arrested a young beggar in Rome, he informed them that the beggars were not well disposed to the Faith: 'among us few practise it, because most of us are worse than Lutherans'. The Spanish writer Pedro Ordóñez observed (1672) of the urban vagabonds that 'they live like barbarians, for they are not known to, nor have they been seen to, go to mass or confession or communion'.

Many minority groups still remained marginal to Christianity. The Gypsies, even when nominally Christian, were unable because of their nomadic way of life to have normal recourse to the sacraments. They were therefore consistently treated as non-Christians by the authorities, and persecuted. The nomadic Cossacks were likewise barely Christianised: some stages of Stenka Razin's revolt in 1670 were directed openly against the established religion. In Spain and Portugal it was known that many *conversos* nurtured hostility to the official faith. But the most notable examples within Christendom were the Islamic communities of the Balkans and of Spain. In regions where the Spanish Moriscos lived, the traveller could pause and wonder as, on the eve of a Muslim fast, every dwelling in sight remained shuttered and closed and no living man could be seen. One hundred years after their forced conversion to Christianity (around 1500), the Moriscos scandalised the conscience of the Counter-Reformation, which in Spain initiated from the 1560s an intense campaign of missionary activity in their areas.

Among the obstacles to reform was the inadequacy of the clergy. Drawing on long experience and on the support of well established institutions, the Catholic Church was able to train and recruit a reformed clergy that surpassed in quality anything the Protestant reformers could offer. But there remained serious impediments, notably that of language. Throughout the continent, missionaries found themselves frustrated by their inability to teach or preach in local tongues. Attempts to introduce the new Protestant English Prayer Book in 1549 to the Cornish people were met by rejection and revolt. In Italy strong official opposition to translating the Bible into the vernacular was backed up by the argument that in reality Italy had no vernacular language.[27] The problem was gravest of all in preaching. In Spain, some Catalan and Basque congregations had to put up in the 1560s with sermons being preached to them in a language they did not understand, Spanish. When in 1620 the Jesuits undertook a mission to the south of Catalonia and delivered sermons for the first time in the native language, the people exclaimed, 'At last we can understand the preachers!'

Missions were a major innovation in Europe. In the early years of European expansion many Catholic clergy – the most famous of them was the Basque Jesuit Francis Xavier – had looked to the 'Indies' of America and Asia as the ideal terrain to seek souls for Christ. With the need to protect souls in Europe against heresy came the realisation that there were also 'Indies' in Europe, primarily among the rural population. As a direct consequence of the Council of Trent, which ended in 1564, Catholic missions, led principally by the Jesuits, began an energetic programme of work in Italy, the Germanic lands and Spain. During the century 1650–1750 the Catholic missions formed a vast network across all Europe.[28] They were no exercise in mere piety, but rather a sophisticated effort to discipline the population by, on one hand, the cleansing rites of confession and contrition, and on the other, a superb display of baroque theatre expressed through music, processions and emotive sermons. For the most part the ritual worked. Though it often had the negative consequence of heightening religious tensions, it would be an exaggeration to describe the campaign as repressive or as an offensive that tried to terrify the masses into orthodoxy.[29] There is little convincing evidence that the process was one in which an elite culture was imposed on a popular culture, resulting in the transformation and sometimes disappearance of the latter. This may have happened, but in very few regions. The argument is perhaps more plausible when applied to external aspects (post-Reformation Catholicism, for example, differed strikingly from the late medieval variety), but again it is important to take account of the continuity in much religious practice.

Whereas the Protestant effort had been split into distinct areas and separate confessional loyalties, the Catholic effort became from the 1560s a vast coordinated campaign backed by pope, bishops, councils and missionary clergy. Literature was examined and purified, plays were banned, popular participation in carnivals and feasts was regulated, a whole range of liturgical customs (like the boy bishop, or dancing in church, or seasonal rites such as the song of the Sibyl in the Christmas service) was rapidly done away with, and statues and paintings were censored. Religious practice was thoroughly revised. The reforms were by no means simply a consequence of the Reformation. Long before Luther, Church authorities had been attempting to impose their preferences on a barely Christianised population. In Mallorca, attempts to control the public celebration of Carnival can be dated back to the fifteenth century. The authorities there banned indecent dances, the donning of clerical dress by carousers, running naked through the streets, and the wearing of masks.[30] We can see the impact in Catalonia, where the bishops and the religious orders eliminated popular religious practices, enforced the new ritual (Catalonia, like England, had had a distinct rite of mass), ordered Sabbath observance, set up Sunday schools, changed the imagery in the churches, and stopped the custom of 'playing the guitar and singing profane songs before the Sacrament' (1610).

Of the several disciplinary tools used by the Catholic reform movement, one was uniquely important: the resort to confession. A respected and traditional sacrament, after the Council of Trent confession was slowly transformed from being a seasonal community ritual (resorted to once a year) into the main ingredient of a new routine of devotion and discipline. Seldom properly understood by the population, it was often used simply as a way of denouncing hated neighbours to the parish priest. Developed in particular by the Jesuits, who used it to remarkable effect in (for example) Austria, Bavaria[31] and Catalonia, confession became the key to moral discipline and official spirituality. In the French Pyrenees[32] and in Spanish Lille,[33] it became the primary weapon of missionaries during the seventeenth century. In Milan the archbishop, Carlo Borromeo, introduced (in 1565) a new structure called a 'confessional' in which penitents could preserve their anonymity while confessing their sins.

The effect of all this in both Catholic and Protestant Europe was comparable. The forms of religious and popular culture were extensively modified within two or three generations. Protestant religious music came to dominate and even replace other forms of melody, filtering down into the everyday singing of ordinary folk. Catholic hymnology was never so successful; on the other hand, Catholics were offered brilliant new music, brighter churches, new devotions, new saints. Even in traditionalist Spain, the new Catholicism was recognisably different, and therefore not easily accepted by either people or clergy. Missionaries of both faiths were concerned to replace a defective culture with a new one. The changes, however, were difficult to enforce. The notion of 'confessionalisation' suggests coercion, but popular culture was flexible and not easily extirpated. Ordinary people by their mere passivity made it difficult for new morality and attitudes to be enforced. After a constant campaign of preaching in a village in Cambridgeshire, the preacher Richard Greenham in 1591 gave up and left, blaming 'the unteachableness of that people'; in 1611 a parish priest in Catalonia explained to his bishop that he did not hold catechism classes because nobody came to them. Despite such failures the frontiers of Christianity were certainly extended. In the mountains of Languedoc, Bohemia, Asturias and

Wales peoples who had not been instructed were slowly introduced to Christianity. In the Western Isles of Scotland, where Presbyterian preachers did not venture, intrepid Catholic missionaries implanted for the first time a Christianity that endures down to today. Reformation and Counter-Reformation merged into each other: overtly hostile, they were in practice part of a single great movement to transform the habits and attitudes of old Europe.

Though changes occurred, it is not clear how profound they were. Since in most of Europe religion and ritual were the preserve of the community, it appears that changes in belief and practice made headway only where the community accepted them.[34] Novelties with which the villages felt uneasy were certainly accepted, but then quietly allowed to relapse. Many changes were never absorbed: 'to the men and women of the villages, official religion played a small role'.[35] If certain traditional practices disappeared, it may have been not because of pressure but simply because the people had adopted newer cultural forms. A case in point is the celebration of Midsummer Eve, the feast of St John. In England the midsummer fires were celebrated until at least the mid-sixteenth century everywhere and in some regions well into the nineteenth century.[36] There was little recorded opposition to the practice after the sixteenth century, and the custom perished through disuse. In Spain, where there was no opposition to the custom, it also perished through disuse; already in eighteenth-century Barcelona a writer could refer to the fires of St John as being a custom of 'the old days'.

Despite the many objectives shared in common by Catholic and Protestant reformers, it is clear that they were working in different directions. In trying to eliminate ignorance and superstition, the two faiths had in mind quite different goals; the Catholics aimed to control and reassert, the Protestants aimed to overturn and rebuild. Despite their efforts, over broad areas of Europe the people remained poorly Christianised, ripe material for the 'de-Christianisation' brought in by the French Revolution and the secular gospels of the subsequent period.

Dissidences: witchcraft

Popular belief in the villages had always assumed that there were unofficial solutions to common problems. A loved one who did not reciprocate, a recurrent illness, a cow that would not give milk: all these could be attended to by the local wise woman (or man), who would offer lotions, unguents or verbal spells. Fortune-telling, love potions, divination for lost goods, were 'white' magic, serving where religion and medicine were unable to. By extension, evil effects could be brought about, such as putting a curse on someone or making their cattle sick: this was *maleficium* (evil-doing), sometimes called 'black magic'. Though both black and white magic had a recognisable function at the popular level, the belief was also firmly rooted in the uppermost levels of society: princes and prelates were known to be interested in the possibilities of supernatural power.

At various times in the medieval period people were tried and condemned for practising *maleficia*. When this involved using alien diabolic help the crime was also called sorcery (*sortilegium*). Nobody questioned that diabolic intervention was possible, since medieval theology and imagery had continually emphasised the reality of the devil. It is more doubtful if the devil played any part in everyday village magic, which was more preoccupied with finding answers to the anxieties and insecurity that ordinary people encountered in their normal activities. From the fifteenth century, for reasons that are still obscure, commentators began to take the notion of diabolic interference seriously. The authors of the German handbook the *Malleus Maleficarum* ('Hammer of Witches') (1486) claimed that witches worked harm 'by the help of the devil, on account of a compact which they have entered into with him'. More than this, it claimed that witches acted communally, by attending midnight meetings called Sabbats at which they worshipped the devil and performed unspeakable rites. The act of fealty to Satan immediately transformed witchcraft into heresy. As evidence from witch trials became available, learned jurists and theologians analysed and identified the problem. Distinguished manuals were written by men such as Jean Bodin (1580); the coadjutor bishop of Trier, Peter Binsfield (1589); the chief justice of Burgundy, Henri Boguet (1591); the procurator-general of Lorraine, Nicolas Rémy (1595); and the Belgian Jesuit Martín del Río (1599). Their works were cited as authority by subsequent 'witch-finders', and gradually the notion of the Sabbat worked its way into general recognition, except in England where the Roman law of the continent was not current and its concepts consequently not used. The learned men by no means initiated or promoted persecution of witches; virtually all denunciations originated from below, where the origins of the phenomenon must be sought.

In early modern Europe tens of thousands of people were executed for sorcery between about 1500 and 1700. Though the numbers of executed have usually been exaggerated, there is common agreement that two thirds of all those condemned were from the German-speaking lands. Some have described it as a witch-craze (*Hexenwahn*), thereby stressing the irrational element. It has also been suggested that since diabolic witchcraft was deemed a heresy, its prosecution conformed to the intolerance of a confessional age. Yet possibly only one heretic died in western Europe for every ten witches executed.[37]

The German historian Hansen pointed out that mountainous areas were particularly affected, notably the Alps and Pyrenees: the name applied to one group of Alpine heretics, the Vaudois, was in the fifteenth century applied also to witches in France and Belgium (in Arras in 1459–61, thirty-two 'Vaudois' were tried and eighteen of them executed). The biggest Spanish outbreak, in 1610, was in the Pyrenees; the most sizeable French outbreak, as recorded by Pierre Delancre, in Toulouse and the French Pyrenees. The great witchhunter Henri Boguet operated in the mountains of Franche Comté in the 1580s. Victims came largely from remote and relatively inaccessible regions with a low cultural level and a poor record of practising Christianity. Where Christ had not reached, the old folk superstitions were still strong. Perhaps the most intensively affected area was central Europe, both by the borders of and within Switzerland. The Valtelline was a hotbed of witchcraft, and so too was Geneva in the time of Calvin. The theory that victims of witchcraft prosecution were mainly unlettered mountaineers out of reach of civilisation is, however, not easy to reconcile with the fact that they were also drawn from lowland areas such as Essex and the Netherlands. Even these might be fitted into a pattern if we accept the view that witchcraft flourished in all marginal, outlying areas, whether mountain or lowland; but this cannot apply to southern Germany, where the phenomenon was frequently urban.

People accused of witchcraft were generally from the lower levels of rural society. 'It is amazing', commented the Italian humanist Galateo when the witch-fear began seeping through southern Italy in the early sixteenth century, 'how this fantasy has seized on everyone through being spread by the poorer classes.' The Italian friar Samuele de Cassinis, the first person to denounce the persecution, pointed out that 'witches' were usually the old and weak-minded (*quaedam ignobiles vetulae, aut personae idiotae atque simplices, grossae et rurales*). An analysis of 366 cases in the county of Namur in 1509–1646 shows that the accused came from the less privileged sectors; and in the Jura region the aged and sick made up most of the victims. It would appear that those least able to defend themselves were singled out. Enclosed and isolated communities were particularly vulnerable, as the cases of 'diabolic possession' at the convent of Nôtre-Dame du Verger at Oisy (Artois) in 1613–15, and at the convent of the Ursulines at Loudun in France (1634) demonstrate.

It was these people, poor, outcast, maimed and afflicted, who were accused of conjurations and crimes so terrible that judges, bishops and even kings bestirred themselves to take part in the work of extermination. *Maleficia* were the most common offence: all but a handful of the 303 people accused in the courts of Essex for witchcraft in 1560–1680 were accused of injuring or killing humans or their property.[38] The accused tended to be women: only one fifth of those accused throughout the period 1351–1790 in northern France were men. The testimonies show that many witches really believed in their own magical powers, and were convinced that they had been transported to Sabbats and had had sexual intercourse with the devil. At the level of folk superstition there was nothing surprising about this. The Italian peasants of this period (from Friule) who believed in the cult of the *beneandanti* were convinced that they had the power to leave their bodies at night and go out and battle against the powers of darkness.[39] The beliefs of the *beneandanti*, however, were a purely local agrarian cult with no associations of *maleficia*. What staggered the courts trying witchcraft was that in case after case the accused came up with virtually identical stories and that these varied very little from country to country, so that right across Europe there emerged the terrifying vision of hundreds of thousands of formerly Christian souls dedicated to the service of Satan. Sex played little or no part in witchcraft, whose whole spirit was against fertility. The alleged orgies of the Sabbat, far from being fertility rites, were in fact infertility rites: congress with the devil, it was well known, froze the womb.

Denunciations of witches, like denunciations for heresy, arose out of antipathies and grievances within the local community. Petty suspicions, jealousies and gossip led to the victimisation of individuals and eventually to their prosecution.[40] In a changing society, the disappearance of traditional neighbourly charity and mutual help might give rise to resentments.[41] The fear of retaliation by witchcraft forced villagers to keep dispensing favours to those who were suspected of being witches or who, to exploit the situation, claimed to be witches. In times of crisis such persons were persecuted and denounced to the courts. Reginald Scot, who argued in his *Discoverie of Witchcraft* (1584) that the phenomenon was a delusion, described one such accusation:

> May it please you to waie what accusations and crimes they laie to their charge, namelie: She was at my house of late, she would have had a pot of milke, she departed in a chafe bicause she had it not, she railed, she curssed, she mumbled and whispered, and finallie she said she would be even with me: and soon after my child, my cow, my sow or my pullet died, or was strangelie taken. Naie (if it please your Worship) I have further proofe: I was with a wise woman, and she told me I had an ill neighbour, and that she would come to my house yer it were long, and so did she; and that she had a marke above hir waste, and so had she: and God forgive me, my stomach hath gone against hir a great while.

But documented cases range far beyond examples of 'charity refused'. Malice between neighbours was a universal phenomenon in witchcraft cases. Community tensions might go beyond the victimisation of one or two individuals: it has been argued that the outbreak in Salem, Massachusetts, in 1692, was provoked by dissensions that went through the entire town.[42]

A curious feature of many cases was the role of children. There were cases in Valenciennes in 1590 and 1662 of children denouncing their own parents; an outbreak at Chelmsford (Essex) in 1579 started with a sick child's accusations, and in the Warboys case the evidence for the prosecution rested principally on the evidence of three children. The important outbreak in Sweden in 1669 revolved entirely round a group of children accused of witchcraft (seventy-five people were executed), and children initiated the Salem trials which ultimately cost twenty-two lives. Perhaps the most bizarre case occurred in Spain when the inquisitor Salazar in 1611 visited Navarre; 1,802 people came forward as self-confessed witches, and of them 1,384 were children aged under fourteen.[43] At Quingey (Franche Comté) in 1657, as two boys of thirteen and eleven were being taken out to execution one of them, dimly aware of the horror into which his statements had led him, cried out to the examining officer, 'You made me say things I didn't understand!' The problems involved in the investigation of such cases go far beyond the merely sociological.

The cost of the witch-craze in terms of human lives was impressive, though contemporaries, especially the great witchhunters, usually exaggerated their figures. Nicolas Rémy of Lorraine claimed to have gathered the materials for his study of demonology from the trials of 900 people he had sentenced to death; the court records suggest that death sentences were really about one seventh of this figure.[44] Boguet claimed to be responsible for 600 executions in 1598–1616; the records reveal perhaps twenty-five executions for that period.[45] Delancre is credited with 600 executions in the Pays de Labourd in 1609; the true figure is closer to eighty.[46] Despite exaggerations, the reality was grim. In southwest Germany between 1560 and 1670 some 2,953 people were executed for witchcraft, four fifths of them between 1570 and 1630; in the Jura over 500 were executed between 1570 and 1670; at the Essex assizes some 110 people were condemned between 1560 and 1680. The figures are often small when set beside regular criminal executions; their significance lies not in numbers but in the interesting origins and character of the witchcraft phenomenon.

If witchcraft was in reality little more than folk superstition, why was it heavily prosecuted in the early modern period alone? Did the increase in prosecutions reflect a real increase in witchcraft? In the early Middle Ages many scholars had rejected the belief in witchcraft, which as unofficial magic threatened the monopoly of the Church. By the fifteenth century, in a trend that culminated in the *Malleus Maleficarum*, writers accepted the possibility of diabolism and then of the Sabbat. Sorcery became politicised, with opponents habitually accusing each other of conspiring with the aid of the black arts. Scotland's first great outbreak of witch mania coincided with the crisis in 1590–7, when the Earl of Bothwell was accused of 'consulting with witches…to conspire the king's death'. In England in 1568–71, plots involving Mary Queen of Scots had important witchcraft complications. In France the wife of the royal favourite Concini was condemned as a witch, and Cardinal Richelieu accused another favourite, Luynes, of plotting 'with two magicians who gave him herbs to put in the king's slippers'. In Russia witchcraft was a regular accusation in political struggles.

The treatises of the great jurists helped give credence to the notions of a Sabbat and a compact with the devil. The idea of a pact with the devil also seemed to proliferate wherever torture was used in trials, because learned interrogators tried to elicit answers that accorded with their own beliefs. In England, where torture was not used in such cases, no doctrine of the Sabbat emerged in witch trials.[47] The merging of learned and popular beliefs was largely precipitated by the same intellectual ferment that gave rise to Renaissance humanism and the Reformation. Elite intellectuals dabbled in sorcery and the occult because they presented paths to knowledge. A typical example of this trend was the late seventeenth-century English freethinker Joseph Glanvill.[48] Others reacted against this and felt that the faith should be protected against the intervention of the devil. It was therefore no coincidence that the high tide of prosecutions occurred precisely during the epoch of Reform and Counter-Reform: in destroying witches the zealots were also destroying superstition and heresy.

Though learned men played a part in the crisis, the effective origins of the witch-craze must be sought in social tensions and conflicts. 'Whence comes the witch?' asked Michelet in his study of *La Sorcière*. 'I say unhesitatingly: from times of despair.' Sorcery, he argued, arose in times of depression, war, famine, economic and social crisis, loss of faith, of certainty and of orientation. In rural areas ravaged by war and food shortage the population victimised those in whom they saw their ills personified. The late sixteenth-century doctor Thomas Platter offered a similar explanation for cases of sorcery in remote areas of Languedoc.[49] In small communities, denunciations for witchcraft often arose simply out of family and communal tensions.[50] The most intensive outbreaks of persecution were in times of agrarian disaster, when local communities blamed the evil influences at work among them. 'Nearly every city, market and village in Germany is filled with servants of the devil who destroy the fruits of the fields', claimed a German pamphlet of 1590. As a result of crop failures in the Schongau in Bavaria, sixty-three women were executed as witches in 1589–91 after petitions by the communities.[51] In Mainz in 1593 a local official wrote that 'the common man has become so mad from the consequences of crop failures that he no longer holds them for the just punishment of God, but blames witches'.[52] The situation was exactly the same in rural Catalonia in 1621, when (as a bishop reported) 'the barons and seigneurs of the villages, on seeing the loss of crops and the clamouring of the people, have supplied a cure for the ills by punishing these women'.[53]

In some parts of continental Europe, learned tradition had never accepted the possibility of diabolic witchcraft: the most striking example is Spain. Though secular tribunals there periodically condemned people for witchcraft, the Inquisition from 1526 onwards systematically refused to prosecute, on the grounds that witches were self-deluded. A discussion paper drawn up for the Inquisition that year stated categorically that 'the majority of jurists in this realm agree that witches do not exist'.[54] From 1526, therefore, the inquisitors refused to take denunciations of witches seriously. In 1550, when the inquisitors of Barcelona gave in to popular pressure and acted against 'witches', they were immediately sacked from their posts. The inquisitor who was sent to investigate the case, Francisco Vaca, produced an unequivocal indictment of witchcraft persecution and condemned the accusations as 'laughable'. A small relapse from this position took place in 1610: as a consequence of a frenzied witchhunt being conducted just across the border inside France by Pierre Delancre, a wave of hysteria swept into Spanish Navarre and led to a number of witches being executed at an *auto de fe*. The inquisitor Alonso Salazar de Frias was sent to inquire into the circumstances and came to the conclusion that 'there were neither witches nor bewitched until they were talked and written about'.[55]

Witchcraft only existed, he felt, if it were prosecuted. As a result, the Inquisition returned to its previous policy and never again tried witches. In 1665 a Catalan widow of Mataró, Isabel Amada, went begging for alms one day where some peasants were tending two mules and a flock of sheep, but was refused any. 'Within three days', testified a witness, 'the two mules died and also thirty sheep. The accused claimed that she had caused the deaths among the herd with the help of the demon.' Isabel told the inquisitors that she had been set upon and beaten by the peasants and had only mentioned the demon to save her life. She was set free.

As in Spain, in the rest of Europe there was an alternative tradition that refused to accept the reality of the Sabbat or the devil's role. Opponents of the witch-craze included scholars from all faiths: Catholics such as de Cassinis (in a work of 1505), Adam Tanner and Friedrich von Spee (1631); and Lutherans such as Johann Weyer, physician to the Duke of Cleve. In his *The Deceptions of Demons* of 1563, Weyer explained that 'I fight with natural reason against the deceptions which proceed from Satan and the crazed imagination of the so-called witches. My object is also medical, in that I show that illnesses which are attributed to witches come from natural causes.' Scepticism over witchcraft cut across religious boundaries. Like Catholic Spain, the Calvinist-dominated Dutch Republic was one of the first states to play down prosecutions for the offence. The last death sentence for witchcraft in Dutch territory was carried out in 1597.[56] Prosecutions continued, but subsequent death sentences were commuted.

One vital factor began to change learned opinion: lawyers and judges became sceptical about the evidence adduced in witchcraft cases. The Parlement of Paris in the late sixteenth century rejected a majority of the prosecutions which reached it, and in the period 1564–1640 confirmed only a tenth of the 1,123 death sentences for witchcraft which came before it as a court of appeal.[57] By 1624, when it ruled that all witchcraft sentences involving the death penalty must be appealed, the offence had virtually ceased to be a crime. In 1644 the Archbishop of Reims protested to Chancellor Séguier against persecution of 'witches' by local magistrates: 'the abuse is so widespread that one finds up to thirty or forty falsely accused within a single parish'. By the 1670s Colbert was intervening to stop any death sentences, and in July 1682 a royal decree forbade further prosecutions, thereby confirming a situation that had been effective for over half a century. In the late seventeenth century scepticism grew also among English lawyers: the last witch condemned to death in England was Jane Wenham in 1712, but she was reprieved; and in 1736 an Act of Parliament stopped further prosecutions. In Hungary, where some 500 witches were executed between 1520 and 1777, the prosecutions drew to an end with new laws promoted by the Empress Maria Theresa in 1758.[58]

4

THE RULING ELITE

In so far as we are born of good lineage, we are the best.
(Stefano Guazzo, *La Civil Conversazione*, 1584)

'We live in a moving reality to which we try to adapt ourselves like algae that follow the thrust of the sea. The Church has been given the promise of immortality; we, as a social class, have not.'
(Don Fabrizio, in di Lampedusa's *The Leopard*)

A mirror to elites

When Sir William Segar wrote his *Honour Military and Civil* (1602) he used the word 'gentleman' to describe the uppermost social category as follows:

> Of gentlemen, the first and principal is the King, Prince, Dukes, Marquesses, Earls, Viscounts and Barons. These are the Nobility, and be called Lords or Noblemen. Next to these be Knights, Esquires and simple Gentlemen, which last number may be called Nobilitas minor.

The one word 'nobility' – *noblesse, nobleza, szlachta* – referred in Europe to the entire status elite and was notoriously imprecise. As new men rose into the elite, it became necessary to define terms. The abstract word 'gentleman' (*gentilhomme* in France, *hidalgo* in Spain) was accepted as referring to a 'true' noble, that is, one who was born such and not created. In the rural provinces of western Europe a knight, caballero or chevalier was likewise normally a representative of the old nobility. Titles were rare, a mark of state favour rather than a guarantee of old nobility.

Wars of the late fifteenth century brought about an increase in the number of those rewarded with noble titles. At this time it was still common to repeat the medieval division of society into three grades – those who fight, those who work, those who pray – and to identify nobles with 'those who fight'. At least for the sixteenth century, the military ideal continued to be a noble monopoly. At the same time nobles tended to be in possession of land, their primary source of wealth, and – more crucially – to exercise jurisdiction, feudal or otherwise, over it. War, land and jurisdiction were three basic and traditional aspects of nobility; though none of them was in fact essential to the *quality* of nobility.[1] Because the medieval ideal had been that a noble should serve his prince, he was also conceded various privileges which were largely upheld in the sixteenth and seventeenth centuries: the exclusive right to carry weapons, to have a coat of arms, exemption from direct taxation, and the right to trial by one's peers were among the more important.

Changing fortunes and social mobility brought controversy into the ranks of the elite. What, it was asked, made a member of the noble elite different from others? Problems centred on three points: the role of the state, of new wealth, and of old blood. The role of the state had been clear since medieval times: only the king could create new nobles. By the sixteenth century, however, many kings had multiplied the ranks of the nobility in order to raise money or simply to build up political support. There were two main methods: royal letters would grant noble status (Louis XIV in the 1690s issued up to 1,000 letters in an attempt to raise money); or status would be granted as an automatic corollary of service to the state (particularly in administration and the judiciary). Though the nobility of the newcomers was never in doubt, critics maintained, in a phrase that rapidly gained currency, that 'the king could make a nobleman, but not a gentleman'. The true quality of nobility, in other words, could not be conferred but only inherited. In the 1500s all monarchies, from England to Russia, attempted to reorganise their elite in order to obtain security for the state. Charles V in Castile in 1525 divided the aristocracy into two: an elite core of (twenty) grandees, and a large group of titled nobles (*titulos*): together with the thousands of *caballeros* and *hidalgos*, these made up the core of Spain's noble class.

Doubts about a state-created nobility were aggravated by the number of those who were rising in the social scale through riches alone. In the sixteenth century a number of writers in Flanders, France and Italy[2] reacted against the parvenus and reaffirmed that the hereditary elite were the true aristocrats (in the original Greek sense of *aristos*, the best). The Monferrat noble Stefano Guazzo claimed in 1584 that 'in so far as we are born of good lineage, we are the best'. Alessandro Sardo in his *Discorsi* (1587) maintained that nobility was conferred not by virtue or service but by birth and lineage, and could not be destroyed even by evil acts. This created a new emphasis, which was to last into the eighteenth century, on origins and 'race'. Nobility could only be transmitted by heredity: nobility, it has been commented, was seminal fluid. The genetic view of status brought with it an extreme concern over marriage and the dangers of *mésalliances*, marrying below one's rank. In order to project the image of a 'race' backwards into the past, myths were created according to which the aristocracy were descended from the Franks (in France and Germany), the Goths (in Spain), and other warlike tribes. The genetic outlook exercised a powerful influence and was inevitably accepted even by the newer nobles, who took care to draw up family trees proving that they were of ancient stock.[3]

At the same time a broad range of social attitudes was created around 'reputation' and 'honour', concepts that gave everyday substance to the status of nobility. Nobility might come through ancient origin, but it was continued and maintained by correct conduct and by the corresponding respect of one's peers and one's community. An immense range of views about what constituted 'honour' came into existence. Merely to be a member of the elite seemed to impose duties in both private and public affairs, giving rise thereby to a sort of official mythology about what it meant to be a nobleman.

In broad terms, one may say that there were three types of honour that a noble needed to cherish.[4] First, he had to preserve the purity of his past lineage ('blood' and 'race'), but even as surely he had to protect that of his present family. Just as it would be advisable to blot out from the family tree any ancestors who might bring discredit, so it was imperative to ensure that present members of the clan followed the accepted rules about conduct, marriage and way of life. Second, a noble had to demonstrate his personal achievement. In traditional Europe it was essential to have performed military service, and no aristocracy admitted into their ranks a family that could not demonstrate experience in warfare. The military ethic was projected into pursuits such as hunting and duelling. At the same time, a noble had to demonstrate his virility, primarily by making a good marriage and siring children, but also by taking part in wars. Third, a noble maintained his honour publicly by playing his correct social role and thereby winning the respect of his vassals and his community. Most notably, he should offer hospitality to his vassals, to the poor, and to travellers and neighbours. He would thereby be honoured as was the seventeenth-century English gentleman who 'kept a very bountiful house and gave great entertainment, lived in great repute in his country and very happily'.[5] Noble households, as many nobles learnt to their cost, were public undertakings, and social duties were expensive.

Many writers nonetheless pointed out that nobility must also be based on virtue and merit. Guillaume de la Perrière in his *Le Miroir Politique* (1555) claimed that 'stock and lineage maketh not a man noble or ignoble, but use, education, instruction and bringing up maketh him so'. The Renaissance emphasis was on virtue, education and service to the state. Girolamo Muzio in his *Il Gentilhuomo* (Venice 1575) began by saying that 'nobility is a splendour which proceeds from virtue'. He felt that the old noble class had long since lost its honour, and that the future lay with a new civic nobility created by the state because of its virtue (i.e. its merits and service). The government must still be aristocratic, though entrusted not to the old militarist nobles but to an aristocracy that had distinguished itself in letters and in laws. This arbitrary distinction between an old elite of 'arms' and a new one of 'letters' had long been a commonplace, even in medieval times, and was moralistic rather than a real analysis of the emergence of a different ethic.[6] In practice, nobles combined all aspects. A noble, wrote the author of *The Institucion of a Gentleman* (1555), 'ought to be lerned, have knowledge of tongues and be apt in arms'. Segar himself observed that the 'endevour of Gentlemen ought to be either in Armes or learning or in them both'. Despite the newer emphasis on virtue considered as education and service to the state, in practice the older concept of virtue as the profession of arms was never superseded.[7] In the eighteenth century Montesquieu was still proclaiming that 'the principal honour of a nobleman lies in going to war'.

The differing views of nobility were evidence of a significant change in both the habits and the social composition of the upper elite, whose overall numbers probably did not vary in the early modern period. The titled aristocracy were always a tiny group, but when we add the fluctuating number of lesser nobles and gentry it is possible to estimate that in Castile those claiming noble status (*hidalgos*) were as much as 10 per cent of the population, and in Poland (the *szlachta*) 15 per cent. By contrast, estimates that are more typical of the situation across Europe suggest around 1 per cent for the upper elite of Venice and Naples, under 1 per cent for France and even less for the nations of northwest and northern Europe.

Power and clientage

When elite and nobles attempted to intervene in affairs of state, they were always at a disadvantage, because their power was inherently local rather than national. It was a factor of which rulers made the most. Governments could feel secure so long as the nobles did not make common cause together. Thanks to divisions among the elite, the state was able slowly to extend its authority and encourage the creation of a national loyalty that transcended local allegiances headed by nobles.

In their provinces, the elite were little kings. Virtually since medieval times, powerful families continued to own the principal estates and control the agrarian life of the countryside. Their feudal links of kinship and influence enabled them to have access to large bands of followers, termed in France *fidélités*. As feudal bonds began to decay, other common contacts brought nobles together. Links between families, based on family and other interests, created a network of 'clientage' and 'patronage' systems that criss-crossed the nation and reached up to national level. In France, where the phenomenon has been most studied, a great noble could call on three main categories of 'client', that is, men who depended on him. First there was his own household and its numerous dependants; then came those who were paid to serve him as soldiers; finally there were the many officials and others who were connected with his estates and offices. All of these in some sense 'belonged' to him and were his clients.[8] The system could be found not only among nobles but also in the extensive bureaucracy of the Catholic Church, and in many ruling oligarchies.[9] The client received the benefits of income and protection, and in return gave the patron his loyalty. In oligarchies and city states, such as in Italy, clientelism depended greatly on kinship and the network formed through family relationships and neighbourhood influence. Beyond the clients, a noble could through marriages, influence and purchase of land build up a series of links with other personages in both Church and state, to form a powerful circle of patronage. The complex links might have feudal connotations, but were more often based on a reciprocity of material interest, established without any written agreements.

When it broke down, the patronage system threatened unrest. In 1575 the Viscount Turenne, feeling that he had not been supported by his patron François Duke of Alençon, forced his way into the presence of the duke with 300 of his own nobles and captains, and formally declared himself to be dissatisfied, or 'malcontent'. The word 'malcontent' was periodically used in French to signify those who demanded by traditional right a redress of their grievances. The same sort of procedure could be used in reverse, to maintain the peace. In 1595 the young Duke of Guise came to submit himself to the king, Henry IV, and brought with him 'as many of his friends as he could gather'.[10] In the language of patronage, a 'friend' was a member of the clan or system of clientage.

It can also be seen that many of the links between nobles were based not on feudal or material obligation but quite simply on friendship and personal commitment based on honour.[11] In France, nobles relied on their standing (*crédit*) with each other in order to form alliances or obtain favours; in their correspondence the words 'friend' and 'servant' indicated willingness to accept a reciprocity of obligations.[12] The elite exercised power not through a chain of command from the greatest to the smallest, but rather through a number of linkages whereby both great and small were bound to each other and received appropriate benefits. In the same way, horizontal linkages created power bases that were not simply local but could extend through an entire province and beyond it.

The system of clientage served principally to help the elites maintain their power, but could be used also to help the administration of the state. In 1656 the intendant of Burgundy, a member of the local elite, wrote to inform Cardinal Mazarin that 'I am using my credit and that of my friends and relatives in this assembly [of the Estates of Burgundy] in order to make the king's intentions succeed'.[13] A nationwide system of patronage helped in this way to further the solidarity of the nation. The links of clientage, kinship and money amounted in effect to a network of influence and corruption. But 'corruption' at that period can be seen as a constructive element in political life. Modern corruption implies a deliberate confusion between private interest and the public interest, to the detriment of the latter. In early modern Europe, by contrast, it was precisely the public interest (in the form of the crown or the government) that made use of bribes or pressure in order to advance state authority. The elites occasionally counter-attacked, as in England in 1701 when Parliament passed a short-lived resolution that 'no person who holds an office of profit under the crown should be capable of serving in Parliament'.

The aristocracy of war

The military significance of the nobles lay in their own private armed retinues as well as in the troops which they called out in the service of the king. Both attributes were feudal, and on both counts the nobility might control most of the fighting forces within the realm. The privilege which made them the only class allowed to bear arms confirmed the fact that they had a near monopoly of violence in early modern Europe. In the Russia of Ivan the Terrible, even more power for violence was put into the hands of the so-called 'service nobility' so as to enable them to extend the authority of the crown through terror. But in the nation states of western Europe private violence was becoming more and more of an anachronism, because it openly contravened public order, the order maintained by the crown.

Arbitrary personal violence by the nobles arose out of community tensions, clan rivalry and simple gangsterism. Ideals such as those present in religious or nationalist wars were superimposed on this local pattern. 'The nobility today is so unbridled and unlicensed', complained the town of Epernay in 1560, 'that it devotes itself solely to the sword and to killings'. François de la Noue, a veteran of many wars, in 1585 condemned gentry who believed that 'the marks of nobility were to make oneself feared, to beat and to hang at will'. During the French civil wars many felt that the nobles were using religion as an excuse for plunder. Was there not ample evidence, claimed a writer in Dauphiné, that the nobles seldom attacked each other's property, even if they were on opposite sides, and only sacked the houses of commoners? The Huguenot and Catholic nobility, it was reported from Languedoc, 'openly help each other; the one group holds the lamb while the other cuts its throat'. The wars bred noble banditry: Claude Haton in 1578 reported the activities in Champagne of a group of seigneurs 'perpetrating unmentionable and incredible beatings, robberies, rapes, thefts, murders, arson and every kind of crime, without any respect of persons'. Supported by local ties of kinship, powers of jurisdiction, and feudal followings (*fidélités*), many nobles were strongly ensconced in their localities. The Duc de la Rochefoucauld raised 1,500 gentlemen within four days for the siege of La Rochelle (1627), and said proudly to the uneasy king, 'Sire, there is not one who is not related to me.' Some local seigneurs were tyrants, like Gabriel Foucault, Vicomte de Daugnon, governor of La Marche, described by Tallemant des Réaux as 'a great robber, a great borrower who never returned, and a great distributor of blows with a club', who rewarded his retainers by granting them other people's daughters whom he had carried off.

The state tried to harness this violence by absorbing it into the national army, but was hindered by the fact that up to the early seventeenth century most armies were still feudal musters. Under Henry VIII in 1523, one third of the total English army was directly contributed by the titular aristocracy. When Philip II invaded Portugal in 1580, much of his army consisted of troops raised by the aristocracy; and the entire force that invaded Aragon in 1591 was feudal and not royal. Up to the reign of Louis XIV, France was still employing the *ban et arrière-ban* (feudal muster); the forces raise by the nobles during the Fronde outnumbered those of the crown. It was not surprising in these circumstances that all rulers feared the power of the aristocracy, in rebellions such as that of the northern earls in England in 1569, and of Montmorency in Languedoc in 1632. Not until the early seventeenth century was a serious move made (by Maurice of Nassau in Holland, by Gustav Adolf in Sweden) to form a national army free of feudal allegiances; and only with Cromwell's New Model Army was a modern national force created. Even then it was inevitable that the nobles and gentry should become the officer class. In the late seventeenth century, with the professional armies of Louvois and the Great Elector, nobles and Junkers monopolised all officers' posts, though this time as servants of the state rather than as commanders of their own forces.

By around 1700, the state was successfully beginning to lay claim to a monopoly of violence. It was more difficult to deal with the limited violence associated with feuds, duels and straightforward crime. The exaggerated concepts of 'honour' which obtained in France and Italy, and to a lesser extent in other countries, encouraged duelling. Every state outlawed the practice (which was also prohibited by the Council of Trent in 1563), but to little effect. In the duchy of Lorraine solemn (and apparently unheeded) prohibitions of duelling can be found in 1586, 1591, 1603, 1609, 1614, 1617, 1626 and so on almost indefinitely. In late seventeenth-century Madrid challenges (*desafíos*) occasioned about a tenth of all prosecutions for crime. The practice was imported from the continent into England in the late sixteenth century, and deemed illegal from the very beginning, but juries normally dealt with the offence lightly and duelling was not formally abolished until 1850.[14] In France, Sully was bitterly opposed to duelling, and Richelieu in 1627 assented, 'for the good of the state', to the execution of the Count of Bouteville, who had flagrantly defied the prohibition against the practice. But though there were numerous French edicts against it between 1609 and 1711, none was ever seriously enforced. The state was, of course, primarily concerned to stop the ruling class destroying itself; 'nothing being dearer to me', as Louis XIII observed, 'than to do all I can to preserve my nobles'. The marshal Duke of Gramont claimed (with obvious exaggeration) that duelling had cost the lives of 900 gentlemen during the regency of Anne of Austria. By contrast, according to Saint-Simon, under Louis XIV 'duels were extremely rare'. The peak period in France came between the 1580s and 1650, when no less than thirty books were published on the subject.[15] During the early eighteenth century duelling came back into fashion in France (the Parlement of Paris dealt with fifty cases between 1715 and 1724), but it had become rather a rite of non-violence than of violence. No longer active in warfare, the nobility used the duel as a way of demonstrating their ability to protect principles of honour without the resort to war.[16]

The aristocracy were tamed, it has been argued,[17] in three main ways: by the deliberate policy of law enforcement adopted by western monarchies, by the gradual impoverishment of many noble families and subsequent economies in retinue, and by a growing preference for litigation rather than brigandage. In 1592 an English judge warned the Earl of Shrewsbury that 'when in the country you dwell in you will needs enter in a war with the inferiors therein, we think it both justice, equity and wisdom to take care that the weaker part be not put down by the mightier'. In 1597, as the reign of Philip II was drawing to a close, a leading jurist in Castile, Castillo de Bobadilla, claimed that the king had humiliated the nobles and 'did not pardon them with his usual clemency, nor did he respect their estates, and there is no judge now who cannot act against them and take their silver and horses'. By the mid-seventeenth century the older aristocracy were beginning to lose their taste for the military ideals they had once cherished. In England, the armaments as well as the retainers kept by leading aristocrats dwindled sharply. In Spain, Olivares complained of a lack of nobles to serve as officers in the army. Only in France, with the Fronde, did the nobles reassert their old habits, and that too was a final gesture.

After the Thirty Years War, the last international conflict to give continuous employment to professional and mercenary officers, the nobles settled down to more domestic pursuits and took advantage of the favourable economic climate. In Siena, which had produced generations of soldiers for foreign armies, they consolidated themselves in the bureaucracy and in the Church.[18]

The nobility in business

Just as they had monopolised warfare, so the nobles dominated the sources of wealth. They owned estates, forests, coastlines and sections of rivers. Their economic power was very great, but at the same time they tended to look down on those who were earning new wealth and rising up the social ladder. The Ferrarese noble Sardo observed that 'inherited wealth is more honest than earned wealth, in view of the vile gain needed to obtain the latter'. This was part of the sixteenth-century reaction in favour of principles of heredity and lineage and against the ascent of rich self-made men into the nobility. Since the new concepts of a 'nobility of race' were largely confined to the Latin countries, it is no surprise to find that the prejudice against earned wealth was strongest there, but not shared by everybody. In Spain the opportunities for trade and industry created by wool and by new wealth from America pushed into the background whatever reservations may have existed. There was not a noble in Seville, observed the writer Ruiz de Alarcón, who did not trade.

In England Thomas Churchyard (1579) distinguished four main types of noble: the governing elite, the soldiers, the lawyers, and 'the fourth are Merchauntes that sail forrain countreys'. Among others who recognised the role of trade was the French jurist André Tiraqueu, whose *Commentary on Nobility* (Basel 1561) claimed that commerce did not derogate from nobility when it was the only way to make ends meet. In Italy the jurist Benvenuto Stracca, albeit representing a more conservative view than had formerly prevailed in Venice, made it clear in his *Treatise on Trade* (1575) that a noble could take part in large-scale trading but not in petty commerce, nor must he participate in person but only as a director. These distinctions were standard ones and widely accepted. Prevailing views were summed up by the jurist Loyseau in his *Traité des Ordres* (1613): 'it is gain, whether vile or sordid, that derogates from nobility, whose proper role is to live off rents'. 'Derogation' (*dérogeance*), a concept which was almost unique to France and unknown in England or Spain, meant loss of noble status for those who participated in money-making or manual labour; wholesale but not retail trade was allowed.[19] Agricultural labour on one's own land was, by contrast, never viewed as derogatory, being considered 'no less worthy for a gentleman in peacetime than that of bearing arms in wartime is glorious'. Like other jurists, Loyseau admitted that to take part in commerce did not result in a loss, but merely a suspension, of noble status: 'all that is necessary for rehabilitation are letters signed by the king'.

Two main influences helped to break down prejudices against nobles in business. The first and most important was the strong wish of the self-made elite to continue in commerce even after they had gained status; the second was the wish of the state to divert the considerable wealth of nobles into trade and industry. In France in 1566 the elite of Marseille had expressly been allowed by the crown to be both noble and merchant. Then in 1607 the royal council informed the merchant nobles of Lyon that 'the king wishes them to enjoy fully and freely the privileges of nobility, as though they were nobles of ancient lineage, and they may continue to do business and trade, both in money and banking as in any other large-scale trading'. In the *Code Michau* (1629), drawn up by Richelieu and Marillac, it was declared that 'all nobles who directly or indirectly take shares in ships and their merchandise, shall not lose their noble status', terms repeated in an edict of 1669. In Spain there was far less opposition than in France to nobles in trade. A Castilian writer of the sixteenth century maintained that 'to labour and sweat in order to acquire riches in order to maintain one's honour' was compatible with the noble ethic; and in 1558 the royal official Luis Ortiz argued in a petition to the crown that all sons of the nobility should be trained in commerce or a profession. In Aragon declarations by the Cortes in 1626 and 1677 stated that there was no incompatibility between manufactures and nobility; and in 1682 the crown, responding to a petition from the textile manufacturers of Segovia, issued a decree that manufacturing 'has not been and is not against the quality of nobility', an important measure that removed all legal obstacles to the social ascent of the new nobility.

Elsewhere in Europe there was so little objection to aristocratic entrepreneurship that we find everywhere nobles involved in industrial and commercial activity. It is sometimes said that, in western Europe at least, the nobles seldom traded and were more concerned with industry. In England Dudley Digges in 1604 claimed that 'to play the merchant was only for gentlemen of Florence, Venice or the like'. If nobles preferred industry to trade, however, there were very good reasons for it. They tended to be landed, and the land produced ore, coal, metals, wood and many similar items which it was only logical for the landowner himself to invest in. Trade, particularly overseas trade, was not always a priority for a man with a rich industry in his own back garden. This did not mean that a noble industrialist was prejudiced against commerce, for very many industrialists also took an interest in exchanging and exporting.

The attempt to alter established attitudes is shown by the existence at this period in both Lorraine and France of the terms *gentilshommes-verriers* and *gentilshommes-mineurs*, which referred to those who enjoyed noble privileges as a result of their participation in the industries concerned, glass manufacture and mining. In England there was little need to break down the barriers. There the nobles distinguished themselves by the exploitation of mines on their estates and by their promotion of mercantile enterprises. In the Elizabethan period the most active entrepreneur in the country was George Talbot, ninth Earl of Shrewsbury. He was a large-scale farmer, a shipowner, an ironmaster, and the master of a steelworks, coalmines and glassworks; in addition he had interests in trading companies.[20] The most prominent aristocratic names in the realm, among them Norfolk, Devonshire and Arundel, were associated with industrial enterprises. The scale of their commitment was not very large. Not all the nobles were direct entrepreneurs: a few merely lent their names. No aristocrat relied on industry alone for his income. The biggest profits were still in land, and it was to urban development and to fen drainage that nobles tended to turn after about 1600. When all allowances are made, however, noble participation in business was still highly significant. The peerage fulfilled a role that no other class, neither the gentry nor the merchants, was able to rival. They risked their money in industrial and trading endeavours to an extent that certainly brought ruin to many, but also helped to pave the way for the later injection of capital by other classes.

In Scotland, the Earl of Wemyss told Cromwell in 1658 that the estate of many Scottish 'noblemen, gentlemen and others doth consist very much in coal-works'. Significantly, the noble entrepreneurs of Scotland relied on a depressed labour force in their coalworks. This combination of feudalism and capitalism was common on the continent, where the wealthy noble merchants and industrialists of Holstein, Prussia, Bohemia, Poland and Russia benefited from the availability of cheap labour that followed changes in the agrarian economy. Heinrich Rantzau, the first and greatest of the sixteenth-century Holstein aristocratic entrepreneurs, made huge profits from demesne farming and ploughed much of this back into industries on his estates. He established thirty-nine mills for the production of lumber, flour and oil, and for the manufacture of articles from copper, brass and iron.[21] Both landed and industrial produce were traded abroad, so that the richest merchants in Kiel, for example, were nobles. After the crisis years of the early seventeenth century, the Holstein nobility tended to withdraw from business and turn to their estates. One of them, the Duke of Holstein-Gottorf, claimed in 1615 that 'trade is not proper for noblemen'.

In the early seventeenth century, possibly the biggest capitalist concern in central Europe was brought into existence in the duchy of Friedland by

Wallenstein. There were unusual features connected with Friedland: it was both financed by and geared to war; and its industries, among them munitions, were not primarily concerned with peaceful trade. But Friedland illustrates the common situation that only the nobles had the means of raising capital and putting it to work. In areas where the bourgeoisie were weak, or in the process of decline, it was the nobility that took control of both trade and industry.

Over the whole of Europe, a significant part of the nobility was active in business, not excluding trade. In Sweden the nobles were prominent as entrepreneurs from the sixteenth century. They tended to work the mines on their own estates – principally in iron ore – and from mining they moved to trade. Trading profits allowed them to accumulate capital, which they invested in forges and manufactories, and also lent out at interest. Their investment in trade was assured by a guaranteed privilege that they could export the produce of their own estates free of duty. Many of the wealthiest nobles consequently purchased ships. The nobility of the German lands varied in their application. In Brandenburg they tended to monopolise both industry and trade. In Lower Saxony, Duke Anton I von Oldenburg encouraged his nobles to take a personal interest in market procedures, from which came a class of noble capitalists. One of these was Stats von Münchhausen, who based his enterprise on land, but then invested his agricultural profits in ironmongery and timber. His fortune grew to be immense: by 1618 he was said to possess over ten tonnes of gold and over one million thaler. Some of this money went into building himself the castle of Bevern on the river Weser. On the Baltic coast, in Pomerania, the family of Loytze from the city of Stettin made themselves into the 'Fuggers of the north' through reinvesting the profits they made from land. When their firm collapsed in 1572, a large number of the nobility fell into difficulties and the chancellor of Pomerania committed suicide because of his losses. 'The nobles in past years', commented a Pomeranian official in the late sixteenth century, 'have not been very industrious and keen to make their living. But now in recent years they have become better at it, and since the country existed the nobility has never been so rich and powerful as nowadays.'

Hungary may be taken as a brief example of the situation in the eastern countries. Since the economy was in no sense industrialised, Hungarian foreign trade consisted in the export of agricultural goods and the import of industrial goods. The nobles were lords of the soil and by extension dominated the trade in its produce. Hungarian seigneurs were consequently both farmers and merchants. A royal decree of 1618 in Hungary confirmed the freedom of the gentry from excise and taxes. In 1625 controls over prices and wages were removed. In 1630 the Diet decreed that the nobles could take part in foreign trade without paying taxes or customs duties. By 1655 a memoir of the time could claim that 'the nobles deal in all kinds of trade', in corn, wine, cattle, honey and so on. How this affected other classes was described by the memoir: 'The seigneurs and nobles take over trading; they seize for themselves whatever they think profitable; they exclude the common people and the merchants; they confiscate everything indiscriminately from the poor, and hold it as their own private property.' In his autobiography, the seventeenth-century Transylvanian nobleman Bethlen Miklos tells us that he took part in the trade of wheat and of wine. Moreover,

> I have traded in salt without losing anything; on the contrary it is by these three items [wheat, wine and salt] that I have gained nearly all my goods, for the revenue from my lands alone would never have met all the expenses I had to make.

Bethlen also traded in cattle, sheep, honey and wax.

In Russia, conditions differed so radically from those in western Europe that a shocked Austrian ambassador reported in 1661 that 'all the people of quality and even the ambassadors sent to foreign princes, trade publicly. They buy, they sell, and they exchange without a qualm, thereby making their elevated rank, venerable that it is, subservient to their avarice.'[22] The tsar himself was the biggest of Russian businessmen, with profitable interests in both trade and industry. Industrial enterprise of every sort existed on the estates of tsars, monasteries and boyars. Among the biggest noble merchants of the sixteenth century were the Stroganov family, whose members had international trade connections.[23] To serve the producing and trading interests of the elite, a labour force of 'state serfs' was brought into existence.

The nobility in business were not necessarily fulfilling a progressive function. In central and eastern Europe the entry of aristocrats into business checked the growth of an independent merchant class (see Chapter 5) and in some cities destroyed an existing trading sector. The manipulation of capital by the feudal classes hindered the development of a strong middle elite, and the rise of landed noble traders led to the decay of urban centres. Only in those countries where the moneyed classes – both noble and bourgeois – cooperated in creative development can the contribution of the nobility be seen as a beneficial step. In any case the positive aspects of noble investment must not be exaggerated: especially in western Europe, the bulk of noble wealth was tied up in a single immobile asset – the land – and dedication to other activities could not have absorbed more than a small proportion of capital.

Estates and fortunes

The one essential mark of nobility was wealth: the aristocracy were the rich. Although sixteenth-century theorists of a 'nobility of race' would have liked to argue that blood was more fundamental, common opinion was against them. As a Spanish writer, Arce de Otalora, observed: 'It is the law and custom in all Italy, German and France, that those who do not live nobly do not enjoy the privilege of nobility.' In Spain, too, the ancient laws of Castile declared that 'if any nobleman falls into poverty and cannot maintain his noble status, he shall become a commoner and all his children with him'. In an age when many men of noble rank were becoming impoverished, it was not surprising that they should cling to the belief that a blood elite did not cease to be an elite simply because it had fallen on hard times.

Certainly, when the noble class was as big as it was in Spain and Poland, poor *hidalgos* and *szlachta* were commonplace. In the former, the theme of an impoverished gentry became standard in literature. In France, the census returns for the *arrière-ban* under Louis XIII show that the provincial aristocracy at its base consisted of a vast number of penniless gentlemen. Despite these cases, the nobles were on the whole wealthy, their resources coming directly from the land. In western Europe the aristocracy were drifting away from their estates and becoming absentee landlords rather than agrarian producers; in the east they were being drawn further into exploitation of the soil. In west and central Europe the sale of land, which received its greatest impetus from the Reformation spoliation of the Church, changed the character of aristocratic income and also facilitated the rise of a new class of nobles. In England before 1600 the receipts of the Earl of Rutland from demesne farming amounted to about one fifth of his income; after 1613, when leasing of land had begun, they fell to about one twentieth. The decay of demesne farming, however, did not mean that nobles lost their grip on the land, merely that they were turning to cash rather than agricultural income. In the seventeenth century, two thirds of the fortunes of the dukes and peers of France were still in land.

The growing role of cash can be seen in some random examples.[24] In 1617 the Marshal d'Ancre, the royal favourite, drew six sevenths of his income from office; in 1640 the Duc d'Epernon, a member of the old aristocracy, drew half his income from office, and the rest from his twenty-three estates; in the 1690s Colbert de Croissy, France's foreign secretary, drew 98 per cent of his income from office. In Spain the Duke of Lerma in 1622 drew two thirds of his income from land; in 1630 the Duke of Béjar drew 35 per cent from demesne and 45 per cent from rents; in 1681 the Marquis of Leganés drew 14 per cent from demesne, 39.8 per cent from rents and cash dues, and 45.5 per cent from state annuities.

Cash came from two main sources: rents (of land and houses), and court pensions. The growth of courts was a logical development from the rise of centralised monarchies. The archetype was Rome, staffed by wealthy aristocrats such as the Colonna and Orsini, dispenser of patronage to the largest bureaucracy in the world, that of the Church. By the early seventeenth century, Europe's other principal courts were in London, Vienna, Madrid and Paris. Each court (Madrid was referred to simply as *la Corte*) was a combination of city and monarch's residence, of political and social life, and above all the heart of the state bureaucracy. The system was based on patronage. Royal patronage encouraged the rise of men like d'Ancre, Buckingham and Lerma. In addition, kings sold or gave away lucrative pensions and offices. From 1611 to 1617 the French court paid out 14 million livres in pensions to nine nobles. In England the gentry received lands in gift or on lease, from dissolved monasteries and from Ireland. They obtained cash (James I in the peak year 1611 gave away £43,600 to Scots favourites) or annuities and secured trade privileges, tax-farms and monopolies to such a extent that the merchant class began to direct its resentment over economic policy against the crown. In Madrid the nobles were given *mercedes* (favours), lucrative offices in Spain and the Indies, annuities and land. The most famous of courts began to be constructed by Louis XIV in the 1670s at Versailles, where in 1682 he took up permanent residence. Thereafter, Versailles became the scintillating centre of patronage, government and culture; an astonishing, indeed unique example of showmanship in the early modern state. In the early eighteenth century the role of the royal court probably declined, but the nobles maintained their inclination for the capital city both as the centre of power and as an alternative to their country seats.

As courts rose, aristocrats seemed to decline. 'The lords in former times', observed Sir Walter Raleigh in the early seventeenth century, 'were far stronger, more warlike, better followed, living in their countries, than now they are'. 'There have been in ages past', claimed Bacon in 1592, 'noblemen both of greater possessions and of greater commandment and sway than any are at this day'. In the United Provinces the aristocracy had lost many estates during the war of independence. In France the civil war helped to bring ruin. 'How many gentlemen', wrote La Noue, 'are shorn of the riches that their houses were once adorned with' under Louis XII and Francis I. The city of Seville in 1627 claimed that the nobility 'have to keep themselves on incomes that will not buy today what could be bought previously with one-fourth of the same'. 'The greater part of the grandees of Spain', observed a French visitor under Philip IV, 'are ruined even though they possess large revenues'.

These comments need to be set in context. Though some great lords disappeared, others took their place; many lesser nobles decayed, but were quickly replaced by rising newcomers. In no European country was there an absolute decline of the noble estate. Their economic problems, however, were real. We may summarise them in terms of conspicuous expenditure, declining estate income and rising expenses aggravated by inflation.

Conspicuous expenditure arose from the need to be seen to live like a noble. The Spanish Duke of Béjar confessed in 1626 that 'everyone judges me to be rich, and I do not wish outsiders to know differently, because it would not be to my credit for them to understand that I am poor'. The system of keeping a large household of retainers and servants was a typical problem. In England in 1521 the Earl of Pembroke had 210 men wearing his livery, in 1612 the Earl of Rutland had 200. Retaining encouraged violence between rival households, kept up the trappings of feudalism, made idleness fashionable and impoverished the nobility. Governments consequently tried to limit it. Bacon commented that the beneficial effect of the English Statute of Retainers (1504) was that 'men now depend upon the prince and the laws'. In Spain a law of 1623 limited personal households to only eighteen persons, yet half a century later the chief minister

Oropesa had one of seventy-four. In Rome the size of households ran into the hundreds. In Poland the French ambassador reported that 'many of the nobles are followed by five to six hundred retainers'. Entertainment was, likewise, a standard item of conspicuous expenditure. The English Lord Hay in 1621 gave a feast for the French ambassador, in the preparation of which 100 cooks were employed eight days to cook 1,600 dishes. When in 1643 the Admiral of Castile gave a great dinner to the ambassadors of the Grey Leagues, 'the other seigneurs', reported a Jesuit, 'who had also been asked to entertain, were fearful of the event because they could not do more than he. The times were not propitious for such excessive expenditure; but if they spent less it would be observed.' Nobles also tried to outdo each other in keeping luxury coaches, which were consequently legislated against in sumptuary laws.

A major item of expenditure was the building of residences. The late sixteenth and early seventeenth centuries were a peak period for investment in houses. 'What has been created in the past is small in comparison with our own time', observed La Noue in 1585, 'since we see the quality of buildings and the number of those who build them far exceed any yet known, particularly among the nobility'. French gentlemen returning home from the wars yearned to build houses as they had seen them built in Italy. In Paris the rebuilding was given a stimulus by Henry IV, who altered the royal palaces and laid out spacious new squares like the Place Dauphine. The nobles built large town houses (*hôtels*), for which Sully set the style with his Hôtel Sully just as Richelieu did later with his Palais-Cardinal. In England the great rural reconstruction of this epoch (several country houses were rebuilt and new ones begun in a process that began in the 1560s, but reached its peak in the 1690s) was paralleled by the work of the nobility. It was the age when Chatsworth, Hardwick and Longleat made their appearance in the world. 'There was never the like number of fair and stately houses', wrote Bacon in 1592. 'No kingdom in the world spent so much in building as we did', reflected another. European courts and capitals blossomed. In London, Somerset House and the Banqueting House at Whitehall were constructed. In Counter-Reformation Rome, Pius IV and Sixtus V attempted to create the most beautiful urban centre in Europe. The sixteenth century saw the building in Rome of fifty-four churches, sixty new palaces – including the Vatican – twenty new aristocratic villas, two new suburbs and thirty new streets. In Valladolid, chief city of the Spanish crown before Philip II made Madrid his seat, some 400 seigneurial houses and palaces filled the city.

Estate income varied widely. Many lords profited from the favourable market conditions of the sixteenth century. In Piedmont the nobles invested in the soil, since other outlets offered limited scope; in the early seventeenth century their annual returns came to over 5 per cent of invested capital. Thomas Wilson testified that in England in 1600 the gentry 'know as well how to improve their lands to the uttermost as the farmer or countryman'. The well administered estates of the Percy family produced an income that rose from £3,602 in 1582 to £12,978 in 1636. Both in England and on the continent, however, there was a strong move to lease out land rather than cultivate it. The leasing of demesne was an old practice, but it was done so extensively in the early modern period that it is possible to consider most of the nobility of western Europe as a rentier rather than a producing class. Where rents could be increased this was done: on the Welsh estates of the Somerset family, rents doubled between 1549 and 1583, and a sample from the estates of seventeen English noble families shows that their rents doubled between 1590 and 1640. On this basis, landlords could keep pace with inflation and even make a profit. English landowners were among the most proficient at increasing their returns. In the period 1619–51 the rents on the twelve Yorkshire manors belonging to the Saviles of Thornhill were raised by over 400 per cent.

However, many rents were settled by feudal custom and written agreement and could not be raised without mutual consent. If, in addition, a tenant of this sort had a long lease, the landlord would be receiving only a fraction of the real rental value. In 1624, for instance, the customary tenants of the Earl of Southampton were paying him a total rent of £272, when the real market value of their tenancies was £2,372. In 1688 the Duke of Infantado's tenants in Jadraque (Guadalajara) were paying him exactly the same cash dues as 100 years before, in 1581.[25] In such cases a lord's income was bound to be severely affected. A powerful lord could use threats to change the terms of tenancy; but equally powerful forces could block such moves: the right of tenants to hold to their customary rent, the danger of rebellion, and the social pressures that demanded good relations between landlord and tenant.

Rising expenses could be blamed in most cases on inflation: the cost of food, building, clothes and luxuries was rising, and could have catastrophic results if there was no proportionate increase in the revenue from rents and demesne. There were, however, also other expenses. Service to the crown in the army and in ambassadorships could involve unforeseen costs. The state repeatedly – in France under Richelieu, in Spain under Olivares – tried to get cash sums from the nobility in order to pay war debts. Payment of dowries could be crippling (41 per cent of the Duke of Infantado's debts in 1637 arose from the dowries of his daughters). Litigation could absorb money and drag on for years.

By the seventeenth century, complaints of aristocratic poverty were universal. In 1591 the Danish historian Vedel deplored seeing gentlemen begging in the streets of Kiel. In 1604 the Danish royal council informed King Christian IV that 'an important section of the nobility already has enormous monetary debts'. Richelieu in 1614 described the French nobles as 'poor in money but rich in honour'. In Venice the nobles had had their fortunes tied to commerce; when that decayed they found it difficult to reinvest. Their numbers declined from a total of 2,090 in 1609 to 1,660 in 1631; as they shrank they became exclusive, caste-ridden and yet more aristocratic. The English ambassador in 1612 observed them 'buieng house and lands, furnishing themselfs with coch and horses, and giving themselves the good time'.[26] In the United Provinces, likewise, the remnant of the nobility had shrunk to a small group who, according to Sir

William Temple in 1673, protected their elitism by refusing to marry below their rank, and by affecting an exclusiveness which showed itself in the adoption of French dress, manners and speech.

The lesser nobility everywhere were the most prominent casualties. In Denmark, where of the approximately 500 noble landowners in 1625 one third held over three quarters of all land,[27] it was inevitable that many should have few means. In France the country gentry (*hobereaux*) were notoriously held to be poor, but in many cases their poverty was, perhaps, only relative. The rise and rapid fall of one French family can be traced in the case of Nicolas de Brichanteau, seigneur of Beauvais Nangis, captain of a troop of fifty men, who died in 1563. His son Antoine rose to prominence in the army, won royal favour and ended up as admiral of France and colonel of the guard. Excessive expenditure in this exalted position began his ruin. His son Nicolas tried to make his way at court but the family's debts caught up with him. In 1610 the estate of Nangis was covered with debts, accumulated at court, of up to four times its value. Nicolas was thereupon forced to retire to his estates in poverty.

In Spain 'the grandees, *títulos* and individual gentlemen who own lands and other rents today', wrote an observer in 1660, 'are completely deprived of any revenue because of the decline in population and in the number of farm labourers, and because prices have risen so disproportionately'. 'Many of the Castilian *títulos*', reported a Jesuit in 1640, 'have excused themselves from court because of the great want in their finances'. Indebtedness since the late sixteenth century is shown by the number of great lords of Castile – the dukes of Alburquerque and Osuna, the counts of Benavente and Lemos, the marquises of Santa Cruz and Aguilar – who feature among debtors to the moneylenders of Valladolid in the 1590s. Alburquerque borrowed to pay for litigation, Aguilar in order to pay a tax, Benavente to pay a dowry. By the mid-seventeenth century the Spanish nobility, including the titles of Alba, Osuna, Infantado and Medina Sidonia, were overwhelmed by debt.

In Naples by the end of the sixteenth century, of 148 noble families as many as fifty were too poor to maintain their rank and position. The Prince of Bisignano, who possessed sixty-five estates in Calabria and other regions, was so burdened by debt that by 1636 all his holdings were sold up. Of twenty-five estates held by the princes of Molfetta in 1551, fifteen were sold by the early seventeenth century. Between 1610 and 1640 alone, in eight of the twelve provinces of the kingdom of Naples at least 215 towns were alienated, by families with names as distinguished as Carrafa, Pignatelli and Orsini.

'How many noble families have there been whose memory is utterly abolished!' wrote an Englishman in 1603. 'How many flourishing houses have we seen which oblivion hath now obfuscated!' In so far as the principal item of wealth passing out of noble hands was land, it was often the urban elite who benefited. In Naples the space vacated by the old aristocracy was filled by Genoese, Tuscan and Venetian merchants, and by Neapolitan bourgeois and office-holders. In Spain the creditors of the nobility were bourgeois and government officials. A Norman noble expressed his hatred of the urban sectors in 1656 by claiming that

> Three things have ruined the nobility: the facility in finding money, luxury and war. In peace they are consumed by luxury; in war, since they have no money in reserve, the most comfortable gentleman can go only by mortgaging his field and his mill. So true is this that it can be proved that since 1492, when money became more common, men from the towns have acquired more than six million gold *livres* of revenues from noble lands owned by gentlemen rendering service in war according to the nature and quality of their fiefs....Men from the towns lend money [and as a result] all the proprietors are chased from the countryside.

But in some parts of Europe it was the lesser provincial nobility – the gentry in England, the *szlachta* in Poland – who profited from the difficulties of the aristocracy. Many of the lesser nobles had originally risen from the landed and trading middle elite and were firmly settled in their new status and life-style: in Italy and Spain they formed the elite in most provincial towns.

The English gentry were not for the most part men of a bourgeois cast of mind. 'I scorn base getting and unworthy penurious saving', wrote one of them, Sir John Oglander, in 1647, thereby disavowing two of the main hallmarks of the capitalist. Their fortune followed much the same lines as those of the higher aristocracy. Some of them fell on hard times, were unable to meet their debts, and sold their property; others prospered from mistakes, invested in land or business at a time when the returns were promising, and founded great fortunes. The gentry increased in numbers and wealth, due principally to the high turnover of land in the property market. How this worked may be illustrated by the sales of land made by Lord Henry Berkeley between 1561 and 1613. Of a total sales value of about £42,000, over £39,000 in land was sold to thirteen members of the higher gentry, the balance being purchased by twenty-five other persons of unspecified rank. Building their fortunes in this way, by purchase of property, many new families made their way up the social ladder. In Wiltshire between 1565 and 1602 no less than 109 new gentry names had been added to the original total of 203. This swelling in their numbers and wealth gave the gentry a new significance in the eyes of contemporaries. The political theorist James Harrington went so far as to claim in his *Oceana* (1656) that the gentry had become the richest estate in the realm: 'in our days, the clergy being destroyed, the lands in possession of the people overbalance those held by the nobility, at least nine in ten'. Another contemporary claimed in 1600 that the richer gentry had the incomes of an earl, and it was said in 1628 that the House of Commons could buy the House of Lords three times over. Like many contemporary claims, these statements have little proof to support them. It is true that the number of gentry increased, and most likely that as a group they held more wealth in their hands by 1660 than a century previously. But there was no radical transfer of power or of wealth from the aristocracy to the gentry.

The emergence of the gentry cannot in any case be measured merely in terms of wealth, for there were still few of them who could compete with the great aristocratic landlords, and even the sales of royalist lands during the republican period did not create a new much-landed gentry class. If their significance is to be gauged, it must be in terms of a steady accumulation of power in the countryside (rather than at court, where few gentry prospered). The power was based largely on land, but was precipitated by the events of the 1640s and also by the devolution of authority, after the later seventeenth century, upon the one class which had maintained its hold on the people of England.

The changing balance between old and new wealth can be see in northern Italy, where the rising classes of industrialists and traders eventually transformed themselves into the patriciate of the cities, reinvesting their money in public office and land. With a few exceptions (Lucca was one) the north Italian cities became re-aristocratised (or 're-feudalised', the term used by some Italian historians). In Milan, families that had made their fortune in munitions in the early sixteenth century had moved out into country estates by the end of the century. Some claimed to exercise feudal authority over their peasantry. The economic difficulties of the seventeenth century, however, began to hit even the new nobility. In one noble estate in Lombardy, state annuities in the period, 4 per cent, promised a higher rate of return than the land, which gave only a 1 per cent annual profit. The restricted social world of the city state limited the intake of new blood, and gradually old and new elites alike began to decay, as in Venice. In Siena between 1560 and 1760 the size of the elite shrank by 58 per cent. Although the city was nominally a republic it had become an aristocratic state, where noble incomes were drawn from land, not from trade, and where by the early eighteenth century the Loggia della Mercanzia ceased to be a meeting place for the business community and became the place where on a summer's day the Sienese nobles might meet to chat.

Most of the observations we have made about the economic difficulties of the aristocracy do not apply to the greater part of eastern Europe. Thanks to the more feudal landed structure in the east (see Chapter 6), the nobles there faced different problems. Nevertheless, in the east as well there was a change in fortunes: the root cause in most cases was political rather than economic. The rise of the Russian gentry is associated above all with the struggle of the boyars and magnates against the absolutism of Ivan IV (the Terrible). Ivan's attempts in 1564–72 to crush the aristocratic opposition ruthlessly by confiscating their lands and destroying their persons was from the political point of view a complete success. His two principal demands were for a reliable military force and adequate revenue. He obtained both by introducing the basic features of the 'service state', in which the state offered protection in return for services performed. In 1556, for instance, the tsar decreed that landlords were to supply one fully equipped horse-soldier for each quantity of land held; alternatively, this service could be commuted into a money payment. This was to introduce feudal principles that were falling into disuse in western Europe. Ivan, however, went further. He arbitrarily divided his kingdom up into a vast demesne territory controlled by a court called an *oprichnina* (comprising half of Muscovy and particularly the area around Moscow), and a territory in which boyar landownership was conceded, the *zemshchina*. Within the *oprichnina* area boyar power was abolished, estates destroyed and opponents executed. To enable this revolution to succeed, Ivan gathered to him the gentry class, the *dvoryanstvo*, who were liberally rewarded out of the land confiscated from the boyars. Writing to the tsar in 1573 of the excesses committed by the *oprichniki*, who carried out Ivan's policies in the *oprichnina*, the opposition boyar Prince Kurbsky denounced 'the laying waste of your land, both by you yourself and by your children of darkness [the *oprichniki*]'. Kurbsky's rhetoric mirrored the very great immediate evils brought about by the *oprichnina*: political and social discontent was widespread, agriculture was ruined, depopulation common, and the military defences of Muscovy were shattered.

On the ruins of this old order, the gentry rose into prominence as the new noble class. The process was continued into the early seventeenth century under the Romanovs. In 1566 Ivan had summoned an assembly called the Zemsky Sobor, consisting mainly of gentry in the service of the crown, to serve as a counterbalance to the boyar assembly. The gentry were also granted estates, but on new terms of tenure; whereas the old magnates had held their lands freely, as *votchina*, the new landowners held it on terms of service, as *pomestye*, and were known as *pomeshchiki*.

As the Russian gentry established their predominance through the land, so too the Polish gentry, the *szlachta*, became the noble class of Poland by extending their control over the soil and over agricultural production. In the early fifteenth century the noble estate was composed, on the one hand, of the great magnates with vast demesnes – families such as the Ostorogs, the Leszczynskis and the Radziwills – and, on the other, of the numerous company of knights and gentry. The latter increased their political power primarily by acting as a body to secure constitutional guarantees of their rights and status, and by establishing their authority at a local level through county committees or *sejms*. By the late fifteenth century the local *sejms* had given rise to a national Sejm or parliament composed of three orders: the king, a senate (consisting of bishops and senior nobles in the administration), and a chamber of deputies (consisting almost entirely of *szlachta*). The constitution of this parliament was officially confirmed by the king in 1505, when he promised not to act on any important issue without its consent. Numerically superior in the Sejm, the gentry inevitably came to dominate its councils and used it to promulgate legislation that served their own interests. By the late sixteenth century, despite the continuing influence of the great magnates, it was the *szlachta* who represented the nobility of Poland.

Like the gentry elsewhere, the *szlachta* were not an economically homogeneous group. Throughout the Polish territories (essentially, Poland and the Grand Duchy of Lithuania) the noble class made up about 15 per cent of the population. But over half of this number were very minor gentry indeed, enjoying noble rights and status, yet possessing little more land than an ordinary peasant. Despite this, it was the land that was the basis of *szlachta* power, and to defend their interests they took care to limit the powers both of the clergy and of the townships. Clerical posts were infiltrated by gentry, and the Church was deprived in 1562 of its disciplinary powers over heresy. In 1565 the Sejm restricted the activities of the merchant class. In this way the so-called 'republic of nobles' came into being, where all gentry, of high and low degree, shared equally in the government of Poland.

In other lands of central and eastern Europe it is also possible to talk of a rise of the gentry, associated with a change in the exploitation of the soil. Perhaps the most outstanding example is East Prussia, where the new nobles, the Junkers, made their appearance in the fifteenth century from the knights, soldiers and adventurers of the German frontier.[28] The process of recruitment of this new landed estate, which must be looked upon essentially as a squirearchy or gentry, since it possessed little of the elitist ethic of the nobility of western Europe, continued throughout the sixteenth and early seventeenth centuries.

The 'land revolution' which followed the price rise was for several reasons no less significant than the price revolution. First, the land protected the privileged. The holders of estates and manors in Germany, France, England, Italy, the noble lords whose soil produced corn, whose fields pastured sheep, whose peasantry brought in dairy produce, kept their heads above the waves of inflation. They raised their rents where possible or necessary, but most important of all began to exploit their resources to benefit from the favourable level of prices. One success story was the Seymour family, whose manorial holdings in Wiltshire produced receipts that rose from £475 in 1575 to £3,204 in 1649–50. The aristocracy – at least the greater part – were not only saved but entrenched themselves even more firmly into the political life of Europe. Second, the sure guarantee offered by land in a world where most other values seemed to be collapsing inspired those who had been successful in their own fragile enterprises – finance, commerce – to think of their families and to buy an estate or two on which to spend their declining days. Land was both the conserver and the solvent of society; while preserving the old forces, it also gave greater opportunities for wealth and mobility to those who had made their fortunes in professions frowned on by the upper classes.

Crisis and resilience of the aristocracy

Like every social class, the upper elite also changed in role and in fortune. Guided to some extent by commentators of that time, historians have often given more emphasis to notable changes (the decline of great lords, the rise of the gentry) and paid less attention to structural continuities. More recent studies accept that changes occurred, but rather as readjustments within the regional and status parameters of traditional society. One result has been to cast more light on the remarkable phenomenon of the survival of the noble elite.[29] In the seventeenth century, for example, up to a half of the Lancashire families (well over 700) claiming gentry status changed, but their overall numbers remained much the same,[30] demonstrating that the elite benefited from social mobility and a lack of exclusiveness, and were capable of continually replenishing themselves.

Observers in early modern Europe frequently commented on the decline in the political function of the great nobles. The Venetian ambassador wrote in 1622 of the English aristocracy: 'the magnates are mostly hated for their vain ostentation, better suited to their ancient power than their present condition'. Similar statements were made at various times of the nobles in the Netherlands, France and Spain. The most visible reason for the decay in noble power was the increase in crown initiative, which affected the elite in three main ways: by a reduction in their military role, by exclusion from high office, and by greater subordination to the law. In all three ways, however, nobles as a class ended up by integrating themselves into the new structure of authority. Their numbers fell dramatically, not least because of a failure to produce heirs, but this too was no obstacle.

The growth of absolutist theory served to support the state, but monarchs were never in principle hostile to the interests of the aristocracy. On the contrary, kings recognised the nobles as the natural and traditional rulers of the people, and the only foundation of the state. They needed them as public ornaments, as administrators and generals, and as pillars of the social structure.[31] Though impatient with the proven incapacity of sections of the elite – 'their contempt of the various branches of knowledge and the little trouble they take to fit themselves for various posts', as the Duke of Sully put it – the absolute monarch never proposed to supersede the nobles in posts of influence. The whole mentality of absolutism was too aristocratic for that. As the state grew in power, therefore, it found itself in an increasingly illogical position. On one hand it relied upon and fostered the hereditary ruling class, and on the other it was obliged to look outside the ranks of that class for the necessary cooperation in setting up a strong administration. This created an internal contradiction within absolutism, one that would be resolved by radical, even violent methods in the course of the seventeenth century.

The first and greatest danger facing the monarchies was the armed might of the nobles, as we have seen above. Much of the success in controlling noble bellicosity must be attributed, first, to the fostering of a strong sense of personal loyalty to the crown, and second, to the gradual absorption of noble forces into those of the state. The results varied from country to country. In England, observed Raleigh, 'the force by which our kings in former times were troubled is vanished away'. Strong crown pressure to keep the peace, the inability of nobles to afford private armies, the relative absence of foreign wars (while three quarters of the titled peerage before mid-century had done some service, by 1576 only one in four had military experience), all helped the English monarchy. In Spain, Philip II drew the nobles into a partnership in which they were given control over all local militia, with each grandee taking command in his own province, while the crown independently recruited the armies serving abroad. Ironically, therefore, in Spain the grandees became militarily more powerful: a notable case was that of the dukes of Medina-Sidonia, whose authority over southwest Spain was extended. The state had no other provincial officials it could use; the peace, therefore, was kept in Spain, but at a price. In France it was the power of the nobles to raise troops in the provinces (the Montmorency rebellion in Languedoc of 1632, the noble Fronde of 1650) that committed Louis XIV to follow a policy different from that of Spain.

Armed rebellions arose in part from noble complaints that they were excluded from high office. In medieval times it had been the right of magnates to give advice to the king, usually through the council, and to hold the chief posts in their provinces. From the later fifteenth century, the crown was forced to exclude over-powerful or unreliable nobles from positions of authority. It was normally impossible to diminish their power in their home provinces; only time would achieve this. At the centre of the administration, however, the state could build up a bureaucracy consisting of lesser men whom it could trust and who did not rely on any great lord for preferment. With few exceptions, this bureaucracy was drawn from university graduates trained in law (see Chapter 9). Though few of the new administrators had titles, by the time they reached the upper echelons of the state and judicial apparatus they were already of confirmed noble rank. All the western monarchies quickly replaced aristocrats with the new trained bureaucrats, but in no sense was this a resort to low class officials: the administrators were of noble status, necessarily so in virtue of the authority that they exercised over others, and many founded dynasties.

Subordination to the rule of law was seldom a matter of law-enforcement, despite the executions of the Duke of Norfolk, the Duke of Montmorency and the Justiciar of Aragon. The state could legislate through the sumptuary laws, could prohibit duelling, could restrict the competence of seigneurial courts; but in practice the rule of law could only operate if the nobles adjusted themselves psychologically to the growing authority of the crown. Governments were aware of the delicate situation and trod carefully. The law of treason, for example, seems to have been applied rigorously only in England. In France, as late as the 1650s the state refused to act with severity against the open treason of the cities of Bordeaux and Marseille (both attempted to ally with Spain). The Prince of Condé, who led a Spanish army against his own country, was eventually pardoned and allowed back into his estates. It was in any case in the interests of the nobles themselves to maintain stability in their territories. The networks of influence in the provinces reinforced the position of both patrons and clients, and maintained the balance of power without necessarily reducing the role of the aristocracy.

The aristocracy began to be tamed, though their power base was never seriously undermined. A census of New Castile in 1597 showed that the lords controlled nearly 40 per cent of the towns and had jurisdiction over 34 per cent of the population. In Old Castile, by the eighteenth century 47 per cent of the population still lived under seigneurial jurisdiction; in the province of Salamanca as many as 60 per cent. Great nobles such as the Constable of Castile and the Duke of Infantado were seigneurs in over 500 towns each. While continuing to exercise extensive authority, however, the Castilian nobility accepted the role of the crown. The partnership between crown and nobles initiated by Ferdinand and Isabella created a political stability almost unique in western Europe: there was not a single noble rebellion between 1516 and 1705.

In England the Tudor monarchy (1485–1603) introduced administrative changes that completely altered the balance of power in the realm. The extensive authority assumed by the royal council in London and in the provinces was wielded by nobles and prelates who had adopted the cause of the crown. But the men on whom the real task of administration fell more and more were the gentry, the class from whom sheriffs and justices of the peace tended to be chosen. The gentry were, in addition, the group that formed the bulk of the membership of the House of Commons, whose constitutional importance grew enormously in the late sixteenth century. Cut off for the most part from participation in local and central government, a task for which they never had much taste anyway, the aristocracy depended for advancement on the great offices of state that lay within the gift of the king – lord-lieutenantcies of counties, posts and sinecures in the royal household and in the military and diplomatic services. The traditional loyalty and deference to peers in their country seats still continued to a very great extent, but even this link was dissolving as feudal tenures disappeared and tenants became less dependent on their lords. Inevitably, then, the peers gravitated towards the court, and it remained for the crown to decide among which groups the favours should be divided. 'Gratify your nobility', Burghley advised Elizabeth in 1579, 'and the principal persons of your realm, to bind them fast to you'.

The efforts of the French monarchy to tame its nobles were constant, from the time of Catherine de Médicis through Richelieu's ministry to the reign of Louis XIV. Under Richelieu plotters were executed: Chalais in 1626, Montmorency in 1632, Cinq-Mars in 1642. Great military commands were taken away from the grandees: the offices of admiral and constable of France were abolished in 1627, and unreliable great nobles removed from the governorships of frontier provinces. In part because of the great size and population of France, the crown was unable to control noble separatism, support for popular rebels and illegal activity; all this made the Fronde possible. Beginning with the introduction of intendants in the 1630s, and the reform of judicial administration in the 1660s, a more stable regime began to be created, in which the nobles were guaranteed all their privileges but effectively excluded from day-to-day government. The absolutism of Louis XIV brought peace not by eliminating the aristocracy but by redefining their function.

Nobles in former times had earned their social ascent through distinction in warfare. The western monarchies now played down the emphasis on war, and preferred to reward on their own terms, which included service to the state in administration, diplomacy and commerce. Thus loyalty to the crown became the major road to preferment. Both old and new nobles benefited. In Spain there had been 124 titled nobles in 1597; by 1631 there were 241, and under Philip IV alone nearly 100 new titles were created. Philip IV in 1625 explained: 'Without reward and punishment no monarchy can be preserved. We have no money, so we have thought it right and necessary to increase the number of honours.' Between 1551 and 1575, 354 new members of the Order of Santiago had been created; from 1621 to 1645 the total shot up to 2,288. Charles II (1665–1700) created during his reign as many new honours for the elite as all his predecessors had done in the preceding two centuries. In Spanish-ruled Naples the number of titled barons increased threefold between 1590 and 1669.

Before the accession of James I to the English throne in 1603, the realm had about 500 knights. In the first four months of his reign he created no fewer than 906 new ones; by the end of 1604 the total of new creations was 1,161. The titled aristocracy were also affected: in the thirteen years 1615–28, James and later Charles I increased their numbers from eighty-one to 126. This increase pales before that achieved in Sweden, where Queen Christina within the space of ten years doubled the number of noble families and sextupled the number of counts and barons. In Hungary the new titles created between 1606 and 1657 tripled the number of higher nobles.

In nearly all cases the noble titles were sold: the creations aimed to raise cash and did not form part of a deliberate policy of social advancement. Louis XIV, as we have seen, resorted to selling titles on a large scale in the 1690s in order to raise money. The flood of new creations, or 'inflation of honours' as it has been called, did not necessarily placate the already discontented peerage. 'It may be doubted', wrote an Englishman of the next generation, Sir Edward Walker, 'whether the dispensing of honours with so liberal a hand was not one of the beginnings of general discontents, especially among persons of great extraction'. In England and in Sweden the resentment led to the overthrow of the ruler, and in France helped to provoke the Fronde. The consequences, however, were not always negative. In both France and Spain the creations helped to raise up a newer class of administrators: the families of Phélypeaux in France and of Ronquillo in Castile were typical of the rising elite of state nobles who served the crown with distinction for over two centuries.

Though the crown appeared to be chiefly responsible for their difficulties, it was also the most reliable ally of the nobles. In the first place, the state guaranteed the integrity and status of the noble class. In France from 1555 to 1632 several edicts legislated a fine of 1,000 livres against any commoner usurping nobility. In 1666 and throughout the reign of Louis XIV, a thorough inquiry into all noble titles was undertaken, and rigorous proofs demanded; intendants were ordered to impose heavy fines. In Spain the inflation of honours led in practice to a more rigid application of the criteria for nobility. Second, the crown extended its system of pensions so as to save aristocrats about to topple into penury: both in Versailles and in Madrid the scale of handouts gave visitors the impression of an impoverished aristocracy. Poor relief for nobles was in fact of long standing: in 1614 the French treasury was giving out sums of ten livres to 'poor gentlemen…to help them live'; and in 1639 Louis reminded his judges 'not to imprison nobles for debt, nor to sell their goods'. Third, the crown gave legal protection to noble property. Several countries had laws allowing only nobles to buy noble land. In Denmark this had the effect of preserving within the class the large amount of land that might have been sold to pay noble debts, estimated in 1660 as equivalent to the value of one third of all their land. A more rigorous form of control was the entail, a legal device disallowing any alienation of property. Known as *mayorazgo* in Spain, the crown from Ferdinand the Catholic (1505) onwards made it obligatory on the grandees. This preserved noble assets and thus allowed the ruling class to serve the state decently. However, precisely because land could not be sold to meet expenses, many lords fell deeply into debt. This made them more dependent on the crown, which in return took exceptional measures to save them. In 1606 the Duke of Sessa died 'out of melancholy at being ruined and because the king did not give him a grant to pay his debts'. In fact, Philip III met one quarter of the dead duke's debts, and settled an income on his widow and son. Entails were common in Italy in the sixteenth century, and in France, Germany and England in the seventeenth. Because of the problems caused by entails (they provoked indebtedness and depressed the land market) primogeniture was preferred in some states. Piedmont attempted in 1598 to limit the period of entails, and in 1648 Charles Emmanuel II issued an edict encouraging the practice of primogeniture, 'since it so concerns us to maintain and develop the splendour of the nobility'.[32]

The power elite also had to evolve their own strategies for survival.[33] A good marriage strategy was essential, in part to produce male heirs and so compensate for the notorious inability of elites to survive over many generations, and in part to restrict any movement outside the closed circle of the peer group. Thanks to state protection and their own efforts, the aristocracy survived. Their estates were favoured by law, their pockets were often flattered by pensions, they were exempted from most taxation, and their persons were frequently immune from criminal proceedings. By the early eighteenth century their life-style and political role had altered, but they remained as powerful as ever; continuity rather than change was their leitmotiv.[34] A comparison of the status of the nobles in Bayeux in lower Normandy in 1552 and 1640 shows that in both years the old nobles controlled four fifths of the total income in the *élection*.[35] In Holland the old nobility retired from active political life but held on to their estates and survived instead of decaying. In a political structure that was actively republican, they kept a hold on power by transforming themselves into rural counterparts of the governing class of patrician regents.[36] For England it has been argued, on the basis of land sales in the counties of Hertfordshire, Northampton and Northumberland, that a solid and unchanging core of aristocrat and gentry families ran the countryside from generation to generation, despite the entry of others (just over 10 per cent) into their ranks.[37] Over and above simple survival, the upper elite succeeded also in communicating to society their scale of values. The middle elite, whether urban patricians or state officials, imitated their behaviour. The nobles, moreover, did not make the mistake of relapsing into indolence. They maintained high cultural standards that set the standard for social taste. In this way they could justify their role in a world that would soon begin to develop more democratic ideals.

5

THE MIDDLE ELITE

'We merchants are a species of gentry that have grown into the world this last century, and are as honourable as you landed folk that have always thought yourselves so much above us.'
(a Bristol merchant, in Richard Steele's *Conscious Lovers*, 1722)

Urban and rural elites; norms and values

In his *Traité des Ordres* (1613) the jurist Loyseau defined bourgeois simply as the inhabitant of a town or *bourg*. More commonly the term referred to the urban elite, and it was in this sense that it was used in Germany (*bürger*) and England (burgher). When referring to the middle section of society, Loyseau talked of 'the Third Estate', which again signified the urban classes, since of the three estates normally represented in parliaments of the time the third was drawn from representatives of the towns. The term 'middle elite' rather than 'bourgeois' will be used here for convenience to refer to the non-aristocratic elites of both town and country, but no single word is appropriate.[1] The upper strata of this elite occupied different positions in the social scale, drew their wealth from different sources, and enjoyed differing privileges as well as distinct norms and ideals. Moreover, the leading citizens of many of the principal cities of Europe were in fact already nobles (as in the case of the elite *capitouls* of Toulouse) or about to become nobles.

Normally the members of this elite did not, like the traditional aristocracy, have a supposed ethic to which writers could devote treatises. But they possessed a coherent pattern of values that defined their conduct and their aspirations.[2] From this point of view, what bound them together were shared values and shared contexts, for example as property owners or as members of professional groups.[3] Since their values always, in the society of that time, involved kinship groups, they strove to give permanence to what their families possessed, through visible proofs such as lineage trees and even coats of arms. The coat of arms, in effect, defined achievement, and helps historians to identify members of the elite. The increase of the gentry class in Warwickshire, for example, can be estimated by the difference between 155 families with coats of arms in 1500, and

288 with the same distinction in 1642.[4] But not all the middle elite, even in England, yearned after coats of arms or lineage trees.

Elites were participants in a process of change, rather than fixed members of a social order; as a consequence, they are difficult to measure in size, role or status. Attrition through lack of male succession, or through rapid mobility from below, might change their numbers radically: new families who had emerged after 1500 formed 80 per cent of those claiming gentry status in Dorset in 1642.[5] In economic terms, the middle elite were thought of as sandwiched between two other strata, those at the bottom who might have to toil for their living, and those who lived off unearned income at the top. At the lowest level they consisted of petty traders, minor officials, prosperous artisans and others who tended to have independent means and were not in the employ of another. Contemporary usage, however, tended to ignore these lower categories and to lay stress on the well off, who were, to cite a statement of the Parlement of Paris in 1560, 'good citizens living in the cities whether royal officials, merchants, people who live off their rents, or others'. All these terms imply the possession of property, leading to the conclusion that though there were different types and status levels among the bourgeoisie, possession of substantial property was always an essential trait. 'Good citizens' signified that in many towns the citizen (*bourgeois*, *bürger*) was one who had been formally accepted into the 'book of citizens', which bestowed several privileges of residence and taxation. In seventeenth-century Lille the inhabitants were divided into 'citizens' (*bourgeois*) and 'commoners'; the former made up one fifth of the population. 'Royal officials' were evidence that as the bureaucracy of state grew, royal officials became more prominent in the towns. Loyseau in his *Traité* placed financial officials and lawyers at the apex of his 'Third Estate'. 'Merchants' were likewise an integral part: Loyseau wrote that

> the merchants are the lowest of the people enjoying an honourable status, and are described as *honorables hommes* or *honnêtes personnes* and *bourgeois des villes*, titles not given to farmers or artisans and even less to labourers, who are all regarded as commoners.

None of these categories was in any sense fixed or stagnant, and there was considerable mobility through the middle ranks of society. Some rose into the bourgeoisie from the shop, some from the plough. In upper Poitou in the sixteenth century, rich peasants put their sons through university, managed to buy them a minor office, and so initiated their rise into the bourgeoisie. In Burgundy in 1515 the Ramillon family were still practising agriculture in the town of Charlay. By the seventeenth century some members of the family had moved to Varzy: there they took up small trading, as butcher or baker. By 1671 Etienne Ramillon had become a merchant draper. In 1712 a grandson of his became an *avocat* to the parlement of Burgundy.[6]

Trade: a classic role

Because of imprecision about status, it is difficult to determine the size of the urban elite. Where figures are available (usually tax figures) they tend to describe a town oligarchy rather than an economic class. In Venice in the late sixteenth century the *cittadini* were 6 per cent of the city's population. In Norwich in the early century the upper middle class numbered about 6 per cent of the population and owned about 60 per cent of the lands and goods for which taxes were paid to the city. A further 14 per cent could be included as coming within the definition of 'middle class', but these were somewhat poorer. In Coventry at the same period 45 per cent of the property was owned by only 2 per cent of the people, among them the grocer Richard Marler, who paid one ninth of the town's subsidy contributions. In later seventeenth-century Beauvais, some 300 out of a total of 3,250 tax-paying families constituted the upper bourgeoisie, but even within these 300 there was a smaller elite of 100 families.

Most of the bourgeoisie achieved status through one of three principal channels: trade, finance and office. By these means they obtained the capital that most came to invest in land. The trading bourgeois was a type that had been known in the Middle Ages and was to be captured perfectly in Dutch seventeenth-century portraits. He could be found in all the major seaports, industrial centres and market towns of Europe: in cities such as Antwerp, Liège and Medina del Campo. Unlike the 'citizen' bourgeois, who was firmly rooted in the confines of his own region, the trading bourgeois had universal horizons, carrying on negotiations with financiers and merchants throughout the country and overseas. He had to be capable of handling large sources of capital, which for him were little pieces of paper (bills of exchange), and of taking risks with his own money and that of his associates. The trading community was already internationalised at the beginning of the sixteenth century, with Genoese merchants in Seville, Spanish merchants in Nantes and Antwerp, and Netherlands merchants in the Baltic. The chief trading nations were all Catholic, with Antwerp at the heart of the system.

The Reformation, by taking over many of the trading routes of the older system, helped to give Protestant enterprise a great stimulus in northern Europe. The growth of Amsterdam was particularly remarkable. Sir William Temple in the later seventeenth century testified to the bourgeois ethic of the Hollanders, 'every man spending less than he has coming in'. Trade, however, was not an assured and permanent source of profits; and as merchants made money they tended to diversify their investments in order to gain security.

In Amsterdam the commercial classes became more exclusive in structure as they grew more wealthy. In part this was because of business marriages, in part because of a wish to conserve control over political life. In 1615 a burgomaster of Amsterdam reported that the elite – the regent class – were still active in trade; by 1652 it was said that the regents were no longer in trade 'but derived their income from houses, lands and money at interest'. Examples from the rest of western Europe show that it is wrong to see the merchant bourgeoisie as one single-mindedly devoted to reinvesting in commerce. All who made fortunes were concerned to diversify their income. In Liège, most big bourgeois in 1577–8 drew their money from both trade and finance. In 1595 a foreigner, Jean Curtius (from the town of Den Bosch), had the biggest single income in Liège, drawn from munitions. During his most active period of capital accumulation, in 1595–1603, Curtius invested in precisely the things that attracted the merchants of Amsterdam: land and rents. In Spain, the financier Simón Ruiz of Medina del Campo belonged to a family specialising in trade with France. He grew rich and founded a hospital for his home town. But from 1576, when the trading world began to get shaky in part because of the Dutch revolt, Ruiz moved his money into public financing. The next generation of his family began to dissipate his wealth and preferred to abandon the money market for the desirable honours of noble status.

These illustrations of a general phenomenon help to place in context Jacques Savary's *Le Parfait Négociant* (1675), where an exaggerated contrast was drawn between the merchants of France and Holland:

> From the moment that a merchant in France has acquired great wealth in trade, his children, far from following him in this profession, on the contrary enter public office...whereas in Holland the children of merchants ordinarily follow the profession and the trade of their fathers. Money is not withdrawn from trade but continues in it constantly from father to son, and from family to family as a result of the alliances which merchants make with one another.

Savary's view was in part anticipated by a report to Richelieu in 1626: 'What has hurt trade is that all the merchants, when they become rich, do not remain in commerce but spend their goods on offices for their children.' It was realised at the time that alternative investments (offices, *rentes*) were attracting money away from commerce. In 1560 the Chancellor L'Hospital had complained that 'trade has decayed greatly because of the issue of *rentes*'. Among the merchant bourgeoisie of Amiens, twenty-seven had been principally active in the textile industry in 1589–90; only six of them were still active thirty-five years later. Of thirty-eight merchant families active in the industry in 1625, only seven remained by 1711. A Lyon merchant of the time protested that 'trade creates wealth; and nearly all the best families of Paris, Lyon, Rouen, Orléans and Bordeaux originate not only from lawyers, notaries and attorneys, but also from merchants....The merchant acquires, the office-holder keeps, the nobleman dissipates.' The complaints about France, if taken literally, would point to decay of the merchant classes by the early eighteenth century, a manifestly absurd conclusion. What happened was a steady move towards securing the future of one's family in terms of tangible wealth and social position. The fortune left by the Beauvais merchant Lucien Motte in 1650 shows the beginnings of this diversification: 4 per cent of his assets were now in land; and 27 per cent in *rentes* and other assets external to commerce.

The trading elite had their own different status levels, determined by wealth and social practice. Large-scale merchants were very clearly distinguished from small traders, a difference perhaps most clearly reflected in the guild system. Large traders in France were organised into guilds known as the 'merchant bodies', *corps de marchands*, while small traders were grouped into 'professional communities', *communautés d'arts et métiers*. There were, inevitably, many variations in practice from town to town and country to country. In seventeenth-century Spain the goldsmiths, for example, were still arguing that they were more than mere artisans, and by the eighteenth century they succeeded in being accepted as capable of nobility.[7]

Elites and financial change

Rentes were loans made by the public to the state, in return for annual payment of interest. They existed in Italy in the Middle Ages, and most other states began to issue them in the fifteenth and sixteenth centuries. In France the *rentes*, though technically a loan to the crown, were issued by the Hôtel de Ville at Paris. In Spain state loans were called *juros*, private and municipal loans *censos*. In Italy the *monti*, as the public debts were called, had long played a part in municipal finance.

These annuities were a tempting form of investment, particularly where the state offered both security and a high rate of interest (about 7 per cent in the late sixteenth century). In an age when banking was relatively unknown, the authorities became bankers, borrowing from citizens and paying them their interest out of taxation. In late fifteenth-century Florence it led to the emergence of a *rentier* mentality among the wealthier bourgeoisie, and to the concentration of financial wealth in the hands of the upper rank of citizens, since it was these who controlled the machinery of state. It is possible that investment in the *monti* diverted capital from entrepreneurial activities. A comparable situation prevailed in other parts of Italy at a later period. In the Como region near the duchy of Milan, a vigorous and wealthy middle class existed. In addition to their other interests, the citizens of Como devoted themselves to moneylending. Their clients were both peasant communities and the government, and from these the bourgeoisie drew their annuities, their *censi*. In 1663 the rural community of Gravedona, one among others, complained that it was crippled by debts because of the *censi* it had to pay to former councillors and officials of the city.

Investment in *rentes* was never in itself open to criticism. Critics were concerned rather with the diversion of funds away from other productive enterprises. The Amsterdam bourgeoisie were a *rentier* class as large as any in western Europe (Louis Trip, for instance, at his death in 1684 left something like 157,000 florins in *rentes* alone). Yet Dutch investment in this sort of commodity took place only after the capital demands of commerce and industry had been met, so that *rentes* tended to eat up only a proportion of working capital. In Germany, France and Spain, on the other hand, the devotion to *rentes* often amounted to a passion.

For many investors in Spain, the *juros* represented quite simply their principal source of income. The nobles invested no less than the bourgeois, and examples of nobles who in 1680 depended on the *juros* alone for their cash income are revealing: the Viscount of Ambite 'whose whole income consisted in them'; the Viscount de la Frontera 'who had no other income to live on'. Innumerable families, particularly widows, drew on *juros* as though they were a pension scheme. Those who lived off the interest from annuities were in effect living off the state, without making any productive contribution to it. Striking examples of this are the city of Valladolid, where 232 citizens in 1597 drew more money from the government by way of *juros* than was paid by the whole city in taxes; and Ciudad Rodrigo, where in 1667 the holders of *juros* drew 160 per cent more from their annuities than the whole city paid in taxes.

The peasantry and the village communities of Europe tended to depend exclusively on the bourgeois moneylenders of the towns for the capital they needed in order to improve their landholdings. The cash available to the peasant was never very considerable; in times of deflation or disaster, when credit was most needed for improvement and survival, the situation became critical. The peasantry inevitably became the largest class of borrowers. The accounts of the Valladolid notary Antonio de Cigales show, for example, that in the years 1576–7 over 51 per cent of his debtors were peasants. The sums were invariably small, but certainly helped the peasant to make ends meet and to develop his holdings when necessary.

It was when the question of payment of annuities and redemption of the loan arose that difficulties occurred. A peasant who did not manage to repay the loan when a good harvest came, often lost the chance forever. A bad year could bring with it the beginnings of an inability to pay; this in turn could lead to permanent indebtedness and final bankruptcy. The *rentier* could step in and confiscate the landholding that had been the guarantee of the loan. In the long periods of agrarian depression that recurred in the rural economy, thousands of peasant holdings passed out of the hands of their owners into those of the urban bourgeoisie. Castile in the seventeenth century was amply populated with towns and villages labouring under the burden of *censos*: one such was Aldeanueva de Figueroa, which in the years 1664 to 1686 alone alienated over one third of its land to the middle elite of Salamanca.

The transference of land from the peasantry is relatively easy to understand, but there were other sections of society that also became indebted to the *rentiers*. In the number of Antonio de Cigales' debtors for 1576–7, about 10 per cent were artisans and 13 per cent were holders of offices, while nearly 3 per cent were nobles. All of these did not necessarily lose their property, but the cross-section of society that did tend to lose land was surprisingly wide. In one of the parishes in the Rouen area in 1521, of a total of 288 people selling their plots of land, 183 were peasant farmers, fifty-two were artisans, twenty were labourers, nineteen were bourgeois and fourteen were priests. The purchasers were almost without exception bourgeois.

Loans, therefore, became an instrument for the deterioration and expropriation of an independent peasantry, and promoted the conquest of the soil by the urban classes. The transfer of land from peasant to bourgeois was not, of course, caused exclusively or directly by *rentes*. The economic circumstances of the early sixteenth century had already given a firm impetus to the process. But peasant indebtedness to *rentiers* certainly played a large part in it. By the mid-sixteenth century, over half the land around Montpellier was said to belong to the city's inhabitants. Whereas tax officials held only six hectares of Montpellier territory in 1547, by 1680 they held 220.

The upper nobility also were prey to the activities of the town moneylenders. The scale of indebtedness of the Castilian nobility was so alarming (the Count of Benavente in the early seventeenth century paid out 45 per cent of his annual income for *censos*) that the crown stepped in to save its ruling class. By royal decrees, individual noble debtors were allowed to seek reductions in the rate of interest they paid; if this was refused by creditors, the nobles were allowed to redeem their *censos* by creating new debts elsewhere in order to repay the old debts. So great was the demand for income from *censos* that reductions were readily conceded by the creditors.

Thanks to the debts contracted by the nobility, the urban class proceeded to take over the ownership of the soil from the nobles no less than from peasants. An extraordinary premium was set on land, as the fortune of Toussaint Foy shows. A tax officer for one region of the Beauvaisis, his fortune at his death in 1660 was made up as follows: lands 55.8 per cent, cash and goods 14.1 per cent, office 5.8 per cent, *rentes* 13.5 per cent, houses 10.8 per cent. The most valued lands were those that carried lordship and seigneurial rights with them; although purchase of these did not confer nobility, it certainly enhanced status. Throughout western Europe the bourgeoisie and the urban elites put their money into soil.

In seventeenth-century Dijon the middle class made up a third of the population. Though the core consisted of officials and members of the court (parlement), there were also several gentry who had moved in from the countryside in search of income from office. In their turn the bourgeoisie moved their interests into the countryside, buying land which would give them the mark of *qualité* that bestowed status. By mid-century, the city of Dijon had obtained a firm grip on the surrounding land.[8] In Amiens at the same period the upper bourgeoisie drew nearly 60 per cent of income from land and rents. A survey in Amiens in 1634 showed that 351 citizens, all commoners, held land ranging from small plots to large seigneurial estates. Of the estates, twenty-eight had feudal jurisdiction, eighteen belonged to the *noblesse de robe* (see below), five to bourgeois citizens and four to lawyers. From Alsace in 1587 came the complaint that 'more and more from day to day grows the unheard-of pace at which houses and holdings pass into the hands of the Strasbourgers'. Soon many bourgeois became the new seigneurs of the soil. One example was Pierre Cécile, a judge of the parlement at Dôle (Franche Comté). By the time of his death in 1587, he was the owner of twenty-five plots of land and meadow, three town houses, three small country houses, and fourteen vineyards scattered through the territory over twenty-five different towns and villages.

The indebtedness of the rural nobility may be studied in the accounts of a leading judge of the Beauvais region. Of those who held *rentes* from Maître Tristan in 1647, nearly three quarters were noblemen, all with distinguished names, including that of the family Rouvroy de Saint-Simon. Nearly all the lands, houses and *seigneuries* that fell into Maître Tristan's hands as a result of his activities as a *rentier* came from noble debtors. From the illustrious Gouffier family, descendants of two admirals of France, a family now overwhelmed by debts and which had sold all their possessions in Picardy to bourgeois, Tristan bought the estates and fiefs of Juvignies and Verderel, which remained in his family for over a century. By the end of the seventeenth century, the Tristans had climbed to wealth over the decayed fortunes of impoverished noblemen, and in the early eighteenth century they obtained noble status through the purchase of an office at court. Their example, one among many even in the confines of Beauvaisis, illustrates the extraordinary extent to which *rentes* served to transfer land and property from the aristocracy to the rising middle classes, and helped eventually to create a new nobility in France.

The acquisition of land by the middle elite has often been looked upon without qualification as a retrogressive, anti-capitalist development, above all since it took money out of commerce. In fact, few bourgeois invested only in land; and the investment in land was in principle highly beneficial. In many regions, only the bourgeoisie had the capital necessary to revive agriculture, so long neglected by aristocrats who had seen their estates as property to be exploited, or by peasant farmers who had been struggling against debts. In the estates that the merchant classes acquired around Toulouse in the mid-sixteenth century, they introduced a rationalisation of labour. The number of tenants was reduced to a working minimum; rents were asked for in kind rather than in cash; and sharecropping (*métayage*) was substituted for less profitable types of tenancy. After the 1630s in Alsace, it was the urban elite of Strasbourg and other towns who helped to restore villages destroyed by war. In the 1650s in the Dijonnais, it was thanks to bourgeois seigneurs that the villages were repopulated, the fields restored, the vineyards replanted and extended, and the cattle brought back. In many areas of Germany after the Thirty Years War, it was the urban merchants who advanced the capital without which rural reconstruction was impossible.

The leading part played by the middle elite in handling money was reflected in their activity as tax-collectors and financiers. Since the Middle Ages, kings and prelates had employed commoners to direct their estates and collect their rents. These administrators were officials of rank and standing, and not modest functionaries; many were already moving into the ranks of the titled nobility. The state preferred to rely on men who could draw upon large reserves of credit rather than on those whose wealth was (like noble wealth) tied up in land. It therefore turned to traders with international connections, which explains the regular appearance of foreigners and Jews in the tax systems of western Europe. In sixteenth-century France, Italians (like Zamet) were prominent in finance; in the seventeenth century Belgians and Germans (like Herwart) became prominent. The Spanish crown relied in the sixteenth century on Germans (the Fuggers) and Italians; in the seventeenth on Italians and Portuguese Jews.

The middle elite were given a major role in financial matters by two interconnected developments: the growth of military techniques, and the greater role of the dynastic state.[9] The needs of war and administration gave new opportunities to merchants who had accumulated wealth in other ways and were now willing to make it available, at favourable rates of interest, to heads of state. The thirty years during which the Emperor Charles V worked in collusion with German, Italian and Netherlands bankers gave a great boost to the rise of an international business class, and also marked a significant step forward in the development of capitalism. The Fuggers, mentioned above, were an outstanding product of the process.

Corporate roles and the function of office

Public position was, at some stage, always necessary to the process of social mobility. By the fifteenth century local elites in all towns had secured a firm hold on administrative posts; where they failed to secure a monopoly, it was because the local aristocracy were powerful or because the older system of open elections was still adhered to. Elite control of local offices created oligarchic rule, but also usually brought continuity and stability into local politics.

Over most of Europe, money was not normally the key to office in the localities, where family influence and other forms of status were more decisive factors. Most local office-holders were untitled and probably commoners, but important sectors (like the gentry in England and the *caballeros* in Spain) were of noble status. The greater the extent of oligarchic rule, the less likely it was that money would play a part in the path to office, whether locally or at government level. In England, posts in Parliament or in county administration, all unpaid, were the reward of status and did not confer status, so that money played only an indirect role. In Venice and the United Provinces, senior posts were controlled by an oligarchy into which it was almost impossible to rise other than by marriage or favour. Sir William Temple observed of the Dutch merchants that

> when they attain great wealth, [they] chuse to breed up their sons in the way, and marry their daughters into the families of those others most generally credited in their towns, and thereby introduce their families into the way of government and honour, which consists not here in titles but in public employments.

The phenomenon of a 'sale of offices' began when the central government, in search of money, began to extend its patronage system. In Venice this resulted in minor offices being put up for sale. In Spain the regular sale of offices was begun in 1540 and pursued by Philip II, principally in towns where the crown controlled nominations to posts. By 1600 in Spain, municipal office represented three quarters by value of all offices sold. Although such sales appeared at first to be a threat to local oligarchies, in the end they merely reinforced oligarchic control, since it was the local elites who purchased the offices. A typical case was that of Josep Orti, secretary to the Estates of Valencia, who in 1696 reported that his family had held the post for over 200 years and that he was about to transfer it to his nephew. In most countries the sales were limited in number; a big exception was France. The initial purpose of the French crown in selling offices was to raise money, but by the sixteenth century this had created major problems. In 1546 the Venetian ambassador reported that 'there is an infinite number of offices, and they increase every day'. Loyseau estimated that in the second half of the sixteenth century about 50,000 new offices had been created. The profession most represented in this spectacular growth was the law, this 'amazing flood of lawyers' as Noël du Fail put it. It was they who thronged the administrative bodies of the state at virtually every level – but only on paper. In practice many of the new officials were absentees, who had acquired the office for social position and a salary. The threat to the state came more from absenteeism than from over-bureaucratisation. Heavy demand provoked an inflation in prices. A judgeship in the Parlement of Paris, officially valued in 1605 at 18,000 livres, was worth 70,000 under Louis XIII and 140,000 in 1660.

For many rising bourgeois, the purchase of office was the first step to nobility. They might then go on to buy land, and the process would be completed by taking up noble pursuits such as military service. These stages might occur in a different order (in Dijon purchase of land normally preceded purchase of office), or together. Offices were obviously valued most if they could be passed on from father to son. In 1604 the French government allowed offices to be inherited on payment of an annual tax, the *Paulette*. Prior to this there had been informal ways of making office hereditary; the new tax legalised hereditary tenure and inevitably provoked an inflation in prices. The part that office might play in incomes can be seen from two examples: in 1589 the fortune of Nicolas Caillot, *conseiller* of the parlement of Rouen and son of a goldsmith, consisted 22 per cent in *rentes*, 33 per cent in rentals and 45 per cent in the fruits of office; in 1629 the Norman official Jacques d'Amfreville left a fortune of which offices made up 30 per cent and land 49 per cent. More generally, offices played a smaller role. Loyseau wrote that the bourgeoisie put

> inheritances [i.e. land] in the first place, as being the most solid and secure property, of which the family fortune should chiefly consist; offices next, for in addition to the profit they gave rank, authority and employment to the head of the family and helped him to maintain the

> other property; and left *rentes* to the last since they merely brought extra revenue.

Through venality of office the bourgeoisie rose to govern France, producing administrators such as Jeannin, de Thou, Séguier, Molé and Talon. They formed the *noblesse de robe*, whom the Duke of Saint Simon castigated under Louis XIV as 'vile bourgeois' but who were in every sense noble. Before 1600 the thirty-strong royal council had consisted largely of the traditional sword nobility (*noblesse d'épée*); by 1624, twenty-four were nobles of the robe.

Mobility of the middle elite

The social improvement of sections of the middle classes was an unquestionable phenomenon of sixteenth-century Europe. In ascending the scale, they altered their status.[10] Those who had made their way in trade, office and land were now concerned to consolidate their gains in social status as well as in political influence. Together with the increase in importance of the urban bourgeoisie went the growing importance of towns in the national economy. It was the moneyed urban classes that began to set the pace, not only in England and Holland but also in other countries where working capital was obtainable only from this group. Their aspirations were widely resented as being subversive of the natural order of ranks. 'Who ever saw so many discontented persons', complained an English observer in 1578, 'so many irked with their own degrees, so few contented with their own calling, and such numbers desirous and greedy of change and novelties?' Even by that date, the process of bourgeois advancement was well under way in countries like France, and a new 'nobility' had come into existence in the form of the *noblesse de robe*. The early modern period was one of rapid social mobility, during which serious inroads were made into the privileged position held by the partly impoverished aristocracy. In Denmark in 1560 the merchant classes still described themselves in a petition as 'lowly branches shadowing under Your Majesty and the nobility of Denmark'. In 1658, however, the bourgeoisie of Copenhagen were openly calling for 'admission to offices and privileges on the same terms as the nobles'.

The evidence, clearly observed by many contemporaries, of new blood, *parvenu* blood, in the ranks of the gentry was enough to arouse condemnation. In October 1560 at a meeting of the provincial estates at Angers, a lawyer named Grimaudet poured his scorn on

> the infinity of false noblemen, whose fathers and ancestors wielded arms and performed acts of chivalry in grain-shops, wine shops, draperies, mills and farmsteads; and yet when they speak of their lineage they are descended from the crown, their roots spring from Charlemagne, Pompey and Caesar.

In 1581 the author of the *Miroir des Français*, Nicolas de Montaud, denounced 'certain gentlemen who have taken the title of nobility as soon as they emerge from their apprenticeships as shoemakers, weavers and cobblers'.

These malicious claims had in them more than a grain of truth. Some bourgeois could work their way up in society in as little as a generation, as with the sixteenth-century Lyon grocer, Jean Camus, whose investments and purchases of land left him at the end of his life in possession of eight noble estates, some of which included villages and towns. In Amiens the rise into nobility took one or two generations. Among the city's *noblesse de robe* in the mid-seventeenth century, office counted for between 30 and 40 per cent of income, but the major part of the remainder came from land and *rentes*. Offices or wealth were not in themselves enough: only 21 per cent of the 544 patents of nobility granted in Normandy between 1589 and 1643 were to office-holders. In the end the decisive criterion was whether a man was 'living nobly'. Those who could prove that their noble style of life had made them accepted as nobles in their communities found little difficulty in being granted status.

The coexistence of old and new nobility was an uneasy one. New nobles and members of the *noblesse de robe* were in all juridical respects fully nobles, equals of the aristocracy. In some cities, such as seventeenth-century Amiens, they intermarried and were virtually indistinguishable. Yet in the 1690s, it was still possible for Saint-Simon to sneer at the ministers of Louis XIV as bourgeois, and in Madrid in the same decade the civil governor, Ronquillo, was despised as a *parvenu* by the grandees even though his family had been noble for nearly two centuries. In France, intermarriage between old and new was deceptive: because inheritance was in the male line, male sword nobles were happy to marry robe daughters, but robe males very seldom married sword daughters, proof that there was active but discreet discrimination.

The nobility in England, though an elite, were not a caste, and it required little effort to become part of their lower ranks. 'Who can live idly and without manual labour, and will bear the port, charge and countenance of a gentleman', claimed Sir Thomas Smith at the time, 'he shall be called master, and shall be taken for a gentleman'. One could become a gentleman simply by living as one, and without necessarily having any landed property. 'In our days', a dictionary of 1730 stated, 'all are accounted Gentlemen that have money'. This was one of several ways in which the landed and mercantile classes became confused, making it difficult to distinguish origins. The confusion was increased by the tendency of gentry sons to engage themselves as apprentices to trade: by the 1630s nearly a fifth of the London Stationers' Company apprentices came from gentry stock.

The middle classes in town and country also supplemented the ranks of the gentry proper. There were two main streams that contributed to this: the successful yeomen of the country and the rising town merchants who purchased land. With the yeoman it was certainly the mobility of land that facilitated social mobility. As independent landholders (though not necessarily freeholders) they benefited from the increased value of the soil, and as a class their average wealth probably doubled in the period 1600–40. Living in the same environment as the country gentry, often more prosperous than many gentry, they rose almost imperceptibly into the higher status group. 'From thence in time', observed a contemporary in 1618, 'are derived many noble and worthy families'. Of the fifty-seven Yorkshire families granted arms between 1603 and 1642, over half were wealthy yeomen. Of a total of 335 gentry in the county of Northamptonshire in the mid-seventeenth century, the great majority were newcomers not only to the county but also to the squirearchy, and at least three quarters of them had only very recently achieved their new status.

Land was important: by the early seventeenth century it was difficult to find a prominent London capitalist who was not also a substantial landowner. The contemporary Stow remarked that 'merchants and rich men (being satisfied with gain) do for the most part marry their children into the country, and convey themselves, after Cicero's counsel, *veluti ex portu in agros et possessiones*'. But though land was clearly a spur to mobility it was often (unlike the situation in France) no more than the last stage in the progress to status, nor did families who obtained land cease to trade. A study of the wealth of seventy-eight gentry families in Elizabethan Sussex shows that among the twenty-five wealthiest families, only four were supported chiefly by land, while the majority had heads who were still – as they had been before emerging as 'gentry' – ironmasters, managers of forges and furnaces, merchants and lawyers. If we look at the greater merchants of the city of London in the early seventeenth century, we find them living in the style of the gentry, with country estates and stewards to manage them, parks and gamekeepers to patrol them, and country houses which regularly dispensed hospitality. But three quarters of them, despite this formal commitment to the country, never moved their roots from London, and maintained both their business and their friends in the city throughout their career.

Many merchants must have hesitated between the choice of profession or status. Claude Darc, a merchant of Amance (Franche Comté) who died in 1597, solved his difficulties in a particularly appealing way. His daughters were married off to legal officials, so that their status was guaranteed. Of his two sons he chose the elder, Guillaume, to remain in the business; but he trained the younger, Simon, to become a doctor of law. In this way, one branch of the family would continue to accumulate wealth while the other sought position. In his will Darc spoke of Simon

> and all the expense he has caused me, both for the pursuit of his studies and for his upkeep these twenty-five years past, and at Paris, Freiburg, Cologne, Rome, Naples, Dôle and elsewhere that he has been up to now, the eight years that it takes to become a doctor; all this has cost (God help me!) more than twelve thousand francs.

He also spoke of Guillaume, who had

> exposed the best years of his youth, and risked his person many times, to the peril and danger of the long journeys he made to distant and strange countries, and in those twenty years he has, by his work and labours, added to and increased the family fortune by much more than the said doctor has spent.

Two widely differing paths, but to each the father gave his wholehearted support.[11]

In the United Provinces, the achievement of national independence left the bourgeoisie firmly in control from the year 1578, when a coup or *alteratie* in the city of Amsterdam led to the overthrow of the old regime, its officials and clergy. The ruling council of the city was thereafter staffed with new bourgeois Calvinist members. In historical terms, the bourgeoisie continued to dominate the United Provinces, because their trading interests had made them support the struggle against Spain. In geographical terms, it was the west and northwestern half of the country that had profited from the war of independence. 'Whereas it is generally the nature of war to ruin land and people', observed a burgomaster of Amsterdam, C. P. Hooft, 'these countries on the contrary have been noticeably improved thereby'. Protected by their rivers and with the open sea before them, the middle elite of Holland and Zeeland had since the 1570s enjoyed virtual immunity from the war, so that while Spain was expending its strength against them in the south, they built up in the northwest a flourishing base on which the Dutch economy was to rest.

The eastern half of the country was, on the other hand, underdeveloped, primarily agricultural and dominated by the noble class. The nobles of Guelderland and Overijssel, in particular, were the main support of the House of Orange in its differences with the bourgeoisie of the west. Their relative weakness in the country as a whole gave control of administration to the bourgeois elite of the cities, the regent class. Senior administrative officers of the towns, the regents were drawn originally either from active merchants or from those who had recently retired from business. Their tenure of office inevitably became a comfortable monopoly and tended to make them withdraw from active trade. The old clash between commerce and office-holding worked to the detriment of the former. By 1652 the Amsterdam merchants were complaining that the regents had ceased to support trade and were drawing their income 'from houses, lands, and money at interest'. The traders of the later sixteenth century had become a *rentier* class in the seventeenth. The de Witts are an obvious example of the drift. Cornelis de Witt, born in 1545, was burgomaster of Dordrecht and a successful trader in timber. The most prominent of his sons, Jacob, continued his father's business, but his growing involvement in public affairs (notably his opposition to William II of Orange in 1650) obliged him to dispose of the family business between 1632 and 1651. Jacob's son Johan, a distinguished member of the regent class, concentrated entirely on the duties of political office.

The Dutch bourgeoisie lived unpretentiously. Sir William Temple testified that

> of the two chief officers in my time, Vice-Admiral de Ruyter and the Pensioner de Witt...I never saw the first in clothes better than the commonest sea-captain...and in his own house neither was the size, building, furniture or entertainment at all exceeding the use of every common merchant and tradesman.

As for de Witt, 'he was seen usually in the streets on foot and alone, like the commonest burgher of the town'. 'Nor was this manner of life', adds Temple, 'used only by these particular men, but was the general fashion or mode among all the magistrates of the State'. This apparent austerity was only the prelude to the adoption of a neo-aristocratic way of life. Social mobility in the usual sense was an irrelevancy, since in practice the regent class by the seventeenth century ranked above the old nobility. In this position, the upper bourgeoisie adopted distinctly conservative habits. 'Their youths', reported Temple, 'after the course of their studies at home, travel for some years, as the sons of our gentry use to do'. When they went to university, they usually read civil law. Johan de Witt was one who read law at Leiden, and did the grand tour with his brother in 1645–7. A patrician class arose, and its rise was accompanied by the abandonment of frugality. 'The old severe and frugal way of living is now almost quite out of date in Holland', Temple complained, having in mind the bourgeoisie of Amsterdam and The Hague. The trend towards luxury was illustrated by a pamphleteer of 1662, who called for the passing of sumptuary laws on the grounds that people were beginning to dress and live above their station.

Sumptuary laws were the standard method of attempting to preserve rank and check mobility, but the Dutch were relatively free of them. Elsewhere in Europe the pretensions of the middle classes were subject to both legislation and comment. 'I doubt not but it is lawfull for the nobilitie, the gentrie and magisterie, to weare rich attire', wrote Philip Stubbs in his *Anatomie of Abuses* (1583). 'As for private subiectes, it is not at any hand lawful that they should wear silkes, velvets, satens, damaskes, gold, silver and what they list.' The abundant sumptuary legislation in Europe at this period is proof that the authorities shared Stubbs' views, though legislation was invariably a failure. The French crown was obliged to issue thirteen sumptuary edicts between 1540 and 1615, but with little success. After 1604, when it repealed all existing sumptuary laws, the English government did not bother to dictate the rules of apparel to its subjects. As Bodin observed of sixteenth-century France:

> Fine edicts have been passed, but to no purpose. For since people at court wear what is forbidden, everyone wears it, so that the officials are intimidated by the former and corrupted by the latter. Besides, in

> matters of dress he is always considered a fool and bore who does not dress according to the current fashion.

The concern with dress suggests that even though it is difficult to define the middle class in terms of status and money, there are good reasons for trying to define it in terms of the culture it possessed. In early eighteenth-century England, for example, members of the middle elite were almost all literate, and the principal patrons of the new communications media of newspapers, the theatre and novels.[12] Through these media, middle-class culture became a determining factor in English civilisation. In London the success of the middle class could be seen concretely in the rising standards of domestic comfort. From the end of the seventeenth century, thanks in part to French influences, the middle classes in their domestic furnishings resorted to china, glass, easy chairs, pictures and clocks.[13] Material comfort became the outward expression of social confidence.

Betrayal by the bourgeoisie?

The bourgeoisie had an essential role to play in the development of the economy. They were the sector in which wealth was created and mobilised; by contrast, the lower classes were unable to accumulate wealth, and the upper classes had already acquired and invested theirs. The commercial and financial life of states was therefore closely related to the activities of the middle class. The commercial success of England and Holland was based on a steady investment of capital by gentry and mercantile bourgeoisie. Out of over 5,000 Englishmen who invested in their country's overseas trading companies in the period 1575–1630, 73.5 per cent were bourgeois merchants, 2.4 per cent were merchants who had been knighted, 9.9 per cent were knights, 9.3 per cent were gentry, 3.5 per cent were nobles and 1.4 per cent were yeomen and men in the professions. Gentry and nobles were prominently active, representing 44.7 per cent of membership of the Virginia Company and 78.9 per cent of that of the Africa Company; in these fifty-six years, moreover, they invested something like £1.5 million in the companies.[14] But it was the bourgeois merchants who were beyond all doubt the foundation of England's commercial greatness. At no time in the seventeenth century did any other European nation match the success of the English and Dutch in mobilising the resources of the middle and upper classes.

Why was this? In his study of *The Mediterranean*, Braudel argued that a conscious 'betrayal by the bourgeoisie' had been a root cause of the decline of the trade of Spain and Italy. Other writers have extended this argument to the trading elite of France and northern Europe. Even in seventeenth-century England, Thomas Mun had complained that 'the son, being left rich, scorns the profession of his father, conceiving more honour to be a gentleman than to follow the steps of his father as an industrious merchant'. In reality, the evolution of the merchant class was more complex than the concept of 'betrayal' suggests.[15] First, most traders and bourgeois were powerless to control the conditions of trade under which they worked; they were not free to make a choice. Second, many – particularly in eastern Europe – were restricted by political environment and an undeveloped society. Third, many who withdrew from commerce in order to invest elsewhere did so because it seemed a rational course to adopt. These points can be illustrated from specific parts of Europe, and go far towards explaining the depletion of bourgeois capital resources.

Spain is the nation about which the most common historical misunderstandings arise. Often presented as an anti-capitalist society, Spain was no less capitalist than other western societies. Its wealth, though limited, came from trade. By the fifteenth century there were active trading links between Aragon and Italy, and between Castile and Flanders. The chief export was raw wool, negotiated by colonies of Spanish merchants in Bordeaux, Antwerp and other cities. Under Charles V and Philip II, the fairs at Medina del Campo made Old Castile an integral part of the west European market, and successful merchants like Simón Ruiz represented the most enterprising section of the Castilian bourgeoisie. The expulsion of a fairly small number of Jews in 1492 – around 50,000 – had done nothing to weaken the middle classes, since *conversos* (Christians of Jewish origin) continued effectively to carry out the roles Jews had fulfilled. The energy of the Spanish middle elite, however, was deceptive. Spain around 1500 was a poor country with inadequate grain output, no significant industry, and with exports consisting almost exclusively of raw materials (wool, agricultural produce). This was too weak an economic base to nourish a bourgeoisie or to foster investment, and the import of foreign manufactures (mainly textiles) to balance raw material exports quickly gave foreign capitalists a big say in the direction of the economy. 'The foreigners do with us what they will', complained Simón Ruiz. The discovery of America temporarily stimulated the Spanish economy but did not improve the industrial situation, and foreign manufactures rapidly took over the American market.

Unable to invest in an economy that did not expand, the Spanish bourgeoisie entered the money market, lending both to the government (*juros*) and to individuals (*censos*). With interest rates at up to 7 per cent in the sixteenth century, it was an attractive outlay. Moreover, *censos* to the peasantry were a form of investment in agriculture, and benefited the rural economy. But writers on economic affairs, the *arbitristas*, were critical of the extent to which the moneyed classes were willing to live off unearned interest rather than invest their money in productivity. Contemplating with dismay the effects of a *rentier* mentality, the Valladolid bourgeois Martín González de Cellorigo in 1600 condemned *censos* as 'a plague which has reduced these realms to utter poverty, since a majority of people have taken to living off them, and off the interest from money'. In a sharply worded passage, he claimed that

> *censos* are the plague and ruin of Spain. For the sweetness of the sure profit from *censos* the merchant leaves his trading, the artisan his employment, the peasant-farmer his farming, the shepherd his flock; and the noble sells his lands so as to exchange the one hundred they bring him for the five hundred the *juro* brings.... Through *censos* flourishing houses have perished, and common people have risen from their employment, trade and farming, into indolence; so that the kingdom has become a nation of idleness and vice.

Price inflation, aggravated later by debasement and monetary inflation, added to the problems of a country where trade was largely in the hands of foreign interests. Spanish bourgeois were active both in commerce and industry, but the scanty resources of their environment and the fact that most American bullion went to pay for foreign imports (hence the continual petitions by the Cortes against the export of bullion) deprived them of investment capital. Inflation periodically wiped out trading profits and made the interest rate on *juros* and *censos* all the more attractive as an alternative outlay. Despite its aggressive imperial role, Spain remained underdeveloped and an economic colony of other nations;[16] it did not decline because there was no level of achievement against which 'decline' could be measured. Not until the late seventeenth century did the bourgeoisie begin to find favourable conditions for investment in trade and industry.

The Spanish experience was reflected in that of Italy, its Mediterranean neighbour. The slowing down of the Venetian textile industry in the late sixteenth century, and its decline after the opening of the seventeenth, could not fail to lead to a redistribution of investment. Increasing difficulties in the Levant trade, and growing commercial rivalry from other Italian cities and from northern countries, made the comparative security of land and rentals more desirable. Nobles, citizens and people of Venice purchased property and estates on the mainland, the Terraferma, particularly at the end of the sixteenth and the beginning of the seventeenth centuries. At the same time in Venice, as in other cities, opportunities to live as a *rentier* were readily available. The decline of commerce, no less than success in business, encouraged the merchant classes to leave their traditional occupations in favour of security and status. Gradually the mercantile oligarchy became a patriciate, as in the city of Lucca. In the city of Como the merchants maintained their business interests but extended their activities into the collecting of interest from loans made to the government or to rural communities. In Milan, many of the great merchants and industrialists of the fifteenth century had by the seventeenth joined the ruling feudal classes. The Missagli family, prominent armament manufacturers of the fifteenth century, obtained a noble title at the end of their period of greatest success, and withdrew their capital from the business. Sixteenth-century merchants like the Cusani diverted their money from trade to the purchase of land. Members of the Milanese elite who had spent their career in the public service (families like the Borromeos, patricians like the Moroni), members of the professions, and office-holders, committed their fortunes to the land, from which they derived noble titles and feudal rents.

The evolution of one family, the Riccardi of Florence, is instructive.[17] Starting in the mid-fifteenth century the family began to buy land: between 1480 and 1517 the output from their holdings increased 3.5 times in grain, 1.5 times in wine. Between 1517 and 1568 their landholdings increased by 250 per cent. From the 1560s they began investing their profits from the land in wool and textiles in Florence, and from 1577 they set up a bank devoted to lending money and investing in trade. In the 1580s the Riccardi were trading both to the Levant and to Spain. In 1600 their business investments – excluding land – were 69 per cent in banking, 16 per cent in wool and 15 per cent in silk. They continued to buy more land and to invest the profits in commerce: clear evidence that there was no formal contradiction between one and the other. By the early seventeenth century, as business declined (Florence had 152 wool producers in 1561 and only eighty-four in 1616) the Riccardi shifted their emphasis to land and the security of social position. In the village of Villa Saletta in 1563 they owned 36 per cent of the land, the Church held 28 cent, and others 36 per cent; by 1620 the Riccardi held 90 per cent, the Church 4 per cent, and others 6 per cent. A member of the family became a senator in Florence in 1596; in 1598 they bought a palace in the city. When Riccardo Riccardi, the head of the family, died in 1612, his fortune consisted 63 per cent in land, 24 per cent in business, 10 per cent in loans and 3 per cent in *rentes*.

Tenure of office characterised the bourgeoisie in most central German cities. An imperial decree of 1530 described the urban middle classes as falling into roughly three categories: the common citizens (including retail shopkeepers and journeymen), then above them the merchants and master craftsmen, and finally the patrician class of office-holders. In smaller towns the last two groups tended to merge, in line with the fact that even self-made men allowed themselves to be attracted by office and by 'living off investment and rents' (to quote the 1530 decree). Merchant families supplied recruits to the class of officials, but the vast majority of them came from the body of university graduates. As everywhere else in western Europe, these tended to study law in order to enter the administration, came from patrician families and were therefore assured of a place in the elite after graduating. In Württemberg in the mid-sixteenth century this group occupied nearly three quarters of the places in public administration. Here was a flourishing middle class, a rising bourgeoisie, yet one that had divorced itself from any part in the production of wealth, and had committed itself to the ideals of office and *rentes*, ideals that in a monarchical regime were a prelude to the attainment of noble status.

The trading bourgeoisie flourished in the early sixteenth century and are best represented by the financial firm of the Fuggers, whose leading members became nobles of the Empire and bought estates in Swabia, where by the end of the century they possessed 100 villages covering about ninety-three square miles.

Good exploitation of these resources brought the Fuggers an annual average 6 per cent return on the capital invested in the land, showing the application of good business acumen. Subsequent changing patterns of trade affected the German elite no less than those of Spain and Italy: the south German towns decayed at the same time as the trade of Italy and Antwerp.

The fate of the central and east European bourgeoisie was linked to one fundamental fact: in a part of the continent with a lower density of population than western Europe, the towns were smaller and weaker, and therefore more likely to be dominated by the rural areas. The long struggle between the traders of the towns and the producers of the countryside (a struggle which in Russia lay behind the great urban revolts of 1648) was eventually resolved in favour of the producers. The feudal structure of Russian society repressed the growth of an autonomous urban elite. There was no field that the traders and merchants could specifically call their own, since the nobility and monasteries dominated large-scale trade and industry. The chief minister Morozov, who fell from power in 1648, traded in grain, mined and produced potash, possessed distilleries and mills, exploited iron mines and ran a metallurgical industry. He was at once a great landowner, merchant, industrialist, entrepreneur and usurer. When princes of both state and Church promoted capitalism to this extent, what function could the nascent bourgeoisie possibly have?

What gave the conflict between traders and producers its peculiar importance was that the latter, owners of the soil and of the peasantry, were the noble class. Strengthened in their possession of land by the seizure of Church property after the Reformation, the nobility gradually came to exercise within the state a political preponderance that no ruler could dispute. At the political level this had a serious effect upon the middle elite, since the rulers repeatedly took the side of the nobles in constitutional disputes with the towns, so that the voice of the towns in the Estates of each realm was progressively weakened. But it was the economic factor that was decisive. The fate of urban privileges in Brandenburg provides an example. As elsewhere in central Europe, brewing was a leading industry of the towns. The nobility enjoyed some exemption from taxes on this commodity, and consequently were able to produce cheaper beer than the urban breweries, in open violation of the law that equalised beer prices. They soon took over much of the rural market and brought depression to the towns: in 1595 the authorities counted 891 ruined breweries in the towns of Brandenburg, while new ones continued to spring up in the countryside. Commerce, long an activity of the town bourgeoisie, suffered similarly. When the nobles began to develop production of corn from their estates, they also began to find ways of transporting it themselves in order to avoid the middlemen in the towns. Despite some attempt to restrict this, by the mid-sixteenth century the nobles were exporting their corn freely. By the early seventeenth century the Brandenburg gentry were claiming that they were entitled to export freely by both land and water, and that they were exempt from tolls and duties.

The result was the decline of the towns and their trading population. At times the towns even had to suffer famine because of the way in which the producers held back supplies in order to speculate in prices. It was not corn and beer only, but all the other produce of the land, in which the gentry began to deal on the basis of the unequal privileges they were accorded. The towns lost their privileged trading and industrial position, and the noble class rose at the expense of the bourgeoisie. The picture was the same throughout the northeast. In Prussia and in Pomerania too, exemption from taxes gave the gentry a clear field in the sphere of corn and beer. After a century of complaints, the great port of Königsberg in 1634 claimed that nothing had been done to remedy the situation. The economic and commercial decay of the towns, and the weakening of their elites, continued through the seventeenth century, and the trend was consolidated in the 1650s and 1660s by the various measures of state control adopted by the rulers of Brandenburg-Prussia.

In the east, the case of Hungary presents a similar picture. Suffering from the burden of the long wars against the Turks, Hungary underwent both a political crisis and a crisis of production. Anxious to rescue their fortunes, the nobles as agrarian producers laid claims to control over distribution as well as over production. Some concessions were made when, in 1563, the kingdom passed a law permitting nobles who were refugees from the Turks to buy houses in the towns and to import wine from the countryside free, provided this was for their own use only. Once granted to a section of the nobility, these privileges opened the way to the nobles as a whole to establish themselves in the towns. Through marriage with the urban patriciate they also managed to take part in the government of the towns. The cities in vain in 1571 presented a demand that landlords should not be allowed to trade in agricultural produce. The Diet ruled that provided the customs duty was paid they could trade both internally and externally in all goods. Inevitably, the towns and their elites collapsed before the economic domination of the gentry.

This glance at different areas of Europe suggests that if sectors of the bourgeoisie failed it was because external conditions, rather than a conscious defection, determined their situation. When they changed their investment pattern, it was because developments presented them with a logical alternative. In Antwerp merchants bought houses and lands (Jacob della Faille in the 1570s owned 800 acres and eleven houses) because these represented tangible wealth as against the intangible wealth of overseas trade and credit. In 1661 the Venetian merchant Alberto Gozzi had 200,000 ducats invested in commerce and industry, but he also had 174,000 invested in land; at this period the percentage return from land was higher than that from trade, so that land was a rational purchase.

At the root of the notion of a 'bourgeois betrayal' is the premise that the bourgeois had ideals or an ethic to which he should have held. In some regions the bourgeoisie certainly showed a clear pattern of behaviour. In Franche Comté they were the most active social group: as traders, they devoted themselves to work, travelling throughout Europe on commercial missions; as landowners, they developed the soil, and went riding and hunting; the men did military service;

their libraries showed a high level of culture; and their sons were educated abroad. The group behaviour of members of the middle elite testifies to a distinctive set of social values by which they lived, but it is more difficult to identify among them a social ethic of aspirations. The private records and wills of merchants and capitalists give only fragmentary hints of their outlook, hopes and ideals. Unlike the nobles, who knew and recognised the ideals of their status, the middle elite felt that they belonged ultimately not to their present condition but to the rank towards which they aspired. Social mobility encouraged them to adopt the ideals of the traditional upper orders. This did not necessarily involve the withdrawal of capital from wealth formation.

The aristocratisation of the middle classes was inevitable. In the Italian state of Lucca the commercial ruling oligarchy which had formerly described itself as *patres, patricii senatoresque*, altered its description by the end of the sixteenth century to *nobilitas*; while the group formerly dignified as *plebs et populus* was downgraded to the rank of *ignobilitas*. The function and status of the new nobility of Lucca were discussed for the first time by the writer Pompeo Rocchi in his *Il Gentilhuomo* (1568). In Holland the social change was commented upon by an English observer in the early eighteenth century: 'their government is aristocratical; so that the so much boasted liberty of the Dutch is not to be understood in the general and absolute sense, but *cum grano salis*'. In France, according to a seventeenth-century robe president of the Parlement of Paris, 'there is only one kind of nobility, and it is acquired through service either in the army or in the judiciary, but the rights and prerogatives are the same'. The notion of service likewise formed the basis of the theories of the Huguenot writer Louis Turquet de Mayerne in his *De la Monarchie Aristodémocratique* (written in 1591 and published in 1611). He claimed that 'birth is neither the origin nor the basis of nobility', and that 'the common people are the seed-ground of the nobility'. 'True nobility has its basis only in good acts; in the work, I mean, of men who deserve well of the state.' 'Proper fulfilment of one's public office ennobles a man.' In a frank justification of bourgeois mobility, Mayerne argued that only the merchant deserved nobility, for he proved it by his worldly success; moreover, he benefited the realm through trade, which enriched the country and also gave him knowledge of public affairs that no other profession had. Arms and war, then, were an ignoble profession; what was noble was trade, finance and agriculture.

Despite obstacles and reverses, the middle elite had no difficulty in 'staying on top'.[18] They did not give up the basis of their success, which was the creation of wealth. But they reinforced it by strategies of ascent: monopoly of offices, careful choice of marriage partners from a closed circle of families, control of inheritances in order to safeguard the transmission of assets, and acquisition of titles and other insignia of social rank. If they decided to adopt, as nobles were doing, a policy of primogeniture to safeguard the family fortune, they also took care to train their younger children in the professions or at least find them an adequate post in the state or even in the Church. In this way, for example, the patriciate of

Barcelona consolidated itself and laid a basis for the subsequent move into the ranks of the aristocracy of the province.[19] In Brescia,[20] part of the Venetian republic, the oligarchies took part in the trend towards converting themselves into an exclusive elite; they produced from their own ranks the lawyers and notaries who staffed the administration; and promoted marriage alliances to confirm their maintenance of control.

6

SOLIDARITIES AND RESISTANCE

> 'Steere said that it would only be a month's work to overrun the realm [England]; and that the poor once rose in Spain and cut down the gentry, since when they had lived merrily.'
>
> (testimony against Batholomew Steere, carpenter, 1597)

Solidarities and honour

The common people in town and country were not a homogeneous sector; they had multiple differences of condition and it is impractical to categorise them together, as we have done for the upper and middle elites. There were, strictly speaking, no 'lower classes' but rather a broad range of conditions associated with recognisable roles. They could possibly be identified by economic function: in seventeenth-century Holland, for instance, one could identify small traders, petty artisans, agricultural labourers, seafaring men, and many others who worked with these or who had no fixed occupation.[1] Women occupied a place in this spectrum, but always at a lower economic level. Since medieval times, it seems, all those exercising labouring functions were allotted a lowly position in the scale of social values. It is impossible to say when this discriminatory attitude became widely accepted, since those who wrote about it varied widely in their judgments. By the fifteenth century, social rules in most European countries agreed that labouring people were a vulgar mass, clearly differentiated from the respectable upper levels of society.[2] Loyseau concluded in the seventeenth century that 'artisans are those who work with their hands [*exercent les arts mécaniques*], any manual work is considered lowly [*vil*] and abject, and artisans are therefore classified as lowly persons'. Daniel Defoe in 1728 felt that 'those concerned in the meaner employments are called working men, and the labouring poor such as mere husbandmen, miners, fishers....Superior to these are the masters in such employments, and those are called mechanics or craftsmen.'[3]

Attitudes to labouring people were complex. Contempt for labour was usually an artificial prejudice, specifically promoted by higher ranks of the social ladder in an effort to justify their exclusiveness. Each rung of the hierarchical ladder professed to despise the rung below it. Lower levels of the ladder, even if despised by the higher, felt that they in their turn had specific standards and status. Some commentators thought that the discrimination against 'mechanical arts' was senseless. The Spanish writer Alvarez Osorio y Redín protested in 1687 that 'all the actions of men are "mechanical", it is mechanical to eat, walk and write, and every movement is mechanical'. The prejudice against 'degrading' work was impossible to dislodge, but it is also true that in many professions and many communities it was not taken seriously. On the northern coast of Spain, in the port of Luarca, the fishermen were considered nobles; their explanation in historical terms was that the apostles of Christ had been fishermen.[4]

Working men could therefore have their own honourable status. Social respect was not a privilege only of the elite and the middle classes. Though the nobility prided themselves on their sense of honour and devoted a substantial literature to the subject, in the societies of Europe 'honour' or its equivalent, good 'reputation', was considered an important quality of all men. The constituents of honour always varied according to rank, circumstance and profession; they were never firmly defined, and were almost invariably identified only when denied, abused or contravened. Honour might be from one point of view inherent in a person, in reference to his moral qualities; from another point of view it was simply the image of that person within his social group, and it was the group that decided his standing and reputation.

In many communities periodic efforts were made to create status distinctions between the sectors of society, sometimes for fiscal reasons and sometimes in the interests of public order, so that each group might know the role it was supposed to play. In towns, a crucial role in determining status was played by the professional bodies or guilds, which controlled many aspects of economic life and gave dignity to all those working people who were unable to rise into the upper ranks of society. Craftsmen enjoyed status and honour because they exercised a specialist profession, and above all because they were economically 'free' and independent; it was in effect the 'free work' that gave them dignity and honour, a status denied to those in lesser professions.[5]

In German towns of the late seventeenth century, the craft guilds maintained the status and honour of specific professions by defining which callings were acceptable in the guilds and which were not.[6] Below the level of these professions came the category of unskilled workers, who enjoyed no status or privilege whatsoever. Not far behind came the very substantial category of servants, until recently usually forgotten by historians but who played a fundamental part in the effective functioning of traditional society. The table of ranks does not stop there. A high proportion of the urban population consisted of rural workers or peasants, who lived in the city but earned their wages in the countryside. These were invariably consigned to the lowest status grade, in consonance with a growing tendency among the elites to look down upon the rural population as 'rustics'. The balance between these different grades affected the infinite variety of politics in Europe's communities. In Frankfurt, for example, the rich elite represented some 5 per cent of households, shopkeepers some 11 per cent, artisans some 56 per cent, general labourers some 12 per cent, and rural labourers some 11 per cent.[7] This profile of a city dedicated to productivity explains many aspects of Frankfurt's stormy history during this period.

In addition to enjoying good status, a citizen might wish to enjoy a good reputation. When used in the context of the elite classes, 'reputation' was identical with the concept of honour. The word *reputación*, as used by Philip II of Spain, even signified the honour of the entire nation of Spain. At an everyday level, it referred to the lesser idea of respect accorded within the local community. The positive aspect of pre-industrial community relations was the sense of welfare and belonging, but a negative aspect was the absence of privacy. Neighbourhoods did not necessarily offer neighbourliness. 'People were constantly observed by their neighbours. Reputation shaped the attitudes of neighbour to neighbour.'[8] Correct behaviour was as a consequence never simply a personal option; it was a requirement imposed and judged by community norms, and regulated according to contexts of religion, gender or economy. Incorrect behaviour, with the corresponding bad reputation, might provoke grave conflicts within the community, and very frequently led to banishment from the community. A woman with a reputation as a 'witch' would be kindly tolerated for many years by her village, but in a year of agrarian crisis she might find that her lack of status would work against her.

The contempt for labour was occasionally extended to the peasants working their fields, an attitude lamented by most writers, who felt that tilling the soil was the most natural and therefore the most honourable of occupations. By far the most important sector of the economy before the era of industrial capitalism was the land; by far the largest and most essential sector of the population was the peasantry. Agriculture was the mainstay of economy, society and state. The peasant classes were correspondingly considered to be the mainstay of all three. In a well known German print of the sixteenth century, the tree of society was illustrated with peasants as the roots and – after the ascent branch by branch through the lower and upper classes, king and pope – even more significantly as the crown of the tree.[9]

By the seventeenth century artists began to represent peasants as drunken, boorish louts, a sign no doubt of a growing lack of comprehension among the expanding urban population. But the respect attached to the status of peasant still retained a powerful influence over social attitudes and political policy. Adam was the first peasant: all men and all nobles were therefore descended from peasants. Far from being a revolutionary assertion, the claim was commonplace. It could be found in the literature of most countries in Europe. In the peasant was to be found those virtues of labour, patience, subordination, duty and piety that every Christian priest praised from his pulpit. The peasant was not sullied by the sins of the townsmen, by the search for profit. He represented a self-contained unit, who lived off no other man, and who trusted in God. Such at least was the myth, and it was by no means a harmless one, for it determined the prejudices of many centuries of Christian civilisation. In economic life the acceptance of subsistence agriculture as natural and good and of trade, particularly trade for profit, as bad, had a persistently regressive effect. Social groups which did not engage in agriculture to any appreciable extent were ostracised as economic parasites who would not soil their hands with true work: hence the popular basis of anti-Semitism, since Jews tended to be an urban minority, and were devoted (many claimed) to the unnatural vice of usury.

The values and honour of peasants and ordinary working people can be approached in several ways: through their own claims and protests; through statements by their superiors; through observations by outsiders; or through the affirmation of certain principles when the norms of correct conduct were transgressed.[10] Lawsuits between artisans in the city of Dijon, mainly to defend themselves against verbal slurs on their integrity, show the concern of working people to protect their 'honour'.[11] Since many slurs were sexual in content, we can see that behind the wish to protect 'honour' there frequently lurked the need to defend male virility. But working men were also concerned to defend social values: time and again, they made claims for 'justice', a value that was impossible to define but that often coincided with 'traditional' ways. The traditions they demanded might often exist largely in their imagination, but served to confirm for them the importance of preserving the means of subsistence. Peasants valued the economic independence of the family household, the *Hausnotdurft* claimed by seventeenth-century Bavarian communities. Where independence was lost, the individual or family had to 'work' in order to live, a situation that immediately demeaned status. Witnesses in the countryside of seventeenth-century Valencia cited examples where the need to work was a sign of poverty. 'He was a poor man', a miller reported of a neighbour, 'so impoverished that in order to maintain his household it was necessary for him to work continuously'. Another peasant was described as being so poor that 'he had to work continuously to earn a daily wage'.[12] At this social level no honour was possible, both because the person was poor and because he was dependent on work for existence. Work was not demeaning in itself, for all professions involved work; but work associated with dependence was always demeaning, and cut off access to honour. Such at least was the burden of much moralistic writing in all countries of early modern Europe. The peasant family claimed economic autonomy in order to preserve their honour, a value that inspired no written manuals but that permeates the surviving court records where ordinary people sued each other for verbal insults that called in question their respectability and honour.[13]

Working men in the cities lived huddled together in restricted space, and enjoyed some types of solidarity, principally those deriving from the family and from the neighbourhood. Perhaps the most appreciated theatre of social activity was, as in eighteenth-century Paris,[14] the tavern, which outsiders looked upon as a den of iniquity and idleness but which played an important part in ordering many aspects of daily life. City councils and even governments made constant efforts to regulate the hours of taverns and to control what went on inside them, but to no avail.

A precarious environment

The dominant feature of sixteenth-century agriculture was the extension of arable land to meet the food needs of a growing population. Claude de Seyssel in his *Grande Monarchie de France* (1519) observed that 'the abundance of population could be observed from the fields, for many places and regions which used to be untilled or wooded are at present all cultivated and peopled with villages and houses'. Attractively high cereal prices encouraged farmers to make profits by putting their land under the plough. There were three main features of the boom: the advance of the plough into forest land, the conversion of common and pasture land to arable, and the reclamation of land from the sea.

The ploughing of forest land was the least significant of these. Though woodland was continually disappearing, causes included not simply conversion to arable but also sales of trees by impecunious owners (including the crown), levelling of woods to lay out parks (a frequent habit of aristocrats), and thefts of timber by peasants. In France and Spain there was continuous legislation to protect forests; in France the crown made its legislation apply to all feudal and private woods, claiming that these were within the scope of its sovereignty. Trees were a major public concern because they supplied fuel, were used in shipbuilding, and helped to prevent soil erosion. Charles I of England seems to have appreciated forests less for these reasons than because they were a useful source of income in sales of trees (the French crown also broke its own laws in this way), and were perfect for hunting. Where woods were destroyed arable crept in: 'the countryside is being deforested', the Estates of Languedoc exaggerated in 1546. In England the argument that arable was of more benefit to the nation than forests began to gather force in the seventeenth century, and found parliamentary expression in the 1653 Act for the Sale of Royal Forests. Despite legislation by conscientious public bodies, the European landscape began to be cleared of trees. The trend had already commenced in the medieval period, but gathered force in some countries in early modern times. It has been estimated that around 1600 one quarter of Denmark was covered by forest, whereas by 1750 only one tenth was. There were significant consequences on the lives of the peasants and even on the quality of the air they breathed.[15]

Conversion of pasture to arable depended on the needs of other agrarian sectors: livestock, for example, was essential for meat, milk, hides and wool, and would have been prejudiced by reduction in pasture. Indeed, herding increased. Cattle figured as 55 per cent of the exports of Hungary to Vienna in 1500 and 93.6 per cent in 1542; the Danish trade in cattle tripled between 1500 and 1600; in Spain the sheep in the Mesta attained their peak numbers in 1550.[16] The emphasis, however, was on grain (though it should be noted that an extension of arable always implied some extension of pasture, since in fallow years the fields were turned from tillage to grass). In East Anglia the rent of arable rose sixfold between 1590 and 1650, while that of pasture rose by only two or three times. Villages and feudal seigneurs extended the plough into common lands: in Spain this occurred in the Tierra de Campos, for example, and around Valladolid. At the same time, in the Mediterranean the culture of supplementary foods was intensified. Vine- and olive-growing areas were extended: at Gignac in Languedoc, olives in 1519 occupied 15 per cent of the tilled soil, in 1534 as much as 42 per cent. In the Basque country wine output trebled during the seventeenth century. The famous wines of Italy and Hungary developed in this period. In the north of Beaujolais vines in 1580 covered 5 per cent of the soil; by 1680 they covered 20 per cent.

Land reclamation was striking evidence of the demand for arable. In the United Provinces between 1565 and 1590, some 8,046 hectares were won back from the sea; from 1590 to 1615 the total was 36,213 hectares, the largest area to have been reclaimed for two centuries. In Schleswig Holstein by 1650 about 25,000 hectares of coast marshland had been drained. Henry IV invited a distinguished team of Netherlanders under Humphrey Bradley to supervise drainage of marshes in France, and it was Netherlanders, profiting from their long experience, who played a leading part in most reclamation schemes elsewhere on the continent, in Italy and Germany. In England under the early Stuarts, Cornelius Vermuyden undertook to drain the Fens, and some 160,000 hectares were eventually reclaimed.

The emphasis on agriculture was accompanied by a spate of farming manuals. In Spain, Alonso de Herrera's *Agricultura General* (1515) held the field for two centuries. In England the outstanding writers were Walter Blith and Richard Weston, both writing in the 1640s. In France the works of Estienne and others were followed by the best-selling Olivier de Serres' *Théatre de l'Agriculture* (1600). In Germany Heresbach's *De re Rustica* (1570) was followed at the turn of the century by Coler's *Oeconomia Ruralis*. Gostomski published the popular Polish work *Notaty Gospodarskie* (*Notes on the Rural Economy*) in 1588.

At least up to the 1570s there was a steady rise in agrarian output. In the villages of Bureba (northern Spain), production in grain between the 1550s and 1580s rose by 26 per cent, in wine by 51 per cent. In Calabria on the lands of the Prince of Bisignano, harvest output rose 75 per cent between the 1520s and 1540s. Output of wheat measured in yield ratios (ratio of grain reaped to grain sown) was fairly high in western Europe, ranging from over 10:1 in Berkshire and Friesland to 6.8:1 in Bureba and 5:1 in Poitou. In eastern Europe yields were lower, as much as 6.5:1 in Masovia (Poland) but below 4:1 in Hungary.

Despite the boom conditions up to the late sixteenth century, no real technical advance in production was achieved. As much as one half of the arable soil in Europe might be vacant in any year, because of adherence to the old method of leaving fields fallow. Manure was scarce and the rotation of root crops did not begin to spread until the end of the seventeenth century; agricultural implements remained primitive and peasant communities resisted innovative techniques. Thus, although two important developments occurred in the early modern period – an extension of cultivated land, involving in some areas (such as land reclamation) a greater investment of capital; and a change in social relationships, which in western Europe meant the decline of feudalism and in eastern Europe the onset of a new feudalism – no substantial change occurred in the character of the agrarian economy.

There were, however, regional variations in this picture. Whereas France appears to have experienced no significant agricultural innovation before the nineteenth century, further north in the Netherlands new methods had been creeping in since the fifteenth century. Population increase and greater urbanisation facilitated the use of manpower in labour-intensive industries. Since the land was not capable of producing an adequate amount of cereals, these were imported in bulk from the Baltic. Available soil could thus be put to alternative use, for intensive dairy farming and other industries such as hops and flax. Where land remained in arable, use was made of convertible husbandry (i.e. alternating crops and grasses), with clover or peas grown in fallow years; turnips were grown as fodder, with turnips, clover and grain sown in rotation in the early seventeenth century in Flanders; and a wide range of manure was applied, including both dung and compost. While the overall output of grain did not apparently increase (and this was never an objective, since the nation relied on imports), yield per hectare was possibly the highest in Europe. For England likewise, it has been argued that the period witnessed an agricultural revolution, most of whose achievements occurred before the 1670s.[17] Changes included the floating of water meadows, the introduction of new fallow crops and grasses, marsh drainage, manuring and stock breeding. Crop yields rose, and in some areas the food production apparently doubled between 1540 and 1700.

The rural community under threat

The soil of Europe was largely in the hands of peasants and rural communities. In France it has been estimated that about half the land was held by peasants, varying from a fifth in Brittany and Normandy to over half in Dauphiné. In Brunswick (Germany) the nobles held only 8 per cent, and the peasants 67.5 per cent of all agricultural land. Such figures are deceptive. The term 'peasant', though its use cannot be avoided, fails to describe adequately the broad variations in tenure and income among the rural classes. Though peasants were the largest social grouping, they were too numerous for the land available, and their holdings were usually inadequate. The average peasant plot was only in exceptional circumstances capable of supporting a rural family comfortably. The division of the soil was normally unfavourable, as at Roquevaire in Lower Provence in 1663, where the clergy owned 1 per cent, the middle class 19 per cent, the nobles 23 per cent and the peasants 57 per cent. The peasantry, on the face of it, got the lion's share. But the landholding community at Roquevaire was made up of nine nobles, twelve bourgeois and over 150 peasant proprietors, so that in reality each noble family held nine times, and each bourgeois family three times as much as the average peasant landed family.

In any case, few peasants actually 'held' land. Peasants were personally free in most of western Europe, but their land was usually not held outright, and they had to fulfil various obligations to a lord; in effect this meant a tenancy, not ownership. The average peasant in Europe was not a freeholder. Where the feudal system and related contractual systems were operative, peasants had to perform services both in kind and in labour, a duty that restricted their own effective freedom. All peasants, whether free or not, were in any case finding that the basis of their independence was being steadily eroded by developments (such as taxation) that were beyond their control. Last, and by no means least, a huge proportion of the rural population held no land at all.

Thanks to the administrative and legal structure of feudalism in England, where the forms of Roman law never took root, the English peasant farmer was almost totally free by the sixteenth century. The landed peasants in some areas continued to pay traditional dues to manorial lords, but the proportion was not numerically or socially significant. Those who did not farm their own land made up a rural labouring sector that formed as much as a third of the total country population. As in any period of change, the peasant farmers developed both upwards and downwards. In the former case, they improved their lot and moved into the yeomanry or gentry; in the latter, they augmented what was, in an age of expanding population, a growing rural proletariat. Generalisations like these become more comprehensible if we look at one detailed example.

The number of households in the village of Wigston Magna in Leicestershire doubled its numbers from about seventy to 140 households in the course of the century 1525–1625, thereby becoming one of the most thriving villages in the English Midlands.[18] A breakdown of the occupation of the villagers in the later seventeenth century shows that 36 per cent depended on agriculture for a living, 30 per cent on crafts and trades connected with the land, 17 per cent on frame-work-knitting. In addition, 16 per cent were simply described as 'poor'. The peasant farmers benefited from the rise in food prices during the century of inflation, and accumulated a comfortable surplus, which in the years up to the early seventeenth century was largely untouched by taxation. The forms of feudal organisation vanished here in 1606 when the last manor was sold by its lord, and the villagers refused to continue to pay the feudal dues to the new occupants. The end of manorial control also meant the end of tenure by copy-hold, for the rolls which proved tenure used to be kept by the lord. All tenure now became freehold. As the village developed, its economic life became more diversified. The peasant farmers grew wealthier, because of the demand for their food produce. But the smaller peasants were unable to compete with the larger producers, and as population increased the landholdings of the smaller peas-antry became even more inadequate. Beside the prosperous farmer there now appeared the beginnings of the rural proletariat. The village world of subsis-tence economy was also being invaded more and more, in proportion to the growth of commerce for the market, by money. Cash transactions became more common, and a ready example can be found in the giving of marriage settlements in cash rather than in kind.

In the Midlands the cost of living for a farm labourer rose sixfold between 1500 and 1640, while his real wages over the same period fell by about 50 per cent. Not surprisingly, economic distress among the rural population was common, and contributed primarily to the growing numbers of landless labourers seeking employment. The situation did, of course, vary widely in other parts of England. There were even a few patriarchal figures such as Sir George Sondes of Lees Court in Kent, who for thirty years spent, in his own words, 'at least a thousand pounds a year' in giving economic help to his farm labourers.

An independent and free community like Wigston Magna serves to illustrate the end of feudal control and the increase of both wealth and poverty. But it is not a clear example of one of the dominant trends of the period, the changes in land exploitation that in their turn provoked social instability. Small farmers and farm labourers had an increasingly difficult time; the former, because it was a constant struggle to make output exceed the level of rents, the latter, because wages fell rather than rose. A small landowner might profit, but he had to compete with the greater marketing power of the larger producers. Lesser tenants had to cope with high rent (the rents at Stoneleigh manor in Warwickshire in 1599 came to £418 and in 1640 to £1,440). They also had to contend with an increase in enclosures (which incurred opposition mainly in the Midlands, where the lands enclosed in Leicestershire rose from 5,870 acres in 1599 to 12,280 in 1607, and in Lincolnshire during the same period from 4,866 to 13,420 acres).

The complex changes on the land did not necessarily bring misery.[19] In the same way, the condition of the peasantry in other countries need not be seen exclusively in pessimistic terms. In most of western and central Europe the peasant had relative security of tenure, even if his holding was small.[20] In Denmark and Sweden agriculture was largely in the hands of peasant producers (in Sweden in 1700 free peasant owners made up a third of all peasants). In an economy where cash transactions were becoming more important, the tendency was for estates held by the upper classes to be broken up into tenancies and for labour services to be commuted to money payments. The advantage of freedom was, however, offset by the burden of taxes. Neither full ownership of the soil (as 'allodial' or non-feudal land) nor security of tenure protected against rising costs. The peasant on feudal soil had to pay dues to a seigneur (these varied, and might include a nominal cash sum, payment in kind such as a proportion of harvest, and taxes on fishing and using the lord's mill to grind corn), to the Church (tithes, not always a strict tenth), and to the state (in France, for example, the *taille*). The peasant on free soil was exempt only from the first of these.

In the Beauvaisis (northern France) in the seventeenth century, a typical village community of 100 families might have two rich peasant farmers (*laboureurs*), five or six middling farmers, about twenty middling peasants (here called *haricotiers*), and a large class of up to fifty farm workers and day-labourers (*manouvriers*). In the Dijonnais in Burgundy these workers were the vast majority of the male adults in the countryside, and totally outnumbered the peasant farmers, who were usually fixed in their residence while the rural workers had no means of their own and were often on the move, particularly into the towns. The average *haricotier* of the Beauvaisis worked about five hectares of land. The payment of taxes to the crown would take up about one fifth of his output (the *taille* accounted for most of this), leaving him with 80 per cent of his harvest. The tithe and Church taxes would take up another 8 per cent of his revenue, and other taxes would account for 4 per cent more, so that eventually the peasant would be left with 68 per cent of his harvest. Another fifth, however, would have to be set aside for running costs and for seed to be sown the following year. This left 48 per cent, and still the outgoings were not at an end, for the landlord's rent remained to be paid. This varied widely, depending on the system of tenure. What the peasant received eventually might be only a small fraction of his original harvest. This, of course, was in a normal year, and takes no account of the possibility that the peasant might have debts to be repaid. If the year had been a bad one, or if his debts were many, the peasant faced disaster.

> If, when he sowed his ground [observed a French lawyer, La Barre, in 1622] the peasant really realised for whom he was doing it, he would not sow. For he is the one to profit least from his labour. The first handful of grain he casts on the soil is for God, so he throws it freely. The second goes to the birds; the third for ground-rents; the fourth for tithes; the fifth for *tailles*, taxes and impositions. And all that goes even before he has anything for himself.

In New Castile the landholding peasant was in a minority, up to 70 per cent of the rural male population consisting of landless agricultural labourers (*jornaleros*). In many villages there were no landholding peasants at all. A census of New Castile drawn up for Philip II in 1575 confirms the plight of the peasant producer, who was obliged on average to consign well over half his harvest to the payment of taxes and dues. The lightest of his burdens tended to be traditional dues payable to the seigneur. Tithes, which were usually assessed at a strict tenth, came to ten times the value of seigneurial dues. After tithes the peasant had to pay his taxes to the crown; these often came to about the same value as the tithes. Finally, and most important of all, came the land rents. In New Castile these took up between one third and one half of a peasant's harvest, and could often amount to three times the value of the tithes. Adding up the rent and the taxes, little could have remained to the producer, as we gather from one village near Toledo which complained in 1580 that 'after paying the rent, nothing was left them'. Nor was this an end to the sorrows of the peasantry for, as we have already seen, those who fell into difficulties borrowed money and found themselves bound by *censos*. 'In short', complained the Cortes of Castile in 1598 when presenting a petition against *censos*, 'everything tends towards the destruction of the poor peasantry and the increase in property, authority and power of the rich'.

In the west German lands labour services formed part of the system of estate economy known as *Grundherrschaft* (some demesne exploitation, but most land leased out). In Brunswick the labour dues were formalised by a law of 1597. According to this the peasantry in that state owed weekly services: an *Ackermann* (peasant farmer) was to give two days' statute-labour with his plough-team; a *Halbspanner* (or holder of half a hide of land) was to give one day. When it came to purely manual labour, the peasants owed services varying from two days to half a day a week. These demands occurred in a system that is usually described as free, in contrast to the serfdom of the east. Labour services with a plough, for example, were onerous, since the team was required to supply two persons and four horses, with a cart. The enormous utility of these services to the landlords is shown by the fact that in the demesne of Gandersheim in the fifty years 1610–60 no workhorses at all were kept, since all the ploughing was done by labour teams. In the year 1639 the demesne obtained 248 ploughing days from labour teams, more than enough for its needs.

The basic problem of peasant obligations was everywhere in mainland Europe aggravated by weather and war, fiscality, and debt. In Spain the burden of rural *censos* provoked depopulation; in France, Loyseau in 1601 observed that 'debts are swollen by interest charges, creditors are more pressing, debtors poorer'. A combination of many factors is shown in the case of the village of Noiron-les-Cîteaux in Burgundy, which suffered badly from the Thirty Years War and had to sell common lands to meet debts. In 1557 it had been a free community with a rich domain and paid only a small *taille*. By 1666 the domain had vanished in alienations, and to the *taille* had been added a heavier *taille*, payments in kind, *corvées* and a tithe. Economic difficulties grew for both rural labourers and smallholders. Three major consequences followed.

First, there was a greater polarisation between rich and poor among the rural classes. A rural elite grew up side by side with a rural proletariat; many middle peasants disappeared. At Chippenham (Cambridge) between 1544 and 1712, the smallholder all but vanished, farmers with over 90 acres increased from 3 to 14 per cent of residents, landless families increased from 32 to 63 per cent. It was a process common to all countries on the continent. A 1667 report on Burgundy observed that 'formerly all or nearly all inhabitants were proprietors of land which they worked, now there are only share-croppers [*métayers*] and labourers'. The landless labour force supplemented its income by seasonal migration in search of work and wages. Second, in regions where peasants lost their lands a concentration of estates took place. In the village of Manguio in Languedoc, in 1595 there was only one estate exceeding 100 hectares; by 1653 there were three and in 1770 eight. Third, as we have seen above (Chapter 5), the urban elite appropriated rural holdings. At Avrainville (a village near Paris) the proportion of land held by Paris townspeople rose from 53 per cent in 1550 to 83 per cent in 1688; by 1680 around Toulouse only one fifth of the land was in local peasant hands. In the Como region (Italy) the expropriation of the peasantry reached its height in the crisis years 1620–50, with most of the land falling into the hands of the urban elite and the Church.

It is evident that these developments must have created a crisis for the European village community. Internally, the community was threatened by the polarisation of wealth and by the consequent social tensions and loss of the neighbour-ethic known in more democratic times. Families drifted away, and within the village there were growing conflicts, leading frequently to riots, between tax-exempt property owners and those poor who had to pay taxes. Externally, there were severe financial problems: the communal debt was always the heaviest burden, sharply intensified in this period by the frequency of war and by the soaring fiscality of the state (in Castile between 1570 and 1670 the tax burden probably quadrupled). Common lands and other assets had to be sold to meet the debts, further weakening the economic position of the village. Finally, in this weakened condition the community was ill equipped to resist continuous encroachments on its privileges by seigneurs, urban landlords and the government. The view, therefore, that the peasant community remained strong in continental Europe, and by its conservatism blocked the agrarian change that eventually became restricted mainly to England,[21] has very little evidence in its support.

In eastern Europe (east, that is, of the Elbe) a substantially different development took place. The sparsity of population (varying from a density of fourteen persons per square kilometre in Poland to three in the Ukraine) meant that with less manpower there were special problems of labour availability. The near-subsistence economy of the region was, moreover, balanced by an extraordinary capacity to supply grain in vast quantities to the west European market. Finally, the machinery of a centralised state had not come into existence in the east. This left the nobility with far greater autonomy than in the west. The predominance of the noble class was a striking feature of eastern Europe. The sixteenth century saw the emergence of the Junkers in East Prussia, the *szlachta* in Poland and the *pomeshchiki* in Muscovy; these gentry now took their place beside the older noble class. The paucity of large towns (of the 700 towns in Poland in 1600, only eight had a population exceeding 10,000), the corresponding lack of a vigorous urban elite, and the constitutional weakness of the Third Estate gave the nobles an inestimable advantage.

Since the fifteenth century the eastern ports had been grain suppliers to western Europe. The produce of eastern estates and the activity of ports like Königsberg and Gdańsk were closely tied to the market demands of the west. With the important exception of Russia, most eastern countries were to some extent part of the European market. This was true even of landlocked territories such as Hungary, since, thanks to its political status as a Habsburg sphere of influence, western Hungary exported agricultural goods through Vienna and south Germany. The rise in cereal and food prices, caused in part by foreign demand, supplied the incentive required by landowners of the east. Moreover, the different price levels between east and west guaranteed a profit for all concerned in the grain traffic, both exporters in the east and importers in the west. While demesne farming declined in western Europe and the nobles attempted to secure incomes from sources other than agricultural production, in much of central and eastern Europe they went back to the land as a source of wealth. On an estate of the Rantzau family in Holstein in 1600, of an annual income of 5,000 marks only 5 per cent came from peasant rents; the rest came from livestock, grain and dairy produce.

Peasant and waste lands were absorbed into demesne, and the production of grain for a lucrative market became a primary occupation. In countries without access to the sea, grain did not necessarily dominate the economy of the great estates. On the contrary, in Bohemia the principal item of production for both the internal and the external market was beer; and in Hungary wine was by far the most important source of income and capital. Both ecclesiastical and secular lords shared in this expansion of production, which increased their capital earnings and allowed them to operate a virtual monopoly over economic activity.

The economic progress of the great nobility was accompanied by the growth of serfdom. The recourse to demesne farming stepped up demand for labour, but peasants were not available in adequate numbers, nor were they all obliged to perform regular labour services. When existing burdens were increased the peasants fled, aggravating the labour problem. Noble influence, therefore, brought in the power of the state. The legislation passed by various governments from the sixteenth century onwards had one aim: to make the peasant's labour available by binding him to the soil and depriving him of freedom of movement.

In Prussia, ordinances of 1526, 1540, 1577, 1612 and 1633 progressively limited the right of a peasant to move from his land or to inherit property. Labour burdens were increased and lords were given the right to exploit the labour of a peasant's children. In Brandenburg, laws of 1518, 1536 and subsequent years likewise tied peasants to the soil, and the question of labour was settled in the early seventeenth century when the High Court ruled that all peasants were liable to unlimited services unless they could prove the contrary. In the Habsburg lands the trend was the same, but the particular problem of these frontier provinces – proximity to the Turks – caused shifts in policy. The general picture can be illustrated by the case of Hungary. Laws of 1514 and 1548 fixed official limits for the labour service (*robot*), but in practice peasants were exploited well above the authorised level of fifty-two days a year. This situation led to the flight of peasants, which in its turn provoked legislation tying the worker to the soil, as measures of 1556 and 1608 stipulated.

Unlike the west, where hired labour was common, many central European estates had to survive largely off feudal services. As in the west, peasant obligations also consisted of tribute in cash and in kind. Since labour rather than tribute was required on the great estates, it became the universal rule in eastern

Europe to commute services in cash and in kind into labour services. This can be seen, for example, in Brandenburg, where in 1608 the Von Arnim family, in the Uckermark, were granted a general permit to use the services of their subjects instead of their rents. Extension of labour services became general in this region. By the end of the sixteenth century most of the villages owned by the cathedral chapter of Havelberg had to render about ninety days' labour in the year. Peasants belonging to the Margrave in the vicinity of Wittstock in 1601 had to serve as much as three days in the week normally, and had to give unlimited service during harvest-time. This process was accompanied by attempts to tie the peasants to the soil. At the end of the fifteenth century a law had declared that any peasant leaving a domain must find a replacement before he could leave. In the sixteenth century this law was made a general rule. In 1536 no peasant was to be admitted to any town or domain unless he could produce a letter from his lord showing he had left with his consent.

The expropriation of the peasantry did not occur in all parts of central and eastern Europe. Free and independent peasant communities were still to be found. In some regions they were few: in Bavaria, by the eighteenth century they numbered only 4 per cent of the peasant population. In specific areas of Poland, however, such as the hills south of Krakow or the lands of the Church in Ruthenia, in the 1660s around half the peasants were free and held over two thirds of the land.[22] A community of free and independent peasantry like the Colmer of Prussia was, nevertheless, exceptional. The majority were economically underprivileged and heavily dependent. In a time of crisis they fell easily into debt and so into the hands of the principal moneylender – the landlord himself. Indebtedness of an impoverished peasantry became one of the essential factors in the evolution of serfdom. There were several categories of dependent peasant, ranging from the relatively free to the wholly servile, but most were reduced by poverty to a common level of existence. The deterioration in status can be seen in Brandenburg, where in 1552 a local writer said in his description of the New Mark: '*Rustici omnes in libertate educati sunt: tota enim Marchia neminem habet servili conditione natum.*' Fifty years later the jurist Scheplitz commented on the same passage: '*vix dici potest*'. In 1632, for the first time, some peasants of the Ucker and the New Mark were classified simply as *leibeigen*, serfs.

It was in Russia that the reduction in status was most marked. Before the final legalisation of serfdom, there had been varying grades of peasants, from slaves and villeins, who were found usually on noble demesnes, to completely free peasants and independent landholders. Between these extremes there were the normal categories of tenants, with different degrees of obligations. The second half of the sixteenth century witnessed a severe dislocation of the Russian state, caused principally by wars and by the *oprichnina* of Ivan the Terrible. In the depression and depopulation that followed these events, the landlords found it very difficult to secure an adequate labour force. Thousands of peasants had emigrated beyond Muscovy, and the attempt by the landlords (the *pomeshchiki*) to exploit those who remained served only to aggravate the flight from the land. As feudatories of the crown, the *pomeshchiki* appealed to it for help. In the spate of legislation that emerged between the late sixteenth and the mid-seventeenth centuries, all categories of peasants suffered, both dependent and free. As usual, the laws concentrated on restricting the peasants' ability to move. The first of these laws was in 1580. Its effectiveness can be seen in the monastery of Volokolamsk, where in 1579–80 as many as seventy-six peasants fled and twenty were attracted in; in 1581 not a single peasant moved.[23]

But it was difficult to obtain satisfactory observance of the law everywhere, as shown by the need for decrees in subsequent years. Of these, the most important were passed in 1597 and 1607. It is important to observe that these laws, unlike similar ones elsewhere, bound the peasants not to the soil but to their lord: the dependence was wholly personal. While this was going on, the liability of the peasants to taxes and to labour services (*barshchina*) was being increased. Labour services were a major obligation not only in central Russia, for as landlords elsewhere found it more profitable than ordinary dues in kind, they began to extend it to their peasants. The mounting difficulties faced by free peasants obliged very many to borrow and hence to fall into debt. A combination of several factors had by the early seventeenth century reduced the Russian peasants to the common status of serfs. Finally, in 1649, this was constitutionally legalised.

In the course of these developments, many of the peasants of eastern Europe lost their land. For the nobles, appropriation of land was nothing new. The spoils obtained from the Church during the Reformation gave them the basis for new extensions to their territory. In 1540 in Brandenburg, the Margrave granted the nobles of the Old Mark, and later those of the whole country, the right to buy out their peasants and to replace peasant holdings by demesne. With the active support of the rulers, who themselves bought land, the nobles replaced smallholdings by large estates. Between about 1575 and 1624, according to a survey of the latter year, in the Middle Mark there was a 50 per cent increase in demesne lands and an 8 per cent decrease in peasant lands. In northeast Estonia, where the landlords likewise took over peasant lands, the number of big estates increased from about forty-five in the early seventeenth century to 135 in 1696. The process of alienation of peasant property can be seen in the Russian district of Varzuga, by the White Sea, where in 1563 the peasants held 95 per cent of the soil, whereas in 1622 they held none directly, and 97 per cent was now owned by various local monasteries.[24]

The new estates were of considerable size, and big estates remained a feature of the eastern economy, whereas west of the Elbe estates were usually much smaller. In Mecklenburg, Pomerania and the central area of East Prussia, over half the estates extended to more than 100 hectares of agricultural land each. In Prussia and Brandenburg between a third and a half were of this size. While the rise of the manorial estate was at the expense of the peasants, the scale of peasant expropriation varied considerably. Even by 1624 in the Middle Mark of Brandenburg, the peasants still technically held four units of land to every one held in demesne. Of the land in Prussia, according to an estimate of the early seventeenth century, the free Colmer held 15 per cent, the nobles 36 per cent and the peasants 49 per cent. In some areas the peasant losses were small. In Saxony the overall loss of peasant land up to the eighteenth century did not exceed 5 per cent of peasant holdings. The peasantry possibly suffered more through deterioration of status than outright loss of land.

What opposition, if any, was there to these developments? The towns and their burghers resented the economic power that the introduction of serfdom granted the nobility. In certain areas of Germany and western Europe the urban elites themselves shared in the expropriation of the peasantry; but in the east this was almost unknown, and indeed there the nobles actually began to expropriate the burghers as well. The towns were therefore in some sense fighting for their own independence. This explains the bitter struggle between the Baltic ports and the noble estate. Among the cities to resist most strongly was Reval, which carried on a long but ultimately hopeless fight against the nobility of Estonia. The burghers objected in particular to the fact that the nobles traded directly with the Dutch, and in 1594 obtained an order prohibiting this, but the order was repealed later in the same year. In the same way the city of Riga was engaged in struggle with the nobles of Livonia. Königsberg committed itself even more directly to protest against the legalisation of serfdom in Prussia. The city refused to observe the terms of edicts that restricted the privileges of peasants, and maintained firmly that all peasants fleeing to it were beyond the jurisdiction of their masters. In 1634 the city authorities in a joint statement claimed that all peasants in Prussia were free and not serfs, and that they and their children were entitled to freedom of movement. After denouncing exploitation by the Junkers, Königsberg went on to reject totally the practice of serfdom. Many burghers from other towns also had the courage to denounce serfdom. Among them was the Stralsund alderman Balthasar Prutze, who in 1614 described Pomeranian serfdom as 'barbaric and Egyptian servitude'.

The state did not always support serfdom. In Electoral Saxony the rulers preferred to 'protect' the peasants, since land passing into seigneurial control became tax-exempt and strengthened the nobles. The Electors therefore bought up land for themselves, both from peasants and lords: between 1590 and 1626, Elector John George I bought up four towns and 108 villages. Meanwhile, successive laws – in 1563, 1609, 1623 and 1669, in particular – restricted the burdens of Saxon peasants and the alienation of their land. In Bavaria there was only a limited move towards serfdom, since the principal landowners were the state and the Church, and neither had any interest in changing the methods of exploitation already in existence.

The Church was among the biggest landowners, and in the eastern countries it contributed as much as any other landlord to the growth of serfdom. The territory held by the Russian monasteries in the 1580s was very considerable: in the Moscow district they held 36 per cent of all arable land; in the Pskov district, 52 per cent. Some of this had been donated during the *oprichnina*, when the nobles, fearing confiscation, handed their estates over to the Church in return for a life tenancy. In 1570–1 alone, ninety-nine such estates went to monasteries in Muscovy. In Poland, the see of Gniezno possessed (by the eighteenth century) scattered holdings that included no less than 426 villages and towns. In Poland and Russia, production on Church estates was directed towards an external market, so that the Church had an interest in controlling mobility of labour.

By the beginning of the seventeenth century, a combination of economic and political factors had reduced the peasantry of much of central and eastern Europe to a condition approaching servitude. Friedrich Engels once described this condition as a 'second serfdom' (*zweite Leibeigenschaft*) since it differed both in time and nature from the early period of European serfdom. There were two distinctive features that created the new serfdom and were essential to its growth: the consolidation of landed power in the hands of the noble elite; and the dedication of the manorial economy to the produce of grain for a (usually external) market.

As in western Europe, the crises of the seventeenth century produced a further severe depression in the condition of the eastern serf peasantry. Two aspects predominated: falling west European demand for grain, and the negative impact of wars. As the west European economy adapted to a falling birth rate and growing sufficiency in wheat, demand for Baltic grain diminished. Between the 1630s and the 1670s the quantity of grain exported out of the Baltic through the Sound fell from an index of 250 to one of 100. To make up for declining income, eastern landlords increased their demands on the peasantry. Dues were increased, and labour obligations made more onerous.

At the same time, the need to have a reliable source of labour continued to be urgent. Earlier attitudes to legislation had been casual and unhurried. When in 1616 regulations for the peasants of Pomerania-Stettin were drawn up, these were described as '*homines proprii et coloni glebae adscripti*', a major change in their status no doubt, but one that was not formalised in any official code. In subsequent years the authorities made every attempt to give formal legal validity to serfdom. In Estonia a law of 1632 began combating peasant flights, and by mid-century stability of the labour force had been obtained. A system of contractual serfdom, based on that practised by the Swedish estates of the De La Gardie family on the island of Ösel, was introduced.

In Russia a major social and political crisis preceded the passing of the Code of Laws, the Ulozhenie, of 1649. As a result of the crisis, in which the victory of the landed nobility was confirmed, the Russian peasantry were fully enserfed. All peasants and their families were declared bound to their masters, with no right of departure, and no right to asylum in the cities. No distinction was made between peasants and villeins: both had to serve on the same terms and with the same obligations and lack of freedom. Like the Ulozhenie, the Recess (or Code) granted by the Elector of Brandenburg in 1653 was influenced by the nobility. For the first time, this edict assumed that the peasants were serfs, and laid the onus on the peasant to prove that he was not one. In the Swedish-occupied territories, such as Pomerania-Wolgast, the Swedish authorities showed energetic opposition to serfdom. But the situation proved uncontrollable, and in 1645 and 1670 laws issued by them gave additional legislative confirmation to the existence of serfdom in Pomerania.

In the long run the serf economy harmed the internal economy by undue emphasis on export; hindered the expansion of urban enterprise; made social change impossible by fixing status barriers; and concentrated wealth in the hands of a feudal aristocracy. Eastern Europe and its peasantry developed in a direction opposite to that of the west. In the west the elites and commercial capital developed hand in hand; in the east they did not merge until the nineteenth century. In the west the peasants were developing towards greater freedom and mobility; in the east it was the reverse.

Solidarities and protest

Historians who look at the events of the past from above have favoured a static view of society, emphasised the continuities in political behaviour, and dismissed the importance of dissent.[25] Others have recognised that stresses and discontinuities play an important role in establishing continuity. Disorder, for example, was a permanent aspect of social conduct, a reflection of stresses and dysfunctions in a usually stabilised society. At a local level it could be provoked by problems in the fabric of traditional social relationships; at a national level, it reflected the conflicting aspirations of status groups. Protest was normal, and therefore frequent. It was an accepted feature of relations between seigneurs and tenants, or princes and their subjects. Social harmony was valued on both sides; but discord became inevitable when attempts were made to alter the traditional pattern of obedience and consultation. Unpopular legislation was, for example, persistently ignored, a situation complacently accepted by the authorities, who would quickly realise that inability to implement a law automatically nullified it.

Resistance to authority was continuous,[26] and often limited in scope, but it formed part of the give and take between governors and governed in pre-industrial Europe. Because it was normally non-violent, resistance was usually resolved through peaceful means, principally through negotiation or through the law courts.[27] The Parlement of Paris, for example, was a forum used regularly in the seventeenth and eighteenth centuries for peasants to resolve their differences with their lords.[28] Even when force was used to put down resistance, the authorities tended to use legal process to restore the peace. Conciliation was always the ideal, not repression. In an extraordinary case in Norway in 1597, a royal commission ordered the restitution of a fine imposed on peasants, and restored the honour of peasants who had been executed for rebellion.[29]

The most typical disorder was the riot, particularly the food riot. Essentially an urban protest, the riot included various modes of action, such as protests against taxes or food distribution, or attacks against specific persons and their property.[30] Riots were not frequent, and authorities always took great care to prevent them ever occurring. It is helpful to ask the crucial question, 'Who really took part in riots?' as a way of trying to resolve the relationship between subsistence crisis and the community. Dearth years were not necessarily years of social conflict,[31] and faced with a natural phenomenon such as starvation the villages seem to have adapted remarkably well to circumstances. When there were food riots, they were limited in place and time, and it is difficult to draw conclusions from them. In certain circumstances rioters might adopt radical measures that indicated their faith in a system of traditional justice and fair shares, what has been called a 'moral economy'.[32]

An even less frequent type of disorder was the revolt, which always included riots but was more extensive in purpose and duration. Revolt might occur against a background of changes in political organisation or fiscal obligation, and a changing perception of social relationships. By the sixteenth century the local communities – the fundamental social units of early modern Europe – were under pressure. Hard times did not necessarily provoke rural populations, and indeed created greater solidarity and a determination among all social levels to step up mutual help and to endure difficulties. The incident at Fuenteovejuna in 1476 (mentioned below) is illustrative. It was a small community acting in unison to eradicate a common problem, but otherwise uninterested in revolt and refusing to combine with other communities in a general protest. Problems that did not threaten the basic structure of society were solved through internal conflict (murder of the lord, riots of taxpayers against tax-exempt, persecution of 'witches') and seldom led to an outward explosion. Rural incidents or riots were infrequent, but 'revolt' was exceptional.

Tensions might turn into revolt under two circumstances:[33] when there was an outrage or threat to the moral conscience of the community; and when the protest escalated from a local to a universal plane. A threat might come in the form of a violation of subsistence norms (crippling taxes and maldistribution of food would both threaten a basic right, the right to exist), and would instantly lower the threshold of violence, precipitating collective action that might not occur at other times. Any violence would naturally be conservative, not revolutionary; it would aim to conserve and restore disregarded norms. The universalisation of protest, by contrast, was a difficult step for the self-centred, conservative local community to take; and tended to happen under the influence of outside ideologies and leaders. Revolt in these circumstances was not a blind, unthinking act of violence, but a carefully coordinated movement, usually agreed by the leadership of several villages at some regional function such as a fair (in Swabia in 1524), a religious festival (Corpus Christi in Barcelona in 1640), or a carnival (Romans in 1580), and carried out with maximum coercion against those individuals or villages that refused to take part.

The apparent tranquillity of the European countryside was permeated with low-level violence, which was employed not to create disorder but to restore social order. A study of the rural communities of Provence has unearthed a total of 374 disturbances, both large and small, over the period 1596–1715.[34] A study of Aquitaine over the same period has discovered some 500 revolts.[35] The overwhelming majority of these incidents were not directed outward at the state but were restricted to the confines of the local community, thereby confirming the apparent peacefulness of traditional society. A recent view is that the 'communities of grain' employed protest as a form of 'representative violence'[36] against social conditions that threatened traditional values. In perspective, it is possible to identify a persistent trend of popular disturbance throughout Europe in early modern times, based always on the values of the community, both urban and rural.

The late fifteenth century set an ample precedent for the social discontent of the early sixteenth. In Spain, the famous incident at Fuenteovejuna (Andalusia) in 1476, when an entire village claimed joint responsibility for the murder of its lord, emphasised the tradition of communal revolt. In Germany there were millennial movements such as that of the piper of Niklashausen (1476) and the Bundschuh (or 'peasant boot') rebellions (from 1493, mainly in the Black Forest). The first big revolt of the sixteenth century was that of the Hungarian peasants in 1514, led by a soldier who was termed 'supreme captain of the blessed army of crusaders subject not to the nobles but to the king alone'. In spring 1520, as Charles V was leaving Spain for Germany, the revolt of the Comunidades ('communities') broke out in Spain. Led by the major cities of northern Castile (and without any echo in the cities of the crown of Aragon), the revolt was a complex blend of political, economic and nationalist grievances, involving all social classes and a strong element of popular rebellion.[37] Incipient radicalism split the Comuneros and frightened the great nobles. These brought in their troops to help crush the main rebel force under Juan de Padilla at Villalar in April 1521.

The classic popular revolt of the early century was that of the 'German peasants' (1525). Confined neither to Germany nor to the peasants, it was in reality a vast unintegrated wave of protest that swept over the whole of central Europe and in some areas was primarily urban. The events have been described in terms of a 'war' or even a 'revolution'.[38] Their long-term cause must be sought in the slow encroachment of seigneurs on the peasant economy: anxious to maintain their income levels, lords enforced and extended their fiscal and jurisdictional privileges. In so doing, they came into conflict with the strong village communities, whose leaders helped to coordinate resistance. The first resort to arms was in June 1524 in Stühlingen (Swabia). By the autumn there were risings all round lake Constance and towards the Black Forest. The core of risings in south and central Germany (February–May 1525) extended into Upper Swabia, then spread along the Danube down to Bavaria and the Alps. From April there were risings by peasants, miners and townspeople in Württemberg, northern Switzerland, Alsace, Thuringia and the Rhineland down to Mainz, the Palatinate and Franche Comté. By summer the revolts had spread to Saxony, Salzburg, Styria and Austria, then into French-speaking Lorraine and Burgundy. In the Rhineland the movement was largely urban, with a notable city revolt in Frankfurt.

Each wave of revolt was distinct in time, motivation, leadership and duration. The heart of the revolution was in Upper Swabia, where the original Twelve Articles of the peasants were drawn up at Memmingen in March 1525 by Sebastian Lotzer, and where the rebels had three armies. In Thuringia the centre was the city of Mühlhausen, where the radical Thomas Müntzer was active; this phase ended in defeat at the battle of Frankenhausen (May), when Müntzer was captured and executed. In the upper Rhineland and in Alsace revolt spread rapidly, but again was broken by a crushing military defeat at Saverne (May). In the Tyrol the rebels were led by Michael Gaismair, who early in 1526 drew up a radical 'Tyrolean Constitution' calling for a communistic type of regime.

This astonishing series of uprisings was led for the most part not by peasants but by artisans, preachers, lesser nobles and bourgeois. Village communities that would in normal times refuse to cooperate with other villages now combined together in a common cause. All groups found a common ideology, a universal legitimation, less in their social grievances than in the appeal to 'God's law'. It was a concept that Luther had pioneered, and many rebels looked to him for support, but he fiercely denounced the uprising. The Twelve Articles combined social and religious demands. 'Henceforth', says the first, 'we ought to have the authority for the whole community to appoint its own pastor'. 'Christ redeemed and bought us all with his precious blood, the lowliest as well as the greatest', says the third, 'thus the Bible proves that we are free and want to be free'. Articles four and five reiterate the claims of the 'whole community' over rights in fishing and hunting. The most persistent demand of the Articles, and of the twenty-five other different versions that appeared within two months in other regions, was that serfdom be abolished. Given the complexity of the revolt, it was not everywhere a failure. In some areas, such as Upper Swabia, peasants obtained written agreements modifying labour services. In the Tyrol some tithes were removed and labour services reduced. In Hesse the Landgrave Philip made important concessions.

Among the notable urban revolts of this time was the Grande Rebeyne at Lyon (April 1529), and the urban revolt at Ghent (1540) in defence of traditional privileges. More broadly based was the Pilgrimage of Grace (1536) in England. Though social protest remained strong within the movement, the Pilgrimage quickly became a traditionalist pro-Catholic rising. In 1548 the first of a series of major uprisings broke out in Aquitaine in protest against the introduction of a salt tax (*gabelle*). Rural areas set themselves up into communes, as at Saintonge and Angoumois, and the revolt (of the 'Pitauts') spread into the city of Bordeaux, which was taken over by the rebels. So extensive was the uprising that a royal army was sent to suppress it, but the demands of the province were met and Aquitaine in 1549 was freed 'forever' from the *gabelle* (which, in fact, was re-introduced without incident during the seventeenth century). Anxiety for regional privileges encouraged rebels to hark back to the myth of a medieval age of freedom 'in the time of the English'. 'Guyenne, Guyenne!', cried the rioters in the streets of Bordeaux.

The mid-1580s, particularly the period 1585–7, were a time of bad harvests. They were years of political crisis throughout western Europe, accompanied by wars in France and the Netherlands. Some of the more savage undertones of popular rebellion came to the fore in these years of blood. In the town of Romans (Dauphiné) in the winter of 1580, a rebellious alliance was formed between the peasants of the countryside (this was a Protestant area) and the artisans of the town, led by a certain Jean Serve or Paulmier.[39] The economic difficulties of the time aggravated discontent. Encouraged by support from the townsmen, the peasants refused to pay their tithes and *taille*. They armed themselves, broke into chateaux, and threw the *terriers* (court rolls) into the flames. In Romans the artisans and peasants danced in the streets, threatening the rich and crying that 'before three days Christian flesh will be sold at sixpence a pound'. The symbolic language was directed at the upper classes of the town, which was now taken over by a popular commune. During the winter carnival Paulmier sat in the mayor's chair, dressed in a bear's skin, eating delicacies that passed for Christian flesh. When they had their carnival procession, the common people under Paulmier dressed themselves up as prelates and dignitaries, crying, 'Christian flesh for sixpence!' The eating of human flesh, here as in other popular revolts, stood for the revolutionary overturning of social values. On the eve of *mardi gras* 1580, the elite classes descended on their opponents and massacred them.

In 1585 in Naples a similar event occurred when, after a bad harvest, the authorities raised the price of bread and authorised the export of flour. In May an angry mob lynched one of the magistrates responsible, named Starace. His body was mutilated (pieces of his flesh were offered for sale) and dragged through the streets, while his house and all his belongings were burnt and destroyed. Nothing was stolen: the proceedings were carried out like a ritual sacrifice. A big urban revolt followed, to cries of '*mora il malgoverno, e viva la giustizia*'. In the inevitable brutal repression that took place, over 800 people were brought to trial between the middle and end of July.[40] In the same epoch, the city of Paris experienced an uprising provoked by the politics of the religious wars. On 12 May 1588, the 'day of barricades', a general rising of the population in favour of the Duke of Guise took place. When the Duke and the Cardinal of Guise were assassinated on the king's orders, authority in the anarchic city devolved on to a commune led by a so-called Council of Sixteen.

The conditions of the 1590s were catastrophic: from 1590 to 1597 harvests were bad, prices crippling. There was famine in 1595 in parts of England, Languedoc and Naples. Prices in Rome in 1590–9 were double those for 1570–9. The crisis[41] touched England, France, Austria, Finland, Hungary, Lithuania and the Ukraine: possibly never before had the timing of so many popular rebellions coincided with each other. In Finland a peasant revolt occurred in 1596–7. A few English labourers in the Midlands attempted a rising in 1596, but it came to nothing. Roger Ibill, a miller of Hampton-Gay, claimed in the autumn of 1596 to have 'heard divers poor people say that there must be a rising soon, because of the high price of corn'. He was joined by Bartholomew Steere, a carpenter, who told him that 'there would be such a rising as had not been seen a great while'. 'He would cut off all the gentlemen's heads', Steere said, and 'we shall have a merrier world shortly'; he also planned 'to go to London, and be joined by the apprentices'. But the authorities responded swiftly, arrested the leaders, and snuffed out the rising.

The great rising of the Croquants in France was concentrated in the years 1593–5. It started in Bas-Limousin, spread throughout Limousin, and at its widest extent covered Périgord, Quercy, Limousin and Languedoc. Originally a peasant rebellion, it became more complex in its social composition and included a large proportion of urban labourers in its ranks. The main grievance of the Croquants was the fiscal system: they firmly opposed both tithe and *taille*, as well as seigneurial taxes. In a manifesto of March 1594 they denounced the soldiery, both Catholic and Protestant, 'who had reduced them to starvation, violated their wives and daughters, stolen their cattle and wasted their land'. They reserved for the urban elites the bitter complaint that 'they seek only the ruin of the poor people, for our ruin is their wealth'. The rebel movement was democratically organised. All religious discrimination was prohibited, and they swore 'by faith and oath to love each other and cherish each other, as God commands'. The programme of social justice and religious unity was one that appealed strongly to the king, Henry IV, and in the early stages of the rebellion he had not disguised his sympathy for the Croquants; but as the rising progressed he and the authorities adopted a harsher attitude. The religious unity of the rebels proved to be their weakest point, which government agents worked to undermine. The main assembly consisted two thirds of Catholics and one third of Protestants. Thanks to the diligent agents, the rebels finally, in 1595, voted to split up into confessional armies. This led immediately to a disastrous defeat by government forces at Limoges. The famine of 1595 marked the end of the Croquant uprising.[42]

Upper Austria, 'beyond the river Enns' (*ob der Enns*), with Linz as its capital, was the theatre of almost continuous peasant uprisings from 1525 to 1648.[43] The risings had a strong religious inspiration, since the territory was Lutheran, but secular grievances were deeply intermixed. The revolt of 1594–7 was a major one that lasted nearly four full years. The pastors urged their Lutheran people to defend themselves against the Counter-Reformation, promoted by Cardinal Khlesl in Lower Austria and Bishop Passauski in Upper Austria from the 1580s. The French historian de Thou reported that in 1595 'the peasants said that they had taken up arms only to free themselves from the unjust taxes with which the nobles oppressed them'.[44]

In the seventeenth century, the first great year of continent-wide rebellion was 1607. In England there were riots against enclosures of land in the Midlands. Rioters assured justices of the peace that their revolt was not against the king 'but only for reformation of those late inclosures which made them of ye porest sorte reddy to pyne for want'. The leader, John Reynolds, was called Captain

Pouch 'because of a great leather pouch which he wore by his side'. Now for the first time, the terms 'Leveller' and 'Digger' appeared in England; 'Levellers' were simply those who levelled down enclosures, without any hint of radical social doctrine. The 'Diggers' appeared in a petition addressed in this year from The Diggers of Warwickshire to all other Diggers. Preaching at Northampton in June 1607, after the suppression of the revolt, a parson claimed that

> they professe nothing but to throwe downe enclosures, but afterward they will reckon for other matters. They will acompt with Clergiemen, and counsell is given to kill up Gentlemen, and they will levell all states as they levelled bankes and ditches, and some of them boasted, that now they hoped to worke no more.

The most important rebellion of these years occurred in Russia. The Bolotnikov uprising of 1606–7 coincided with the dynastic struggle that followed the death of Tsar Boris Godunov in 1605. In 1606 the boyar Prince Shuisky seized the throne, but his rule was opposed by other nobles, who raised armies and marched on Moscow. The core of their support was the peasant movement led by Bolotnikov, a former slave who had fled from his master, been captured by the Turks, and after adventures in Italy and Germany had returned through Poland to Russia. Identifying himself with the opposition to Shuisky, Bolotnikov became allied to the noble party and raised the peasants for them.[45] In the spring of 1607 he and his forces found themselves trapped in the fortress town of Tula. After a long and cruel siege Tula capitulated in October. Bolotnikov was captured and executed.

In Upper Austria in 1626 the biggest popular uprising of the entire Thirty Years War period took place.[46] Nearly all the nobility of Upper Austria were Lutheran, and their religion was guaranteed by the emperor. But in the early seventeenth century the *Land ob der Enns* was put under Bavarian administration, and a Catholic reaction took place. In 1624 the exercise of the Protestant religion in Upper Austria was prohibited by decree and the old faith was introduced with the use of force, provoking several of the bourgeoisie and nobility of the region, including the Count of Ortenburg and the Freiherr von Zinzendorf, to plot rebellion. The revolt began in May 1626 when the peasants along the Danube were rallied together by their two principal leaders, Stefan Fadinger and Christoph Zeller. They waged a full-scale war against the imperial armies, laying seige to several towns and at one stage besieging Linz itself. It was during this siege that Fadinger was killed. He was the true inspiration of the rising, a folk hero whose memory remained for centuries among the people of Upper Austria. His place as leader was taken by a nobleman, Achaz Willinger. By spring 1627 the rebellion was over: in March Willinger and nine other leaders were executed. By the end of the war over 12,000 peasants had been killed, and numberless others crippled or driven into exile.

The 1626 peasant war was widely publicised throughout the German lands.

News-sheets were issued in Linz, Augsburg, Frankfurt, Vienna and other cities. The peasants themselves had their own publicity, in the form of songs which they sang when they marched or when they rested. The most famous of these was their theme, the 'Baurenlied' or 'Fadingerlied', which celebrated the end of the old order, the destruction of lords and priests, and the emergence of the peasant as master:

> Das gantz Landt muss sich bekehren
> weil wir Bawrn jetzt werdn Herrn,
> können wol sitzen im Schatten
>
> (The whole country must be overturned
> for we peasants are now to be the lords,
> it is we who will sit in the shade)

The day of clerical tyranny was over:

> Die Pfaffen sollen ihre Closter lassen,
> die Bawrn seyndt jetzundt Herrn
>
> (The priests must quit their cloisters,
> for the peasants are now the masters)

The land had passed from the seigneurs to the peasants:

> Jetz wollen wirs gantz Landt aussziehen,
> unsere aigne Herrn müssen fliehen
>
> (Now will we sweep throughout the land,
> and our own lords must flee)

In France, thanks to Richelieu's need for money to finance diplomacy and war, the tax burden in real terms doubled between 1630 and 1650. Up to the period of the Fronde there were four main waves of revolt: in the Quercy region in 1624; in several provinces of the southwest in 1636–7; in Normandy in 1639; and in areas of the south, west and north in 1643–5. By their nature urban revolts were more frequent (and briefer) than rural revolts; they can be found in many large towns and cities of France for every year from 1623 to 1647.

Aspects of the French risings can be illustrated by looking at the two largest outbreaks, that of the Croquants in 1636, and the Norman revolt of 1639. The date 1636 helps to explain popular discontent, for this was the year after the entry of France into the Thirty Years War. The correspondence of government officials in the provinces (above all in Burgundy and Picardy) reported widespread misery and anger caused by the plague, by poor harvests and by the passage of troops. Already in 1635 there had been a series of uprisings in the cities of the south, notably in Agen. The Croquant peasant revolt broke out in May 1636 and was crushed only in November 1637. It came to cover so wide an area – most of the territory between the Garonne and the Loire, an area approximating to a quarter of France – that it may well be regarded as the biggest peasant rising in French history. It was not a unified, organised revolt, but consisted of the sporadic activity of numbers of wandering bands. The first explosion was in the city of Angoulême and its region, where a massacre of royal tax-agents occurred. In one town, twelve tax officials were murdered, and one (in Saintonge) was cut to pieces while alive. The uprising became so great and widespread that only a royal army could have crushed it, as one of the intendants reported to Richelieu. But the army was occupied elsewhere, in defending France's frontiers, so the government was obliged to arrive at a compromise. In August 1636 the governor and the intendant of Angoulême opened talks with the rebels. Several tax concessions were made, which pacified the rising for the winter. In spring it broke out again, largely provoked by the fact that the intendant had used troops to help him collect taxes. The new centre of the rising became Périgord. There nearly 60,000 cried 'Vive le Roi sans la gabelle! Vive le Roi sans la taille!' The leader of the movement, and ultimately of the greater part of the Croquants, was a nobleman named La Mothe La Forêt. In the summer of 1637 the repression started. The Duke of La Valette caught the peasants in the town of Eymet and left over 1,000 dead on the ground. By November further action had crushed all but isolated groups of Croquants.

Normandy, where the *Nu-Pieds* rebellion broke out, was one of the most heavily taxed provinces in France. Sully once boasted to the English ambassador that the king drew as many taxes from Normandy as from all the other provinces together. Under Richelieu's fiscal regime, the complaints of the estates of Normandy against the burden of *tailles* and *gabelles* went unrelieved. In 1638 the estates were told that circumstances made relief impossible. A rumour in 1639 of an increase in the tax on salt, which was one of Normandy's chief products, proved to be the last straw. In July 1639 an officer named Poupinel, arriving in the town of Avranches on some other business, was mistaken for a *gabeleur*, and gravely wounded during a riot created by the salt-producers. A few days after Poupinel's death a sheet of verse was found fixed to his tomb. The last stanza ran:

Si quelque partisan s'arreste
Pour s'en informer plus avant
Di luy que *Jean Nuds piedz* s'appreste
Pour luy en faire tout autant

(If any tax-collector [*partisan*] should pause
In order to find out more
Tell him that Jean Nu-Pieds is ready
To do as much to him)

The reason for the choice of the pseudonym *Nu-Pieds* was apparently because taxes had reduced the people to barefoot beggary. Unlike the Croquants, the

Normans were well organised. The peasants were formed into an army called the Army of Suffering (*Armée de Souffrance*) and their leader signed himself 'General Nu-Pieds'. Both Caen and Rouen had popular riots which put them for a while under rebel control. The uprising was ended in 1640 by bringing over troops from Picardy. The revolt in Caen was crushed, then the royal troops met the main rebel force near Avranches and annihilated it, killing most of the leaders.

The years 1647–8 were ones of agrarian crisis throughout Europe. In England there were bad harvests from 1646 to 1649; the winter of 1647–8 was particularly wet, and in London prices rose in 1647 to their highest level prior to 1661. In Andalusia, thanks to the rains of 1647, there was a severe bread shortage in 1647 and 1648. In southern Italy and Sicily the heavy rains of February 1647 were followed by a drought and therefore by famine conditions in 1647 and 1648. In Russia, too, the years leading to 1648 were ones of bad harvest. Throughout Europe, the distress and protest were concentrated in the major towns.

In England, the Leveller movement, under the leadership of John Lilburne and of his colleagues, including Richard Overton and William Walwyn, made its first effective appearance in July 1646 when it published a *Remonstrance of Many Thousand Citizens*, which called for a republican democracy and religious toleration in England. From this time, the Levellers published successive policy programmes, drawn up in the form of a national constitution: each of these statements, of which the first appeared in 1647, was called the *Agreement of the People*. Because the Levellers failed to create an insurrection, it is often easily forgotten how close they came to creating a revolution.[47] In the critical year 1647, when the army quarrelled with Parliament both over policy and because it had not been paid, the Levellers succeeded in infiltrating the army and in dominating all its proceedings. In October the General Council of the army was obliged to sit down at Putney, near London, and discuss plans to adopt the *Agreement of the People* as the basis of future policy. Only the ruthless hand of Cromwell succeeded in breaking the Leveller threat. Facing an attempted mutiny by some regiments in November, he arrested the ringleaders and had one shot. In April 1649 he arrested a group of Leveller mutineers and had one, Robert Lockyer, executed; a month later, at Burford, he executed three soldiers.

Cromwell wisely did not underrate the strength of the Levellers, whose popular support in London could be seen clearly by the great crowds that turned out for Lockyer's funeral on 29 April 1649, and by the thousands who greeted Lilburne's release from arrest by the magistrates. From 1647 to 1649 the Levellers' support could be seen in the volume of protest they managed to stir up, not only in London but also in the provinces. They made ample use of the presses, dispatched thousands of leaflets throughout the country, and had their own newspaper, the *Moderate*. Lilburne and his friends made use of the strategy of petitioning Parliament, the only sovereign the Levellers recognised. Their petitions give valuable evidence of their support. Four days after the arrest in

March 1649 of Lilburne and other Levellers, a petition bearing the signatures of 10,000 Londoners was presented to Parliament; proof not only of support but of the remarkable speed of Leveller organisation. In September 1649 the Levellers produced their most revolutionary pamphlet, *The Remonstrance of Many Thousands of the Free People of England*, which was signed by nearly 100,000 people.

In these years the Spanish monarchy was shaken by disaster both within and without the peninsula. In its Italian possessions the crisis led to major revolts in the two largest cities of the south – Naples and Palermo. Reacting to the famine of 1647, in May a popular procession marched into the cathedral in Palermo and stuck a pole crowned with bread on the high altar.[48] There were shouts of 'Long live the king and down with taxes and bad government!' Mobs set fire to the town hall, opened the prisons and demolished the tax offices. In August a popular leader emerged in the form of a goldsmith named d'Alesi. However, when quarrels within the popular movement produced fighting at the end of August, the authorities seized their opportunity. D'Alesi was murdered, and in September Spanish troops entered the city. The Palermo revolt exhibits the three main features of the urban troubles of 1647–8: a food shortage triggered the uprising, the main grievance was against taxes, and the most active enemies of the people were the nobility.

The problems of Naples were very much those of Spain, its overlord. Administratively the Spanish crown had only limited control over the kingdom, which was in the hands of its feudal lords. In 1638 a Spanish official noted of them that 'the tyranny and injustice in that kingdom deserve severe punishment'. But taxation for the Spanish war effort was also extremely heavy. The main fury of the people of Naples on 7 July 1647, the day that a riot in the city market-place exploded into a major revolt, was directed against the *gabelle*, the salt tax.[49] Though the illiterate fisherman Masaniello emerged as the popular leader, the real power behind the rising was his adviser, the elderly (86 years old) priest Giulio Genoino. Masaniello's murder in mid-July did not check the revolt, which now spready rapidly to other parts of southern Italy. The rebels, under a new popular leader Gennaro Annese, celebrated their victory by declaring a republic, under the protection of France. French support was only half-hearted, thanks in part to problems at home, and by April 1648 the Spaniards were back in control.

Spain, reeling from the loss of Portugal and Catalonia and from noble plots in Aragon and Andalusia, also suffered instability. There was a potentially dangerous uprising in Granada in 1648. On 18 May the poorer people of the city, chanting 'Long live the king and death to the bad government', began a peaceful agitation that swelled the crowds in the streets; they managed to get the civil governor (*corregidor*) replaced. These years of famine and plague helped to precipitate further risings in 1652 in Granada, Seville and Córdoba.[50] In both Seville and Córdoba the people formed a commune, chose their own *corregidor*, and set up a popular militia to keep order in the city.

The Frondes in France were the most important of all the urban revolutions of the year 1648, but the popular struggle never assumed significant proportions.

Even the famous barricades in Paris, which were erected on 26 August 1648 and stayed up for three days, were not a purely popular phenomenon, and were firmly under the control of the city elite. The Fronde in Bordeaux had more popular elements. The first serious disturbances there, in August 1648, were precipitated by the export of wheat from the city at a time when, as in the rest of France, starvation was beating on the doors. The parlement of Bordeaux joined the rebellion and outlawed the governor, the Duke of Epernon, as a public enemy. This first stage of the Bordeaux Fronde ended with a peace in January 1650. The city was next caught up in the Parisian struggle when the Princess of Condé won the leaders of Bordeaux over to her party. From 1651 a new force entered the struggle. The Ormée, a mass movement named after its initial meeting place near some elm trees, was based on popular support but had very divergent aims. It absorbed the Condé party and by June 1652 had set up a commune in the city. The Ormée had a membership of thousands and appears to have had genuinely radical views: 'it is equality that makes for perfection', claimed one of its pamphlets, 'The real cause of sedition and political strife is the excessive wealth of the few.'[51]

The risings of 1648 in Muscovy were, in their political effect, among the most important to occur in Europe. Over the whole administrative area of Moscow there were about thirty urban uprisings from 1630 to 1650; in the city of Moscow itself the greatest cluster of riots was in the summer of 1648.[52] From 1645, Russia had been ruled nominally by the 16-year-old Tsar Alexei Romanov, but the real power was wielded by the boyar Morozov. Taxes rose steeply under his regime and the burgher class was the first to protest. Opposition focused on the new salt tax, first levied in 1648. Poor harvest conditions, and military reverses in the fight against Turks and Tatars, helped to foster discontent. In June a riot broke out in Moscow. When the royal musketeers (the *streltsy*) were ordered to break up the crowds, some of them retorted that 'they did not wish to fight for the boyars against the common people'. A foreign eyewitness reports[53] that

> the Streltsies or life guard, consisting of some thousand Men, took the Commons part, and thereupon in the afternoone they seized on the Court of Morozov....The sayd Court they plundred totally, all the stately and pretious things they found they hewed in pieces...the plate of gold and silver they did beate flat, the pretious pearles and other jewells they havc bruised into powder, they stamped and trampled them under feet, they flung them out of the windowes, and they suffered not the least thing to bee carryed away, crying alowd: *To Naasi Kroof*, that is to say, this is our blood.

Officials were murdered, and Morozov was exiled. Moscow, meanwhile, caught fire in the riot and a large part of the city was destroyed. As a gesture to the populace in Moscow and other cities, the government agreed to a summoning of the Zemsky Sobor. This met in 1648–9. It was one of the last moments of Russian constitutionalism.

The Swiss cantons were not free from agitation during the Thirty Years War. The peasantry benefited from the rise in prices caused by the influx of refugees from Germany, but the coming of peace reversed the trend: prices tumbled, leading to an agricultural slump and currency devaluation (1652–3) in Bern, Lucerne and other cantons. Unfamiliar with the economics of devaluation, the rural classes rose in revolt.[54] The protest movement was led by Johannes Emmenegger, a wealthy peasant who owned 100 head of cattle and drank out of a silver goblet. His friends called him the *Edelstein der Bauern*, the jewel of the peasants. Other leaders included Niklaus Leuenberger, a wealthy peasant who later became supreme head of the whole movement, and Christian Schibi, military commander of the Lucerne peasants, who was looked upon as a magician and sorcerer. When the Lucerne peasants failed to get the devaluation revoked, their leaders met in January 1653 in the town of Entlebuch and took an oath to struggle together for freedom. At the meeting they also drew up a protest song, the 'Tellenlied' (song of William Tell), which was to become the anthem of the peasants as they marched to war. In March 3,000 peasants under Schibi marched to Lucerne and forced concessions; similar concessions were made in April by Basel and Solothurn. On 23 April a mass rally of several thousand Swiss rebels was held in Sumiswald, and decided to take the field against their enemies. The main body of their army, led by Leuenberger, exceeded 24,000 men. By the end of June, however, they were defeated and in disarray. Schibi was executed in July, Leuenberger in September.

The indomitable spirit of the Cossacks troubled Russia in the 1660s with the rise of Stepan (Stenka) Razin, leader of a section of the Cossacks of the river Don. Razin began raiding in 1667, when he announced that 'I have come to fight only the boyars and the wealthy lords'. Fired by the old dream of uniting all Cossacks, he was by March 1670 at the head of 7,000 Don Cossacks and in open revolt against Moscow, his professed aim being 'to remove the traitor boyars and give freedom to the common people'. His following soon became immense, swollen by the nomadic populations of the Don and Volga. Many monks and clergy rallied to his cause; as literate men, they helped to draw up the propaganda that was circulated through the countryside. In September 1670 the royal army scattered his forces, with a bloody repression of his humble followers. Next spring he was betrayed by dissident Cossacks and handed over to the government. Taken to Moscow in a cage, he was tortured and then quartered alive (June 1671). The most popular folk hero in all Russian history, his stature may be measured by the legends and *bylini* devoted to him. Revered as the 'shining sun' (*krasnoe solnyshko*), he was believed by his followers not to have died but to be in hiding, waiting for the call of his people.[55]

In the France of Louis XIV, the peasant tradition of revolt seemed to collapse. A revolt in the region of Boulogne in 1662 was brutally crushed. The main disturbances during the reign were in 1675, directed specifically against taxation. In Bordeaux tax riots in March led to street riots, and for over four months the city remained under popular rule, with the number of urban and peasant rebels estimated at several thousand. The government took a harsh view of what it regarded as complicity by the city in tax-protests, and exiled the parlement. In Brittany, where tax revolts broke out in Rennes in April 1675, the movement became an extensive rebellion against taxes and seigneurial oppression and in favour of regional liberties. In Lower Brittany, where chateaux were pillaged, a 'Code Paysan' was drawn up by delegates of village communities of the 'pays armorique'. They wanted social peace on the basis of inter-class marriages, a revision of peasant labour services, abolition of the *corvée* as being against 'Armorican liberty', and all legal proceedings to be free, with judges being elected by peasants. The peasants wore red bonnets as symbols of the liberty of the province. It was the last great regional revolt of Louis XIV's France.[56] Only towards the end of the reign, with the spread of urban disorder in the great subsistence crises of 1693 and 1709, did rebellion again attain the ascendancy it had held during the early century.

Peninsular Spain experienced some of its most threatening insurrections at the very end of the century. In 1688 the first stage of a prolonged revolt broke out in Catalonia. Since 1640, when social order in the principality had almost totally collapsed,[57] the Catalan communities had lived in peace. The approach of war with France renewed the problem of contributions for the troops, and minor clashes with cavalry provoked a chain of uprisings. In April 1688 all the villages of lower Catalonia rose, and a peasant host of 18,000 besieged Barcelona. The crisis continued into late 1689 when once again the peasants laid siege to the capital. This time, however, energetic action by a new viceroy pacified the rebels and scattered their leaders. A few years later, in 1693, the communities of central Valencia rose in protest at their seigneurial burdens and formed themselves into an 'Army of the Germanías' (after the movement of 1520), but were easily suppressed.

Characteristics of communal revolt

In early modern Europe the precipitants of revolt can be reduced very generally to three: bad harvests, extraordinary taxation and the soldiery. The causes of revolt did not necessarily coincide with these precipitants. Food shortages did not by themselves cause discontent; bad harvests were a normal occurrence, and so long as the common people could see that everyone else was starving they were long-suffering. Only when it was clear that others were profiting from distress did they rise: food exporters and food hoarders were the target in Naples in 1585, Bordeaux in 1648 and Córdoba in 1653. In 1566 in Antwerp, and in 1648 in Granada, riots occurred after the food crisis had passed; in the latter, reported a witness, 'the supply and price of grain improved, but disorder in the quality and supply of bread increased', causing indignation where there had been none during the actual shortage.

Extraordinary taxation features in nearly every revolt as a direct or proximate cause; in France, thanks to Richelieu's war policy, the fiscal burden quadrupled between 1620 and 1641. Though taxes may have been the provocation, they were invariably no more than a trigger to release other long-standing grievances. Few revolts can be considered merely fiscal in scope. Soldiers were also a notorious cause of protest. Troop billeting provoked the rural uprisings in Catalonia in 1640 and 1688. In some cases the soldiers were an indirect aid to risings. A report on the French northeast border in 1645 noted that 'the administration of justice has been interrupted, through the passage and lodging of armies which have caused such disorder in the country that the peasants refuse to allow any judicial action to be taken, and instead rebel even against the judges'.

The tradition of revolt featured as a strong aspect of many insurrections. Geography was important: banditry tended to recur in mountainous areas (the Catalan Pyrenees, the Polish Tatr mountains), and frontier areas (such as the Habsburg frontier with the Turks) had a continuous history of agitation. Certain localities seem to have been in the forefront of rebellions: the little town of Gourdon in Quercy (France) was at the centre of peasant agitation three times in three centuries; the 1648 uprising in Seville started in the same quarter that had supported the Comuneros in 1520. On a larger scale, endemic regionalism was a self-evident reason for the persistence of a tradition of rebellion. In Spain, Catalonia was always looked upon as a source of disorder; in France, Marseille from 1591 to 1596 maintained itself as an independent state of the Catholic League, and again in 1650 declared itself independent. At times the tradition took the form of a myth: names like Croquants, Levellers and Germanías were adopted repeatedly by subsequent rebels, as if to draw legitimacy from their predecessors. In Spain the tradition of Fuenteovejuna was invoked frequently. In 1647 in the village of Albuñuelas (Granada) an official reported an uprising to the Duke of Béjar, lord of the village, and stated that 'those arrested say they are Fuenteovejuna, and the judges don't know how to deal with it'.[58] In the village of Aldeanueva de Ebro in 1663 the residents cried out, 'Down with the bad government! Fuenteovejuna, Fuenteovejuna!'[59] The urge to legitimate a rebellion by establishing continuity from a respected past was constant. The Swiss rebels of 1653 appealed directly to the national hero, William Tell, as the words of the 'Entlebuch Tellenlied' make plain:

> Ach, Tell! Ich wollt dich fragen
> Wach auf von deinem Schlaf!
>
> (Tell, I beseech you
> Wake up from your sleep!)

The leaders and inspirers of uprisings were drawn from the rural elite, urban artisans and, at the topmost level, nobility. This was not surprising since many major revolts, once they had transcended the local level of grievances, mushroomed out to become large movements embracing all classes and interests. The lords were in addition keen to protect their communities. In Normandy in 1643 it was reported that 'the gentry and seigneurs of the villages support and protect the revolt of their vassals'. Nobles also wished to rescue their people from the taxation and political authority of the state. Frequently rebels chose leaders from the upper classes: only nobles had the requisite military expertise, and only they had the status necessary to give respectability to the rebel cause.

Clergy were prominent participants and leaders. In the rebellion in Angoumois in 1548, the vicar of Cressac marched at the head of his parishioners 'in a green bonnet and blue sandals, with a large beard and a two-handed sword'. A Croquant priest in the same region justified his role 'because priests are not forbidden to go to war…and he was defending the public good'.[60] In Spain clergy had a long tradition of rebellion: the preaching of friars in Salamanca in 1520 put the city firmly on the side of the Comunidades. The populist role of clergy is deceptive; priests and friars participated less for ideological reasons than because their primary loyalty was to their flocks. Their function in revolts was social rather than religious.

Town and country had varying roles in uprisings. In eastern Europe the rural economy dominated the life of the people and the towns, whereas in the west the towns and the bourgeoisie or nobility controlling them had begun to dominate the rural areas. In the east, therefore, the conditions of social conflict were radically different: the revolutionary impetus had to come not from the towns but from the countryside. When the common people rose in the east it was under leaders like Bolotnikov and Khmelnitsky, men who had lived all their lives outside the towns. In the west, the radical movements tended to originate in and emerge from the towns, and as a rule they had a considerable bourgeois component. A brief look at the French revolts of the early seventeenth century is enough to establish that every significant outbreak began in a town, expanded its support from the town, and maintained its strength so long as it had urban help. By the 1640s all the major risings in the west were urban – in Naples, Paris, Granada and Bordeaux. The townspeople were beginning to take the initiative. In eastern Europe no such trend was forthcoming.

In the preceding outline it has been assumed that rebellion was an expression of community solidarity against outside pressures. But many conflicts also arose within the broad limits of the local community, where some interests were directed against others. An analysis of seventeenth-century Castilian towns suggests that conflict was often provoked by struggles for power between urban oligarchies.

Popular agitation has often been viewed as fragmentary and short-lived, and consequently of no political importance. The duration of revolts depended in part on the solidarity of the local community. Where community structures were weak or even nomadic (as on the Russian frontier), peasant risings degenerated into skirmishes, all too easily suppressed. Where they were firmer, protracted struggle was possible: near Linz the peasants of Wildeneck maintained a ceaseless fight from 1601 to 1662 against the monastery of Mondsee.[61] When communities and towns resolved themselves into 'communes' and held together, a revolt might survive for some time: the Catalan revolt of 1688 lasted for nearly two years, as did the Croquant rebellion of 1594; and the Austrian peasant rising of 1594 went on for three years. In numbers, too, the uprisings could not be ignored, rebel armies amounting to 24,000 in Switzerland in 1653 and 40,000 in Austria in 1595.

A common misapprehension about popular uprisings is that they were sanguinary. Luther denounced the peasants as 'murderous', but the reality was different. Most rebels respected both life and property. The Austrian rebels of 1595, far from resorting to an orgy of looting, maintained 'perfect discipline'; and in one remarkable incident that year they did not kill the soldiers who were sent to attack them but merely disarmed and beat them, a practice repeated by the Catalan peasants in 1689. During the Spanish urban risings in 1648 and 1652, not a single death was caused directly by the populace.

The violence of revolts was none the less distinctive. The primary purpose of rebellion was always to achieve justice: justice was therefore visited, in a primeval and almost symbolic way, on doers of evil and enemies of the community. Tax-collectors, particularly those who originated from outside the community, were regular victims. Bodily mutilation, as practised at Agen in 1635 (the private parts of a tax-collector were cut off), was common. The ritual of cannibalism as practised at Romans in 1580, and ritualistic mutilation of the sort committed on Starace in Naples in 1585 and at Saintonge in 1636, were further examples of a savagery that was little more than a resort to a form of justice older than civilisation.

Property likewise was an object of popular justice, the emphasis here being on purification rites. The scene at the destruction of Morozov's palace in Moscow in 1648, with rioters throwing valuables out of the windows to cries of 'This is our blood!',[62] can be found also in the Starace incident at Naples and in the Seville rising of 1652. The refusal of outraged rioters to touch tainted property was one of the most striking aspects of the purification ritual of popular rebellions. It can be seen in the Naples riots of 1647:

> It was admirable what a regular method they observed in their fiery executions: for they used first to take all the goods out into the Market place to be burnt, crying out it was the blood of the people of Naples, and 'twas death to embeazle the least thing; insomuch that one who had stolen but a peep of Sausage was like to be hang'd by Masaniello; nor did they spare either gold, silver or jewels, but all was thrown into the flames, as also coaches and horses were burnt alive, most rich Tapistries and Pictures; but they saved books and pieces of Piety, which they sent to several Churches.

These unusual rites of protest were not mere play-acting. The ritual of rebellion has sometimes been analysed as though it were more significant than the actual rebellion.[63] In reality the popular classes, lacking the means of coercion, had little option but to resort to symbols of coercion: 'cannibalism' was employed as a threat because no other violence was available.

All rebels took great pains to establish their legitimacy. Lacking any basis for their authority, they appealed to history, to myth and to God. Side by side with this pseudo-ideology went a formal belief and trust in the king. Most movements appealed over the heads of local superiors to a distant ruler. It was rare for them to question the existence of monarchy, hence the shock felt throughout Europe when the English in 1649 got rid of theirs. It is exceptional to meet cases, such as that recorded by Marshal Monluc in his *Commentaires*, of peasant rebels in the late sixteenth century who reacted to a mention of the king by saying, 'What king? It is we who are the kings; the one you speak of is just a little turd.' Role reversal of this type – peasants as kings – was commonplace in most uprisings. Rebels might dress themselves up as lords and clergy, men might dress up as women (in the Forest of Dean in 1627 and 1631 the male leader of the revolts assumed the name 'Lady Skimmington', a skimmington being one version of the charivari). The symbolism was subversive, but modelled on the otherwise non-subversive role reversal practised in carnivals. Turning the 'world upside down', a common enough symbol of the carnival tradition,[64] became a logical recourse of rebels. But though social protest can fairly be presented as an array of symbols, it departed radically from symbolism when it had recourse to violence.

Failing secular legitimacy, rebels appealed to God. The religious radicals of the German Peasant War wanted to bring the kingdom of heaven down to earth. The bandit Marco Sciarra titled himself 'the scourge of God, sent against usurers and hoarders'. Captain Pouch in the 1607 Midlands revolt claimed 'that he was sent of God to satisfie all degrees whatsoever, and that in this present worke hee was directed by the lord of Heaven'.[65]

Authority, however, must be proved by deeds and miracles. The rebel leaders consequently became invested with supernatural powers in the eyes of their followers, and on occasion deliberately fostered this sense of magic. In the Normandy rebellion there was more than one mysterious Jean Nu-Pieds: a leader who was known yet unknown, who was one yet many, who was here yet also everywhere; this was the consciously cultivated image that made the leader appear ubiquitous, elusive, immune to all danger, immortal. In the folk songs, Stenka Razin hurls back the bullets fired by his enemies. Wherever the 1607 rising broke out, in the south, in the Forest of Dean, it was reported that Captain Pouch was there. In addition to this ubiquity Pouch was able to grant immunity,

> because of a great leather pouch which he wore by his side in which purse hee affirmed to his company, yt there was sufficient matter to defend them against all commers, but afterward when hee was apprehended his Powch was seearched and therein was onely a peece of greene cheese.

The Lucerne peasant leader Schibi was famed as a magician and warlock. His superior, Leuenberger, maintained his authority by an outward symbol. He had been given a red cloak by the peasants of Entlebuch, which he wore wherever he rode. 'He had only to beckon with his hand', reported a Solothurn chronicler, 'or scribble a word and men, women and children would go by day or night through rain, wind and snow, to deliver his message'. Catherine de Médicis observed in 1579 of Paulmier, leader of the commune at Romans, that 'he has such great influence and authority that at his slightest word all the people of the town and round about will bestir themselves'. The Fugger correspondent at Linz in 1596 wrote of the Austrian rebels that

> they seem bewitched, for as soon as the word is given, even in this cold, they leave their wives and children, hasten from their houses and farms, yet attacking neither towns, castles nor even villages. They tell the populace, whom they drag along with them, that for all they care horses, oxen and cows, even the women, may perish and they pawn their cattle and drink away their gold.

How revolutionary were rebels? Most, necessarily, looked to restore what had been lost, not to gain what they had never had. The widespread Croat rising of 1573, which involved up to 60,000 peasants, demanded little more than the restoration of 'ancient rights'. One of the lords reported how his peasants came to him and asked him 'not to ally with anyone against them, since they had not risen against their lords, but only that their ancient rights be restored to them'.[66] However limited their aims, they nonetheless, and despite themselves, threatened the social order. The Croat rebels demanded a reduction of taxes and the abolition of tithes; had either been granted the structure of authority would have been shaken. Moreover, the cry of 'ancient rights' was revolutionary because it appealed to a near-mythical age of freedom.

The yearning for equality was of course perpetual. In 1679 we encounter in Germany the couplet which John Ball had preached through England in the fourteenth century:[67]

> Da Adam ackert und Eva spann,
> Wer war damals ein Edelmann?
>
> (When Adam delved and Eve span,
> Who was then a nobleman?)

Egalitarianism was not new, but in many risings it became commonplace. 'We bear the nobility on our shoulders', observed a pamphleteer in Paris in 1649, 'but we have only to shrug our shoulders to throw them on to the ground'. An Essex labourer asked in 1594, 'What can rich men do against poor men if poor men rise and hold together?' The oppressors were not shaken off, and the optimism of the rebels never bore fruit. Bartholomew Steere in 1596 informed a friend that 'he need not work for his living this dear year, for there would be a merry world shortly'.[68] Despite all millenaristic hopes, this merry world receded further and further into the future, until overtaken by the gaunt realities of the Industrial Revolution.

7

GENDER ROLES

> In these days the view that men take of us is so adverse that we can neither win them over with our patience nor impress them with our innocence.
>
> (María de Zayas, *Desengaños Amorosos*, 1647)

Women, like men, had a recognised place in traditional society, but their specific role varied across the spectrum of social forms to be found in pre-industrial Europe. Their gender marked them out for functions – in the family, at work – that were generally considered subordinate, and in some measure decided their status. But they also had the possibility of rising above allotted roles. Male dominance was in no way universal; in the simpler societies of village and countryside, women had a greater share in tasks and their status was less restricted, whereas in complex urban societies they tended to be more disadvantaged.[1] The position of men was based on two decisive roles: the private one of head of the family, a position which in European society was traditionally allotted to the patriarchal figure; and the public one of warrior, who not only protected society but also enshrined the ideals of honour and status on which society rested. Women were never able successfully to challenge the male monopoly in these two areas. Their formal roles, accepted in the literature of the time, were three: as unmarried women, as wives, or as religious persons. But at various stages of their life cycle, and in select communities of Europe, they were able to exercise choices that gave them some freedom of movement within the apparently firm restrictions imposed by males. Moreover, as parents or as mistresses or as property owners they were frequently in a position of authority that clearly contradicted the formal gender role allotted to them.[2]

In literature of the time the notion of a war between the sexes was commonplace. Allusions to the theme, as in the works of the seventeenth-century Spanish novelist María de Zayas, were numerous and reflected a widespread view of gender roles.[3] The 'querelle des femmes', as it was termed in French writings, was for the most part a literary conceit,[4] a device used by male authors to assert their supremacy in specific spheres. Literary works were full of complaints by males that women were seeking to transcend the limit of their sexual roles and invade or even take over the male domain. Women hate all subjection, was the theme; they desired, in the words of the playwright Lope de Vega, 'to assume the reins that God put into the hands of men'. There was typically among English writers 'an acutely felt anxiety about how women could best be governed and controlled'.[5] Excessive sexuality on the part of women was, for example, a threat to the virility of men, who might not have the potency to satisfy their women. All the critical attitudes adopted by men were therefore, María de Zayas perceptively noted, motivated simply by the concern 'to make themselves more secure'.[6] The security was deemed to be basic to the functioning of society. Transgressing the role was a fundamental threat to patriarchal relations. Though there were multiple modifications to this scenario, received opinion had changed very little by the time that Rousseau declared in *Emile* that 'la femme est faite pour plaire et pour être subyuguée, elle doit se rendre agréable à l'homme au lieu de lui provoquer'.

When examining the role of women in early modern Europe, it is impossible to be sure of the extent to which literary references reflected social reality. A common opinion was that women were more independent and perhaps freer in northern Europe than in the Mediterranean. Both Spanish and English visitors remarked on the autonomy of Dutch women.[7] German literature referred regularly to the uncontrollable aspects of women.[8] But it may be seriously misleading to construe such references as proof of a social scenario in which all women were considered responsible for disorder and subversion. Though authority in traditional society was firmly in the hands of men, they did not consistently wield the authority against women. Court prosecutions for crime do not show a direct bias against women.[9] Surprising testimony can be found even in the Mediterranean to an assumption that the man–wife relationship was not based on conflict, nor even on an absolute authority exercised by one over the other, but on a fulfilment of complementary roles.[10] Among Spanish writers of the Counter-Reformation who dealt with domestic roles, Cristóbal Acosta affirmed (1585) that the duty of a man was to 'honour woman and never speak ill of her; employ the eyes in looking on her, the hands in serving her, the property in giving her gifts, the heart in making her happy'. Marco Antonio de Camos (1592) maintained that the wife is 'neither superior nor inferior but equal in love and companionship'.[11] In parts of France and Spain it was common for the wife to control the household money, which the husband was by custom obliged to hand over out of his wages. These attitudes referred only to the domestic sphere; outside it, women were notoriously disadvantaged.

The notion of a 'war' was of course not far from some aspects of social practice. In all classes, men outwardly professed an apparent disdain for the 'inferior sex'. In the eighteenth-century elite, in both Paris and London, it was the fashion not to admit to being in love with one's wife.[12] In public life – a custom practised down to our own day – women were regularly separated from men. In churches women were not permitted to occupy the same section as men, largely because of the supposed dangers of physical contact. At some public events, such as theatre-going, the sexes had different entrances and seating. The practice was medieval in origin. During the later sixteenth century it was generally practised in Rome and Milan, and apparently enforced in the Netherlands in both Catholic and Calvinist churches. But attempts to extend it to churches in Spain seem to have failed, despite great efforts by the clergy.

Matrimony

Artistic representations of woman from the Renaissance onwards tended to follow the stereotypes determined by Christian tradition – woman as saint, woman as sinner – and can seldom be accepted as reliable images of social reality. Even the image of the good housewife to be found in Dutch paintings of the seventeenth century tended to appeal consciously to the image of the virtuous wife in the book of Proverbs. Because of this, prescriptive writings of the period are possibly a surer guide to changing conceptions of a woman's role. There were many of them, instanced on the Catholic side by the treatise of Juan Luis Vives (1523) and on the Protestant side by the Puritan Thomas Becon's *Book of Matrimony* (1562). In the post-Reformation period, the views of all Christian writers tended to converge: they recognised that women must be shown love and respect. The treatises, inevitably, limited their scope to one principal role: that of the married woman. It was the function that determined most aspects of woman's life in traditional Europe.

Though girls might marry late (we have seen that the mean age for first marriage in western Europe was around twenty-five years), all those early years were a mere preparation for, and widowhood a mere postscript of, the condition of matrimony. Life outside marriage was, for most women, almost inconceivable. Even the male-dominated Catholic Church of the Counter-Reformation conceded that though chastity in the religious life was a high calling, the married life might be an even higher one. For the majority of women, the norm was matrimony.

Exceptions to the norm, one must say at the outset, were considerable. In the 'northwest European pattern' a high proportion of females, possibly up to one fifth, abstained completely from marriage; whereas in eastern Europe virtually all women married. For example, in northwest Spain in the early eighteenth century 16 per cent of women remained celibate.[13] The perceived presence of single women in a community was often higher than this, because of other factors such as the high number of widows. At any given moment in the west, and thanks to religious ideals (entry into convents), economic disability, widowhood or simply the unavailability of men, nearly half the women under fifty years old might not be in a state of matrimony. Although in general the population was fairly balanced between male and female, the men too would suffer difficulties in finding mates. Rome in 1592 had only fifty-eight women for every 100 men, and in Nördlingen during the Thirty Years War the authorities allowed unlimited immigration to women (even before the war, in 1581–1610, immigrant girls were 22 per cent of brides) but restricted entry of males.[14] There were also special circumstances, such as the seasonal emigration of males in search of employment, that might leave villages almost entirely without young males for several weeks.

We have seen that, depending on a broad range of factors that included above all the permission of parents, a girl might have considerable freedom in choice of a partner. Ironically it was in the upper classes, where property questions were paramount, that girls might find the choice made for them against their will. In their case marriage was an investment, and they were the marketable commodity. In the lower classes a greater laxity of social control, and more ability to move around within the region, produced a greater freedom of courtship.

But what could a woman contribute to matrimony beyond her person, in a traditional society that was male-dominated at every level and where gender roles were exclusively decided by men? In reality, within the framework of male domination there could be considerable variation of roles; and a woman's contribution to a marriage could be very important indeed, both in terms of the property she brought with her, and in terms of the practical work experience she might provide. She was, above all and traditionally, the mother, the bringer of life to the household.

The dominance of man in a traditionally patriarchal society was reaffirmed during the confessional age. In the interests of stability of property and family, the laws strengthened the role of the husband. Both tradition and common practice tended to give wife and children a very subordinate role. In 1587 a jurist of Tours commended 'domestic discipline where the father is as a dictator', and in 1622 an English writer described the husband as 'a king in his owne house'. There were extreme cases where customary law allowed men to beat their wives or kill them for infidelity. But by the early seventeenth century, some attitudes in western Europe were changing. The three great controls over family behaviour were the state, the Church and the community; all three modified their attitude between the fifteenth and the eighteenth centuries. Perhaps the most significant influences at work derived from the Reformation and the Counter-Reformation, whose leaders attempted to bring some order into the rules of marriage. The Reformation, which ceased to recognise celibacy as an ideal state, put more emphasis on the status of marriage; but in practice both Protestants and Catholics were working with the same problems of human conduct and came up with virtually the same solutions.[15]

The intervention of the state aimed invariably to strengthen the patriarchal authority of the father, with particular concern for the protection of family property. A revival of Roman law among jurists stressed both the rights of property and the father's authority over his family. In some parts of France disobedience to parents came to be regarded as a crime, and in Spain the Madrid city police arrested disrespectful sons. On the other hand, the state ceased to tolerate the power over life and limb that husbands had once exercised over wives and children; and 'divorces' or legal separations were granted by state and Church courts both in France and Spain, when the wife could prove systematic beating. It is significant that over 70 per cent of the petitions for divorce in the archdiocese of Cambrai in 1710–36 came from women.[16] The majority of petitions for separation in Spain cited marital violence as the reason. There were two principal grounds for granting separation in a Catholic country, if we go by the practice in Catalonia.[17] First, if either spouse threatened the life and honour of the other (a wife from Sitges stated in 1660 that 'she is mistreated by her husband who threatens to kill her and beats her with his fists and kicks her'). Second, if the spouse refused to give economic support (the same wife stated that 'her husband refuses to work and to give her the necessary maintenance'). Impotence (that is, inability to fulfil marital duties) tended to be cited not in pleas for separation but in pleas for nullity. Impotence was difficult to prove on personal evidence alone, and more weight was put on the testimony of the community. In one case in Catalonia in 1596, the parish priest testified on behalf of the wife that 'he has heard people say many times in the village that the husband didn't have much of a member'.

Catholic practice was that couples might be separated but could not marry again, for the original marriage was binding. The Protestants, in contrast, gradually came to accept remarriage after divorce, but were by no means eager to condone it. Protestant Basel, where divorce was granted to 16.7 per cent out of 1,356 marital cases in 1550–92, and the parties were allowed to remarry after a year, seems to have been exceptionally liberal. As a rule all Christian denominations discouraged divorce, and preferred to preach the merits of a good marriage. Anglicans reacted against Catholic teaching on the virtues of chastity by stressing the high calling of marriage, 'a state' (according to the Puritan William Perkins) 'in itself far more excellent than the condition of a single life'.

The pleas for divorce and separation are a reminder that the state of marriage in traditional society was not as harmonious as once believed. Though the duration of marriage between a couple in western Europe was (as we have seen for the area of Basel) around twenty years, after which death would intervene for one of the partners, in practice very many Europeans were unable to last the course. Stability in marriage was a desired ideal rather than a daily reality. In post-Reformation Germany, the attempt to affirm marriage discipline was a constant challenge, with the Lutheran courts particularly active in the mid-sixteenth century.[18] 'It is no surprise', a Spanish priest observed in 1588, 'that in our time there is such unhappiness in marriages'; and another the following year commented that 'it is a disgrace to see how openly and unashamedly so many adulteries are committed'.[19] The fact is that in traditional Europe the marriage bond was not always seen as indissoluble.[20] Like any other secular contract, marriage could be annulled if certain conditions, such as the payment of a dowry, were not complied with. Because the contract carried no commitment to permanence, many felt themselves free to break the bonds by mutually agreed separation or even by bigamy. In the sixteenth and seventeenth centuries, the offence of bigamy constituted 5 per cent of all the cases prosecuted in Spain by the Inquisition. The nature of matrimonial unhappiness varied greatly, then as now, and had a broad range of scenarios, with physical violence as a constant component.[21]

Historians have frequently presented the traditional family as one in which wives suffered, children were beaten, and husbands ruled. Though all this undoubtedly happened, it is important to remember that a profound control was exercised over marital conduct by community norms. No village remained ignorant of the virtues or misdeeds within families, which were always vulnerable to the interference of kin and neighbours. In 1617, when the villagers of Yardley in Worcestershire petitioned against a householder, they included the accusation that he 'did beat his wife most cruellie'. Throughout western Europe the custom of the charivari (see Chapter 8) allowed members of the community to deride cuckolds, henpecked husbands, second marriages and unfaithful spouses. Community control of other types survived: in Granada, for example, the people annually elected a *juez del barrio* (suburb warden) whose task it was to oversee the behaviour of families, and battered wives in the same region could obtain the arrest of their offending husbands. At the very time that the process of social and political change began to diminish the influence of the community over the lives of families, other moral norms were being brought into play. The Puritans in England and America may not have innovated radically in their approach to marriage, but they certainly shifted opinion towards a more respectful relationship within families.

The Council of Trent also had a decisive influence: manuals for confessors published before its sessions contain no references to the duties of parents, whereas all manuals published thereafter devote considerable space to the subject.[22] Cardinal Richelieu reflected the new trend when writing that the commandments impose 'obligations not only on children towards their fathers, but also on fathers and mothers towards their children, inasmuch as love should be reciprocal'. One of the most influential Catholic works exalting marriage was St François de Sales' *Introduction to the Devout Life* (1609): for him marriage was 'a great sacrament, to be honoured by all and in all ways'. The position of woman was firmly defended in a pioneering work by the Spanish Dominican Vicente Mexía, *Salutary Instruction on the State of Marriage* (1566). He defined the relation between husband and wife as one of 'equals in everything: equals in honour and service and ownership of goods and whatever pertains to the husband: all of this the wife has equally and without distinction'. The wife, he said, was 'not a slave or servant but a free woman, lady of the house and estate and goods and whatever else he has, with the one obligation of obeying him'.

Affection and love had always been important in matchmaking,[23] though there was never any assumption that they were necessary or could affect the nature of the marriage contract. Prescriptive writings, however, began to admit that there should be a basis for stability within marriage. Church manuals before the mid-sixteenth century did not use the word 'love' in a conjugal context; by the later seventeenth century most did so. In the early sixteenth century it was almost impossible to break an engagement to marry; by 1665 in France it was possible for Jeanne Pluot to be officially released from her engagement on the grounds that she 'has never loved and still does not love the said Lasnier, and would choose death rather than marry him'.[24] Normally, however, 'love' was not a criterion accepted by the courts, which used other principles to guide them when they sanctioned the separation of couples. When the courts failed to satisfy, couples all over Europe seem to have done what came most naturally: they simply separated.[25] In rural Catalonia, the incidence of separation, apparently accepted by communities, was so high that the bishops placed it at the top of their list of moral failings among the people.

The encouragement of intra-family respect and affection by the Reformation and Counter-Reformation was one of the ways in which broad external influences helped to modify the character and development of the family. The evolution of work patterns was another powerful influence. Before early modern times there was no significant distinction between place of work and place of leisure: the family worked where it lived, as peasant families would continue to do for centuries to come. As work became dissociated from the home (through urbanisation and later through industrialisation), the family evolved into a centre where the wage earner retreated for leisure. This helped to privatise the family; and servants, who had hitherto always been considered members of the family-household, were gradually excluded from the domestic circle.

Women and property

A woman with property possessed both status and independence; she also surmounted the weaknesses of her sex. She became a highly desirable commodity in the marriage market; her male peers accepted her on terms of equality; and in certain societies she had the right to political representation that came with her property, especially if she were effective head of the household. In some village communities, female heads of household enjoyed the same status as the males; in some parliaments of Europe, women could attend as members. None of this is surprising if we remember that in most countries (not in France, where the Salic law excluded them) women could transmit noble titles, and frequently succeeded to thrones in their own right. In practice, however, the wide variety of legal systems in Europe, and even differences between Church and state laws, created important modifications in the relation between women and property.

Property determined the possibility of marriage, and a girl with a fair dowry could always find a husband. Among the lower orders the wife brought little dowry to a marriage; a small sum of money, perhaps, or in country areas a farmyard animal. The existence of the property was vital. In the poor French village of Sennely en Sologne in 1700, the priest complained that his younger parishioners 'get married out of financial interest rather than any other inclination.

Most of them when looking for a bride only ask how many sheep she can bring to a marriage.' The transference of property through marriage dowries assumed crucial importance among the richer classes, and was regulated by complicated arrangements to ensure the correct disposal of the property. Women consequently became a key link in the forging of political and economic alliances between families, as in Brescia where the dowry was an essential element in the strategy of property accumulation practised by the elite.[26]

Women might possess property and yet not be in a position to control it. In England, control of property passed to the husband; and the common law dictated that inheritance passed to the eldest son. These rules affected the elite, who owned the bulk of landed property. However, among the greater part of the population, who owned little land and were unaffected by the strict laws governing elite inheritance, the legal system functioned more along lines of common sense, and working women were able to achieve a surprising degree of equality in the distribution of settlements.[27]

The weaker position of women in questions of inheritance affected their ability to remarry if they were widowed. A widower usually enjoyed control of his late wife's property, and therefore had the means to seek out a new woman to take care of his household. Fortunate indeed were those widows who retained property from the marriage, and in addition had no children; for them remarriage was never a problem. Since the majority of widows were not in this happy position, they remained single. In Coventry in 1523, there were nearly nine times as many widows as widowers among the registered households.[28] Across rural Europe, widows were a significant proportion of the population profile. But they were not necessarily poor or idle. With no man to earn the keep, they struggled through on their own resources. In the villages of Zamora (Spain) in the 1560s, there were several widows who put their children to work: one widow had two sons, and (she said) 'she had them with her sometimes, and at other times they were off earning their living, because they owned no property'.[29]

Women and work

The preparation for marriage obliged all women, rich and poor, to acquire some experience with which they could bring benefit to the family household. It was normal for women to do work in the house, and also frequently out in the field.[30] The process started from the early years, when rural families sent their daughters away from home, to spend a number of years in life-cycle service in the towns. The female presence in the urban labour market was always important. In the textile town of Leiden in the 1580s, 10 per cent of the labouring population were independent women workers, and a further 20 per cent were women in menial employment.[31] Since life-cycle workers had the specific intention of serving for only a short while, until they had saved money (for their dowry) or learned a trade, there was a rapid turnover in their numbers. In the Spanish town of Cuenca, over one third of servants left their jobs annually, and a further one sixth changed their dwellings every year.[32] In global terms, country girls employed in domestic service in the towns were a significant long-term feature of the European labour market. They 'accounted for 13 per cent of the population of any city north of the Loire'[33] in pre-industrial times. The high proportion of girls in such employment contributed to the gender imbalance in many European cities. For every 100 women, Venice in 1655 had seventy-nine men, London in 1695 had eighty-seven men, and Zürich in 1671 had seventy-four men.[34]

The degree of participation by women in work depended logically on the nature of local industries. Production based on the domestic loom could be dominated by women, as in Cologne where it was reported in 1498 that 'in our city the craft of silkmaking is carried on mainly by women and very rarely by men, with the result that the women are much more knowledgeable about the trade than the men'.[35] Silk was an exceptional case of an industry in which women continued to play a predominant role. In Bologna in the 1700s, when the industry was in decline, women ran two thirds of the production centres. In this case the women were not of humble origin, but came from the middle classes, and acted as producers and guild members while their husbands acted as merchants and purchasers of raw materials. In Polish cities of the seventeenth century, by contrast, women producers and traders were few. Their role was confined largely to small retail trade,[36] and even to moneylending: of a sample of small loans made in seventeenth-century Gdańsk, three quarters were made by women.[37]

Women were, by custom, excluded from most occupations where men were the traditional wage earners. By extension, this meant that women were normally excluded from guild membership and its corresponding status. In many towns in Germany, Poland and the Netherlands, however, where family links helped them to participate, they were accepted often into guilds and became apprentices. If the family controlled a textile firm, they naturally played a significant role in production.[38] In small crafts not controlled by guilds, such as printing, they had a useful role. In some family businesses, women attended to all the public and sales activities; in others, they did the bookkeeping; in others, they conducted the business correspondence.[39] The Englishman Fynes Morison, visiting Holland in the 1590s, was of the opinion that in small businesses the men wasted their time doing nothing while the women took care of all the work. Though pushed into the background by social custom, wives and daughters were frequently the mainstay of productivity. In early eighteenth-century London, women played a significant role directing small businesses. On the basis of fire-insurance policies taken out by them during the period 1726–9, it can be seen that 37 per cent of the women concerned were active in food and entertainment (taverns, grocers, coffee-houses), 31 per cent in textiles (as drapers and milliners), and 11 per cent in pawnbroking.[40]

Moreover, women played a fundamental role in the local economy. Excluded from most professional activities by the guilds, they were an essential part of the agrarian economy, not only in the tasks of planting, weeding and harvesting, but also in transporting produce and in buying.[41] At every social level, whether managers of farms or field labourers, whether as dairy-farmers or as keepers of animals, their role was extremely complex and is difficult to define in statistical terms.[42] In some peasant societies, they worked side by side with men. In the Basque lands and in northern France, women were an important element in agriculture. In the Mediterranean area, on the other hand, they appear to have been discouraged from working in the fields, as this was held to endanger the man's honour. Only men, it was felt, could direct the agrarian economy. Even so, a Catalan writer (1617) reflected the classic male attitude in claiming that 'the woman has to be the first to start work and the last to leave off, the first to get up from the bed and the last to lie down in it'.[43]

Some recent studies of women in work have adopted the view that work was a great liberating force that made women more equal in a very inegalitarian society, and gave them social advantages. It is not easy to apply this optimistic view to the realities of pre-industrial society, where work could be neither pleasant nor rewarding, nor necessarily enhanced the status of women. The widespread norm of exclusion from guilds, together with the frequent restriction of women to domestic obligations, have on the other hand often given rise to the pessimistic conclusion that women played only a marginal role in work activity. Some scholars go so far as to suggest that restrictions on the role of women in work had worsened their status on the eve of the Industrial Revolution. This view may be seriously incomplete. Women, both unmarried and married, participated to a remarkable degree in all aspects of work, even though they thereby earned no status separate from that of the menfolk, nor earned comparable wages. If women's role declined in some work sectors, it may not reflect any worsening of their status, but rather have been because of changes in those industries, or because of changes in family structure that removed women from the workplace.

In many respects, woman's part in work during early modern times may have remained constant (for better or worse) simply because it was often shared. In societies where the economy was based on the household, much work was necessarily allotted among members of the family.[44] Women played their part and husbands often appreciated what they did. In 1600 a Salisbury man, Thomas Reade, left all his property to his loving wife, who 'by her joint care, travail and industry hath supported and augmented my estate'. By contrast, in urban centres most working wives did not share their men's work, and were correspondingly subjected to the demeaning conditions of the market.

Motherhood and the family

It was commonly recognised at the time that woman's role as mother was the most trying of her several duties. It began with the mortal risk of childbirth. In the upper elites, where it was important to produce a male heir to take over the family property, women were under constant pressure to give birth. The pleasure of becoming a mother was superseded by the obligation to deliver (male) heirs. 'Always going to bed, always pregnant, always giving birth', the Polish princess Marie Leszczyńska, wife of Louis XV, is reported as saying resignedly. It was no exaggeration. At a time when giving birth was still both painful and a risk to life (both of mother and of child), aristocratic and royal wives complied with their duty and ran the risk. The constant need to produce live births was of course a result of the very high rate of infant mortality, in which possibly one out of every three children died in infancy. Elite wives had to remedy the default, particularly if they kept on producing girls and were unable to achieve the desired goal of a male heir. In Spain the young (and subsequently notorious) Princess of Eboli, who consummated her marriage with the prince of that name in 1557, when she was seventeen, produced ten births over the subsequent dozen years. She was hardy enough to survive. By contrast, three of the four wives of Philip II of Spain died as a consequence of childbirth complications, and the king's second daughter Catalina died young of the same cause. The proportion of women dying in childbirth at that period is not clear, but it could have been as high as 10 per cent in some areas of France,[45] much less so among the peasantry than among the elite. For England it has been estimated that childbirth caused up to 20 per cent of all female deaths between the ages of twenty-five and thirty-four.[46] The well known advice (1671) of Madame de Sévigné to her daughter, who had just given birth, that she should abstain from sexual relations for a while, demonstrates a common awareness of the risks involved.

One of the greatest aids to a woman in childbirth was the midwife, whose services were clearly essential to human survival. The remarkable memoirs of a seventeenth-century Dutch midwife, Catharina Schrader, who began her notes in 1693 and continued them until her death in 1746, reveal the experiences and trials of a career in which she assisted at about 4,000 deliveries.[47] The midwife, as a bringer of life, was a socially respected figure (in 1704 in Chester the local midwife was the mayoress!),[48] and was also a valuable witness used by courts investigating cases of rape and infanticide.

As an extension of the view that love and affection were slow to develop in western society, scholars from Ariès onward have frequently affirmed that maternal love towards infants was rare in traditional Europe. The view was reinforced by research that showed, as we have seen, that one in every two infants did not survive into adulthood; mothers, it was presumed, accepted the inevitable and suppressed their affective feelings. The common practice in eighteenth-century France of upper-class mothers leaving their infants in the (often unreliable) care of wet-nurses seemed to supply a concrete example of the general trend. Some feminist historians also suggested that if maternal affection was sometimes in evidence, it was the simple consequence of males enforcing a 'motherly' role on women.

These views have been convincingly questioned. In all pre-industrial societies, concern for infants was the natural rule, and Europe could not have been an exception.[49] The evidence of a large number of surviving first-person accounts[50] from England reveals beyond any doubt that among the literate classes affection for children, and corresponding grief over their deaths, was the norm. Children, it seems clear, were both wanted and cared for.

Women in religion

Throughout Europe women continued to enjoy an important role in religion. Their first and most important role was in the religious practice of the family and the upholding of family virtues; by extension they also played a major role in community religion. At home they cared for the upbringing of the children; in the community they played a full part in festivities and were normally those who arranged the cleaning and decoration of the church. Going to church seems moreover to have been considered the special function of women; at least in the Mediterranean countryside, the men stayed outside the church, playing at dice and waiting for their women to come out.

The Protestant Reformation had an ambiguous impact on the position of women in the family and in religion. The agreed view is that it 'both expanded and diminished women's opportunities'.[51] Women could be found in the vanguard of the Protestant movement, and insisted on their right to participate equally in the cause with men. 'Do we have two gospels', the ex-nun Marie Dentière protested, 'one for men and the other for women?'. Despite opposition from males, women made a profound impact on the course of the Reformation. In France, they played a major part in religious changes. Marguerite of Navarre and Jeanne d'Albret gave their support to Calvinism. It was of course inevitable that noblewomen should exercise considerable influence. But in terms of suffering the ordinary women had the more heroic role: one fifth of the martyrs in the Marian persecution in England were women. The abolition by Protestants of clerical celibacy and of enclosed convents gave a new dimension to women's social role, but without necessarily improving it. There were indeed many negative trends. In traditional society women had been active in festivals, processions and other community functions; the abolition of these celebrations by the Reformation sharply reduced the public activities in which females might participate.

The same ambiguity could be found on the Catholic side, with the essential difference that Catholics did away with no structures – as the Protestants did with celibacy – and worked within traditional parameters. Catholic villages continued to accept the need for clergy to take 'housekeeper' mistresses, in part because they felt that the women contributed a practical experience to the often sheltered world of celibate men. In Barcelona in 1561–2, the vicar general issued fifty-seven warnings to clergy of the diocese over their concubines, and in 1613 the Inquisition in the same city disciplined thirty-eight of its clergy for the same offence.[52] A Catalan priest went so far as to affirm in 1539 that 'clergy may in good conscience marry [he meant 'cohabit'] even if they are priests'. The staunchly male-orientated Church of the period after Trent marginalised women in some respects but in others firmly recognised that, for example, women had a key role in parish life. Women's guilds were the mainstay of several aspects of church activity. Above all, women were the majority of churchgoers. The outstanding role of Catholic women can be seen in the French Counter-Reformation, which produced a crop of canonised noble ladies (such as Jeanne Françoise de Chantal), important spiritual leaders (such as Angélique Arnauld of Port-Royal), and a number of highly successful women's religious orders.

There were, arguably, some negative trends on the Catholic side. The priority given to an all-male priesthood may have prejudiced the previously significant role of females in the religious life of the community. The Church after Trent also tried to minimise the part of women in religious services. Religious reforms brought order into the chaotic world of convents, but enforcement of the strict cloister may have excluded women from a public spiritual role. Against this, however, must be set the major contribution made by the many new female religious orders, as well as by individual Catholic women such as Mary Ward, who modelled themselves on the Jesuits and carried out notable spiritual and charitable work. Ward argued that she saw 'no such difference between men and women that women may not do great things'.[53] The supreme achievement was that of Teresa of Avila, whose influence permeated the religious reforms in both Spain and France, and who was subsequently proclaimed patron of her nation.

On both the Protestant and Catholic side, spirituality was a route through which women succeeded in affirming their interests and making a very special contribution. This was not wholly surprising. In traditional Europe women had stood out in popular experience as hermits and visionaries, and continued to carry out the role at all social levels. Holy women, such as the *beatas* in Spain, exercised a strong spiritual influence over local communities and even, in exceptional cases, became the privileged advisers of kings. María de Agreda, a nun in a little Aragonese town, was visited by Philip IV of Spain in 1643, and came to exercise a profound influence over the king, advising him on the highest concerns of state. But religious women were symbols of power in their own right as well: many famous convents were governed by influential abbesses and female superiors, and noblewomen played a distinctive role as patrons of religion and of the religious orders. These favourable aspects coexisted in society with the usually unequal position enjoyed by women in family and economic life. The revolutionary religious changes of the sixteenth century quite simply continued the ambiguity of women's role.

From the seventeenth century onwards, by contrast, an extraordinary initiative was gained for women through their activity in minority religious groupings that had themselves asserted their autonomy from established structures. The pioneers were the Quaker movement in England, and the most active of the first Quaker women was Margaret Fell, wife of a member of the Long Parliament. Women took part notably in the more radical activities of the movement, such as in public preaching, and also in their support for the activities of the enthusiast

James Nayler,[54] but on the whole they kept within the bounds of discipline. By the mid-seventeenth century the Quaker women were sufficiently organised for 'above seven thousand handmaids of the Lord' to petition Parliament against payment of tithes.[55]

The purely spiritual contribution of women may best be seen through their extensive impact on religious ideas. Teresa of Avila's influence spread rapidly through Spain after her death, and her books became best-sellers in the southern Netherlands. In France her writings were adopted as the basis for religious reform from 1603 onwards. France likewise was the centre for the great mystical controversies that centred round Madame Guyon. Such famous women, however, were no more than the sign of a broader tendency. Throughout social Europe, religion in the post-confessional age was increasingly gravitating away from men and towards women. In Spain it was notoriously the women who went to mass and to missions, more than men. In early eighteenth-century Germany, women played a significant part in the Pietist movement. Among the Methodists in England, 'where statistics for chapel attendance exist, women outnumbered men by nineteen to one'.[56] Through their role in the Christian family, and despite a Church organisation that remained almost exclusively in the hands of men, women were both moulding and determining the shape of western religious attitudes.

Private and public escapes

Women in traditional society led enclosed lives: when unmarried they were constantly chaperoned, and when married their position seldom improved. A sixteenth-century Spanish Jesuit suggested that young women might be taught to read but not to write (to avoid writing notes to lovers). Moreover, they 'should not go out to see other women, should not dance, should not go to public parties, should not drink wine and should not stir from the house'.[57] Girls in Spain were often not even allowed to go to mass, a restriction much denounced by some clergy. Though the cloistering of women was most practised in the upper classes, women of all conditions evaded it at every turn, and the participation of girls (always criticised by moralists) was one of the delights of public festivities in the Mediterranean. Perhaps the most significant escape, ironically, was religion: women went to church in order to find company, both male and female. Women in general became the mainstay of parish congregations, organisation and festivities.

Education was the most important escape accessible to women, but it was rarely available outside the noble classes. The first girls' public school to be established in France was the college of Saint-Cyr, founded by Madame de Maintenon in 1686 for daughters of the nobility. At the same period girls' finishing schools were developing in Restoration England. The majority of elite girls were tutored at home or, in Catholic countries, in convent schools. Education was normally limited in scope, and directed to prepare young ladies for their social duties. In France the Franciscan educator Jacques du Bosc in

1632 stressed that for girls, 'music, history, philosophy and other similar exercises are more in accord with our design than those of a good housekeeper'.[58]

Like men, women were free to achieve considerable mobility. America is a significant example. Of those Spaniards who registered formally as emigrants to the New World from Seville, women constituted no more than 5 per cent prior to 1519, but by the 1550s they were some 16 per cent, and in the 1560s they were as many as 28 per cent. Most were single; in the new lands they carved out their own destiny, fighting where necessary alongside the men. Women who went to English America entered a somewhat different society that was still strongly regulated by the customs of the Old World, but there were still benefits. They were liable to find greater opportunities for marriage, encountered greater possibility of social mobility, and encountered less male arrogance.[59]

Some elite women were constantly active in public life and politics, which gave them an escape normally reserved for men. At the highest level, the role was based on matriarchy. Ladies such as Margaret, Countess of Salisbury, or María Pacheco, leader of the Comuneros in Toledo in the 1520s, were fulfilling roles created by their family position rather than by the accident of their sex. Even in wholly traditional societies, kinship and matriarchy allowed women to dictate family politics, down as far as the context of the village community. On occasion they might direct military campaigns, as the Princess of Condé did during the Fronde in the 1650s.

Blood, rank and kinship allowed noble women to play a much larger part in post-medieval politics than is commonly accepted by traditional accounts, which have tended to emphasise only male roles. While Philip II of Spain's son-in-law the Duke of Savoy was away at the battle-front in the 1590s, his place as chairman of the state council of Savoy was regularly, and with great effectiveness, occupied by his wife Catalina. The number of such women is legion. The many heads of state who were women were by no means deprived of their gender. It is true that their role-function was essentially as males, for the crown was considered to be a male symbol. But the attendant support given to their role usually emphasised their female gender, notably in the active propaganda created around Elizabeth I of England as personification of the goddess Astrea.[60] In the mythical speech that Elizabeth is said to have made at Tilbury in 1588, she claimed that 'I have the body of a woman, but I have the heart and stomach of a king'. It was a clever publicity exercise on the theme of gender.[61] Elizabeth was celebrated by poets and artists not only as a symbol of imperial, dynastic and religious power – all of them normally the preserve of men – but also as a virgin, a goddess, and an ideal of male chivalry.

It is important to emphasise, consequently, that the exercise of power by women at every level was widely accepted in early modern Europe. There was not, as sometimes suggested,[62] a permanent male dominance. The vocabulary of politics was normally expressed in the person of the male, for all language was (until our own day) predicated on the male; all civil authority, moreover, was normally patriarchal. But female rule was respected wherever it operated, whether in the cult of Elizabeth in England or that of Isabella in Castile. The frequently quoted attack of John Knox against Mary Stuart and Mary Tudor, in his *First Blast of the Trumpet Against the Monstrous Regiment of Women* (1558), was wholly exceptional and motivated by religion. Political theorists who based their idea of power uniquely on patriarchy, such as Filmer or James I, were untypical and had few followers. The only western state that insisted on applying principles of male dynastic power (the so-called Salic law) was France, where ironically, women dominated the political scenario for the best part of the century 1558–1651. The problems implicit in female rule over the state arose less from the sex of the ruler than from related questions, notably the issue of hereditary succession. Doubts over the succession, and therefore over political stability in the state, plagued the exercise of power by Mary Stuart, Elizabeth and Catherine de Médicis. The failure of Isabella of Castile to produce a reliable heir handed her country over to a foreign dynasty, the Habsburgs. There were, obviously, female rulers who flopped, but they appear to have done so less because of their sex than because of their own independent attitudes. Christina of Sweden is an outstanding example of a woman with great personal gifts but an equally great inability to accept the limitations imposed on her by an overwhelmingly male power apparatus.

But women also had an important cultural role, whose possibilities were determined always by the social level to which they belonged. Either personally or through their husbands, women in sixteenth-century France played an extraordinary part in the dissemination of ideas sympathetic to Calvinism, particularly in the merchant and professional classes.[63] The cultural role continued to be one of the most profound contributions made by educated women in Europe.[64] The literary salons of seventeenth-century Paris were pioneered by that of the Marquise de Rambouillet, frequented by the great names of the time: 'she taught good taste to all her contemporaries', it was commented.[65] The tradition continued into the early Bourbon period. In the same way, Sophie Charlotte of Brandenburg-Prussia became patron to the philosophical and musical circles of Berlin. Numerous individual women successfully made their way as creative persons in their own right. The painter Sofonisba Anguissola in the Spain of Philip II, and the writer Aphra Behn in seventeenth-century England, both of whom made their living exclusively through painting and writing respectively, were pioneers of the new category of professional women. Others were less successful with their writing but no less determined to succeed. 'Since all heroic actions and public employments are denied our sex', wrote Margaret Cavendish, Duchess of Newcastle, in the seventeenth century, that 'is the cause I write so much'. Despite their signal contribution, creative women were living in an environment where male values dominated; they were therefore either mocked, as Molière mocked at the late seventeenth-century group associated with Mlle de Scudéry, or not taken seriously. The English, however, were generous enough to agree that Aphra Behn be buried among the immortals in Westminster Abbey.

Outside their public role, women significantly made their mark on subsequent generations through their private escapes into the intimacy of diaries. In England, known diaries began in the seventeenth century, and women who kept them were exclusively from the elite classes. Perhaps the most remarkable case was that of Lady Margaret Hoby, of Yorkshire, who between 1599 and 1605 kept the first known diary in English by a woman. Her pages reflected her life as a country lady but managed also to exclude virtually all reference to her husband. By contrast, most lady diarists reflected clearly their close dependence on the men in their household, whether father or husband. A few managed to write principally about themselves. The first extant autobiography in English by a woman was that of Lady Grace Mildmay, written in 1619.

Women, honour and the law; crime and witchcraft

Men controlled early modern society, but women were not excluded from their proper social roles, which included protecting their own honour and that of the community. As we have seen above, honour was a protean concept with constantly changing rules. Its relevance to women also varied according to time and place. Some traditional attitudes held that exclusively men possessed honour, and that women partook of it through obedience. 'Your sex', the Marquis of Halifax informed his daughter, in a tract that was published in 1688 and ran through seventeen editions in a century, 'wanteth our Reason for your conduct and our Strength for your protection'. On this view, a woman's good reputation depended on her acceptance of male power, and her fulfilment of the roles assigned to her. In marriage, for example, perfect fidelity was required of a woman, whereas infidelity in a man was not normally deemed dishonourable; in compact communities men might on occasion be publicly criticised for infidelity, but women ran the risk of an unwanted birth that could bring lasting shame. In work, certain professions were held to be an exclusively male domain, and women were relegated to marginal activities.

This patriarchal and male-dictated concept of honour, however, did not always square with what happened in the complex real world. Social practice at every level, from court down to village, often gave many women an opportunity to assert their own honour, without thereby presenting any threat to male hegemony. Chastity, for example, was traditionally considered a fundamental part of female honour, and women who lost it outside the normal course of marriage were 'dishonoured'. Women who habitually resorted to sex without marriage were of course quite dishonourable, or 'whores'. In reality, these attitudes persisted only in small or simple societies. In more cosmopolitan societies, such as Restoration London,[66] it was possible for high-class whores to be honoured and respected because their social rank gave them honour. In cases of adultery, the so-called 'double standard' did not always operate. The offending woman clearly invited shame, especially if she gave birth to an unlawful child. But the husband was also seen, by many authoritative commentators, to have acted dishonourably. Women were dishonoured by a husband's adultery, the Spanish writer Vicente Mexía argued, and could legitimately plead for a separation. Another Spanish authority, writing in 1593, affirmed that a wife could refuse to have any sexual intercourse with her husband if he had committed adultery.[67] It seems fair to conclude that the official Christian view, whether Protestant or Catholic, 'never accepted the double standard'.[68] Women, especially among the popular classes, were often capable of prevailing against the dominant male ethic. They might turn against a man the reputation he sought to preserve, by accusing him publicly of violence and rape; in other cases they might blackmail him. Though normally at a disadvantage, women too had their weapons, and the 'double standard' operated by males did not always predominate.[69]

At the same time, male dominance carried with it certain responsibilities, and men who did not fulfil them were called to account. Wife-beating is a prominent example of a practice that was usually criticised by moralists, frowned on by neighbours, and prosecuted (though with negligible penalties) by legal systems.[70] Though always permitted, it came to be viewed as dishonourable conduct for a man. The diocesan courts in sixteenth-century Catalonia made it clear that beating one's wife or failing to support her with the means necessary to her sustenance were infringements of her honour and adequate grounds for legal separation. In this sense, a wife asserted her honour through her husband's dishonour; she vindicated herself simply by the shame the husband brought on himself. In all other aspects of the marital relationship, the woman equally had an opportunity to demonstrate that her role invited respect.

Similarly, a husband who failed to perform his sexual duties was seen to have acted dishonourably. Village rituals, such as the charivari, exposed his shame and thereby vindicated the wife. Traditional societies also sharply criticised husbands who allowed their wives to dominate them. In all the foregoing cases, a man's reputation was in some sense dictated by the woman, and it was the community that judged whether the man was fulfilling his gender role adequately. In these circumstances, the patriarchy of man in the household and in society was not absolutely assured, but was frequently threatened and had to be examined and revised. The seventeenth-century theatre in England, as instanced in productions of Shakespeare's *Taming of the Shrew*, reminded the public of the problem.[71] Some men undoubtedly took precautions to ensure that all domestic roles, male and female, were adequately performed. Few perhaps were as conscientious as the Puritan Nehemiah Wallington, who in 1622 drew up rules for the conduct of his household, which he had signed by his servants and apprentice as well as by his wife.[72]

The complex relation between sexual roles and honour was, in the final instance, more favourable to the man. Men could suffer grievously in their honour because of impotence or sexual misdemeanour or mistreatment of their wives, but there were other extensive areas where they were free to play different roles and vindicate themselves, such as in politics or in war. Women, by contrast, had a smaller choice of roles and therefore fewer opportunities. 'Whereas for a woman sexual reputation was the whole of her reputation, for a man it was merely one part.'[73]

There were certain very limited areas where women might assert their social position, even against accepted male norms. The unique role of women as providers for their children gave them a voice in times of social discontent. As key participants in many of the riots and rebellions of the period, they were in a sense the upholders of the community and its norms.[74] Their role is most clearly illustrated by the significant part they played in urban riots. One example is that of the city of Córdoba, where in the spring of 1652 a poor woman went weeping through the streets, holding the body of her son who had died of hunger. Other women responded to the scene of misery, and persuaded their men to join the protest. By the end of the morning a popular rising took over control of the city.

In riots and disorders where food supply and therefore community survival was the main issue, women played a key role. They were prominent in seventeenth-century English food disturbances.[75] Similarly, they participated actively in protests made under cover of ritual community celebrations such as carnivals. In these events they were responsible for some of the more ferocious excesses, but more normally their role was a ritualistic defiance of the forces (inevitably male) of authority and of repression. Female violence frequently took the form of ridiculing the enemies of the community, so much so that a folklore tradition consented to males dressing up as women (as in the case of the Lady Skimmington, used in the west of England) in order to perform the same function. By contrast, women had a purely ancillary role in extended popular risings, where the emphasis was for the most part on military action.

Woman's status and honour evidently depended on an infinite number of contexts, varying according to class and community. Cases where women appealed to or came into conflict with the law highlight the ambiguous situation in which they stood over their social reputation. The primarily domestic situation of women meant that they appeared very little in statistics of public crime: most serious and violent crime was male, frequently with women as victims. By contrast, women were prosecuted for special lesser offences, usually related to their domestic and sexual role. It does not appear valid to say that they were unequal (to men) before the law, since in cases of serious crime such as murder they were treated with equal severity. On the other hand, certain social attitudes affected them more directly: in Renaissance Italy, only women appear to have been prosecuted for infringing the sumptuary laws regarding dress in public.[76]

A special crime for which women alone were indicted was 'infanticide'.[77] It could represent as much as 10 per cent of detected homicides, and in some jurisdictions such as in northern France the rate was much higher. The typical accused woman was of low social ranking and was unmarried or a widow; she was treated with the rigour of the law if she could not prove that the death was accidental. Death by accident was normally the consequence of bad treatment or neglect, or simply of having put the infant out to nurse. Deaths that had the appearance of being deliberate were, according to the records, caused by mothers who had illegitimate children. The offence led in England to a parliamentary Act (1624) 'to prevent the murthering of bastard children'. The crime was, until a change of attitudes in the eighteenth century, normally dealt with severely, and possibly more women were executed for it than for any offence other than witchcraft.

Women were most vulnerable in criminal cases involving sorcery. There were exceptions to this rule, as in northern France and in Aragon, where during the sixteenth century more men than women were prosecuted for the offence of witchcraft. Normally, females predominated among the accused. The fact that they made up the overwhelming majority of those prosecuted in Europe was due less to the prejudice of the law than to the nature of the local societies within which the accusations originated. Several scholars have emphasised recently that witches were persecuted not because they were women but because they were witches. The writings of those who attacked witchcraft at the time show no firm prejudice against women as women.[78] There were, certainly, cultural and sexual considerations that put women more at risk. A woman's role as creator, as midwife, as healer (the 'wise-woman' of the village), as visionary, provided points at which an anguished male-dominated society might choose to victimise her for sudden disasters caused by crop failures or epidemics. Any analysis of the phenomenon of women in witchcraft persecution must look equally at the problems of the accusing society, and the vulnerable position of the female accused. For though males featured frequently as accused, all the treatises of the time have no hesitation in categorising the victims as female. One of the most adamant opponents of the witch persecution in seventeenth-century Spain was the Jesuit Pere Gil, who knew many of the accused and described them (1619) as 'simple-minded women of little intelligence, feeble and timid, most of them poor, untaught in Christian doctrine and easily deceived'. 'There is little opposition', he wrote, 'when the villages and people say of the witches that they do infinite ills and deserve a thousand deaths. For since they are poor, exposed, simple-minded and ignorant in the Christian religion, no one takes their side.'[79] Gil's analysis, it should be noted, refers to such women because they were a disadvantaged population in the villages, not because they were women. The majority of female accused were old, often marginalised by their communities. But a few were also young, either victims of village tensions or involved through accusations levelled against relatives. Pere Gil gives the interesting information that members of their own family in fact denounced many accused. In some witchcraft cases in Augsburg, accusations reflected deep antagonisms among women themselves, and often the operating motive was simply envy.[80]

8

SOCIAL DISCIPLINE AND MARGINALITY

> Though the number of the poore do dailie encrease, all things yet worketh for the worst in their behalfe.
>
> (Thomas Dekker, *Greevous Grones for the Poore*, 1622)

Community discipline and sexual morality

Traditional communities, anxious to conserve their social norms and good order, attempted to correct divergent behaviour and remedy failures of conduct. In a changing world, the means to achieve this were not always available: policing systems, where they existed, had limited authority. Moreover, there were no commonly accepted norms about what represented incorrect behaviour, or in what way it could be regulated. Long before the sixteenth century, small societies in Europe had used their local processes of control to regulate conflict and instability. In fourteenth-century Norfolk, the local court prosecuted operators of brothels less because of moral concern than because it 'caused controversy and discord between neighbours'.[1]

One of the novelties of the early modern period was the appearance of writings that, for the first time, attempted to grapple with the issues. There was concern, for example, about the decay of the habit of neighbourliness. Many claimed to observe a decline in good manners and courtesy. There were laments about the end of traditional hospitality. All these old customs had regulated relationships in the traditional community, preserving the framework of known society. Their breakdown was seen as the end of an era. Controversies arose, moreover, about whether one should give food and alms to the indigent. In Reformation Europe, where religious change also precipitated changes in the relationship between lords and vassals, and between neighbours in the same village, the breakdown in social relations came sooner than in the Mediterranean, where change was slower. Hospitality in the era of confessional conflict was unlikely to be extended to those of another religion. Because of this, minority communities (such as the Huguenot immigrants in England) tended to evolve their own systems of mutual help, and as a consequence groups such as Huguenots, Moriscos and Jews tended not to have any visible poor. Among lords and gentry the custom of keeping open house – defined in England in 1698 as 'a liberal entertainment of all sorts of men at one's house, whether neighbours or strangers, with kindness, especially with meat, drink and lodgings'[2] – was eroded by social changes and rising costs. But hospitality continued as a primary obligation of all social relations, not only among the elite but also within the village community, where every rite of passage was a public event that required the dispensation of neighbourly kindness in the form of food and drink.[3] In the Mediterranean, hospitality appears to have been less susceptible to decay, and traditional attitudes survived. In Languedoc the model of *honnêteté* involved respecting and performing one's duties to others, and behaving correctly to them.[4] In Valencia the principal grandee, the Duke of Gandía, was still in the 1660s spending large sums at his palace in Gandía (where he did not normally live, since he was resident in Madrid) on maintaining an open table of meals for his vassals and for travellers.

Discipline involved also the regulation of relationships within the community, above all those affecting sexuality. Traditionally the community had taken an interest in the moral behaviour of its members, and had expressed its preferences about who married whom. If a new bride came from out-of-town, the young men of the village would state their approval or disapproval through time-honoured rituals such as demanding a nominal payment at the church door before the girl could be allowed in to get married. In southern France,[5] parish standards were enforced by the youth confraternity known as the *garçons de la paroisse*, who for a year after the marriage ceremony supervised the progress of the couple, to see that the husband behaved and that the wife was dutifully pregnant. Wherever sexual norms were broken, such as if the husband allowed himself to become henpecked, the youths would stage a farce known in one form or another throughout western Europe, and termed 'charivari' in French-speaking lands. Taking the form of discordant noise or 'rough music'[6] performed by groups of youth beating on utensils, the charivari was most frequently staged as a social protest against the remarriage of widows and widowers.[7] The custom was testimony to continued community vigilance of the rites of marriage, which were deemed to affect not merely the couple but the whole parish.[8] But in the confessional age the official Church, which would have preferred to exercise control itself, did not look with approval on community regulation of marriage and morals. From the 1540s in Spain there were firm episcopal prohibitions of the charivari, and the Inquisition occasionally prosecuted those who performed it. The prohibitions were largely ineffective. Charivaris were practised in England and in France through the eighteenth century, and in nineteenth-century Valencia a traveller testified to their survival. The intervention of the ecclesiastical authorities was, however, a pointer to a new and significant trend.

Questions of conduct and morality began to appear in the law courts. Church tribunals, or consistories, had traditionally dealt with issues of morality; but a novelty of the age of religious conflict was the attention given by them to sexual questions. The Protestant Reformation seems to have taken considerable initiative in the matter. The Reformation secularised the consistory courts by removing all their clerical members and appointing only laymen: this happened, for example, in Neuchâtel and Augsburg. The same moral discipline prevailed, but this time under Protestant control. In Neuchâtel the seigneurial consistory at Valangin prosecuted 2,355 persons in the period 1590–1667: the offences included fornication, insults and drunkenness.[9] Attempts to control sexual morality loomed large in the programme of the Reformed churches in Scotland.[10] In Sweden the prosecution of sexual offences increased in early modern times as a consequence of the Reformation.[11] At the same period the Counter-Reformation also put sexual discipline at the top of its agenda. In Spain the Inquisition began from the 1550s to intrude into spheres of personal conduct that had never before been the subject of enquiry.

The attempt to improve sexual manners was part of the programme of all religious reformers, both Protestant and Catholic. We may choose one aspect at random. Community tradition had sanctioned a number of celebrations during which there might be contact between the sexes, notably the village fair or dance. Dancing had featured in traditional festivities, both popular and sacred.[12] In the Mediterranean, the custom also existed of priests dancing before the altar in church, perhaps in imitation of David dancing before the Ark of the Covenant. From the sixteenth century, zealots considered dancing of any kind indecent and attempted to prohibit it. In Holland the Calvinist pastors issued injunctions forbidding dancing at weddings.[13] In Spain some of the clergy attempted to prohibit dancing in popular processions, and banned village dances. One Franciscan friar took the view that any dancing between males and females was sinful, and that it was only permissible for women to dance with women or men with men.

There were periods of severe sexual repression in specific societies, such as seventeenth-century England during the years when the Puritans were in control of the machinery of state. But it would be misleading to consider that Puritans were looking only at the sexual side of misconduct. John Milton in 1641 considered that 'discipline is not only the removal of disorder, but the very image of virtue', and that it affected all aspects of social and political conduct.[14] It is doubtful if the intrusion of religious authorities into the sphere of public morality had much effect,[15] except where the community gave full support. Community norms rather than religious belief had always governed sexual conduct, and this continued to be the rule. In the eighteenth century, examples from France and Germany show that dancing continued as an uninterrupted feature of social life, but under the vigilant eye of local people.[16]

Controlling poverty

The decline of neighbourliness was perceived acutely by contemporaries in their response to growing poverty. The numbers of the urban poor alarmed Juan Luis Vives, who censured them for entering churches while the faithful were at prayer:

'they push through the congregation, deformed by sores, exuding an unbearable smell from their bodies'. Sixtus V in 1587 complained of vagrants in Rome who 'fill with their groans and cries not only public places and private houses but the churches themselves; they provoke alarms and incidents; they roam like brute beasts with no other care than the search for food'. Pierre de l'Estoile reported of Paris in 1596 that 'the crowds of poor in the street were so great that one could not pass through'.

But who were the poor, and how were they defined? A reliable measurement of 'poverty' at that period is difficult to come by.[17] In a town those who were registered to receive poor relief were normally categorised as poor, but a further number considered to be indigent might also receive relief in dearth years, and beyond these were the families who were possibly exempt from taxation because of their lack of means. Thus in Augsburg in 1558, 5 per cent of the citizens were in regular receipt of poor relief, a further 5 per cent might need help in crisis years, and in total 47 per cent of the citizens were considered too poor to pay taxes.[18] In western Europe over one fifth of a town's population might consist of the wholly poor. In Louvain in the mid-sixteenth century, the 'poor' constituted 21.7 per cent of the population, and in Leiden about 40 per cent. In Brussels the proportion was 21 per cent, and in Segovia in 1561 one sixth were registered as poor, without counting vagrants. In Elizabethan London, the poor were about 14 per cent of the population.[19] In the towns of Leicester and Exeter, an estimated half of the population lived below the poverty line. In Bergamo in 1575, 35 per cent of a population of 20,000 were registered as poor, a minimum figure that included 'the aged, the sick, and children aged fifteen or below'.

While poverty was an undeniable feature of the towns, with their large numbers of unemployed, it was not only an urban phenomenon. Many of the poor came originally from the countryside. In Normandy in the early 1500s a contemporary census of forty-six rural parishes described 24 per cent of the families as 'poor and beggars'. An estimate for eighteen villages in Lower Saxony suggests that the poor were nearly 30 per cent of the population. For both town and country, poverty was a normal experience. In the villages around sixteenth-century Valladolid, up to one fifth of the rural population was poor. A pamphleteer of 1641 estimated that 'the fourth part of the inhabitants of most of the parishes of England are miserable poor people and (harvest-time excepted) without any subsistence'.

As towns grew, classes became economically segregated. In Exeter there was a nucleus of wealthy residential areas in the city centre, in the parish of St Petrock, surrounded by a ring of poorer districts, some outside the city walls. In Valladolid and in Amiens, the centre was held by the propertied classes and the poor lived in the outer parishes. When poor relief was handed out, women and children featured as the majority among the registered poor. Of the 765 people qualifying for relief in the parish of St Gertrude in Louvain in 1541, over half were children. In 1561 in Segovia, women were 60 per cent of the adult poor and in Medina del Campo 83 per cent. Of the poor registered in Norwich in

1570, nearly half were children; in Huddersfield in 1622 children were 54 per cent. The children were normally under the age of fifteen, a section of the urban poor that was unable to find employment or was orphaned through the death of their fathers. Logically, they featured prominently in schemes for poor relief. An impressive body of writing was dedicated to the education of young people and to the rescue of abandoned infants. Spanish writers were second to none in their concern. Luis Vives devoted a chapter to children in his study on the poor, leading clergy founded hospices for infants, the royal physician Luis Mercado published a work (1611) on the education of children, and the monk Pedro Ponce de León devised in the 1580s a method for teaching deaf and dumb children to communicate.[20]

'Poverty' was the result of an imbalance in the distribution of resources. It was aggravated in the sixteenth century by economic developments that converted it into a permanent feature of western civilisation. The change that provoked most comment at the time was the rise in prices, sometimes identified by historians as a 'price revolution'. In Spain Alonso de Herrera claimed (1513) that 'a pound of mutton now costs as much as a whole sheep used to'. Jean Bodin in France testified (1568) that 'the price of things fifty or sixty years ago was one-tenth what it is at present'. All classes suffered: the famous Italian engineer Antonelli, on contract to Philip II, claimed (1581) that in Spain 'the prices of goods have risen so much that seigneurs, gentlemen, commoners and the clergy cannot live on their incomes'. Nearly all the items that made up the ordinary stock of consumer goods rose appreciably in cost. Because the inflation was imperfectly understood, it was blamed in the first place on speculators and hoarders of food. But price changes were also provoked by currency devaluation, which all over Europe accelerated monetary inflation. Meanwhile, in 1568 Bodin published a tract arguing that 'the principal and almost the only' cause of the price rise was '(a reason that no one has yet suggested) the abundance of gold and silver' from America. His argument (which in fact had been proposed already in 1556 by the Salamanca jurist Martin de Azpilcueta), was to become the classic exposition of the origins of the price revolution.

In a less flexible economy than ours is today, the impact on incomes was severe. 'In times past', observed an English commentator in 1581, 'he hath been accounted rich and wealthy who was worth thirty or forty pounds; but in our days the man of that estimation is reputed next neighbour to a beggar'. In the city of Speyer between 1520 and 1621, wages nearly trebled but over the same period the price of rye, a basic staple food, increased by fifteen times, that of wheat thirteen times, that of peas fourteen times, of meat sixfold, and of salt sixfold. In Poitou a farmhand's wages in 1578 could purchase only 52 per cent of what they could have bought in 1470. In Languedoc, agricultural wages that stood at an index of 100 in 1500 fell to an index of 44 by 1600. All sections of the labouring class were severely hit.

There were many workers for whom a money wage formed only a small part of income, since they were paid in kind – usually one or two meals daily – and were consequently less dependent on ready cash. This group often included the unskilled labourers in the towns, and over large areas of Europe formed an absolute majority of the rural working population. Many serfs, for example, were paid entirely in kind. The social problem in the sixteenth century was not, therefore, so much one of wages (since so few depended entirely on wages for a living) as one of rents, prices and debts, issues which affected both the skilled craftsman and the unskilled wage earner. Thanks to being paid in kind, and perhaps enjoying fixed rents, some workers might even be cushioned against inflation. There is no real doubt, however, that among the lower classes as a whole incomes were a serious casualty of the price rise.

The process of change on the land produced a considerable number of casualties. In England the independent small farmer, the yeoman, sometimes improved his lot and rose economically, but tended equally to suffer distress. Even in lands which, like Sweden, had a relatively free peasantry, changes in land values and soil exploitation led to the expropriation of a section of the peasant class and to the growth of unemployment, both urban and rural. Landlessness became a prime consequence of the rise in land values (in Myddle in Shropshire only 7 per cent of the population were without land in 1541–70; in 1631–60 the proportion was 31.2 per cent). At the same time vagrancy increased and agrarian conflict intensified.

Two widely differing views of the poor were held in this period. One, of an old humanist and Christian ancestry, felt that the poor deserved well of society since society had not done them well. The other, which obtained greater currency after the Reformation, was that the poor needed reforming, since their own incapacity had put them where they were. Martin Bucer declared that 'such as give themselves wilfully to the trade of begging be given and bent to all mischief'. The opposition to public charity, based on a concern for social order, was elsewhere reflected in a strong belief that class distinctions had been created by God, and that the poor must stay in their place. 'God hath made the pore', observed Sir John Cheke to the rebels in Kett's revolt, 'and hath made them to be pore that he myght shew his might and set them aloft when he listeth, for such cause as to hym seemeth, and pluck down the riche to hys state of povertie, to shew his power'. Others felt that rebellion was proof of the unwillingness of the poor to turn their hands to any useful thing. In England some Puritans (such as William Perkins) felt that to be poor was to be wicked, in conformity with a general belief that idleness was evil. For Perkins, vagrants were 'a cursed generation'.

Unemployment fed the political fear that 'idleness' bred mischief, which must be disciplined. The Elizabethan annalist Strype condemned vagabonds as 'lewd idle fellows…who run from Place to Place…to stir up Rumours, raise up Tales.…devising slanderous Tales and divulging to the People such kind of News as they thought might most readily move them to Uproars and Tumults'.[21] The fear of rumour, common to Elizabethan England and discernible in Shakespeare's plays, was fed by the conviction that the poor and simple were easily stirred to rebellion. Archbishop Whitgift observed that 'the people are commonly bent to novelties and to factions, and most ready to receive that doctrine that seemeth to be contrary to the present state and that inclineth to liberty'.

In the bigger towns a high level of unemployment might give justifiable cause for concern. Amiens in 1578, a city of perhaps 30,000 people, was stated to have had as many as 6,000 workers 'supported by the alms of the well-to-do'. In these circumstances charity could be seen as an attempt to stave off social unrest. In Troyes in 1574, those poor who came from outside the city were, according to a common practice, given leave to stay no more than twenty-four hours. The reason given was that 'the richest citizens began to live in fear of disturbance and of a popular riot by the said poor against them'.[22] Unemployment and poverty explains what happened in the city of Tours at Pentecost in May 1640. About 800 to 900 silkworkers who were dissatisfied with their wages staged an uprising. Soldiers were called in, and when these proved inadequate some royal troops were called as well. To penalise the people a tax was imposed. This led to another rising in September, when several tax officials had their throats cut, and the rioters threatened to put the city to the torch. The risk of riots was higher in Lyon, probably the biggest industrial city in Europe. Two thirds of its population of 100,000 were workers, some living in extreme poverty and many regularly unemployed. In 1619 about 6,000 of the workers were in receipt of poor relief of some sort; in 1642 the figure was 10,000. The lesson that unemployment bred insurrection was not forgotten in Spain. In 1679, the authorities in Granada, Spain's largest industrial centre, which had a population of some 100,000, estimated that the number of poor who depended on labour in the silk industry for their daily wage exceeded 20,000. Mindful of a previous uprising in 1648, steps were taken to relieve the distress, occasioned this time by the plague. When unemployment in Toledo threatened their livelihood in 1699, the silkworkers of that city protested that although over 3,000 were out of work, no steps had been taken to come to their aid. If this situation were to continue, they threatened,

> it would not be surprising if in order to obtain bread they were to resort to all the means permitted by natural law, and even to those not so permitted. The people have no wish to be angered nor to cause riots or scandal; all they desire is that their lot should be bettered.

The social tension brought about by unemployment was well described by an English writer in 1619: 'The poor hate the rich because they will not set them on work; and the rich hate the poor because they seem burdenous.'

Feared by their betters, the poor were still essential to their spiritual welfare for, as Catholic tradition proclaimed, to succour them was an act of charity. Since charity was given, the protagonist in *Guzmán de Alfarache* (1599) argued, less for the material welfare of the recipient than for the spiritual welfare of the donor, it might as well be given to the false poor as to the real. In the old medieval attitude to poverty, since poverty could never be eradicated ('the poor you have always with you', Christ had said) it must be used as a means of obtaining spiritual graces. Outdoor relief, later attacked as a positive encouragement to mendicancy, became a corporal work of mercy. Rich men prepared their way to heaven by leaving sums for the poor in their wills. In sixteenth-century Valladolid, the consciences of the rich were eased by the unusual practice of having an entourage of paupers bear the candles at the funeral; some pious rich even had themselves interred as paupers.

In the early sixteenth century the first studies on poverty appeared. The humanist Juan Luis Vives was the first to outline a methodical approach to poor relief, in his *De Subventione Pauperum* (*On the Relief of the Poor*) of 1526. His view of charity was the classic Christian one: the poor have a right to aid, and the propertied have an absolute moral obligation to help them. But he went beyond previous practice by opposing begging and rejecting the view that charity was mere material relief. Hospitals must be set up to take the poor off the streets, and relief must consist 'not in mere almsgiving but in all the ways by which a poor man can be uplifted'. The Christian state had a duty to maintain its less fortunate citizens and the task should not be left to private charity. Other Spanish writers addressed themselves to the problem.[23] Juan de Medina, in his *Plan of Poor Relief Practised in Some Spanish Towns* (1545), outlined a scheme to abolish begging and to hospitalise the sick and needy. His plans were apparently already being practised in Valladolid, and seem to have been partially successful. Domingo de Soto in the same year produced his *Considerations on the Poor*, and in 1598 came Cristóbal Pérez de Herrera's *Discourse on the Assistance of the Poor*. Juan de Mariana, in his *De Rege et Regis Institutione* (1599), confirmed the new emphasis on state intervention by urging that 'piety and justice necessitate relieving the poverty of invalids and the needy, caring for orphans and aiding those in want. Among all the duties of the Sovereign, this is the chief and most sublime.' The example of Spain contradicts a common assumption that it was the Reformation that was responsible for the laicisation of charity and the substitution of municipal for clerical relief.

There had always (it seemed) been poor, but contemporaries agreed that mass beggary was new; and there had always been vagrants, but mass vagabondage was apparently recent. The publication in Germany in 1510 of the *Liber Vagatorum* (*Beggars' Book*), which till then had circulated in manuscript; the expulsion of vagabonds from Paris by the Parlement in 1516; the beginning of urban poor relief in the 1520s; all seem to point to a specific period when people became more conscious of a problem. Harrison, in his *Description of England* (1577), identified the period of origin precisely when he claimed of organised beggary that 'it is not yet full threescore yeares since this trade began'. The Reformation and other religious changes played their part: Robert Aske, leader of the Pilgrimage of Grace, claimed that 'in the north parts much of the relief of the commons was by succour of abbeys', but this had vanished at the dissolution of the monasteries.

Public action over the rootless poor began in the early years of the sixteenth century.[24] A Vicenza noble wrote in 1528: 'you cannot walk down the street or stop in a square or church without multitudes surrounding you to beg for charity'. There was a surprising unanimity about the measures of control adopted. Augsburg in 1522 banned street begging and appointed six 'poor guardians' to supervise relief. Nuremberg followed suit, so did Strasbourg and Breslau in 1523, Regensburg and Magdeburg in 1524. Luis Vives was the direct inspiration for a scheme put into practice at Ypres in 1525. Between 1522 and 1545 some sixty towns on the continent (about thirty in Germany, fourteen in the Netherlands) reformed their poor relief system. Luther in 1523 helped to reorganise the system in Saxony, Zwingli did so in 1526 in Zürich, in 1541 Calvin passed an ordinance on relief in Geneva. All these schemes, both Catholic and Protestant, stressed three new principles: a ban on begging, centralisation of relief in civic hands, and compulsory work for the able-bodied. In 1528 Venice, where previously the religious fraternities (Scuole Grandi) had supervised charity, began a system of hospitals for the poor. In 1531 the civic authorities in Lyon, learning from the urban riots of April 1529 (the Grande Rebeyne), started to establish the famous Aumône Générale, which centralised relief and laid particular emphasis on the creation of jobs for the workless.

Many traditionalists deplored the new attitude. The Sorbonne in 1531 declared the ban on begging to be 'uncatholic', the mendicant orders were inevitably hostile, and the Anglican annalist John Stow lamented the passing of the 'ancient and charitable custom' of outdoor relief. On the other hand, Ignatius Loyola was so impressed by what he saw of the new system that when he returned to his Basque home town of Azpeitia in 1535 he helped introduce it there. By the mid-sixteenth century, the Counter-Reformation was giving its support to a revision of the medieval attitude. Relief was in future intended to secure the spiritual welfare of the recipient; his bodily welfare was only secondary, as was the spiritual benefit obtained by the donor. The recipient was required to mend his ways, resume his religious duties, and seek employment in order to help his dependants. Hospitalisation was meant to help him achieve all this, through giving him a bed, proximity to a chapel, and access to job-training schemes. Though the Church cooperated closely in all the new relief projects, in principle they were controlled and financed by the municipality or state. Charity was not therefore 'secularised', but it was largely taken out of private hands.[25]

One initial problem was to stem the flow of vagrants and localise the problem of the poor. The earliest control measures consisted in granting beggars a licence to beg within a certain area only, usually the place of their origin. In London in the 1520s, genuine local paupers were given licences and identification discs: all others were to be whipped out of town. The purpose of this was to dissociate begging from vagrancy. As the poor realised they could only beg in their own localities they would cease to drift, and vagrancy would soon cease. Charles V in Spain restricted beggars to an area within a radius of six leagues from their home towns. Under Philip II this method of control was centred on the parish:

the parish priest alone issued begging licences, each parish created officials to superintend the poor, and an attempt was made to register all vagrants. The system of licences failed completely, partly because it was easy to counterfeit them. In Scotland, the laws restricting beggars to their native parishes were passed in 1535, 1551 and 1555, and not renewed thereafter. In 1556 the Cambridgeshire authorities banned all begging whatsoever and suspended the licence system. Norwich followed this example. By mid-century, the licence system was being discarded.

At about the same time the local authorities resorted to the dual system of institutional care and outdoor relief.[26] Institutional care was provided through hospitals: in 1544 the great pre-Reformation London hospital of St Bartholomew's was re-founded, and by 1557 there were four 'royal' hospitals in the city – St Bartholomew's, Christ's, Bridewell and St Thomas'. In order to help pay for such institutions, a compulsory tax for poor relief was decreed in London. Other local authorities followed suit. In order to maintain its workhouses or 'houses of correction', Norwich in 1557 issued regulations for compulsory taxation. In France a similar procedure was followed. The Paris authorities in 1554 set up their first poor hospital, at Saint-Germain; this was subsequently called the Hôpital des Petites Maisons and lasted till the end of the *ancien régime*. Hospitals were meant almost exclusively for the invalid poor; for the able-bodied, workhouses were set up in all the major towns of England and France. They offered refuge and employment, neither in a very appealing form, to those who had no other way of earning their living. Like England, France delegated control of poor relief to the localities. The ordinances of Moulins (1566) and Blois (1579) stipulated that local authorities should raise money through parish collections and tax levies. Lyon was perhaps the earliest of all French cities to provide for the unemployed, and seems to have been the first to set up workhouses: the Aumône Générale was in existence as early as 1533, and was replaced in 1614 by the much larger Hôpital Général de la Charité.

The English poor relief system mirrored those on the continent. Harsh laws were passed against vagrants; a pamphleteer of 1580 denounced 'that loathsome monster idleness'. In 1547 a statute specified slavery as one penalty for vagrancy. Two years later the slavery clauses were repealed, but in 1572 another harsh proposal became law. By this act a vagrant could be whipped and bored through the ear on the first offence, adjudged a felon on the second, and be punished by death on the third. All these penalties were repealed in 1593.

To preserve public order and to keep the poor honest, work must be made available. 'This is the best charity', wrote a seventeenth-century Puritan, 'so to relieve the poor as we keep them in labour. It benefits the giver to have them labour; it benefits the commonweal to suffer no drones, nor to nourish any in idleness; it benefits the poor themselves.' The famous Statute of Artificers (1563) was an elaborate scheme to put the able-bodied to work. Then, at the end of the reign of Queen Elizabeth, a comprehensive act to regulate poor relief was passed. This, the Act of 1597–8, was amended and re-enacted in 1601.

Together, the legislation of these years formed the basis of poor relief in England for the next two centuries. Poor relief was localised: it was placed in the control of churchwardens of the parish and four overseers of the poor appointed every Easter by the justices of the peace. The poor were divided into categories, each of which was to receive particular treatment. The able-bodied poor were either to be put to work or confined in houses of correction; children were likewise either to be set to work or apprenticed; and the sick and maimed poor were to be housed and cared for 'at the general charges of the parish, or otherwise of the hundred or the county'. Begging and vagrancy were prohibited. To finance the work of the Act, a compulsory poor rate was to be raised in each locality. This legislation was devised to meet a severe emergency, for these were years of great economic distress throughout Europe. Predictably, its success was only partial. The harsh regime of the workhouses or houses of correction resembled prison life, and were hated more than prison: their purpose clearly was to make life so unbearable that inmates would prefer to seek work outside. A Somerset Justice of the Peace, Edward Hext, cited some vagrants who 'confessed felony unto me; by which they hazarded their lives; to the end they would not be sent to the House of Correction, where they should be forced to work'. The machinery to run the Poor Law was not always adequate. An observer of the situation in southeast England in 1622, Thomas Dekker, reported that 'though the number of the Poore do dailie encrease, all things yet worketh for the worst in their behalfe. For there hath beene no collection for them, no not these seven yeares in many parishes of this land, especiallie in countrie townes.'

The resort to houses of correction has been seen as the first stage of 'the great confinement'.[27] On this view, there was an increasing move in western Europe to criminalise poverty and resolve it by shutting the poor away. Up to the mid-eighteenth century, however, there is very limited evidence for the thesis. Houses of correction were limited to a few major cities; they consequently catered for only a small proportion of the poor; and many countries had no such institutions. The vast mass of the poor, whether beggars or criminals, operated freely outside the ambit of corrective institutions. The Amsterdam workhouse in the seventeenth century, for example, had room for only seventy persons, by no means an adequate response to the social problem it was supposed to confront.

Institutionalisation of relief was only one of the many solutions used to tackle the problems of poverty and mass unemployment. Regulation of wages and prices was also necessary. Outdoor relief and food subsidies continued: in 1623 the bailiffs of Derby reported that 'wee have at the charge of the cheife and ablest inhabitants of this Burrowe provided 140 quarters of corne which wee weekely afford to the poore as their necessities require under the common price of the markett'. Sometimes the drastic measure of forced emigration was proposed. In 1617 one London parish contributed 'towards the transportation of a hundred children to Virginia by the Lord Mayor's appointment'. Vagrants were occasionally transported, and on one occasion during the Protectorate it was suggested that prostitutes be expelled to America. Numerically, however, compulsory emigration was not significant. Instead, further changes were introduced into the poor relief system. At Bristol in 1696, for example, John Cary modified the organisation of workhouses.

French practice followed the same general lines, but lacked the important central direction provided in England by Privy Council and Parliament. Compulsory hospitalisation of the poor was ordered in a decree of 1611, but discontinued as general policy after 1616, though there were subsequent efforts (as in the 1629 Code Michaud) to impose the principle on municipalities. Each region and city continued local practice. In Aix-en-Provence, for example, a general hospital or Miséricorde was founded in 1590 and designed to help both disabled and able-bodied poor. In 1640 alone three important charities were founded in the city: the Charité (a general hospital), the Refuge (for prostitutes), and the Providence (for homeless women). Large general hospitals were established in Paris in 1612 (the Pitié) and in Lyon in 1614 (the Charité).

No significant progress towards change was made in France until mid-century, when the religious grouping known as the Company of the Blessed Sacrament turned its considerable energy and wealth to the problem of poverty. The Company was firmly committed to incarcerate the disorder of the poor. The establishment of a branch at Aix in 1638 was primarily responsible for the hospitals set up there in 1640. Other hospitals were set up at Marseille in 1639, Orléans in 1642, Grenoble in 1661, and in other major cities. The plan for the Company's Aumône at Toulouse revealed its hostility to traditional almsgiving, which was regarded as useless to protect 'the poor, who by birth should serve the rich'.[28] In 1656 the Company founded the Hôpital Général des Pauvres at Paris. The institution was made deliberately unpleasant. The inmates could be punished by the directors of the hospital, all their activities were timetabled, and they were to be 'clothed in grey robes and caps and have each on their robes a general mark and a particular number'.

A collaborator of the Company, St Vincent de Paul, became the best known of all Christian servants of the poor. Combining both a devotion to the medieval ideal of poverty and a commitment to the reforming concepts of the Counter-Reformation, he distributed outdoor relief on one hand and founded hospitals on the other. His hospital for beggars, the Nom-de-Jésus (1653), provided both shelter and obligatory work. Throughout the north of France in the worst years of the Thirty Years War and the Fronde, St Vincent and his helpers were everywhere present to save lives as well as souls. 'For the last two years', states a letter of 1653 to Vincent,

> the whole of Champagne and this town in particular have lived only from your charity. All the countryside would have been deserted and all the inhabitants dead from hunger if you had not sent someone to relieve them from poverty and give them life.

From the 1650s, when better times returned to France, the government turned to a policy of hospitalisation. Colbert later stated that 'nothing is so detrimental to the state as the begging of able men'. An edict of 1662 prescribed the establishment of a general hospital in every city and large town. The policy was reaffirmed in a 1676 circular letter to all bishops and intendants, and after 1680 hospitals were founded with more frequency. In 1666 the Salpêtrière hospital in Paris housed 1,900 inmates, of whom 110 were blind and paralysed, eighty-five were imbeciles, ninety were infirm aged, sixty were epileptics, and 380 were aged over sixty. But only a fraction of the poor could be accommodated. Moreover, the milder regime of 'hospitals' was reserved mainly for women and younger persons; the few men who accepted charity were put into the harsher 'workhouses', from which they escaped if they could.

In Catholic and Protestant countries alike, it was principally the urban elite that gave to charity. In the United Provinces, where workhouses were established from 1589 after the publication of Dirck Coornhert's *Discipline of Knaves* (1567, published 1587), an English traveller observed in 1685 that 'there is nothing shows more the charitable inclination of the Hollanders than their great care in relieving, maintaining and educating their poor, for there are no beggars to be seen anywhere in the streets'. In England the London merchants distinguished themselves in giving to charity. One of the most significant aspects of the gifts made by London burghers was the so-called 'secularisation' of their donations. It has been estimated that over the period 1480–1540 the lesser merchants of London gave 61 per cent of their gifts to religious purposes and only 18 per cent directly to the poor. From 1601 to 1640, on the other hand, religion was given no more than 9.8 per cent, while the poor were given 52.4 per cent.[29] The figures do not prove that the poor benefited: in the earlier period money donated to religion often found its way to the poor, while in the later period it seldom reached the poor directly and went to institutions. But they demonstrate a growing concern with a grave social problem. In seventeenth-century Milan, private donations were by far the most important source of income for the poor. Milanese merchants gave large sums to the hospitals; among them was Giulio Cesare Lampugnani who, besides giving 90,000 lire in legacies to two charitable institutions, left, in his will in 1630, 196,000 lire in goods and 63,500 lire in capital for supplying the poor with bread, rice, coal and clothing.[30] In Spain, secular donations appear to have played a smaller part in financing poor relief. The example of Zamora, where religious confraternities were the principal donors, reflected a common pattern.[31] On the other hand, in seventeenth-century Madrid several lay brotherhoods came into existence, devoted to caring for the poor, paying for their education, and feeding, clothing and burying the indigent. The most active was the Brotherhood of the Refuge, which was founded in 1618 and went through its most flourishing period in the 1670s.[32]

The most striking aspect of the new poverty was its mobility. Many of the wandering poor were simply looking to earn their living. Subsistence migration, on the increase in the sixteenth century, was tied closely to the agrarian cycle. Evidence for England in the 1570s suggests that movement was at its highest in

August and September, at the end of the harvest, and then in April and March, at sowing time. In contrast with traditional seasonal migration, where workers moved to harvest areas in summer and then back to their villages in autumn, the new migrants were often rootless, like Nicholas Lawrence of Thanet, who explained that 'he is a poor labouring man and is sometime in one place and sometime in another'.

Migrants and vagrants were astonishingly mobile, travelling across nations and across seas. In the sixteenth century Valladolid received migrants from Galicia; Exeter had migrants from London. Of a sample of vagrants who passed through Amiens in the early seventeenth century, 20 per cent came from Normandy, 4 per cent from Franche Comté. The Irish, all too often involuntary migrants from their homeland, fled for economic relief to the land of the oppressors, England. There they met draconian poor laws. 'Philip Maicroft and his wife', says a record from Kent,

> were whipped the 8th March 1602, and had granted unto them six dayes to be conveyed from officer to officer out of the country of Kent, and then to be conveyed to Bristol, the place (as they say) where they landed, from thence to be conveyed to Dungarvan in Munster in Ireland, the place (as they say) of their birth.

The emigration from Ireland, especially in times of famine, could not be stemmed. In 1629 the mayor of Bristol reported that 'the scarcity of corn in Ireland is such that the poor people of that realm are enforced...to come over into this kingdom'. In 1633 the Somerset justices complained of a 'troop of Irish, that begin again to swarm out of that country'.

In western Europe the direction of movement was north to south, towards the Mediterranean. Between France and Spain the movement was almost exclusively southwards, dominated by the host of seasonal workers, often indistinguishable from vagrants. Fernández de Navarrete in the 1620s claimed that 'all the scum of Europe have come to Spain, so that there is hardly a deaf, dumb, lame or blind man in France, Germany, Italy or Flanders, who has not been to Castile'. It was reported of the hospital in Burgos (with considerable exaggeration) that 'every year, in conformity with its rules, it takes in, cares for and feeds for two or three days, from eight to ten thousand people from France, Gascony and other places'.

Criminal activity was popularly associated with two groups: vagabonds (and *picaros*), and beggars. The vagabond *picaro* was a literary type rather than a historical figure. He emerges as one of the preponderant themes in the literature of Spain's Golden Age. Mateo Alemán's *Guzmán de Alfarache* (1599) is commonly regarded as the earliest novel to describe the amoral vagabond life of the *picaro*. But already in the *Lazarillo de Tormes*, which appeared half a century earlier in 1554, the main features of the picaresque life were described, though without actually using the word *picaro*. The next famous work of this genre was Quevedo's *Buscón* (1626). The picaresque world of thieves, vagabonds, prostitutes and swindlers was not confined exclusively to Spanish society. Italy, Germany and France were no less afflicted by the same social type, and translations of the Spanish novels found a ready market in those countries. The *Lazarillo*, for instance, was translated into German in 1617, *Guzmán* two years earlier in 1615. Though the *picaro* was a literary creation, he was born out of a social context in which war, displacement, economic crisis and demographic disaster were endemic. But in literature the features of the delinquent were romanticised and his basic criminality glossed over.

The literature on beggars was even more exotic than that on *picaros*. From the late fifteenth century written sources speak of a strange and mysterious organisation called the Beggars' Brotherhood, with vagabonds and professional criminals under its sway. Romantic and imaginative literature on the Brotherhood, which appears to have been little more than a myth based on the late medieval predilection for the vagabond life, ranges from the anonymous *Liber Vagatonum* in Germany, to the *Vie Généreuse des Mercelots, Gueuz et Boesmiens* (1596) of Pechon de Ruby in France, and *Il Vagabondo* (1621) by the Italian, Rafaele Frianoro (a Dominican friar whose name in religion was Giacinto de Nobili). Many other writings, including several in English and Spanish, were also published on the same theme.[33]

Beggars had their folklore, their methods, and their impostures.[34] In Rome in 1595, when a youth was arrested for begging he informed the papal police that 'among us poor beggars there are many secret companies, and they are different because each has a distinctive activity'. He went on to name nineteen different types of imposture: the *famigotti*, for example, were beggars who pretended to be invalid soldiers; the *bistolfi* wore cassocks; the *gonsi* pretended to be rustic idiots. By 1621, when Frianoro was writing his book, the Italians had twenty-three categories of imposture; there were similar categories in other nations. Not all the details given by contemporaries about the beggars can be written off as fruit of a romantic imagination. The world of the Brotherhood was a recognisable 'underworld'. The seventeenth-century historian Henri Sauval testified that the beggars did not practise marriage nor did they frequent the sacraments, and if they entered a church it was only to cut purses. They were an anti-society, organised against it, disbelieving in its ethics and religion. They were also separated from it by the jargon, called *cant* in English, *Rotwelsch* in German, *argot* in French, *jerga de la germanía* in Spanish. Cant had a virtually international vocabulary. The first comprehensive account of it in English was Harman's *Caveat for Common Cursetors* (1567). In France *Le Jargon de l'Argot Réformé* (1628), and in Holland Adriaen van de Venne's *Tableau of the Ridiculous World* (1635) summarised both the language and the customs of the beggars.

The romantic legends about the beggars presented them as essentially vagabonds, tied to no locale, with their home in any nation they chose to reside in, true citizens of the world. In each major city, so the mythology went, they had a regular place of assembly, the so-called 'Court of Miracles'. Most frequently it was in the heart of the slum quarter. In Paris, Sauval tells us, 'it was in a very large square at the end of a large, stinking, noisome, unpaved cul de sac'. There, according to one legend from which the Court derived its name, all the poor and maimed who entered in emerged healed and upright. But, according to another version, the true miracle was that there 'the poorest among them is deemed the richest'. The need for beggars to resort to trickery and crime was explained by Rob Greene in his *Defence of Conny Catching* (1592): 'This is the Iron Age, wherein iniquitie hath the upper hande, and all conditions and estates of men seeke to live by their wittes, and he is counted the wisest that hath the deepest insight into the getting of gaines.'

The vagrant problem was also in part a gypsy problem. Gypsies appeared in eastern Europe in the fourteenth century, and in west and central Europe in the early fifteenth. Their coming coincided with the rise of organised begging and the persecution of witches, so they were often identified with both. They were repeatedly arrested and accused of sorcery because of the way in which they dabbled in magical cures and fortune-telling. In Hungary and Transylvania they were enslaved from the fifteenth century. In Moldavia they were sold at slave markets. In Germany in 1540 Agrippa denounced them because they

> lead a vagabond existence everywhere on earth, they camp outside town, in fields and at crossroads, and there set up their huts and tents, depending for a living on highway robbery, stealing, deceiving and barter, amusing people with fortune-telling and other impostures.[35]

In 1560 the Estates General at Orléans called on 'all those impostors known by the name of Bohemians or Egyptians to leave the kingdom under penalty of the galleys'. In Spain the harsh legislation included a 1633 decree ordering them 'no longer to dress as they do, and to forget their language', with bans on public assembly.

Disciplining crime

The disciplining of conduct, we have seen, entailed the disciplining of morality. In the sense that immoral conduct (what we might define as 'sin') was an offence against society, it was seen as a 'crime', and in effect many tribunals throughout the early modern period made no firm distinction between the two concepts. There was also no clear perception of what acts were legal offences: different social levels had different views. Was vagrancy, for example, a crime before certain laws made it so? The English Parliament in 1650 declared adultery to be a crime: was it therefore a crime? The enormous problems confronting any discussion of crime[36] are seen most clearly when attempts are made to measure it. Statistics for crime in pre-industrial Europe are notoriously incomplete: there were few policing bodies, arrests were easier to make in towns than in the countryside, and a large number of offences went wholly unpunished, creating a substantial 'dark figure' of undetected crime.

The existence at that time of multiple jurisdictions, with different courts competing to try the same offence, reduces seriously the significance of available statistics. In broad terms, the bulk of cases tried by European courts were crimes against persons or against property. The former usually took the form of violence, or the resolution of personal problems through injury; in large measure they were attacks and mutilations provoked by insults, dishonours and brawls. The picture has led many scholars to assume that early modern society, particularly in its lower echelons, was oppressively violent. If this is true, violence can be seen as a hallmark of a traditional society. By contrast, crimes against property have sometimes been seen as typical of a modernising society, where the accumulation of wealth and the growing gap between propertied and propertyless could lead to social conflict. The idea of an evolution of misdemeanours in western society from crimes of violence to crimes of theft, however, is not always sustained by available evidence. Moreover, it is incorrect to assume that the courts (and by extension members of society) were preoccupied only with offences involving theft or murder. At the Essex quarter sessions in 1629–31, some ninety-three cases of theft were prosecuted, but 698 people were also prosecuted for failing to observe work obligations, and 652 more were accused of offences in the drink trade.[37]

The statistics are clear on perhaps only one point: who the alleged offenders were. Of some 2,000 persons arrested on criminal charges in Cologne between 1568 and 1612, the majority (five sixths) were men, and of dependent or lowly status.[38] By contrast, the perspective of offences varied considerably. Violence was a constant of life in *ancien régime* Europe, notably for example in the rural Haute Auvergne in France, where between 1587 and 1664 two thirds of recorded offences involved violence against persons, and only one third were against property.[39] The scale of violence here led eventually in 1665 to the installation of special royal courts, the famous *grands jours*, to stamp out crime. Evidence for other tribunals suggests that offences against property may by contrast have been more preponderant, but always within the context of changing agrarian conditions.[40]

Historians are aware that the 'dark figure' of undocumented crime in early modern Europe is very large. Towns may have been adequately policed, but the greater part of the countryside lacked police forces or systems for enforcing law and order. Some basic problems may be summarised. In the first place, prosecution of crime was always selective. In many societies, such as in the Mediterranean, coercive violence was seen as acceptable because it was used as a mechanism to regulate social relations, protect personal and public honour, and control misdemeanours. In such an environment, some types of violence would not be seen as crimes. In the same way, when offences against persons and property were committed by those who controlled power, namely the nobility, they were not prosecuted. As the example of southwest France shows, nobles were responsible for a high proportion of rural violence.[41] 'You will see no one but poor and humble thieves being hanged', commented the bandit Oliver in

Grimmelshausen's *Simplicissimus* (1668). 'Where have you ever seen a person of high quality punished by the courts?'

In the second place, the offences prosecuted were usually *public*, those that occurred in public places and affected public order.[42] There is no guarantee that they represented the bulk of committed offences. A large number of 'crimes' that did not occur in the public domain, such as violence between persons and within the family, did not arrive in court. These private offences were not the sole preserve of the lower classes but common to all levels of society. In any case, then as now the parties to a conflict would make efforts to resolve their problems without recourse to the law. Prosecution through the courts can in some measure be seen as exceptional; it was certainly more common for rural communities to seek other solutions for offences.[43]

Third, there were many 'crimes' that did not fall within the jurisdiction of the governing authority. Early modern Europe was a mass of conflicting jurisdictions, with state, Church and seigneurial courts sometimes overlapping in authority (for example, the offence of sorcery might be subject to either a Church or a civil court, or to both). Some crimes make no appearance at all in the historical records of a court, simply because another local court (whose records may have disappeared) exercised authority in the matter. In France, a substantial number of disputes involving crime (theft, insults, assault) could be settled by the local public notary, and so seldom made their way to the criminal court;[44] for the historian who consults only court records, these cases never happened. In many regions the nobles still exercised authority over all justice, and even retained the power to pass death sentences. The confusion of jurisdictions often caused prolonged quarrels over competence. As the centralised state attempted to impose an acceptable system of law and order, it began to phase out the confusions, introduce its own norms, and reserve powers of punishment to itself alone. In the process it partly superseded community systems of law, which, however, continued to exist throughout Europe in many forms. Since law officials were few and normally non-resident, rural communities were often left to police themselves. This meant that, for lack of law enforcement machinery, many 'crimes' were never punished or prosecuted,[45] and apparently tranquil communities may well have experienced more lawlessness than the records show. On the other hand, in certain rural areas community controls were exercised over offences that may not have been formal 'crimes', but that threatened to disturb social order. In the province of Santander in northern Spain, this form of social discipline and policing was the predominant one in the pre-industrial period.[46]

Moreover, even if offenders were arrested, the courts themselves might decide not to prosecute in order to save costs. It was also common for the local community to block official penalties that it considered inappropriate. In Spain, though rape was officially punishable with death, it was more common to force the rapist to make restitution in the form of cash or marriage. In England, local magistrates and juries conspired to make several harsh laws inoperative. Of nearly 1,000 cases coming before the Maidstone quarter sessions in the late sixteenth and early seventeenth centuries, in none was the death penalty applied when it should have been. Faced with the letter of the law, juries preferred to acquit rather than condemn. The attitude of both witnesses and jurymen in Somerset in 1596 was described by a local magistrate, Edward Hext:

> Most commonly the simple Countryman and woman, lokynge no farther then ynto the losse of ther owne goods, are of opynyon that they wold not procure a mans death for all the goods yn the world, others uppon promyse to have ther goods agayne wyll gyve faynt evidence yf they be not stryctly loked ynto by the Justyce.

What the propertied classes considered as 'crime', therefore, was not always seen in the same way by the lower orders; for these, 'social crime' was a tolerable aspect of conduct, not deserving of prosecution. Poaching and banditry often fell into this category. In countries where there was little chance of popular attitudes influencing the courts, hostility to the harsh laws intensified opposition, as we can see by the actions of the rioters in Seville in 1648:

> They went to the offices of the secretaries of the criminal courts, broke them open, seized all the papers and burned them in the middle of the square, in full view of all the judges. They did the same with the gallows and ladder in the same square, and with the torture-rack and all the instruments of the executioner. They also burned at the same time the committal records that contain the names of all those imprisoned in all the gaols. But great care was taken not to burn the civil records.

The real level of crime in pre-industrial Europe is therefore impossible to establish with any confidence. The apparent absence of violence in the countryside was probably, as we have mentioned, deceptive; and in any case formal prosecutions tended to be directed against outsiders rather than members of the local community. In the Kentish countryside, most of the prosecuted crimes involved theft rather than violence, and appear to have been committed not by local people but by outsiders and travellers, by soldiers in transit to and from Dover, and by gangs operating from London. Records from other regions of England agree that theft predominated, but show that local people featured. Two thirds of the 3,129 indictments presented at Essex assizes in 1559–1603 were for theft;[47] it was the same in Wiltshire, where twenty-three out of eighty-two indictments in 1615, and forty-two out of 103 in 1619 were drawn up against local people for this offence. Second only to theft in Essex came prosecutions for witchcraft; some court cases concerned violence, but tended to involve mostly kin groups within the villages. The level of violence in rural England can appear to be deceptively low if only the higher courts are consulted. Between 1615 and 1660, for example, only twenty-three cases of violence from the village of

Preston turned up at the local quarter sessions. But there happened also to be a manorial court at Preston, and of the 4,758 cases with which it dealt over the same period over 26 per cent involved assault, a far surer guide to the degree of village conflict.

In rural France, of 400 cases tried before the courts in Angoulême in 1643–4, 23 per cent concerned trespass and other property offences, a further 22 per cent involved personal wrongs such as marital infidelity, drunkenness and sorcery; thefts answered for 16 per cent, and violence occurred in 18 per cent of cases. In Spain violence seems to have been more common. In the region known as the *montes* of Toledo, of 1,988 cases covering the period 1550–1700, over 42 per cent concerned violence in various forms, and only 10 per cent involved petty theft. Partial evidence for the late seventeenth century in Valencian and Catalan villages shows a similarly high level of violence within the rural community, aggravated by the widespread possession of firearms: in 1676 the Viceroy of Catalonia deplored 'the many great and enormous crimes perpetrated in the principality'.

A possibly moderate level of crime in the countryside must be contrasted with the situation in the large towns, where problems of housing, food and employment were severe. The figures are, however, frequently misleading. Police officials were particularly harsh to off-duty soldiers and to outsiders, two categories that consequently appear with frequency in the records. Of those condemned to corporal punishment by the municipal court at Bordeaux from 1600 to 1650, nearly 52 per cent were vagabonds and other outsiders. Urban crime was violent, at least in Spain. In 1578 the municipality of Valladolid had to appoint two extra law officers to deal with the increase in theft and murder. For Madrid, the reports present a frightening picture. 'Not a day passes but people are found killed or wounded by brigands or soldiers; houses burgled; young girls and widows weeping because they have been assaulted and robbed', wrote a witness in 1639. 'From Christmas till now', wrote another in June 1658, 'there have been over 150 deaths and no one has been punished'. An analysis of Madrid crime in the late seventeenth century gives some support to these accounts. In 1693, one of the peak years for violence in the period, repeated street-brawls led to the arrest of over 300 persons for disturbing public order; there were twenty-nine recorded murders and fourteen cases of rape. The municipal police were unafraid to act against nobility, who that year were implicated in incidents of assault, rape, brawling, theft, wife-beating and murder. The authorities initiated 382 criminal prosecutions during the year, but 212 of these could not be proceeded with because the accused had fled the city. Over the period 1665–1700 crimes of violence represented about half of all detected crimes, sexual incidents came next (rape, sex crimes and marriage quarrels), and cases of theft last of all.[48] In some towns historians have been able to identify the emergence of a real underworld of organised crime. In London in the 1720s, a petty criminal called Jonathan Wild rose to become an Al Capone-type boss who directed the activities of a network of accomplices.

The Madrid figures seem to emphasise the pervasive violence of traditional society; but at no time was violence deemed acceptable, as private memoirs of the time demonstrate. Moreover, in a society where there was no active police force and prosecutions were initiated on the basis of denunciation, the activity of courts was little more than a reflection of what people chose to denounce. In sixteenth-century Rome, the courts were frequently mere tools used by malicious neighbours to take vengeance on each other.[49] Many communities took their own policing measures to control crime. Above all, the civil authorities and the state attempted, by passing laws and sometimes by direct intervention, to eliminate violence. We have seen that the taming of the great nobles and the formation of state armies were essential parts of this programme.

Popular discontent might erupt into uprisings; but it also expressed itself on a smaller scale in a resort to crime. The frequency of banditry was another symptom of those very conditions that could cause mass rebellions: heavy taxation, agrarian distress, class resentment. In general all banditry, both aristocratic and popular, was criminal; but it was a form of crime that rose out of political and social crisis. Viewed as crime, aristocratic and popular banditry also shared the common factor of thriving in areas usually inaccessible to the government, such as in mountainous regions and in woods.

Beyond this common ground, the two sorts of banditry differed widely. Aristocrats who operated robber bands were reverting to a purely feudal defiance of the state. This was the case with the great bandit-lords of central Italy in the late sixteenth century, most notable of whom was the Duke of Montemarciano, Alfonso Piccolomini, who for thirteen years from 1578 was the supreme head of the brigands in the Romagna. Several other distinguished nobles followed Piccolomini's precedent, not always with success: in 1587, when the Grand-duke Ramberto Malatesta began to operate as a bandit the Pope had him seized and executed. Piccolomini himself was hanged at Florence in 1591. So severe were the Pope's measures against the bandits that 'this year', reported a Roman newsletter of September 1585, 'we have seen more heads on the Sant' Angelo bridge than melons in the market'.[50]

Popular banditry, on the other hand, tended to originate as a protest against misery, and seems to have thrived most in periods of economic crisis. Unlike rebellions, which aimed to secure broad support, banditry was at its strongest when its support was purely local. The men who fled to the mountains to join the bands were usually those whose crimes, although culpable in the eyes of the state, had not received general disapprobation in the locality. Regional sympathy defeated all the efforts of governments to annihilate banditry. The mountainous regions of central France and the Pyrenees were prominent in the sixteenth century as centres of banditry. When Charles Estienne published his *Guide des Chemins de France* in the mid-sixteenth century, he took care to list some of the roads that were infested by brigands. Catalan banditry south of the Pyrenees had its heyday in the period stretching from the French civil wars to the revolt of 1640.[51] The peak period for activity here was in the reign of Philip III, under whom the most famous of all the Catalan bandits, Perot Rocaguinarda, began his career in 1602. Much of his fame derives from the appearance he makes in Cervantes' *Don Quixote*. A diarist of his day reported that 'Rocaguinarda was the most courteous bandit to have been in that region for many years: never did he dishonour or touch the churches, and God aided him'. He ended his career in what became a traditional way, accepting a pardon in 1611 and going overseas to Italy to serve with the troops.

As in Catalonia, the Italian bandits emerged from an agrarian background, and periods of agrarian crisis seemed to provoke further bandit activity. The critical years of the 1580s, followed by a harvest crisis in 1590, initiated widespread disturbances. A Roman newsletter of 1590 reported incidents in the Romagna, where 'numerous peasants have joined the bandits, and commit murders publicly in the streets'. The resurgence of banditry was part and parcel of an agrarian revolt. One of the most prominent leaders to reflect this was Marco Sciarra, a native of Castiglione, who had been a bandit since 1585, when he emerged as the leader of a group which had its headquarters in the Abruzzi. For nearly seven years this group's activities were viewed as an anti-Spanish revolt, which helped to bring him popularity. More significant was the fact that he practised a redistribution of wealth that was the classic hallmark of the 'Robin Hood' type of bandit. He was loved by the poor of Naples 'who used to say', reports a contemporary, 'that he would soon come to occupy Naples, and make himself king'. The combination of peasant agitation and banditry can be seen in seventeenth-century France, where the regularity of popular uprisings gave ample scope to rebels. In Périgord in this period, the principal bandit was Pierre Grellety. He was never caught and eventually in 1642, in the now accepted way, took up a military commission to serve in Italy, which Richelieu had offered him.

The Spanish bandits of this period operated not only in Catalonia but also in Valencia, Murcia and Castile. Their lives displayed a curious mixture of crime and charity, religion and impiety, the very combination of opposites that made social banditry a unique phenomenon. One bandit of the time of Philip II was called *El Caballero de la Cruz*, because he always left a crucifix on the grave of his victims. Most bandits wore medals and scapulars around their neck, and practised the official religion; but they also drew on popular superstition, and were known to recite prayers to make themselves invisible to their pursuers. Women were sometimes leaders of the bandit groups, as happened in Granada. One of the more curious groups active in the early century in Andalusia operated in the Sierra de Cabrilla. They dressed as gentlemen, were always kind and courteous to their victims, and robbed them of only half their goods: this charitable form of property redistribution earned them the title of *Los Beatos de Cabrilla* – the Holy Ones of Cabrilla. Of a bandit active in Castile in 1644 it was reported that 'he never kills anyone but only takes part of their money, leaving them with enough to continue their journey; he borrows money from villages and individuals, giving his word as a pledge, and is punctual in payment'.[52]

The Russian state and its frontiers were the principal victims of brigandage in the east, for two main reasons. First, many of the bands were tribal and racial groups that were actively at war against Muscovy. Both the Tatars and Cossacks were long-standing enemies. All the major peasant revolts in the Russian lands and in Lithuania and the Ukraine were made possible because of the active help of the Cossacks. Banditry became an essential arm of agrarian revolt, and the bandits in turn were accepted as defenders of the people, heroes of a popular tradition in Russia.[53] The second reason for the strength of banditry was the chaos caused in Muscovy by the growth of feudalism and the bitter internal struggles of the period. The breakdown of order during the Time of Troubles, for instance, was particularly fruitful in promoting brigandage; the schism in the Russian Church likewise drove many clergy and others to the same occupation. Peasants fleeing from feudal obligations were perhaps the largest single group of people to swell the growth of banditry. In popular estimation, the work of the bandits was a form of social justice, since their principal victims were merchants and other rich travellers, government officials and tax-collectors. In the songs devoted to their deeds, the *bylini*, they emerged as folk heroes whose work to redress the evils of the time earned them legendary status.

Crime and punishment

The ruling authorities had always claimed a monopoly over violence: this took its most notable form in the exercise of the right to punish. During the confessional period of European history, from 1520 to around 1650, the crime most conspicuously punished (not in numbers but in social impact) was that of heresy, which normally earned the death penalty. Heresy had emerged as a significant crime only in the thirteenth century, but was dealt with most cruelly during the epoch of the Reformation. Executions were deliberately staged as public spectacles, meant to edify and therefore to deter. In Catholic states they were normally managed by bishops' courts (as under Mary Tudor) or by special courts of the Inquisition (in Spain and the Netherlands), that by canon law could not shed blood and therefore handed condemned persons over 'to the secular arm'. The majority of deaths for heresy in Europe were decreed not, as commonly thought, by ecclesiastical tribunals but by state and urban courts, responsible between them for the majority of known executions. In France the Chambre Ardente, set up by the crown in 1547, became for a while the chief court used against heretics. The punishment of heresy became, in effect, a means through which emergent state power could assert itself. From 1520 to about 1560, possibly 3,000 persons were executed for heresy by the state courts in western Europe. Two thirds of them were Anabaptists, sentenced mainly in the Germanic lands and the Netherlands.[54] Significantly, it was only in this period, precisely in 1559, that the Spanish Inquisition began to mount its famous public *autos de fe*.[55] The spectacle (in which executions never played a part, since they were carried out separately) immediately became equated in the Protestant mind with religious fanaticism.

The repression of religious dissent reminds us that historians normally ignore a significant category of crime, namely verbal offences. Blasphemy, often punished with the death penalty, was the gravest of all offences, for it was a public crime against God. But an extensive range of other verbal offences continued to occupy the tribunals.[56] Sedition, or fomenting discontent against the authorities, was always punished harshly. In the same way, fomenting discontent against other people in society, sometimes through the written word but more normally through verbal slander or defamation, was treated seriously because it affected personal honour and could give rise to violence. The importance of verbal offences makes it quite logical that the Spanish Inquisition should have devoted a good part of its activity in early modern times to this type of crime.[57]

The punishment of everyday crime was handled by a multitude of local courts in villages and towns, and supervised by various local jurisdictions. The consequence was an alarming inconsistency in the punishment of offences, with the quite arbitrary exercise of the death penalty. From the sixteenth century, state authorities intervened regularly in private jurisdictions in an attempt to control the situation, but made slow progress. The efforts made in the Massif Central of France to impose the *grands jours* of Auvergne (1665–6), referred to above, are often seen as a significant step forward, though the real success of such campaigns is open to doubt. There were three main components of the official programme: an attempt to reserve the death penalty to the government alone, a clearer definition of which offences were criminal, and the gradual elimination of many traditional punishments, some of them popular in nature, some of them extreme. Various important changes were also introduced into the nature of trials.

Public executions for secular crimes were staged (like the Spanish *auto de fe*) as a public spectacle, but with a greater display of ferocity, intended to dissuade members of the public and bring home to them the consequences of crime. Executions of notable political figures had often, in England for example, been revoltingly brutal. The brutality appears to have intensified as state control advanced: both in England and in Germany in the eighteenth century criminal executions were ritualised spectacles.[58] It has been argued that the almost theatrical ritual of executions was in effect a conscious effort by the authorities, both urban and state, to impose a system of control and repression.[59] But by the mid-eighteenth century public executions and their attendant barbarity were no longer in favour. Certain punishments, such as mutilation, were discontinued. Torture was still sanctioned, but a growing body of legal opinion argued fiercely against its use. In accord with social usage, legal concepts of punishment began to change.

It is possible to take the view that public executions were infrequent. Both in Nuremberg and in Amsterdam in the late seventeenth century and early eighteenth century, the number of criminals executed averaged only four a year.[60] Since each town had its own criminal jurisdiction, however, it would be more revealing to estimate the total number of executions in a sample of adjacent towns.

Perhaps the most important aspect of punishment in pre-industrial Europe was also, to modern eyes, the most surprising: criminals were not as a rule incarcerated. Though gaols existed everywhere, they were employed as temporary residences until the fate of the condemned person could be decided. At the Old Bailey in London, for example, prison sentences represented around 1 per cent of the sentences passed in the mid-eighteenth century. The normal punishments in Europe included corporal chastisement (flogging, mutilation), banishment from the community, and execution. Prisons and the penitentiary system did not come into existence until the nineteenth century.

The English introduced a special form of banishment that had no precedent in Europe: transportation to the colonies. In 1718 Parliament passed a Transportation Act that permitted the authorities to send convicted felons overseas to America. It was a highly convenient innovation that saved having to incarcerate or execute criminals. Over the next two generations some 50,000 convicts, mostly young males, were obliged to make their homes in the New World.

Physical punishment was the most drastic of the disciplinary solutions offered for controlling social disorder. It can often be easily identified in the surviving court documentation, and consequently appears to be the logical response of pre-industrial society to crime. But there were also other solutions, not often visible in court documentation and therefore unduly forgotten by historians. Three such solutions, whose impact was in the long run no less important, may be noted: marginalisation, exclusion and confinement. They were responses that aimed not at a cure but rather at expelling what did not fit into the confines of the accepted, or what appeared to be a social threat. We have seen that the poor and vagrants and gypsies were at one time or another subjected to these solutions. Witches were evidently another social grouping that faced the same policy of incomprehension and rejection.

A final response also deserves its place in this picture: pardon. Traditional society was far readier than our own to pardon and reconcile. In an age when very many offences were religious, involving wrong attitudes or wrong beliefs, the authorities were willing to forgive if there was genuine repentance. The practice had its roots in medieval society, but all ecclesiastical tribunals in early modern Europe adopted it as standard procedure. The medieval Church, basing itself on the sacrament of penance, also habitually encouraged malefactors to atone for their crimes by going on pilgrimage, which was specified for offences such as murder, incest, bestiality and sacrilege.[61] In fourteenth-century Flanders, the secular courts seem to have used pilgrimage as an all-purpose penalty for violent crimes. Completing the penance meant that the crime was 'satisfied', though those who were found not to have done the penance were harshly treated. The Inquisition in Catalonia in the sixteenth century still regularly condemned minor offenders (guilty, for example, of swearing) to go on pilgrimage, invariably to

Montserrat. It is in Catalonia too that we find an unusual procedure known as a 'pardon', based on the premise that society needed to forego violent revenge against a murderer in order to save itself from worse ills. As practised here, the Church intervened directly to exact a promise from the family of a murdered man that they would not seek personal vengeance on the man's identified murderer or on the murderer's family. Punishment was to be left to the appropriate jurisdiction. In this way the threat of a blood feud was warded off, and social order preserved. Similar procedures of reconciliation can be found in France among both Catholic and Protestant communities. The disputants were encouraged to make peace together before the community, usually in church, and to take communion together.

Marginalisation: slavery

There were, broadly, two types of slavery in Christian Europe: the 'colonial' and the 'feudal'. The 'colonial' type of slavery was the predominant one in western Europe, and owed most of its vigour to practice in the Iberian peninsula. There the *Reconquista* – the reconquest of Muslim territory – had since the later Middle Ages led the Christian races to dominate and exploit the defeated Moors. So-called 'Saracen' slaves were a commonplace in central and southern Portugal and Spain in medieval times. The struggle between Christian and Muslim extended beyond the peninsula, and it was through sea warfare that the institution of slavery continued to perpetuate itself. Muslim corsairs were operative throughout the Mediterranean in the sixteenth century, and collected Christian slaves from as far afield as Russia and England. The Christian powers, in turn, did not scruple to enslave any Moors they could lay their hands upon. With this experience behind them, the Iberian powers accepted slavery as a standard feature of their public life. The medieval laws of both Spain and Portugal sanctioned the holding of slaves.

Spanish slavery had been firmly Moorish, and continued to be so even after the expulsion of the Moriscos in 1609. The only Moriscos not expelled from Spain were those being held as slaves, who must have numbered several thousand. After each Morisco rebellion in the sixteenth century, particularly after the rising in the Alpujarra region in 1569, large numbers of rebels, reportedly running into thousands, had been sold into slavery. This native source of labour (used mainly for domestic work, but also for the galleys and for forced labour in the mercury mines at Almadén) was supplemented from abroad. The battle of Lepanto brought many Turks into Spanish households; slave raids were also fruitful, as with the expedition made in 1611 by the Marquis of Santa Cruz to the island of Querquenes, when he captured 400 slaves.

When the age of discovery began, Iberian slavery took on a new texture. From being a Mediterranean institution it became an Atlantic one. The geographical change also implied a racial one: in the place of Moors, black Africans were traded. In both quantity and quality a new era had commenced, for not only were the blacks enslaved in numbers that exceeded any previous practice, but they were employed primarily to serve the needs of the colonial economy in America. The logic of this was that countries which resorted to slavery in their colonies – Portugal, Spain and, later, France and England – tended to accept the extension of slavery in their own metropolitan territories, thus introducing into Europe the colonial pattern of race relations.

Portugal, the first of European countries to develop the new type of slavery abroad, was the first to be inundated at home. By 1553 a Belgian humanist, writing from Evora, could report that 'Portugal is so full of slaves that I could almost believe Lisbon to have more slaves than free Portuguese'. In 1551 Lisbon was calculated to have one slave for every ten free Portuguese; by 1633 the estimate was of 15,000 slaves in a city population of 100,000, with a further 2 per cent consisting of free coloureds. In the whole of Portugal, which had a population of just over a million, slaves and blacks constituted about 3 per cent of the population, the largest ratio of any European nation.

The development of black slavery in America had a direct effect on Spain. A Flemish observer reported in 1655 that 'the American trade has given new life to the institution of slavery in this country, so that in Andalusia one sees few servants other than slaves, mostly Moors as well as blacks'. The slave population tended, as elsewhere in the Mediterranean, to concentrate on the seaports. Seville in 1565 had 6,327 slaves (7.4 per cent of the population), most of them black; Cadiz in 1616 had 300 Moorish and 500 black slaves. In Spain slaves were normally domestic servants. There was initially very little racial prejudice against coloureds or blacks, as shown by the case of Juan Latino, whose parents were both black slaves. He began his career as page to the Duke of Sessa, managed to enter the University of Granada, graduated from there in 1557, finally obtained a chair in Latin and married the daughter of a noble family.

Outside the Iberian peninsula, Mediterranean slavery could not rely on the colonial system and owed its continued existence almost exclusively to piracy. In France, the ports of Marseille and Toulon inevitably had to harbour the booty of slave-hunters. Beyond these Mediterranean ports slavery was very rare in the country. There were recorded cases of slaves in Roussillon (which became French in 1659) but they were nearly all Moorish, an overspill from Spain. In theory slavery was illegal. In 1571 the parlement of Bordeaux, ruling against a slave-trader, declared that 'France, the mother of liberty, does not permit slavery'. 'All persons in this realm are free', wrote the jurist Loisel in 1608, 'and if a slave reaches these shores and gets baptised, he becomes free'.[62] The growth of the overseas empire, however, militated against statements like this, and as colonial slavery grew so did its acceptance by metropolitan France, which imported coloured labour mainly through La Rochelle and Nantes.

Piracy made Venice, Genoa and other Italian ports into leading slave centres.[63] A slave cargo brought back from the Levant by four Florentine galleys in June 1574 totalled 300, made up of 238 Turks, thirty-two 'Moors', seven blacks, two Greeks, five Arabs, five Jews, five Russians and six Christians. They were taken to the market at Messina, where 116 were sold and most of the Christians freed. Slaves were purchased for galley and domestic service. The navies of the Italian states and of Spain were heavily dependent on slaves for rowers. An agent for the Spanish royal galleys, shopping for slaves in Genoa in 1573, bought 100 slaves in February and another thirty-two (these last from Hungary) in April. At this period the cost of each slave was about 100 ducats. Their places of origin – Aleppo, Salonika, Istanbul, Algiers – point to the overwhelmingly Muslim character of slavery in the Christian Mediterranean. In the Arab Mediterranean, of course, Christians were the slaves. In 1588 it was estimated that over 2,500 Venetian subjects were scattered throughout the Mediterranean '*in misera captività*'.

In Italy, as in Spain, domestic slavery predominated. A prince of the Church like Cardinal d'Este was said in 1584 to have had fifty Turkish slaves in his villa in Tivoli. But though slavery was accepted in practice, the laws were equivocal, and a fugitive slave (and, in particular, a baptised slave) was legally entitled to be free. Servitude was looked upon as a temporary condition, a result of adverse fortune such as being captured in war. Being temporary, it could not be inherited. It was in those very Mediterranean countries where slavery was most in use – Spain, Italy and France – that Catholic theology and public law conspired to guarantee the dispossessed their right, both as men and as Christians, to manumission and social equality. In normal circumstances this would have meant the gradual disappearance of slavery from Europe. But new life was given to the institution by the growth of colonial economies dependent on cheap labour.

'Feudal' slavery in Europe was associated with the availability of labour. Scotland's most capitalised industry, mining, was introduced to the profits of slavery in this period. Colliers had been personally free up to 1605. Then in July 1606 an Act of Parliament forbade them moving their labour elsewhere and also in effect froze their wages. The 1606 Act applied to coalmines, another in 1607 applied to metal mines, and in 1641 a statute extended these terms to factory workers.

In Russia slavery was a standard feature of the rural scene. The slaves (*kholopi*) performed essentially the same function as serfs, their distinctive feature being the loss of personal freedom. One could become enslaved by contract for a limited or unlimited period, or be enslaved through war, or fall into servitude because of debt. Non-Russians were also enslaved: Polish slaves rose to positions of responsibility in noble households, and there was a brisk trade in Tatars captured on the frontier. In the steppe, where many estates had no peasants, slave labour was common; the proportion of slaves to free peasants in some districts was as high as 50 per cent. The importance of slavery in the Russian state is shown by the fact that 200 of the 940 clauses in the Ulozhenie of 1649 were concerned specifically with it. Paradoxically, slavery disappeared as it intensified. The distinction between a slave and a serf had always been slight, and as both categories became depressed in the course of the seventeenth century they tended to be legally merged into one. The last great distinction between the two was the exemption of slaves from taxation. Laws of 1680 and 1724 made the landless slave as liable to taxation as the landed serf; with these measures slavery became merged into the larger institution of serfdom.

The enclosed: madmen

Traditional society had few solutions for those who did not fit into standard categories. All irrational behaviour was considered, in juridical terms, simply as the absence of rational behaviour; it could not therefore be made the basis of a judicial decision. The situation provided a convenient escape route used by both assassins and heretics when they wished to avoid the penalty of the law. Since the madman did not legally exist, and a state of madness in a person was difficult to prove or disprove, the problem was pushed aside.[64] Despite its absence from the juridical canon, irrational behaviour was frequent enough to be accepted as a commonplace in the literature of the time, and served to amuse theatre audiences.[65] Judges and doctors, and the public too, recognised that madness was a serious condition; but it was commonly assumed to be temporary, and those guilty of irrational conduct were locked up until they came to their senses. The notion of madness as demonic possession was a special development that may have made its appearance fairly late. In parts of sixteenth-century Germany, the view of the madman as a devil seems to have been propagated by preachers, and was not originally present in popular culture.[66]

The availability of public correctional institutions for the mentally unfit made it possible for families under pressure to exercise control over relatives who were becoming an embarrassment. Confinement in institutions was a form of disciplinary action that attempted to remedy disorder within individual families and within urban society. Rowdy individuals, drunken women, violent husbands were denounced and put into correctional institutions for a few weeks or months. It was a practice used increasingly, for example, in eighteenth-century Antwerp and Brussels.[67]

9

MODERNISATION AND THE INDIVIDUAL

> The art of Printing will so spread knowledge that the common people, knowing their own rights and liberties, will not be governed by way of oppression.
> (Gabriel Plattes, *A Description of the Famous Kingdom of Macaria*, 1641)

At the heart of both great and small movements in European history lay the activity of countless individuals. The contribution of the 'common man' has been seen as a crucial factor in the making of the Germanic Reformation.[1] More than a century after the Reformation, radicals in England claimed a place in society for the common individual: 'the poorest he', Colonel Rainboro asserted at the debates among army officers at Putney in 1647, 'hath a life to live as the greatest he'. Was the ordinary man finding his voice? Were Europeans moving slowly away from the communal world into the freedom of individualism, the assurance of greater privacy, the seclusion of personal life?

Evidence for the expression of individualism can be found as far back as the written records take us. Scholars have claimed to see extensive individualism in societies with considerable mobility of land and of persons, such as England.[2] In this sense, individualism seems to mean a freedom to make personal and economic decisions. Others have looked at individualism in terms of an emerging distinction between what might be 'public' concerns and what might be more specifically 'private'. Some intellectuals were probably aware of a significant difference between their private thought patterns and the alien world outside. 'In order to master the sciences', the humanist Ficino argued, 'it is necessary for the soul to withdraw from the external to the internal'.[3]

These differing views about the 'modernising' aspects of pre-industrial society have their own different perspectives and emphases. A distinguished historian sees an emergence from the later seventeenth century in England of a trend towards interest in the individual personality, and a demand for more privacy and self-expression.[4] At a private level the trend might include emphasis on personal sexuality, at a public level it might involve a move towards toleration of different opinions. The scope of the concept, it is clear, can be vast.

Most scholars, for all that, appear to be sceptical about the evidence for a move towards 'privacy'. Some deny categorically that individualism increased.[5] The evidence for a growth in privacy has come so far mainly from England and has referred principally to its upper classes. The few comparable studies available for other societies in Europe have not offered convincing support for the thesis. The norm in European pre-industrial society was always the group rather than the individual person. Even the apparently individual affirmation of the Reformation – personal salvation based on a direct relationship with Christ – was given meaning only within the community of believers, the 'Church'. The joining of two people in matrimony was likewise not usually private, but subject to the will of parents and the interests of kin groups. Within the communal context there had of course always been scope for individual affirmation, such as through the assertion of individual affection or 'love'. It is more doubtful whether such individual tendencies can be viewed as part of a more general move towards individual expression.

At the level of social development, some historians have considered that events in early modern Europe can be seen as part of a process of 'modernisation', marking the transition from a traditional, agrarian and religious society to one associated with expansion, mobility, literacy and secularism. Marxist scholars gave particular support to 'modernisation', which seemed to confirm the advance of society towards the socialist millennium. The concept is a suggestive one, but extremely difficult to demonstrate by the evidence available for Europe prior to the late eighteenth century. Despite the extent of change in all spheres, pre-industrial society managed to retain its fundamental characteristics unchanged for longer than is often thought, and it would be mistaken to apply to the whole continent conclusions that might in part be valid for one fraction of it, namely England.

Privatisation and the family

At the core of social life in pre-industrial Europe, in the domestic group, the rules of conduct were related fundamentally to the whole family and not to its individual members. Individual interests, even when they existed, were subsumed in those of the family, the household and the wider community.[6] Nor did the place of work permit any serious divergence from the rules, since for most people the place of work was also the place of residence, unlike the twentieth century where very many people perform their work and their leisure roles in two distinct environments. Even more securely, legal systems normally recognised only the rights of the group; private contracts took place (as many still do) within a context affecting all members of the public. It follows that standards of conduct and morality did not usually give scope for individual deviation. Despite the apparent rigidity of this situation, however, there can be little doubt that there were new trends, particularly among the upper classes, where a so-called 'civilising process' has been identified,[7] seen on one hand in greater courtesy, discipline and cleanliness, and on the other in greater scope for individual expression.

A small but significant example is the case of suicide. Suicide in early modern society was always looked upon with great horror, and treated by the courts as a crime (canon law forbade church burial, and some laws forfeited the suicide's property). For England it has been suggested, on the basis of data from late sixteenth-century Kent,[8] that suicide was more common than homicide, and that its incidence was very similar to that of the twentieth century. The suicide was generally seen not as an individual within society, but as a satanic deviant who had put himself outside it. All the same, by the eighteenth century in England a significant change was taking place in educated opinion on the subject.[9] Juries in the courts began to reject the idea that suicide was a crime, rationalist thinkers rejected the view that suicide was satanic, and passive acceptance of the (suicidal) rite of duelling eased the way to accepting self-killing as a fact. The new approach was echoed by the city council of Geneva, which in 1735 declared that suicides were in fact insane, and therefore not to be further castigated in their goods or their honour.[10] The Genevan attitude needs to be set beside the fascinating data for the other Swiss city of Zürich, where it appears that suicides among the population increased from the seventeenth century onwards, at the same time that homicides seem to have decreased. Some 511 suicides are recorded for the period 1500 to 1800, rising from one a year in the 1630s to four a year in the early eighteenth century.[11] In general, the Zürich authorities did not rule against the victims.

Though there was no formal recognition of the social role of the individual, there was a growing acceptance of the freedom to express individual preferences – what may in a limited sense be called 'privacy'. The world of the 'private' took several forms, among both men and women. It was to be found more among the privileged classes, and can be defined broadly in two areas: in the arrangement of personal ideas, and in the arrangement of personal space. We have already seen that the development of personal ideas was visible in literary expression, in the writings of memoirs and diaries, and in the rise of interiorised religious forms such as Pietism. Personal space was re-arranged mainly within the context of family life, with changes in house construction and the allotting of specific functions to rooms in the building, of which one consequence was that the elite family (at least in England) began to be visualised as a 'private' rather than a 'public' sphere. 'As every man's house is his castle', Richard Braithwaite affirmed in 1630, 'so is his family a private commonwealth'.[12] At the elite level, the family continued still to be a broad concept that might include both kinfolk and house servants; but it was also seen often as a terrain in which the state should not intervene. It might possess many of the aspects of 'privacy', but the privacy was shared with other members of the family grouping. Privacy was, in this sense, less individual than collective.

Among working people, if there was a degree of privacy it was always conditioned by restrictions on space in the household, and by the intrusion of the neighbourhood. In the neighbourhood, where gossip was supreme,[13] it was difficult to maintain a way of life that did not conform to standards laid down by the local community. Sexuality remained a public matter in all small communities. Collective values dominated rather than individual values. In this sense, traditional society did not yet accept any effective separation of what was private from what was public.

Scepticism, secularism and privatisation of belief

The age-long failure of official religion to penetrate down into the people gave rise to a surprising persistence of non-religious attitudes. Drawing on the evidence of literary culture,[14] scholars two generations ago decided that irreligion was not possible within the context of those times but a later phenomenon based on a reasoned rejection of dogmatism. Scepticism, where it existed, was based on belief and arose out of the same attitude that inspired members of the elite to dabble in magic. Intellectual curiosity impelled the learned to resort to alchemy, astrology and magic. The link with witchcraft could be seen in the art and iconography of the age, most notably in the artist Hieronymous Bosch, and in the scientific endeavours of Elizabeth of England's court magician John Dee. The Renaissance encouraged inquiry and therefore doubt; the true scholar must maintain a mind open to all sources of knowledge, which might include dabbling in the occult and the Hermetic tradition of allegedly pre-Biblical science. The Faust story, concerning a doctor who sought knowledge outside the bounds of dogma, reflected this background: the account was published in Germany in 1587, translated into English and Dutch in 1592, and into French in 1598. Though early science was inevitably concerned with magic (such as the attempt to transmute metals), it was a magic that had nothing in common with naive popular beliefs. Intellectuals were pursuing a truth that did not contradict or conflict with Christianity. Many (like Paracelsus) pursued their work outside the normal academic frontiers, others worked within established circles.

In Prague, Emperor Rudolf II (d. 1612) gathered round him a circle of scientists ('magicians') and freethinkers. In England, Sir Walter Raleigh and his friends denied the reality of heaven and hell, claiming that 'we die like beasts and when we are gone there is no more remembrance of us'. In France, after the excesses of the civil wars there was a reaction that made La Noue observe that 'it was our wars of religion that made us forget religion'. The epicurean court of Henry IV, like that of James I in England, encouraged speculative thought or 'libertinism'. Some made a profit out of their irreligion, like Jérémie Ferrier, a Huguenot pastor who abjured his faith in 1613, drew large pensions as a priest till his death in 1626, and claimed that for fourteen years he had preached Christ without believing in him. Most unbelievers kept their attitude concealed. This was advisable, particularly after the shock felt in French society in 1623, when the poet Théophile de Viau was arrested for blasphemy and later condemned to death, a sentence subsequently commuted to banishment. The result was, as

Pierre Bayle claimed, that many 'die like everyone else, after confession and communion'. 'Unbelief', the sieur de Rochemont wrote in 1665, 'has its laws of prudence'.[15]

But reasoned unbelief was rare. Most 'sceptics'[16] were seeking new intellectual frontiers within the confines of traditional belief. The most famous French sceptics frequented the literary academies, such as the Rambouillet; or the philosophic academies such as that of the humanist brothers Dupuy. Among them were the doctors Gabriel Naudé (d. 1653) and Guy Patin (d. 1672), and the priest Pierre Gassendi (d. 1655). The most active influences still came from Italy, which Naudé claimed was 'full of libertines and atheists and people who don't believe anything'. Among the restless spirits in Italy was the adept of Hermetic lore, Giordano Bruno, who proclaimed that man had 'by the light of sense and of reason, with the key of most diligent enquiry, thrown wide those doors of truth which it is within our power to open'.[17]

These searchers after truth attempted to find a reality beyond official dogmas; they were excited by the possibility of rediscovering ancient lost arts. Freemasonry, which became historically significant only in the early seventeenth century, attracted many because of its implied access to long-hidden knowledge. It was this that led the English antiquarian Dr William Stukeley to join the movement and 'to be initiated into the mysteries of Masonry, suspecting it to be the remains of the mysteries of the ancients'. Perhaps the most remarkable of the groups that practised the new mystification were the Rosicrucians. Their supposed existence was announced with the publication in 1614 of the *Fama Fraternitatis*, a work that provoked widespread excitement and came out in nine editions in three years. Descartes, who was living at Frankfurt in 1619, tried in vain to join the group and concluded that it did not exist; Leibniz at the end of the century proclaimed it to be a fiction. The myth was created by the Lutheran thinker Johann Valentin Andreae, probable co-author of the *Fama*; according to it, a fifteenth-century German nobleman, Christian Rosenkreuz ('rosy cross'), had been given access to the ancient lore of Persia and India.[18]

Elite belief thus had its marginal zones, in which individuals indulged their private views. A newer development was the wholly non-theistic philosophy of the Levellers and Diggers. Gerrard Winstanley, the Digger leader, defined religion only in terms of social justice: 'True religion and undefiled is thus: to make restitution of the Earth which hath been taken and held from the common people by the power of Conquests formerly, and so set the oppressed free.' Two centuries before Marx, Winstanley described religion as the opium of the people:

> This divining spiritual Doctrine is a cheat; for while men are gazing up to Heaven imagining after a happiness, or fearing a Hell after they are

> dead, their eyes are put out; that they see not what is their birthrights, and what is to be done by them here on Earth, while they are living.

The viewpoint appears familiar, but in practice it is almost impossible to identify the existence of any systematic alternative to the theism of western philosophy. The authorities would continue to burn select figures for what they called 'atheism'. Jacques Gruet was burnt in 1550 at Geneva, Geoffroy Vallée in 1574 at Paris, Noël Journet in 1582 at Metz, Giordano Bruno in 1600 at Rome, Cesare Vanini in 1619 at Toulouse; and young Thomas Aikenhead, a student at the university, was executed at Edinburgh in 1697. But philosophers had not yet fashioned the conceptual tools necessary for defining unbelief. It was not until the late seventeenth century that the emergence of probability theory introduced the notion of degrees of assent.[19]

The intellectual context of irreligion seemed to point directly towards the age of individual reason and Enlightenment. Recent studies have made it clear, however, that scepticism and irreligion also had popular, non-intellectual roots that long antedated intellectual scepticism. In Spain, where the coexistence of three world religions may have fostered relativism and indifference, scepticism about heaven, hell and salvation was commonplace, and continued to be so for generations more. An Andalusian villager maintained in 1524 that 'we are born and die and nothing more'. A Catalan peasant asserted in 1539 that 'there is no heaven, purgatory or hell; at the end we all have to end up in the same place, the bad will go to the same place as the good and the good will go to the same place as the bad'. Another Catalan stated in 1593 that 'he does not believe in heaven or hell, and God feeds the Muslims and heretics just the same as he feeds the Christians'.[20] Exceptionally, this sturdy rejection of the official cosmology might invent its own scheme of things, as in the case of the Italian miller Menocchio, from Friuli, who at the end of the sixteenth century explained to the startled inquisitors that the universe was not created the way they thought but evolved through a process of fermentation, like cheese that produces worms.[21] None of these affirmations indicates any tendency to privatise religion or assert the independence of individual belief. Scepticism about religion and the afterlife was so widespread in the early modern Mediterranean that we may assume it to have been ingrained in popular traditions of belief, rather than being a private deviance. Certainly the Spanish Inquisition did not take seriously the cases of those denounced for scepticism, and attributed the errors to simple ignorance.

Privatisation of belief was, in its most concrete form, a legal one. The legal right to dissidence of belief had a long and respectable history. Massacre and intolerance in the Netherlands and France were the ugly face of confessional conflict, but represented only one side of a complex picture. In Poland, the Confederation of Warsaw (1573) accepted a situation of mutual toleration between different ideologies. But this was no novelty. As a Polish Lutheran stated in 1592, there was nothing new about diversity of religion in Poland. 'Apart from the existence of Greek Christians, pagans and Jews have been known for a long time and faiths other than Roman Catholic have existed for centuries.'[22] After the persecutions of the Reformation period, religious pluralism became slowly accepted again. In France toleration of dissidence became common from the 1570s and legally guaranteed for nearly a century after 1598. In the hereditary Habsburg lands, at one time or another all the religions were tolerated. But in all these cases the toleration was extended only to community groups.[23] Even among the Grey Leagues in Switzerland, where communes of different faiths coexisted in the sixteenth century, no dissidence was permitted within each commune.[24] Respect for the individual conscience, passionately demanded by Sebastian Castellio after the execution (1553) in Geneva of Miguel Servet, was not recognised legally anywhere in Europe. Individuals and small groups were tolerated sporadically, but usually for practical reasons and not by the legal system. The step from community norms to individual norms of worship was a large one that was not taken until well into modern times.

The most significant moves towards individualism in belief were made in the seventeenth and the eighteenth centuries by mystical sectarians, who had in common a rejection of the dogmatic structure of the official Churches. For the same reason the Catholic Church always considered with suspicion the constant re-appearance of mystical persons and groups. Pietism, which began like Lutheranism in the heart of Saxony but then spread throughout the western world, was perhaps the most powerful of all the individualising tendencies in early modern religion. Viewed from a modern perspective, it may appear that – in Protestant countries at least – religion was changing its character and also its role in society. The increasing importance given to individual piety is beyond doubt. But religion, even individualistic religion, was always firmly anchored in families and small communities, where the scope allowed to 'private' faith was usually restricted. It is, consequently, doubtful whether any meaning can be given to the idea that society in the early eighteenth century was moving towards 'modern' criteria or that it was by degrees becoming 'secularised'.[25]

Privatisation of knowledge: literacy and the people[26]

Probably the greatest spur to individual expression, and in historical terms the most valuable evidence of how individuals liberated themselves from their traditional cultural environment, was the extension of literacy. Although knowledge of reading and writing was considered desirable in medieval Europe, it was still looked upon largely as a practical skill, a qualification rather than a cultural necessity. Many medieval monarchs and even prelates of the Church were illiterate: they were not however uncultured, for they had readers who read to them and scribes who wrote for them. The importance of literacy as a practical qualification is reflected in the statutes drawn up by an archbishop of York for a college he founded in 1483, in which one of the purposes of the foundation was said to be that 'youths may be rendered more capable for the mechanic arts and other worldly affairs'. The Church valued the technical importance of literacy, for only a literate clergy could be the arbiters of religious (no less than social) life. In a very special sense, literacy was the preserve of the Church, which in Catholic Europe had a monopoly control over education.

The invention of printing, involving quicker and cheaper methods of book production, revolutionised illiteracy. Living in the century immediately after the development of the printing press by Gutenberg, Francis Bacon described it as one of three great inventions (the others were gunpowder and the compass) which had 'changed the appearance and state of the whole world'. In at least three respects – the promotion of education, propaganda (mainly religious) and the development of popular taste – literacy and the printed book affected the cultural level of the public.

The advent of the printed book could not by itself promote literacy. Books were not widely distributed, and in the villages people had to rely on obtaining them from strolling pedlars. These in any case carried booklets ('chapbooks') and fly-sheets rather than weighty tomes. Printed matter, moreover, was expensive; so that the public resorted less to quality books than to the cheaply produced tales of love and adventure, known in seventeenth- and eighteenth-century France as the Bibliothèque Bleue (Blue Library – from the colour of the binding), that pedlars hawked around. The greater accessibility of reading material helped to inspire an upsurge of interest in education. The theory of teaching developed significantly from the Renaissance onwards: possibly the most outstanding contribution came in the seventeenth century from Comenius. A literate education came to be considered desirable, not solely because literacy was useful but because it was right and proper to acquire knowledge. There is evidence that, in England at least, the essentials of reading and writing were being communicated to a high proportion of the common people. In the city of Norwich, there was free elementary education for the children of the poor.

A writer in central Sweden in 1631 reported that the people were 'so fond of letters that although public schools are very few nevertheless the literate instruct the others, with such enthusiasm that the greatest part of the common people and even the peasants are literate'. What, however, did it mean to be literate? Historians formerly judged literacy for this period by the ability of people to sign their own names. But it is now clear that very many who knew how to sign were otherwise unable to write or read, like the Spanish travelling actor who in 1663 admitted that 'he can sign but cannot write' or read.[27] Even the possession of books was no proof that one could read, as in the case of clergy who relied entirely on memory rather than on their mass-books for saying the mass (in a Latin they did not understand) and other prayers. The unreliability of the available evidence makes it difficult to measure 'literacy rates' during the early modern period.[28]

Signatures and books remain, of course, useful evidence of a certain cultural capacity. Of the 126 people in rural Surrey in 1642 who protested their loyalty to the government on paper, one third signed their names and the rest made a mark. The variation in signatures according to social class was quite notable. In the English village of Limpsfield, only 20 per cent of the servants but 62 per cent of the householders signed their names. In the Narbonne area in late sixteenth-century France about 90 per cent of the bourgeoisie signed their names; among the urban artisans about 65 per cent did so, and among the rural population the rate varied from 10 to 30 per cent.

In Durham in about 1570, a fifth of the lay witnesses in a church court were able to read; by the 1630s the proportion was 47 per cent. In Sweden the Lutheran Church insisted on literacy as a condition of active membership: in one seventeenth-century parish (Moklinta) 21 per cent of adults were able to read in 1614, and 89 per cent by the 1690s. Yet 'reading' in such a case might amount to no more than ability to decipher a catechism. Most people who 'read' seem never to have been in contact with a book. An examination of 2,843 cases for New Castile in the period 1540–1817 suggests that 45 per cent could read and write, yet only eight people out of this total confessed to possessing a book.[29] Nearly everywhere until the eighteenth century the transmission of culture remained oral. Moreover, a constant rise in possible literacy cannot always be assumed. It improved in some social sectors but not in others, in cities but not in the countryside. London in the 1640s had a literacy rate of 78 per cent, but in the counties it was never higher than 38 per cent. Evidence for England and Spain[30] suggests that some groups were actually more illiterate in the seventeenth than in the sixteenth century, because educational opportunities had not been expanded for them.

Promotion of literacy among the common people was undertaken most seriously in Protestant countries. The Bible was the basis for faith, and the Bible must be read. 'The Scripture', Luther argued passionately, 'cannot be understood without the languages and the languages can be learned only in school'. Much of the success of the Reformed movement in France was based on effort at promoting literacy. Elementary textbooks and alphabet manuals were distributed among the population. By the end of the seventeenth century the Protestant countries were arguably the most literate in Europe. In England by the 1650s there was a school for every 4,400 of the population. In Catholic countries there was no lack of emphasis on education either. By 1700 most parishes in France were equipped with a school (59 per cent in the diocese of Toul, 87 per cent in that of Paris), though literacy still varied a great deal. In the Beauvaisis 60 per cent of men could sign their marriage acts, but less than 10 per cent could in the Limousin and Brittany. Literacy tended to be much higher in the north than in the Mediterranean south. Religious reformers on both sides were concerned to educate their people to read the Bible and manuals of instruction.

Elementary education was not necessarily a step towards greater literacy. In most countries the 'grammar' taught at school, as an adjunct to reading and writing, was Latin grammar. The use of Latin was deliberately fostered by writers who believed that knowledge was the preserve of the few, and even innovators like Copernicus preferred to use Latin in the belief that the mysteries of science should not be communicated to the common public. Latin became a symbol of obscurantism to the Protestant reformers, who felt that it prevented the people gaining access to the truth. Vernacular sermons and books therefore assumed a greater importance than ever before. When Thomas More in 1533 claimed that nearly three fifths of the English people could read English, and hence could read a vernacular translation of the Bible, his purpose was to express alarm at the evil that could be done by unlicensed literature. More's figures were certainly wrong, but the fear of literacy in the native tongue persisted.

Private and public education, and the state

So many new universities were founded in the age of the Counter-Reformation that it was as though a new age of learning were coming into existence. In Germany there were Dillingen (1554), Jena (1558), Helmstedt (1569), Würzburg (1582) and several others; in the United Provinces there were Leiden (1575), Groningen (1614) and Utrecht (1636); in Britain there were Trinity College Dublin (1591), Edinburgh (1583) and the new Protestant College at Aberdeen (1593). The expansion of universities took place throughout Europe. In the old universities new colleges were founded and the total student membership rose: Cambridge had 1,267 students on its books in 1564 and 3,050 in 1622.

The notable expansion of universities presents all the appearances of a boom in higher education. The truth is that, to some extent, the statistics of expansion are misleading. A great number of the new universities were foundations artificially created to serve an immediate religious or political bent, and without any real hope of attracting students. Of the twenty-two new German universities created between 1540 and 1700, only seven survived into the nineteenth century. Some of them never attracted more than 100 students, and served a purely local demand. The principal reason why many new foundations came into existence was not primarily an increased demand for education, but because Catholics and Protestants refused to attend each other's universities, and instead set up their own rival colleges. The new establishment at Leiden was created because Louvain and Douai (the latter founded in 1562) were both in the Catholic southern Netherlands. The Lutherans had obviously taken care to fortify themselves in the institutions that passed to them at the Reformation, and the same was true for the Anglicans. Where the need for denominational education was still felt, establishments such as Strasbourg (1538, created a university in 1621) filled the gap. The Catholics in their turn had to create colleges for their refugees. The first great university created by the Counter-Reformation was Würzburg, which was under close Jesuit control and staffed principally by former professors of Louvain. In Germany the two most famous Jesuit-orientated universities were Ingolstadt (a pre-Reformation university) and Dillingen.

The coincidence of the rise in the volume of higher education, with the revolutionary changes of the post-Reformation period, might suggest that the educational impulse was breaking new ground. Once again, on the whole, this was not so. The education offered by the many new places of learning was very much a repetition of old methods and syllabuses. The increase in the number of schools and universities was not accompanied by any corresponding change in the methods of teaching. Hartlib and Comenius were still struggling in the mid-seventeenth century to bring in that 'revolution' in education which had till then occurred in numbers alone.

Part of the reason for the decay of academic learning in the universities was the rising tide of demand for civil office. Study of the liberal arts was neglected in favour of the two disciplines – civil and canon law – that offered a promising career. In the German universities the cultivation of the philosophical and natural sciences, of mathematics no less than of biology, was neglected. A fleeting stay at college became one's passport to a career. Besides, wealth could purchase degrees. The Wittenberg professor and poet Frederick Taubmann wrote in 1604 that 'nothing is easier today than to gain a doctorate, if you have money. Anyone can become a *doctor*, without being *doctus*.' There were numerous complaints of the type of education that Oxford and Cambridge offered. Giordano Bruno in 1583 described Oxford as 'the widow of good learning in philosophy and pure mathematics'. Chemistry and experimental science were apparently neglected and, reported William Harrison in 1587, 'arithmetic, geometry and astronomy...are now smally regarded'. 'The secrets of the creation', Gerrard Winstanley complained, 'have been locked up under the traditional, parrot-like speaking from the universities'. Aspects of the decay in Spain may be seen from the case of Salamanca university, which ceased teaching Hebrew in 1555, a year when only one student registered for it. In 1578 the chair of mathematics had been vacant over three years. By 1648 the arts faculty there was described as 'totally lost'.[31]

Until recently historians took a pessimistic view of the cultural role of the universities in early modern Europe. Scientific method rarely advanced there. The great pioneers – Copernicus, Brahe, Kepler, Peiresc – were often educated at universities but did not hold chairs and pursued their researches in a more independent environment. Perhaps the only significant exception was Italy, where the pursuit of knowledge in universities lingered on. Torricelli was professor of mathematics at Florence in the mid-seventeenth century. Padua, thanks mainly to Vesalius, remained the principal medical school in Europe, and it was to Padua that Harvey went as a young man. On balance, however, it must be recognised that universities were the base on which all other achievements were built. Over 87 per cent of the scientists born between 1450 and 1650 were trained at university.[32]

From the later sixteenth century, private groups of scholars took over some of the learned initiative from the universities. Literary salons and philosophical circles were commonplace in late sixteenth-century France and Italy. By the early seventeenth century the scientific academies were much in evidence. The two outstanding Italian ones were the Lincei in Rome (founded in 1603), which counted Galileo among its members, and the Cimento in Florence (founded in 1657), which included Borelli and other scientists. In England, 1660 witnessed the formal establishment of the Royal Society, which could trace its origins back over a decade earlier. Many of the first members of the Society had been professors of Gresham College, an independent institution set up in 1596 to provide an alternative to the education offered by the major English universities.

Renaissance ideals of culture and education were certainly influential in the vogue for improvement, especially among the gentry and rising men who wished to give their children the best. In 1614 Sir Thomas Fairfax asked a Cambridge college to allocate a good tutor to his son, for 'my greatest care hitherto hath bene, and still is, to breed my sonne a scholar'. But higher education was never regarded as an unmixed blessing. At the French Estates General of 1614, some deputies of the clergy complained that higher education

> burdens the state with too many educated people, weakens the armed forces, destroys trade and the arts, depopulates agriculture, fills the courts with ignorant people, diminishes the *taille*, inflicts simony on the Church, supernumerary officials on the state, wages and pensions on the Exchequer, and in brief overturns all good order.

Cardinal Richelieu was strongly opposed to more education: 'the commerce of letters would totally drive out that of merchandise', he claimed in his *Political Testament*. A French writer of 1627 thought that the schools 'have produced a great number of literates but few educated people. If someone learns three words of Latin, of a sudden he ceases to pay the *taille*.' Education, it was felt, made one a privileged person. Not surprisingly, many political commentators blamed political turmoil on the pretensions of the great number of shiftless educated. The Swedish statesman, Magnus de la Gardie, claimed in 1655 that 'there are more literati and learned fellows, especially in politicis, than means or jobs available to provide for them, and they grow desperate and impatient'. 'It is a hard matter for men', Hobbes was to point out, 'who do all think highly of their own wits, when they have also acquired the learning of the university, to be persuaded that they want any ability requisite for the government of a commonwealth'. His conclusion in respect of the events of the year 1640 was simple: 'The core of rebellion, as you have seen by this, and read of other rebellions, are the Universities....The Universities have been to this nation, as the wooden horse was to the Trojans.'

This exaggerated viewpoint does not coincide wholly with reality. Students went into higher education to serve, not to overturn, the state. If they were to be criticised it would be for a lack of interest in academic studies: 'the love of letters', observed a high court judge in Valladolid in 1638, 'brings only a very few to the colleges'. In most universities in central and western Europe two subjects predominated: canon law (in Catholic countries) and civil law. Then as now, the legal profession was the gateway to employment by the state. Marburg had been the first post-Reformation university founded (in 1527) with the express aim of producing graduates to serve the government; other German universities followed the trend of specialising in law. In Salamanca in the sixteenth century, enrolments for canon law exceeded those for all other faculties together; in the early seventeenth century civil law became popular, taking about half as many students as canon law. In England, those who did not go to Oxford or Cambridge went to the Inns of Court in London; many (50 per cent of entrants to the Inns) went to both university and Inns. The governing class in England became more educated: of 420 members of Parliament in 1563, 110 (or 26 per cent) had matriculated at university; by 1642, out of 552 members the figure was 276 (or 50 per cent). Most of the local justices of the peace in the country had by the 1640s been either to university or to the Inns.

The increase in university enrolments shows a consistent pattern in England, Germany and Spain; one may presume that it was the same elsewhere. Figures rose during the sixteenth century, with a pronounced increase from the 1550s until the second decade of the seventeenth century. Very roughly, matriculation totals doubled in Spain between about 1560 and 1590, in Oxford between about 1550 and 1580, and in Leipzig between about 1560 and 1620. The common people did not, of course, participate in this increase. In England peasants were 70 per cent of the population, but at Cambridge they were only 15 per cent of the student body.

Though law was the main subject taught in most places of learning, the universities did not become the training-ground for a bourgeois bureaucracy. The middle elite in Germany and Spain were conspicuous by their virtual absence from places of higher learning, and in England they were only a small proportion. Everywhere the nobles and gentry were in ascendance. The Venetian ambassador in 1612 reported that the Inns of Court contained 'five hundred of the wealthiest gentlemen of this kingdom', and records of the Inns confirm that between 1570 and 1639 gentry were over 80 per cent of entrants. At Oxford, 39 per cent of those matriculating in 1575–9 were gentlemen, and by 1600–9 the proportion was 52 per cent; correspondingly, the number of students of plebeian origin fell from 55 per cent in 1577–9 to 37 per cent in 1637–9 and 17 per cent in 1760. At the same time scholarships that had been reserved for the education of the poor were seized by the privileged. The picture was repeated in Germany: at Leipzig 289 poor students had matriculated in 1421–5, but only seventeen in 1556–60; at Cologne there had been 743 poor students in 1486–90, but only ten in 1556–60. It was the same in Spain, where in the course of the late sixteenth century the sons of the poor were crowded out of the places originally reserved for them. The university of Geneva (that is, Calvin's Academy, founded in 1559) had by the early seventeenth century become firmly aristocratic, the resort of the Calvinist nobility of Germany and France and of the premier families of Britain (Beauchamps, Cavendishes, Cecils, Douglases and Drummonds). Leipzig became dominated by the patriciates of central Europe and Poland: in the period 1559–1634 its students included six dukes of

Saxony, four princes Radziwill, one crown prince (of Denmark) and numerous other higher nobles.

For the gentry, university was a convenient finishing school.[33] William Harrison said in 1577 that 'they oft bring the university into much slander' with their extravagant way of life. Few bothered to stay the course and take a degree: this applied to half of all those enrolling at Cambridge in 1590–1640. Of the thirty-five government officials in the 1584 English Parliament, only thirteen had been to university and only four had a degree. In Heidelberg between 1550 and 1620 the proportion of matriculands taking their final degree never exceeded 5 per cent.

Nobles usually had private tutors for the formative years of their education. Universities – particularly foreign universities – were fitted in at the end in order to 'finish off'. Hence the Grand Tour, a product of the Renaissance which flourished no less in this period of confessional strife. When Sir Philip Sidney undertook it in 1572, the main aim was travel. 'Your purpose is, being a gentleman born', he was later to advise a younger brother, 'to furnish yourself with the knowledge of such things as may be serviceable to your country'.[34] Leaving England at the age of nineteen in the company of a tutor and three servants, Sidney travelled to Paris, Frankfurt, Heidelberg, Strasbourg, Vienna, Hungary, Padua, Germany, Poland, Prague and Antwerp, an absence of three years, only some of it spent in study. The '*nobilis et erudita peregrinatio*', as Justus Lipsius described it, was in practice fashionable only among the elites of northern Europe; French, Spaniards and Italians did not take to it. Manuals were written, such as Jerome Turler's *De Peregrinatione* (1574), and another by Thomas Palmer in 1606 that was prepared expressly 'for the youngest sort of such noble gentlemen as intend so recommendable a course'.[35] Public service no less than personal edification was the purpose, if we judge by Sidney's remark above, as well as by Sir Thomas Bodley's comment in 1647:

> I waxed desirous to travel beyond the seas for attaining to the knowledge of some special modern tongues and for the increase of my experience in the managing of affairs, being then wholly addicted to employ myself and all my cares into the public of the state.[36]

In the late sixteenth century, Italy was the most popular country visited. John Evelyn wrote in 1645: 'From the reports of divers curious and expert persons I've been assured there was little more to be seen in the rest of the civil world after Italy, France and the Low Countries but plain and prodigious barbarism.' A tour might often be rapid (a German noble journeying abroad in 1578–80 spent, during his visit to Italy, a few days at Bologna, a few weeks in Perugia, three months in Siena and then one year in Padua, having probably inscribed himself at all these universities without necessarily studying anything). The Austrian nobility were one group to broaden their cultural horizons: the Protestants journeyed abroad to Wittenberg, Jena and Marburg universities, the Catholics to

Vienna, Ingolstadt and Louvain; those of either faith who wished to study law went to Padua, Bologna and Siena. Through these travels they extended their knowledge of the romance languages (Spanish was in any case a requisite at the court of Vienna), and contacts with Italy brought them into the sphere of Renaissance literature. In private libraries of the Austrian nobility, three books – all Latin in culture – took pride of place: Cicero's *De Oficiis*, Petrarch's *Canzionere*, and Ariosto's *Orlando Furioso*.[37]

The practice of the tour shows that even in the age of ideological conflict the universities had not lost their international character. The rise of state barriers, of *cuius regio eius religio*, did not peremptorily destroy the international republic of letters. Protestants still went to Italy; Calvinism helped universalise academic study by opening the doors of its universities to all nations. Of the 161 names enrolled in the *Livre du Recteur* of Calvin's Academy at Geneva in 1559, nearly all were foreign to Switzerland. Of the 110 who matriculated at the Academy from late 1584 to early 1585, nine were Genevan, ten Polish, twenty Netherlandish, three Czech, three British, and nearly all the rest from France or Germany.[38] As late as 1653 a Genevan pastor complained that 'there come to this city a great number of foreign nobility, who live in great licence'. Attendance in the late sixteenth century at Heidelberg, perhaps the most important of the Calvinist universities, included about 39 per cent foreigners.

Leiden university can serve to illustrate the continuing internationalism of higher education. Founded in 1575, it remained open to both Catholics and Protestants, but flourished chiefly as a centre of Calvinism. In its first twenty-six years, 41 per cent of its registered students came from outside the United Provinces; in the subsequent quarter century over 52 per cent were from outside the country, more than half of them from Germany. In 1639 there were possibly more Germans matriculating at Leiden than at any German university.[39]

During the seventeenth century universities went into decline, for two quite distinct reasons. Demographic stagnation led to falling enrolments: in Spain matriculations nose-dived after the 1620s; and in Germany the disruption of the Thirty Years War created a huge drop in admissions between 1620 and 1645. The second reason was that by becoming channels for the bureaucratic elite and leisure resorts for the aristocracy, universities suffered a lowering of standards and ceased to be desirable centres of learning. In Salamanca, for example, faculty chairs were prized because they were stepping-stones to high office: one chair of canon law was filled sixty-one times in the course of the century. Those, even from the aristocracy, who wished to offer their sons an academic training, would send them to private academies or hire private tutors.

Private culture: diaries

To the historian, the most visible sign of literate individualism was the keeping of diaries. There had been medieval precedents, in the form of business accounts or agrarian journals, in which personal annotations had sometimes been made.

By the sixteenth century many Catholic parish priests, inspired no doubt by enforcement of the regulation that they should keep church records, used the opportunity to scribble memoirs. From the period of the Reformation, spiritual concerns were the chief motive for diaries: Ignatius Loyola kept a spiritual journal. John Evelyn commented on 'the infinite benefit of daily examination, comparing to a merchant keeping his books',[40] and kept detailed notes of the sermons at which he assisted. The frequency of diaries among Puritan gentry and clergy was testimony to the importance of spiritual concerns. But most diaries were short-term records, not written up continuously, and may consequently be aggregated to other similar first-person writings such as memoirs and autobiographies, which evolved at about the same time.

The best known diaries come mainly from the literate male elite, and mainly from northern Europe, where literacy seems to have been higher and the privatisation of lay spirituality more advanced. The superb seventeenth-century diaries kept by the Englishmen John Evelyn, Ralph Josselin and Samuel Pepys all share a deep preoccupation with spiritual matters. Over a broad perspective, however, first-person writings were not limited to males, nor to northern Europe nor to spirituality. Women, as we have seen (Chapter 7), were from the seventeenth century significant diarists. In the Mediterranean, a rich spirituality produced remarkable personal memoirs (such as the *Life* by Teresa of Avila). But the genre of a personal record was also intimately allied to that of autobiography, supplying us immediately with significant exceptions to the primary theme of spiritual matters.

Moreover, the genre of a purely personal record was broadened into that of public autobiography and memoirs, in which the writer used his own life as the basis for a narrative of his experiences and of the important people with whom he had come into contact. Though such writings cast interesting light on the writer, they shed even more light on the society of the time. The principal articulate gentlemen of Renaissance France (such as the Duke of Sully or Pierre de Brantôme) wrote their memoirs when they had retired from an active military or political career. Their motives were usually the same as those that prevail today among public figures: a wish to correct the record and justify their actions retrospectively. Seventeenth-century French noblemen and ladies conveyed their thoughts to paper extensively, and perhaps permitted themselves to doubt at a private and intimate level what their society at a public level took for granted.[41] Examples of such non-spiritual diaries have surfaced also in the Mediterranean, such as the extremely valuable memoirs of the Catalan Jeroni Pujades.[42]

Finally, numerous humble people all over Europe, from parish priests to artisans, kept little diaries that have fortunately survived, though only a few have been published. The form of such writings is at first glance individualistic, for the act of committing thoughts to paper was a clear affirmation of personal preferences, and the subject matter of diaries always reflected an individual point of view. But there are good reasons for doubting whether they were pioneer expressions of individualism. 'Perhaps the most striking aspect of early modern autobiographical writing at all social levels', it has been pointed out, 'is its relentless focus on externalities'.[43] With rare exceptions, autobiography was rooted in the environment that produced it. Though it spoke often of private griefs and public quarrels, it was seldom introspective. The writer yearned perhaps to escape from his or her personal condition, and took to writing as a means of affirming it, but in general continued to be tied down to the reality of everyday circumstance rather than to inner experience. Even the spiritual and mystical writers were less concerned with their own condition than with the great experience towards which they aspired.

Early modern personal documents often explored the world of the individual but differed from post-industrial autobiography in three main ways.[44] They paid less attention to sentiment and the interior self; they were never conscious of the external pressures of the world of the work-ethic; and they paid little attention to wider social problems. First-person writings have traditionally been used as invaluable sources for every aspect of social history, from family life to descriptions of the plague (the latter in Daniel Defoe's famous *Journal of the Plague Year*, published in 1722 but describing the London plague of 1665). They remain invaluable tools for exploring the evolving individual and inner world of the people of pre-industrial Europe.

The development of private opinion

From the time of the Reformation, public authorities became aware of the importance of private opinion and took steps to influence it. Luther addressed himself at an early stage to individual Germans, hoping thereby to bypass the existing structures of authority. In an age of low literacy, the most direct contact with the common man was made through the spoken word, in the pulpit.

In medieval times the pulpit had been the chief moderator of public opinion. From the sixteenth century both Protestants and Catholics rediscovered the potential of the sermon. The Jesuit Peter Canisius is said to have preserved Vienna for the faith by his preaching. It must not be supposed that successes were easily achieved. Most clergy, Protestant and Catholic, did not know how to preach: in pre-Reformation Europe sermons may have been frequent in the large towns but they were rare in rural areas. Congregations were quickly bored: in one parish in Cambridge in 1547, 'when the vicar goeth into the pulpit, then the multitude of the parish goeth straight out of the church, home to drink'. All over Spain in the 1560s pulpits had to be erected in parish churches where preaching had been unknown. Congregations had to be enjoined to listen reverently: silence in church[45] was one of the great innovative achievements of the period of confessionalisation. Since no other effective control was available over what half-educated clergy preached, the services of the Inquisition were called upon to discipline sermons.

Ecclesiastical permission was required in order to preach. The continental Reformation liberated the pulpit from Church control, but in episcopal England the bishops still kept a tight rein on the public expression of dissenting views. This encouraged Puritan communities to appoint unofficial 'lecturers' who, because they were not formally parish clergy, did not require a licence to preach and might often put forward theological views that differed from those of the official Church. As a result, Puritan attitudes were disseminated with impunity from hundreds of pulpits throughout the country, and threatened to subvert the established order. Lecturers, stormed Archbishop Laud in 1629, 'are the people's creatures and blow the bellows of their sedition'. The struggle for the pulpit was a struggle for men's minds.

The spoken word was powerful, but transient. It was the permanency of the printed word that alarmed the authorities, encouraging them to repress and control information. Printers were in the front of the ideological firing line. In the post-Reformation era many emigrated from Catholic to Protestant countries; from south to north Germany, from France to Geneva, from Belgium to Holland (among the exiles from Antwerp was the firm of Elsevier).

The battle of the books continued to be a religious one. Though there were opportunities for works on literature, travel, law and history, the religious book (devotional or controversial) was seldom displaced from its leading position. Of 169 books published in Paris in 1598, 32 per cent were in belles-lettres, 29 per cent on religion, 16 per cent on history, and 13 per cent on arts and sciences. In 1645, of 456 works published 38 per cent were on religion, 24 per cent in belles-lettres, 18 per cent on history, and 7 per cent on science. One third of the books published between these two dates were on religion. This may have been influenced by the high tide of the Counter-Reformation in France, but even outside France religious controversy (Arminianism, Jansenism) continued to dominate.

Books were not the ideal vehicle for controversy or propaganda. They were still comparatively expensive, and tended to be published in small editions (about 1,250 to 1,500 copies). The Bible was always a best-seller (possibly a million copies of Luther's Bible alone were printed in the sixteenth century). Devotional works sold well. The *Imitation of Christ* (*c.* 1418), the great product of *devotio moderna* spirituality, went through innumerable editions in the course of the sixteenth century, and in France alone from 1550 to 1610 was issued in thirty editions. St Francis de Sales' *Introduction to the Devout Life* (1609) totalled over forty French editions by 1620, and by 1656 had been published in seventeen different languages. But books in the vernacular were often in a minority, judging from the catalogues of the international book fair at Frankfurt. From 1564 to 1600 this fair, the largest in Europe, displayed nearly 15,000 books of German origin. On average, no more than a third of these were in the German language. In 1601–5, of 1,334 books at the fair, 813 were in Latin and 422 in German. Only after about 1680 did books in German come to be in the majority. In England the vernacular had a stronger hold on publishing, but despite this there was no notable attempt to use books in the moulding of opinion.

The literate public was less likely to read weighty books than chapbooks, pamphlets and fly-sheets. Short, well phrased tracts with a clear argument and simple language became the staple fare of the ideological conflict. From the pamphlet war of the Reformation to the often cruel propaganda of the Fronde and the Thirty Years War, it was this category that came closest to providing some sort of material for the masses to read. The fly-sheets usually contained satirical illustrations brilliantly calculated to attract a reader's attention. In most cases the text was a piece of doggerel verse, often several stanzas long. Though the entire early modern period was one of strife and controversy, pamphlet propaganda was not a continuous part of it. The overwhelming majority of surviving pamphlets date from one central epoch only, the middle decades of the seventeenth century, and are concerned with three key events: the Thirty Years War, the Fronde and the English Revolution.

The vast majority of German leaflets dealing with the Thirty Years War attempted to present the justice of one cause and the excesses of the opposing side.[46] The volume of literary output that this involved signalled the emergence of a particular kind of writer: the professional publicist. The Germans were to produce many such in the course of the conflict, notably Kaspar Schoppe, who wrote for the Catholics, and Hoë von Hoënegg, court preacher to the Elector of Saxony, for the Lutherans. All the techniques of crude propaganda – distortion, exaggeration, plain falsehood – were employed generously by these writers. Small wonder that to the historian the most interesting of the fly-sheets are not the blatantly partisan ones so much as those which react against all the protagonists and plead wearily for peace and humanity. Typical of these is one of 1642, protesting bitterly against the sufferings endured by the peasants at the hands of the nobles and soldiery:

> The splendour of the land can no longer be seen,
> War, robbery, murder and arson are laying it waste,
> The free Roman Empire is falling to barbarians.

The literature associated with the English Revolution and the Fronde was, like the propaganda of the Thirty Years War, produced for the most part by a handful of skilled publicists. To contemporaries one of the most alarming aspects of the troubles in England and France was that the rebel leaders had invited the common people to partake of mysteries forbidden to them. 'The people entered into the holy of holies', Cardinal de Retz was to say with satisfaction of the Fronde. In England, Clement Walker in his *History of Independency* (1661) criticised the proceedings of the Independents: 'They have cast all the mysteries and secrets of government before the vulgar, and taught the soldiery and the people to look into them and ravel back all governments to the first principles of nature.' Another English contemporary denounced 'the tumultuous risings of rude multitudes threatening blood and destruction, the preaching of cobblers, feltmakers, taylors, groomes and women', a list drawn up no doubt in ascending order of outrageousness.

But despite such testimony, pamphlet literature was not always an expression of 'popular opinion'. The pamphlets of the Fronde, produced systematically by the dominant political groups, were an attempt to win support and not a spontaneous outburst of popular sentiment.[47] In Paris the pamphlets circulated principally in the period from January 1649 to October 1652. Moreau's catalogue of these Mazarinades (so called after the best known pamphlet, *La Mazarinade*, dated 11 March 1651 and directed against Cardinal Mazarin) lists over 4,000 items.[48] It seems likely that the actual total was about twice that figure. There was also a lively run of leaflets in Bordeaux during the Fronde there. The circulation of pamphlets was not restricted to France; the Dresden library, for example, possesses over 3,000 items presumably collected within Saxony and Germany. Each pamphlet was carefully calculated to entertain the reader and to destroy the opposition through rumour, derision or simple false information. 'We felt', de Retz noted proudly in the spring of 1651, shortly after he had sent fifty of his men out to distribute his latest pamphlet, 'that we were masters of the street'. They were influencing and creating public opinion.

In the English Civil War the output of pamphlets was higher than any known in Europe. The British Library collection lists nearly 2,000 for the year 1642 alone, an average of nearly six pamphlets a day. For the years 1640–61 the total of surviving pamphlets approaches 15,000. In general, the pamphlets in England were not sophisticated propaganda nor the handiwork of experienced publicists. In both England and France many writings were totally irrelevant to the crisis that produced them, and simply doggerel. Among the rest, despite their ephemeral character, were a great many that through the medium of propaganda attempted to reflect the attitudes of the common people: pamphlets full of proverbs, slang, vulgarities and outright obscenities. For sheer volume of publicity, the seventeenth century was one of innovation.

The activity meant a very busy time for the presses. A Paris printer commented with exaggeration in 1649: 'One half of Paris prints or sells pamphlets, the other half writes for them.' As the leaflets rolled off the press, distributors would be on hand from early morning to take them out to the streets. After the capital came distribution to the provinces, carried out with striking efficiency. Mazarin complained in 1649 of one pamphlet that 'they have sent more than six thousand copies of the leaflet against me and d'Hémery [the finance minister] into all the provinces'. Since censorship regulations were theoretically still in force, pamphleteers always needed to be wary. The Levellers were among the most devious and successful publicists of this time. John Lilburne made himself a thorn in the side of authority by his ability to produce unlicensed pamphlets: 'I am now determined to appeal to the whole kingdom and Army against them [the Presbyterians]', he proclaimed in 1647. From 1648 to 1649 he was helped by the existence of a newspaper, the *Moderate*, which presented most of the principal Leveller news to the public. It was one of the first instances of a close-knit revolutionary group making extensive use of the press in order to change the climate of opinion.

Incomparably the most important propaganda centre in Europe was the

Dutch Republic. In Amsterdam and in Leiden the presses served the demands of nearly every leading European language. Amsterdam had a virtual monopoly in the production of anti-French propaganda, and subversive literature was also smuggled regularly into England, Scotland and other countries. With the freest press in Europe, the Dutch threatened the security of every state practising censorship.

The history of pamphlets overlaps that of the periodical press. The function of both was to appeal to the public forum, and a pamphlet that appeared periodically (the earliest example in England was the series of Marprelate tracts in 1588 and 1589) was already setting a precedent. The real distinction between the two, however, was that the periodical aspired to give news and was, in effect, a news-sheet. In the sixteenth century, on the other hand, as in some modern authoritarian states, news could be dangerous. A printer could be accused of betraying information to the enemy, or of deliberate distortion and slander, or of inflaming the people by seditious publication. The penalties for sedition could be severe: in England in 1637 William Prynne had his ears cut off, was heavily fined and then imprisoned. In Rome in 1572 the Pope waxed so indignant at the hostile tone of the *avvisi* that he forbade their publication, and his successor passed an edict against the spreaders of false and malicious news. One of the journalists who fell foul of these regulations in 1587 had his hand cut off and his tongue cut out, and was then hanged.

The *avvisi* were principally merchants' newsletters, and were the earliest form of Italian journalism. Those sent from Venice to the Fuggers in Augsburg in 1554–65 were among the earliest, but the first regular series were those sent from his agent in Rome to the Duke of Urbino over the years 1554–1605. The information was collected by journalists called *menanti*. The best known missives were the Fugger newsletters, to which correspondents from every part of Europe contributed. They were not limited merely to business news, but gave information about everything that the writer considered worth reporting. The *avvisi* appeared infrequently; by contrast the appearance of newspapers is measured by frequency. The official *Mercure Français*, published at the beginning of the seventeenth century, was issued only annually. By general agreement the first 'newspaper' is dated to the early seventeenth century. This was the monthly *Relation*, first produced by the Strasbourg printer Johann Carolus in 1609 and distributed also in Augsburg. It contained news reports from seventeen different European towns. Another contender for the title of first newspaper is the *Avisa, Relation oder Zeitung*, which appeared at Helmstedt in the same year 1609. A weekly seems not to have existed until the appearance in 1615 of the *Frankfurter Zeitung*, published by Egenolf Emmel. Germany may rightly claim to have been responsible for both the invention of printing and the beginnings of journalism. The first French newspaper was published in 1620, not in France, however, but in Amsterdam. It was in Amsterdam, too, that the first English newspaper came out, in the same year 1620. This was the *Corrant out of Italy, Germany etc.*, which gave regular news reports on the Thirty Years War.

Two considerations gave a great impetus to the growth of proper newspapers. In the first place, the state was concerned to publicise its views. Copies of state edicts were printed and distributed (for the years 1598–1643 alone, the National Library at Paris possesses over half a million different printed papers issued by the state). The desire to have a regular platform for official views led Théophraste Renaudot to found in 1631, with the support of Cardinal Richelieu, the *Gazette de France*, as a journal for 'kings and the powers that be'. But the *Gazette* was also intended to be a straightforward supplier of information for the average citizen, so that

> the merchant will no longer trade in a besieged and ruined town, nor the soldier seek employment in a country where there is no war: not to speak of the comfort for those writing to the friends, who were formerly forced to give news that was either invented or based on hearsay.

It came out weekly and consisted of four (later eight) quarto pages. Other states followed suit. Florence got a weekly gazette in 1636, Rome in 1640, Genoa in 1642, the States General of the Dutch Republic in 1649, and in Spain the *Gaceta de Madrid* was first published by royal order in 1661.

News became particularly desirable during a political crisis, and any sort of information was seized on with avidity. 'From the great to the small', says a report on Paris during the Fronde,

> everyone discusses what is going on only through the *Gazette*. Those who can afford it, buy copies and collect them. Others are satisfied to pay in order to borrow and read it, or else they group together so as to buy a copy.

In England the breakdown of censorship during the Civil War gave scope to an unprecedented flood of news-sheets: in the Thomason collection at the British Library there are only four newspapers for 1641, but 167 for 1642, and 722 for 1645. The two most important were the royalist *Mercurius Aulicus* (edited from Oxford) and the parliamentarian *Mercurius Britanicus*. The circulation of the former in London alone was about 500 copies, but each copy was read by several people; if other papers sold as many copies, the total public they reached must have been large. Censorship was re-imposed with the Licensing Act of 1662, but in the later century, when political parties appeared, the demand for tracts was even greater. The common people of London (where the number of printing presses trebled from 1662 to 1695) became sensitive to the great issues of the day, particularly after the Licensing Act of 1695 abolished pre-publication censorship.

Censorship had been strict in the early sixteenth century, as it had been in medieval times even before the invention of printing. Printing was seen as a major threat to established authority: it 'opened German eyes', wrote the

German historian Sleidan in 1542. John Foxe commented that 'either the pope must abolish knowledge and printing or printing must at length root him out'. This optimistic view is reflected also in Gabriel Plattes' claim (1641) that 'the art of printing will so spread knowledge that the common people, knowing their own rights and liberties, will not be governed by way of oppression'. Every country had firm controls: in England the first list of prohibited books was issued in 1529, and in 1530 a licensing system was introduced. The notorious Star Chamber decree was passed in 1586. One of the first opponents of licensing was the Leveller leader Walwyn, who demanded in 1644 'that the Press may be free for any man that writes nothing highly scandalous or dangerous to the state'. John Milton made the same demand in his *Areopagitica* (1644). On the continent the Roman and Spanish authorities published guide-lists of forbidden books in their famous *Indexes*. The *Index* ironically became useful to bibliophiles seeking details of anti-Catholic publications: in 1627 the Bodley's librarian at Oxford suggested that it be consulted as a guide to books worth buying.

The spread of literacy and printing had very complex consequences. It did not replace the primacy of oral culture, which remained dominant, for example, throughout the Mediterranean and the Russian lands until well into the nineteenth century. With good reason during the confessional period in Germany did the Jesuits direct their emphasis towards the theatre and the Lutherans towards hymnology.[49] The book was a fruitful instrument, but its successes lay in the future. Educated elites everywhere improved their grasp of learned culture, but continued to share the same human environment as the less literate, so that it is not easy to determine whether differences between elite and popular cultures were made sharper. 'By itself, literacy does nothing.'[50] It could accompany change but not initiate it. It had a perceptible influence on the spheres of information and administration, but in pre-industrial times had no measurable impact on the level of culture or the development of individualism.

Printing appears not to have disturbed the levels of popular preference. Readers chose escapist literature, 'lewd Ballads', 'merry bookes', 'corrupted tales in Inke and Paper', to cite English critics of the genre. The 'Blue Library' in France consisted of romantic fiction of this sort. Attempts were of course made to change popular taste. Intellectuals in Spain, most of them clergy, claimed repeatedly that the suppression of superficial literature was one of the most useful roles of censorship. Romances of chivalry were the most criticised. In Spain the poet Alvar Gómez de Castro felt that 'since they are without imagination or learning and it is a waste of time to read them, it is better to prohibit them'.[51] Fortunately for the public, who would otherwise have had to feed on very dull fare, censors in practice paid less attention to superficial than to ideologically dangerous literature.

After the Restoration in England there was a sustained attempt to appeal to popular opinion. Though licensing of publications was imposed in 1662, after 1695 the licensing system was abandoned. Some restrictions continued, but with sufficient liberty for a vigorous political press to emerge. Journalism became a respectable profession. When Defoe founded his *Review* (1704) he proposed 'to open the eyes of the deluded people', and went on to achieve remarkable success. A contemporary reported that 'the greatest part of the people cannot read at all, but they will gather about one that can, and listen to the *Review*, where all the principles of rebellion are instilled into them'.[52]

Private and public dreams: the discovery and loss of Utopia

At a time of rapid social change and shifting beliefs, one aspiration remained constant: the yearning for a better world in which man would cease to make mistakes and justice for all would be achieved. The search for a just society drew on ideas of the late medieval millenarians (particularly Joachim of Fiore), on classical mythology, and above all on the tradition of the simplicity of the early Christians.[53] Successive thinkers and social rebels looked back to a mythical 'age of gold' which was, assuming that history moved in cycles, to come again. They contrasted it with their own 'age of iron' or 'iron century', in which strife and injustice were rampant. When they proposed improvements, however, their ideals tended inevitably to arrive at a confusing compromise between the unattainability of perfection and the reality of man's limitations.

In 1516 Thomas More published in Latin a little study called *Utopia*, which was not translated into English until 1551. The book described an imaginary society on the island of Utopia ('Nowhere'); to this More later added an introductory dialogue between himself, some friends and a traveller called Ralph Hythloday, on the main topics of the time. Inspired by medieval monastic ideals and by the communism of Plato, More presented his Utopia as a place where men lived in conditions of equality, elected their rulers freely, were all obliged to work, were guaranteed security, education and leisure, coexisted peacefully with other states and worshipped without dogmas. *Utopia* was an exercise in imagination, not a blueprint for a communist paradise; it made no attempt to be explicitly Christian because the author was writing in the non-ideological humanist environment that preceded the Reformation.

The study had been provoked by tales of the lands discovered across the Atlantic. When Columbus and the early Spaniards reached the New World they were astounded by its felicity. The perfections of America appealed immediately to those who wished to compensate for the evils of the Old World. Montaigne evolved his myth of the 'noble savage'; others resurrected legends of the 'earthly paradise'. The reality after the conquest was different: the Indians were ravaged by disease against which they had no immunity, their lands were taken away, their villages broken up and the men taken off to perform labour services. Spanish missionaries who still treasured the early vision were horrified. Schooled in the humanists and in Erasmus, they tried to recreate for the Indians the environment they had lost. Vasco de Quiroga, first bishop of Michoacán, had spent some time reading and annotating *Utopia*. As a result he set up at Santa Fe an entire community based on the practicable principles of More's book: all property and land were held in common, labour was communal, government was through elected representatives. For the first time in history, Utopia was actually put into practice. Similar programmes were attempted by Las Casas in his settlement of Vera Paz (True Peace) in Guatemala in the late 1530s. But one by one these schemes collapsed.

After the 1550s the Utopian vision faded, to be overtaken by an epoch of inflation, epidemic and continuous religious conflict: for contemporaries this was the core of the 'iron century'. The only significant idealist scheme of the period was offered by an Italian bishop, Francesco Patrizi, in his *La Città Felice* (1553).[54] Scholars were more concerned to salvage some order out of the ruins of their war-torn countries. When Jean Bodin published his *Six Books of the Republic* (1576) he disavowed any intention of writing about an impractical ideal state, 'a republic in the imagination and without effect, such as those which Plato and Thomas More have imagined'.

The years of strife were not without practical experiments. After the disastrous episode of Münster (1535), Anabaptists set about constructing peaceful communities in central Europe, notably in the mountains of Moravia. Meanwhile, Giordano Bruno in his *Expulsion of the Triumphant Beast* (1584) presented a proposal for sweeping changes in society. His radicalism of outlook, however, tended to be anarchical. The practical Utopias of minority groups were, by contrast, strictly regulated. All Utopias, whether theoretical or practical, depended for their existence on rigid seclusion from the rest of the world, total uniformity of thought and action, with a minimum of free choice; collectivisation of functions, and in extreme cases even of the family; abolition of distinctions of rank and wealth; and an extensive system of education for all. These principles might work among small groups in Moravia; they were more difficult to put into practice in South America, where the grandest of Utopias was created by the Jesuits.

In seventeenth-century Paraguay (a large area covering a third of Spanish territory in South America) the Jesuits attempted to liberate the Guaraní tribes from the colonial labour system. In 1611 the local authorities prohibited Indian slavery and permitted the Jesuits to set up Indian settlements (*reducciones*).[55] By 1676 the Society had twenty-two *reducciones* with a total of over 58,000 Indians who held land in common, were given arms to defend themselves against marauding settlers (all whites other than Jesuits were excluded), and had black slaves to do the heavy labour. The experiment continued until the Jesuits were expelled from America in the late eighteenth century. In one sense it was not a Utopia, for the Jesuits were doing little more than fulfilling local legislation in respect of the Indian. While it survived it seemed to work, and stimulated the interest of social thinkers in Europe.

In the early seventeenth century the accumulation of crises seemed to provoke a resurgence of Utopian literature. All the significant writers were convinced Christians, yet curiously none of their projects was explicitly so.

Common to the schemes of Campanella, Andreae, Bacon, Hartlib and Vairasse was an emphasis on rational order and a scientific structuring of society. Knowledge (and therefore education) became the key to a well ordered state. Comenius described this outlook as 'pansophism', a term he borrowed from the *Pansophia Sive Paedia Philosophica* published at Rostock in 1633 by Peter Laurenberg, which drew heavily on the ideas of the medieval Catalan philosopher Ramon Llull.

Tommaso Campanella (d. 1639), a native of Calabria, was a man of contradictions. A priest of the Roman Church, his fundamental commitment was to astrology and magic; a protagonist of Spain's universal dominion, he spent over twenty years in a Spanish prison in Naples; defender of Rome's supremacy, he was imprisoned by the Pope and fled to France after three years in a Roman gaol. These contradictions emerge in his *City of the Sun*, which he wrote during his imprisonment from 1602 to 1626. Presented as a dialogue between a Grand Master of the Knights Hospitaller and a Genoese sea-captain, it describes an ideal society without private property, which is abolished because property encourages acquisitiveness and self-love. 'But when we have taken away self-love, there remains only love for the state.' All things are held in common, all activity done in common. Living, sleeping, eating are mass communal activities. The family is likewise abolished, and procreation is controlled by the state. Work is held to be noble: because everyone works, tasks are completed rapidly and the average time worked is four hours a day. There is universal education from very early youth, and the sciences are encouraged. There is no explicit reference to Christianity, and magistrates who possess the names of the principal virtues govern the city. The physical layout of the city is magical and astrological. The chief priest who governs the city represents the sun. Procreation is undertaken at the right astral conjunction, and the careers of inhabitants are decided 'according to their inclination and the star under which they are born'.

When Johann Valentin Andreae (d. 1654) published his *Christianopolis* in 1619, his aim was not to describe an ideal state so much as a tiny community of like-minded people. He conceived of a settlement no larger than a small village: 'about four hundred citizens', he wrote of Christianopolis, 'live here in religious faith and peace of the highest order'. There was no private property, and 'no one has any money, nor is there any use for any private money'. Manual labour was honourable: everyone took part, and the working hours were short. After what we have already seen of Andreae's Rosicrucianism, it seems that Christianopolis was really an exclusivist society, and the citizens an elite of savants. Education was universal, and even 'their artisans are almost entirely educated men'. Despite the name of the city, Andreae's concern was with learning rather than religion.

It was the service of learning that also influenced Francis Bacon to describe the mysterious island of *New Atlantis* (written in about 1624, published 1627). The work was left unfinished, and is not strictly Utopian. New Atlantis was a monarchy which still possessed the standard features of property, wealth and rank, and Bacon showed little interest in discussing social improvements. Its main interest lies in the secret scientific society (the members of Salomon's House) that enjoyed a privileged position in the state. Its members could withhold scientific secrets from the state, and periodically sent agents out into other countries to learn their secrets. Most commentators have seen this as a prefiguration of the Royal Society of London, founded in 1660.

Samuel Hartlib (d. 1662), of Baltic origin but resident in England after about 1628, was interested more in education than scientific learning. A member of his cultural circle, Gabriel Plattes, published in London in 1641 *A Description of the Famous Kingdome of Macaria*, which took the form of a dialogue between a scholar and a traveller, on the theme of an ideal society. Macaria was a monarchy, with a Great Council that sat annually for a short period. Below this Council were five lesser councils, dealing respectively with husbandry, fishing, trade by land, trade by sea, and overseas plantations. One twentieth of the income from husbandry was taken by the state to finance improvements. Nobody in Macaria held more land than he could exploit. The kingdom was armed, in order to secure peace through strength. A college of medicine looked after the health of its inhabitants, and medicaments were distributed free. In many respects all this seems more modern than Utopian. We are also told, however, that there were neither Papists nor Protestants in Macaria: all were non-sectarian Christians. 'There are no diversitie of opinions among them', and a divine who comes up with novel opinions 'shall be accounted a disturber of the publick peace, and shall suffer death for it'. New opinions could not be published, but had first to be debated before the Great Council, which decided whether to sanction them.

The authors we have noted were men of learning, experience and liberal views, but their Utopias were less a reflection of society's shortcomings than of their own private vision. Andreae and Bacon were frankly elitist, Campanella openly exotic. Plattes' *Macaria* was by far the most sober blueprint for society, but it is possible that concern for reunion among the churches (one of Hartlib's chief aims) was the chief rationale for the work. The only writer to base his scheme for the future squarely on the errors of the present, and to locate his ideal state not in some distant island but in his own native country, was Gerrard Winstanley, whose last and most important work, *The Law of Freedom*, was published in 1652.

Winstanley's career with the Diggers had been spent in trying to persuade the authorities to bring freedom and equality to England. Now in 1652, after the collapse of the Digger cause, he presented to Cromwell in book form a summary of his ideas for the new society. 'I have set the candle at your door', he addressed Cromwell, 'you have power in your hand to act for Common Freedom, if you will'. *The Law of Freedom* lacked some of the fire of his earlier published tracts, but in outline it presented most of Winstanley's essential ideas. All land and resources would be held in common by all the people. The economy would be mainly agricultural, practising barter and exchange, but there would be no commerce and no money. The family unit would remain sacred, and so would family property. Government would be under a parliament, elected annually.

Knowledge would be made available to all, and education would be free and compulsory. Information would be circulated throughout the country, and general (rather than just religious) instruction would be given through the pulpit. Law would be codified and not depend on man's interpretation. These radical proposals contrast sharply with the more conventional ideas of James Harrington, whose *Oceana* (1656) was essentially a set of moderate constitutional reforms, based on the same scientific principles that inspired his colleagues in the educated elite.

The conservatism of late seventeenth-century society was not fertile ground for political innovation. The crisis of absolutism in Louis XIV's France was responsible, however, for a revival of speculative Utopias. Over a dozen projects appeared in French, the majority written by Protestants who used the genre as an oblique way of criticising the regime. The Huguenot exile, Denis Vairasse, presented his *History of the Sevarambians* (1675 in English, 1677 in French) as a travel tale of Europeans shipwrecked in Australia who stumble across the people of Sevarambia. There are echoes of Campanella in the fact that worship of the sun is central to Sevarambia; government follows regular Utopian lines in being communistic, and all education is controlled by the state.[56] The device of a travelogue was also used by Archbishop Fénelon of Cambrai in his *Télémaque* (1699), which followed the hero as he wandered through various countries and polities in search of his father Ulysses; but Fénelon's scheme was less Utopian than conservative, a summons to the classical virtues of the traditional pastoral way of life.

Utopian ideas were a reasoned response to the social and political problems of the time. Underlying the dreams was a desire to advance beyond contemporary illusions to the achievement of a perfect science and a just society. Winstanley, who had seen deliverance from the age of iron and from 'the great red Dragon' within the people's grasp, had most cause to hope still for the achievement of his vision: 'that we may work in Righteousness and lay the foundation of making the Earth a Common Treasury for all, both rich and poor'.

10

THE ABSOLUTE STATE

> The great and chief end of men uniting into commonwealths, and putting themselves under government, is the preservation of their property.
>
> (John Locke, *Of Civil Government*, 1690)

Economic stability was a prerequisite of political stability. Europe in the late seventeenth and early eighteenth centuries emerged into a more quiescent, more stable epoch. Over most of the continent, levels of fertility appear to have stagnated or fallen (an exception was Spain, where the birth rate rose as though in compensation for repeated epidemics). Scattered evidence exists of a new tendency to restrict family size by marrying later (between the sixteenth and the late seventeenth centuries the mean age of brides rose in Normandy from 21 to 24 years, in Amsterdam from about 24 to over 26 years, in Colyton from 27 to 29 years). The move to later marriage helped to stabilise population levels at a time when the dreaded bringer of mass mortality, plague, had been banished from northern Europe and would soon (after 1721) disappear from the Mediterranean. Subsistence crises were also much fewer in the late century. There were natural disasters – 1693 and 1709 in France, 1696 in Finland – but on a more regional scale.

Falling demographic levels were accompanied by falling prices. In southern Europe agricultural output decayed (again, with the exception of Spain): in Languedoc yield ratios of nearly 7:1 in the early century fell in the 1680s to under 5:1; in the Roman Campagna they stagnated at about 6.5:1. In northern Europe the response to what looked like recession was different. Yield ratios in England were maintained at about 8:1. Since prices were falling and demand decreasing, rather than cut back on production tenants and landlords preferred to improve and innovate. Ironically, therefore, the difficult economic climate in England encouraged investment in the soil. Agriculture benefited from manuals such as Weston's *Discourse* (1645) and Houghton's *Letters for the Improvement of Husbandry* (1681); new field (clover, lucerne) and fodder (turnips) crops; and mechanical innovations (Jethro Tull's seed-drill, patented 1701). The diet of the poor improved, English corn output rose.

Though the late seventeenth century displays some of the characteristics of a depression, therefore, there is no sign that the economy was contracting. Falling prices did not dampen business; indeed, in northern Europe business activity increased. Bullion from America, far from decreasing in quantity as historians once suggested, actually increased. The metals did not, however, push up prices as in the inflation of the sixteenth century, but were re-exported out of Europe by the English and Dutch to pay for their purchases in Asia. The English East India Company in 1700–1 alone exported over £700,000, and Dutch bullion exports to Asia rose from half a million ducats in 1618 to 1.25 million in 1700. It was a period when the foundations of Europe's domination of the world economy were laid: the English, in particular, made spectacular gains in the Atlantic slave trade, the Asian trades, and the re-export trade from the colonies. Within Europe, bills of exchange were made more generally negotiable, and bank-cheques began to be issued (by the Bank of Amsterdam in 1682). In 1694 the Bank of England was founded; it issued 'bank-notes' and offered attractive interest rates to investors.

The economic difficulties of the early century seemed, then, to be largely surmounted in the period after 1660, which was an epoch of consolidation. Lower grain prices benefited the working poor and in effect raised real wages. Entrepreneur farmers, faced with limited profits, turned their energies to innovation and improvement.[1] Regular popular revolts were becoming a thing of the past: regimes now enjoyed greater security. In most western states, the government began to legislate for social stability on the land and in commerce.

State intervention: land and mercantilism

Political stability in both eastern and western Europe favoured the consolidation of the social regime. Gentry and bourgeoisie committed their fortunes to the land, as the necessary prerequisite for social position and political office. In an economic climate where direct exploitation of the soil was costly, emphasis shifted to indirect exploitation through rentals; in the east, meanwhile, serfdom was intensified. The state stepped in to protect the landed regime of its elites.

In eastern Europe the ascendancy of the nobles was not new, for they had long been the natural rulers of the soil. The novelty was that this ascendancy was confirmed by the state in conditions where an extension of state power might have been expected. The noble classes were the backbone of the economy, and rulers such as the Great Elector of Brandenburg-Prussia chose to ally with them against the towns. In Brandenburg after 1660 excise taxes were levied on the produce of the towns but the nobles were exempted, giving them an obvious advantage. In Prussia the Estates granted the Elector an excise in 1662, but this likewise was used in favour of the nobles and against the towns. The story was repeated in Russia and other eastern lands.

In England, feudal tenures and the Court of Wards were abolished by Parliament in 1646. This meant that the crown ceased to be the ultimate landlord in the realm. Landowners now gained full ownership of their estates. In 1647 a law of entail was first brought in: owners could settle their land on their eldest son and prevent alienation of the family estate. This prepared the way for the great consolidations of property in the eighteenth century. When an act was passed in 1660 to confirm the measure of 1646, no additional privileges were extended to lesser landowners. The smaller men failed to win that security of tenure which the big landowners had obtained, and the way was prepared for expanding the land market, which had been boosted by the land sales of the interregnum in the 1650s. In that period Royalist sympathisers alone (this does not include crown or Church lands) had suffered confiscation of estates to the extent of about £1.25 million, and a further £1.5 million was lost in fines. A number of people lost their land permanently in this way, but no revolution in ownership occurred. Many bought back their own property, and what was unredeemed often went to members of the same social class. Perhaps the most important result of the sales was the acceptance of greater mobility in agrarian relationships.

The sum total of this in England was a situation favourable to the interests of the big landowner. A property franchise made sure that only those with a material interest could vote for the government of England. To protect those whose incomes came from the soil, Corn Laws were brought in. In 1670 grain exports were allowed, and in 1673 bounties were granted on export shipments; finally in 1689 duties on corn exports were removed and were instead imposed on imports.

In Piedmont it was also a period of aristocratic consolidation on the land. The noble class – recruited both from the old families as well as from successful bourgeois – continued to accumulate estates, and at the same time provided most of the capital for the bonds issued by the state from 1653 onwards. Clergy and aristocracy together provided two thirds of these loans to the state. It was to preserve the economic power of this class that Piedmont introduced legislation to protect noble holdings. The most important step was the edict of 1648 favouring inheritance by primogeniture. At the same time the burden of taxation on noble lands was lightened, until by the eighteenth century they were paying virtually no taxes. The power of the aristocracy was strengthened in all walks of life. Only under Victor Amadeus II in the early eighteenth century were any steps taken to reduce their hold on political life, but their economic and landed predominance remained undisturbed.

Whether freed from feudalism (as in England) or subjected to it (as in the east), the land became the mainstay of an aristocratic regime. State protection became normal policy, because the state protected the interests of the landed elite. Colbert's famous 1669 Ordinance on Waters and Forests restricted the rights of the non-propertied to cut wood, just as the English Game Law of 1671 restricted the rights of the rural lower classes to hunt. The unprecedented legislative activity of the state also had an effect on the formulation of 'mercantilist' policy.

'Mercantilism' did not exist as a formal theory: there were no specifically mercantilist writers and no governments consistently practised mercantilist policies. In retrospect, however, some historians have suggested that the word may be usefully applied to a number of principles that the emergent nation states of western Europe were putting into practice. The state seemed to be intervening for the first time in the formulation of economic policy, and the interests of the state therefore seemed to be coinciding with the wishes of the merchant oligarchies and the elite producers. In England and Holland there is clear evidence that commercial companies exercised influence on the formulation of foreign policy.

The state intervened in economic policy for three virtually self-explanatory reasons: to protect the sources of tax income, to control the movement of bullion, and to protect the trade of its merchants; in three words, fiscality, bullionism, and protectionism. All three aims are most commonly identified with the economic policy of France under Colbert, but can be found also in aspects of the policy of most other states, such as Piedmont under its minister Truchi. In practice the operation of these policies varied considerably. England and Holland gave less importance to 'bullionism', because their enormous entrepôt trade made it necessary for them to let a multilateral system of financial exchange come into existence. France, however, with a simpler trade system, wished logically to maintain a reasonable trade balance, and consequently limited the exit of precious metals.

Social structure and absolutism

Political institutions reflected the disposition of social forces. In England and a few other nations in the north of Europe and to the east of the Elbe, the medieval elite maintained their unity in the face of the king, who was consequently obliged to consult a bicameral body consisting of the landed classes (the lords) and the great cities (the commons). In France and most of the German lands the elite became split into interest groups, in accordance with feudalism in its most developed form: parliaments therefore became tricameral, with nobles, prelates and commons. Together, king and consultative bodies represented an alliance of interests, a 'commonweal' (to use an English term). The tasks of government were minimal: to maintain the proper relationship between elites (that is, to secure order and protect property), and to defend the commonweal.

From the late fifteenth century the collapse of feudalism resulted in greater emphasis on the role of the 'prince'. Renaissance writers such as Machiavelli, Castiglione, Seyssel and Erasmus looked to the prince to bring some order out of the conflict created in post-feudal Europe. The excellent advice they tendered was, however, often wishful thinking. The princes of this time were like an only infant in a domestic nursery: despotic and destructive in the little zone to which he is confined, but powerless to range over the family house where he is by common consent the most important resident. France and Spain were still only embryonic nation states, and their rulers had very limited powers in finance and administration, but in theory their authority was considerable. Late medieval ideas, adapting the language of Roman law, had accepted that the crown should be absolute. Isabella of Castile referred repeatedly to her 'absolute royal power', a phrase which recurs several times in her testament. In France it had been held since the late thirteenth century that the king 'holds his power of none save God and himself'; and later theorists emphasised that he was the source of laws and not subject to them. There was a vast gap between such claims and political reality, but the long-standing theory helped to justify subsequent efforts by princes to free themselves from the control not only of their elites but also, most importantly, of the Church and papacy, which had also made far-reaching claims to political authority.

In the course of the sixteenth century princes tried to put their claims into practice. The first great casualty was the papacy, which everywhere found its authority contested not only by nations (it was against the papacy that Thomas Cromwell claimed that 'England is an empire' or sovereign state), but also by its own bishops in each nation. Prelates trained in law maintained in France, Germany, Spain and England that within the realm the crown had broad temporal authority over the Church. The Spanish monarchs by about 1510, and the French crown by the Concordat of Bologna in 1516, won extensive control over their respective churches. The Reformation, when it came, took several other churches completely out of papal control. The crown did not benefit from these changes as much as it might have expected. Indeed, the social changes of the sixteenth century seemed to pose new threats to orderly government: economic and social mobility gave a stronger voice to interests, notably the rural and municipal gentry, that sought political power; the price-rise created difficulties for state finance; in some countries (France, Germany) religious differences threatened to bring anarchy.

Ferdinand and Isabella, who were feudal rulers and in no way 'new monarchs', adopted a wholly feudal solution to their problems by allying with their noble and municipal elites. For later European rulers the situation was more complicated. Among the developments which helped them was the emergence of sedentary royal 'courts', with their ritual and chivalric glamour, which created a visible centre of authority; the reorganisation of laws and the legal system, which confirmed that legislation emanated from the prince; the growth of a bureaucracy, trained in the law faculties of the expanding university system; and the evolution of a modern army under the central command of the state, in place of the old feudal musters. Even while these steps were taking place and writers such as Bodin (*Republic*, 1576) were maintaining that sovereign power was absolute and entitled the king to raise taxes, make war and peace, and so on, in practice rulers were careful not to move a finger without receiving support from sections of the political nation. Autonomous sovereignty was still only an aspiration; 'absolutism' was an ideal construction, in which thinkers attempted to create order out of the disorder they saw around them.

The persistence of absolutist theory, however, is proof that Europeans felt a deep longing for order and peace. In this sense, the theories are a significant attempt to deal with a real problem. Governments were obliged to handle their aristocrats carefully. The Reformation was a powerful spur to the process of power-sharing between the princes and their elites: land-hungry gentry became natural allies of a prince who guaranteed them the property they had seized from the Church. At the same time the images of royal authority (in France, for example, the magical 'king's touch' which was supposed to heal scrofula) became divorced from the Church and more laicised. In England, Shakespeare argued for a 'deputy anointed by the Lord' whose authority came from God but was not mediated by the Church; and Elizabeth I declared (in 1585) that 'sovereigns are not bound to render the reasons of their action to any other but to God'. Despite such claims the rulers of the time acted with remarkable circumspection. Machiavelli in *The Prince* (1514) had been impatient with the weakness of rulers, and kings thereafter increased their personal authority significantly, but all as a rule operated within the limits sanctioned by tradition, with few forays into *raison d'état*.

At the dawn of the seventeenth century, nation states were emerging but the power of the ruler was still inadequate. Kings were forced to contend with dissension, revolt, separatism and war at a time when the means available to them, in terms of both cash and personnel, were exiguous. Kingship itself was shaky: England and France survived a disputed succession, but the northern Netherlands had rejected their prince (Philip II), and the elective monarchies of Bohemia and Poland continued to suffer political uncertainty. Muscovy achieved peace in 1613 only after selecting a new dynasty, the Romanovs. All over Europe the privileged classes, sitting in their regional and national assemblies, continued to dispute authority with their rulers. In Upper Austria in 1610, a Protestant lord actually claimed in the Estates that 'the people chose their prince and can also reject him, the territory decides for itself whether the ruler shall be hereditary'. Princes naturally responded to such claims with doctrines of absolute power. James I, when king of Scotland, produced his *Trew Law of Free Monarchies* (1598), and when king of England engaged in a spirited controversy with the papacy and its theorists (Bellarmine and Suárez) over the right of kings to demand an oath of loyalty. Although undoubtedly important at the time, the controversy was over an issue (the relative spheres of papal and kingly authority) that became quickly outdated. The loyalty of nationals to their ruler, regardless of his religion, was never again seriously undermined by papal claims.

In a world of shaky authority, rulers asserted their status in at least two ways: by the imposition of solemnity and emblems; and by the encouragement of political theorists. The development of emblems,[2] cultivated at every level by municipalities and lesser nobility, became in the hands of the monarchy a projection of the image of power. From the publication in 1531 of a book by the humanist Alciati on images and heraldry, to the creation in 1663 of Louis XIV's famous device of a sun with the words 'nec pluribus impar', there was a systematic development of the emblems of state power. A French writer observed in 1671 that 'ever since the king adopted the sun as his symbol, enlightened people have taken him to be the sun. To think of one is to think of the other.' The solemnity of power was asserted in part by court ritual, but above all by the construction of luxurious residences, of which the most notable was Versailles.[3] In Versailles, art became a strategy of power, a pointer towards new frontiers of authority, for the palace and its gardens kept on expanding continuously until the king's death in 1715.

The early seventeenth century was the high tide of absolutist theory in most countries, with the notable exception of Spain, where Mariana and a small group of others reacted against Protestant regalism by proposing instead the democratic foundations of political authority. 'The king', Mariana wrote, 'must be subject to the laws laid down by the state, whose authority is greater than that of the king'. 'The subject is obliged to obey in accordance with his own conscience', argued another Spaniard, Cristóbal de Anguiano. In France, the reaction against the assassination of Henry IV encouraged more extreme absolutist theories than were current elsewhere. Notable among the several works that came out was Le Bret's *De la Souveraineté du Roi* (1632), which held that 'the sovereign command resides in a single person, and obedience in all others'. In these same years attempts were being made – by Strafford in England, Richelieu in France and Olivares in Spain – to harness and rationalise the resources of the state and strengthen the power of the king. Claude Joly remarked later during the Fronde that 'France has never been a despotic government unless it be in the last thirty years, when we have been subject to the mercy of ministers'. His sentiments are in some degree testimony to the success of the western European experiments in absolutism.

Conflict was inevitable because there were multiple and sometimes contradictory sources of legitimate authority. Many petty princes and small state assemblies also laid claim to sovereignty. In Germany, while the theorist Reinking in 1619 defended the emperor as being an absolute monarch, Hippolitus a Lapide in 1640 claimed the same absolute power for each state and for the Imperial Diet as a whole. In Aragon the kings were unable to interfere with the absolute powers (including powers of life and death over their peasants) of the nobility; and even in Castile many lords were virtually sovereign in their own estates. In Poland the nobles exercised sovereign power in their lands and blocked the emergence of a strong central monarchy. 'Absolutism', in short, was not exclusive to the crown; it was not a form of state government, but merely one way in which power could be exercised. By the mid-seventeenth century, indeed, in England and Holland some thinkers had moved towards absolutist republicanism. In the decade after 1640, the English Parliament exercised powers far more absolute than any that the Stuart kings had dared use, and Henry Parker in various writings claimed for Parliament the ability even to abolish Magna Carta. In 1649 the Rump Parliament resolved that 'the Commons of England...being chosen by and representing the People, have the supreme power in this Nation'. In Holland, Spinoza (*Tractatus Politicus*, 1677) argued that 'absolute sovereignty is the sovereignty held by the whole people', and Ulrich Huber (*De Jure Civitatis*) held that the absolute rule of the upper classes was superior to monarchical absolutism because more broadly based and therefore more stable.

Even while advocating royal claims, theorists were aware of traditional and practical restrictions on the exercise of authority. Many apparently extreme writings can, when read carefully, be seen within their context to be realistic. A good example is Charles Loyseau, who in his *Traité des Seigneuries* (1610) announced that 'sovereignty consists in absolute power, that is to say in full and complete authority in every respect, and is consequently without superior'. 'However', he goes on,

> since only God is all-power the authority of men can never be entirely absolute. There are three kinds of law which limit the sovereign's power without affecting his sovereignty: these are the laws of God, the natural rules of justice and the fundamental laws of the state.

Similarly Le Bret in 1632, while declaring royal sovereignty to be unlimited, went on to specify that the monarch must respect private property, could not alter the succession to the throne, and could not issue a command contrary to divine law. Bossuet, well known as an exponent of Louis XIV's absolutism, declared (in a work written in 1679 but not published until 1709, after his death) that the absolute sovereign must abide by the laws of the kingdom. An absolute ruler claimed to be free (*absolutus legibus*) from subjection to the law, but only because he was the fount of law, not because he intended to break the law. Absolute power implied autonomy of sovereignty, not despotism.

Were any acts of European rulers 'absolute'? The question is potentially a philosophical rather than a historical one. In practice it would seem that any royal decrees issued on the prince's sole authority might be *ipso facto* absolute, hence the strong suspicion with which lawyers in Tudor and Stuart England regarded the crown's right to issue proclamations (as confirmed in a statute of 1539). Outstanding among occasions when governments in western Europe acted alone and without consultation were those when *raison d'état* permitted political assassination (the murder of Wallenstein is a good example). Louis XIV's revocation of the Edict of Nantes, often quoted as an absolute act, is a particularly weak example of absolutism: it came only at the end of a decade or more of persecution, and merely set the seal on a process that had originated not with the crown but in the lower levels of the administration. In practice 'absolute' acts are as difficult to identify as 'infallible' papal decrees. Contemporary critics of Philip II, Charles I and Louis XIV felt on surer grounds when they condemned 'tyranny', a familiar Graeco-Roman concept, whereas 'absolutism' fell into no recognised category and so could not be easily identified.

By the same token, though 'absolute' princes preferred to rule without

Estates, government without Estates did not in itself signify absolutism. Bourbon France after 1614 had no Estates General but was by no means short of representative assemblies. As a general rule, no western governments thought they were free from the need to consult at least some of their traditional institutions. In France, though the Estates were not called, Richelieu convoked the Assembly of Notables; and though Habsburg Castile had no Cortes after 1665, the cities represented in the Cortes were directly consulted. In a society that was a complex amalgam of many different interests, representative bodies were not the only guarantors of the rule of law. Rulers had to be wary of the Church, of city corporations, and of regional assemblies. States that were beginning to evolve some form of central apparatus were far from achieving any authentic centralisation, thanks to the existence of other autonomies within the nation. By the early seventeenth century, the western monarchies all had consultative and executive bodies in their capital cities, but in the absence of a national bureaucracy they were virtually body-less heads. Even more important was the fact that the social structure proved an obstacle to the centralisation of power.

It is too often assumed that where absolutism flourished the ruling elite were crushed, their privileges removed, the Church subjected, the common people overwhelmed by taxes. This negative view identifies state power with coercion. Yet perhaps the two most successful rulers in the period covered by this book – Isabella of Castile in about 1500, and Henry IV of France in about 1600 – became living legends and won the hearts of their subjects precisely because they used a minimum of coercion. There is therefore good reason to argue that consent rather than coercion was the basis on which the power of the emergent state came to rest. If the seventeenth century was more absolutist than the sixteenth, it has been pointed out, it was not because the laws had been changed to make them more oppressive, but because the old laws were reasserted and made more effective; any change was political, not legal.[4]

Perhaps the most convincing way to view royal absolutism is as an overall supervising authority arbitrating between conflicting interests. Theorists such as Loyseau and Le Bret felt a need to elevate the executive authority of the crown, and in so doing they expanded on medieval principles of sovereignty. But at every stage they recognised that interests such as the Church, the nobility and the law must be respected. In practice, of course, kings in countless individual instances broke all the rules: they usurped ecclesiastical rights, arrested and executed nobles, levied taxes, and broke laws ranging from regional laws to laws regulating the succession. They were able to do this not because they were strong but because they were able to play off interests against each other. A particularly telling example is the way in which the crown at the French Estates General of 1614 was able to divide the Estates and annihilate their role in politics; thereafter the First and Second Estates were summoned separately, the Third not at all. Similarly, the monarchy survived the Fronde not because it was strong but because its opponents were divided. From the early sixteenth to the late seventeenth centuries, the undoubted increase in royal authority was achieved without any significant diminution in the power of elites. This was possible because power shifted *within* the ruling class from the traditional to the recently ennobled aristocracy. The state was able to exploit this shift of power and use it to its own advantage.

The power of elites altered but did not diminish. In part this was because the nobility everywhere retained their monopoly of the bulk of national wealth; in part also because newer status groups – the *noblesse de robe*, the gentry – broadened the hold of the upper classes on political and economic life. In these circumstances the crown could hold and increase its authority only as an arbiter between interest groups, gratifying sections of the elite with honours and offices while taking care to protect its own position as the source of patronage. Progress towards 'absolutism' thus involved compromises at every stage. In times of strained relations the elite took refuge in traditional laws, thus making the crown seem to be the aggressor. In Aragon the appeal (in 1591 and 1640) was to the *fueros*, in England a tradition of common law was felt to be the force by which (Parliament declared in 1642) 'the nobility and gentry enjoy their estates, are protected from any sort of violence and power, and differenced from the meaner sort of people'. These, the meaner sort, in their turn responded by rebellions that could be used by some of their leaders (as Mousnier argues) against the fiscal pretensions of the 'absolute' state.

It has rightly been argued that the power and role of the state in the sixteenth and seventeenth centuries were enhanced by the regularity of war. The declaration of war was reserved to the monarch alone; he obtained sole right to command the nation's armed forces; and military needs provided a pretext to raise extra taxes. Possibly three quarters of a state budget might be allotted to war (including defence and diplomacy). In the process, important structural changes would occur. New administrative personnel would be required; the armed forces might (in what has been called a 'military revolution') be made more professional, cutting out reliance on mercenary troops; the regularity of conflict would stimulate back-up industries (uniforms, weapons, food supplies) and so give an added boost to nascent capitalism. Though war might promote state initiative and administrative change, however, it did not necessarily lead to princely absolutism. No modern state could wage war properly without training an officer class, and in every case the increase in military activity boosted rather than diminished the power of the traditional elite. In Spain Philip II decentralised defence and put it in the hands of the local grandees; in Brandenburg the Great Elector relied on the nobles for the efficiency of his army organisation. Moreover, the soaring costs of war, far from stabilising the state, caused profound social conflict over fiscality and eventually provoked revolutions against the monarchy.

One contradiction in early absolutism, then, was that more authority was being gained by the crown (in France, for example, aristocratic criminal activity declined during the seventeenth century), but effective political power remained in the hands of both the old and new elites. Attempts by the crown to achieve greater autonomy led everywhere to a crisis confrontation. The outcome has sometimes, and unsatisfactorily, been presented as a victory of constitutionalism over the prince in part of northern Europe (England, the United Provinces), and of the prince over the constitution in the rest of the continent. In practice there was no outright victory by either side. Though revolutionary acts did take place – in England the abolition of the system of conciliar government, in France the subordination of the Parlement of Paris and later of the provincial estates – the social structure remained untouched and immobile, thus guaranteeing both continuity and stability. In the more favourable economic conditions of the late century, 'absolutism' changed its character. In the early seventeenth century absolutism was an extension of earlier attempts to consolidate authority in the person of the monarch. In the later period it had become a device to consolidate authority jointly in the monarch and the political nation.

The drift towards the newer absolutism (William III's coup in Holland in 1650, undertaken against the wishes of the bourgeois elite, was atypical) was accompanied by the demise of representative government. But the disappearance of traditional institutions was not necessarily a sign of tyranny. The Diet in Brandenburg lost its effective power after 1653, the Estates of Prussia after 1663. The last Zemsky Sobor met in Russia in 1653, the last Danish parliament in 1660. The Parlement of Paris was silenced in the 1660s, the French provincial Estates in the 1670s. Habsburg Castile had no Cortes after 1665, Sweden and Piedmont became absolutist in the 1680s. It would appear that freedom was being silenced all over Europe. In reality most of these bodies concurred (with an occasional protest) in their own demise. Their disappearance did little to change the balance of power. In the provinces the local elites were still in firm control. And even when there were no active Estates, every rational government had to continue to consult regularly with municipal corporations, courts of justice, trade guilds and other national and regional bodies. 'Absolutism' therefore succeeded for a while because it appeared to reconcile the interests of the elite and of the state. Only when it failed to keep in touch with opinion (this was why criticism arose in the later years of Louis XIV) did it begin to seem tyrannical.

No political class in Europe would have been so foolish as to sign away all its political privileges, and no king was so foolish as to believe that absolute power gave him the right to act against the economic interests of the elite. The theoreticians, like Spinoza in his *Tractatus* (1677), or Schumacher in the Danish 'Lex Regia' of 1709, envisaged the monarch as an epitome of state power: the king was the state, in the sense claimed by Louis XIV. But as with the omnipotent modern state, the absolute monarch was meant to be a reconciler of interests. In practical terms this meant that he must respect the interests, above all the property interests, of the elite. This is what Bossuet, Louis XIV's greatest apologist, meant when he argued that 'what is termed legitimate government is by its very nature the opposite of arbitrary government'. Viewed in these terms, the most realistic political philosopher of the new type of government was not the idealistic Hobbes with his *Leviathan* (1650), but the non-authoritarian Locke, with his claim in the *Second Treatise of Civil Government* (1690) that 'the great and chief end of men…putting themselves under government, is the preservation of their property'. Despite the many conceptual differences between Locke and the continental Europeans, his was the most faithful expression of the views of the propertied elite. And despite institutional differences, the social basis of authority in England was not greatly different from that in France or Denmark. Certainly, the propertied citizens of these countries were no more enslaved than Englishmen were, despite the decay of their representative bodies. The rhetoric of absolutist theory should not therefore be confused with the reality of social experience. Though absolutism might mean the rule of a single person, that person could not maintain his power without the aid of the social structure: it was the governing class that supplied officers for the army and administrators for the machinery of state. Agrarian developments of the seventeenth century gave landlords a greater part in profits and in the political process: the state seemed to work hand-in-hand with the producing elite, thereby assuring dominance to the gentry in England, the Junkers in Prussia, the rural nobility in France. The stability of the late seventeenth and the early eighteenth centuries arose from a broadening of the previously narrow social base on which state power had precariously rested. Rebellions by the elite were now virtually a thing of the past: social and political relationships settled into the mould from which they were to be rudely shaken only by the French Revolution.

NOTES

1 IDENTITIES AND HORIZONS

1 Braunstein, Philippe, 'Confins italiens de l'Empire: nations, frontières et sensibilité européenne dans la seconde moitié du XVe siècle'; and Denis Crouzet, 'Le concept de barbarie', in *Conscience Européenne au XVe et au XVIe Siècle*, Paris 1982.
2 K. M. Panikkar, *Asia and Western Dominance: A Survey of the Vasco da Gama Epoch of Asian History 1498–1945*, London 1953.
3 Werner Sombart, *Der moderne Kapitalismus*, 3 vols in 5 parts, Munich-Leipzig 1916–27, vol. II, part 1.
4 Geoffrey Parker, *The Grand Strategy of Philip II*, New Haven 1998, 52.
5 Charles Tilly (ed.), *The Formation of National States in Western Europe*, Princeton 1975, is a brilliant range of essays, written from another perspective.
6 Wolfgang Reinhard (ed.), *Power Elites and State Building*, Oxford 1996, 3–4.
7 Charles Tilly, *Coercion, Capital and European States*, Cambridge 1990.
8 Christian Desplat, 'Louis XIII and the union of Béarn to France', in M. Greengrass (ed.), *Conquest and Coalescence: The Shaping of the State in Early Modern Europe*, London 1991, 68.
9 Cf. Desplat, 'Louis XIII', 81.
10 Cf. David Rollison, *The Local Origins of Modern Society: Gloucestershire 1500–1800*, London 1992, ch. 5, for the national and local interests of the Trotman family.
11 Peter Sahlins, *Boundaries: The Making of France and Spain in the Pyrenees*, Berkeley 1989.
12 Benedict Anderson, *Imagined Communities*, London 1991.
13 A recent but somewhat confused discussion, by a non-historian, is Adrian Hastings, *The Construction of Nationhood*, Cambridge 1997.
14 Cf. the discussion in Eugen Weber, *Peasants into Frenchmen: The Modernization of Rural France, 1870–1914*, Stanford 1976, 113.
15 R. A. Houston, *Literacy in Early Modern Europe: Culture and Education 1500–1800*, London 1988, ch. 9.
16 Peter Burke, 'A sketch for a social history of post-medieval Latin', in P. Burke and R. Porter, *Language, Self and Society*, Cambridge 1991, 34.
17 Cited in Klaus Garber (ed.), *Nation und Literatur im Europa der Frühen Neuzeit*, Tübingen 1989, 439–41.
18 G. Marker, *Publishing, Printing and the Origins of Intellectual Life in Russia, 1700–1800*, Princeton 1985, 25.
19 Jane Dawson, 'Anglo-Scottish protestant culture and integration in Britain', in Steven Ellis and Sarah Barber (eds), *Conquest and Union: Fashioning a British State, 1485–1725*, London 1995.
20 P. Higonnet, 'The politics of linguistic terrorism', *Social History*, 5, 1980, 49.

21 Cited in Fernand Braudel, *The Identity of France*, vol. I, London 1988, 86.
22 Yves Castan, *Honnêteté et Relations Sociales en Languedoc (1715–80)*, Paris 1974.
23 Jonathan Steinberg, 'The historian and the Questione della Lingua', in P. Burke and R. Porter (eds) *The Social History of Language*, Cambridge 1987.
24 Cf. R. Scribner, 'Communities and the nature of power', in R. Scribner (ed.), *Germany: A New Social and Economic History*, London 1996.
25 Quoted in Keith Wrightson, *English Society 1580–1680*, London 1982, 62.
26 Randolph C. Head, *Early Modern Democracy in the Grisons*, Cambridge 1995.
27 Cf. Peter Blickle, *Communal Reformation: The Quest for Salvation in Sixteenth-century Germany*, Atlantic Highlands, NJ, 1992, 178.
28 Cf. S. Imsen and G. Vogler 'Communal autonomy and peasant resistance in northern and central Europe', in part I of Peter Blickle (ed.), *Resistance, Representation and Community*, Oxford 1997, 15.
29 Jerome Blum, 'The internal structure and polity of the European village community from the fifteenth to the nineteenth century', *Journal of Modern History*, 43, 1971.
30 Sheilagh Ogilvie, 'Institutions and economic development in early modern central Europe', *Transactions of the Royal Historical Society*, 6th series, 5, 1995, 230.
31 J. Smets, 'Les chemins du pouvoir dans le village Languedocien', *Libertés Locales et Vie Municipale*, Montpellier 1988, 187.
32 Hilton L. Root, *Peasants and King in Burgundy: Agrarian Foundations of French Absolutism*, Berkeley 1987, 22–44, 208–30.
33 Heidi Wunder, 'Peasant communities in medieval and early modern Germany', *Recueils de la Société Jean Bodin*, vol. XLIV, Paris 1987, 46.
34 Henri Cavaillès, 'Une fédération Pyrénéenne sous l'Ancien Régime: les traités de lies et de passeries', a classic study of 1910 republished in *Lies et Passeries dans les Pyrénées*, Tarbes 1986.
35 Christian Desplat, *La Guerre Oubliée: Guerres Paysannes dans les Pyrénées (XIIe–XIXe Siècles)*, Biarritz 1993, 47.
36 Peter Clark (ed.), *Small Towns in Early Modern Europe*, Cambridge 1995, 1.
37 Cf. Gerhard Dilcher 'The Social and Institutional Structures', in part V of Blickle (ed.), *Resistance, Representation*, 219.
38 Mack Walker, *German Home Towns: Community, State and General Estate 1648–1871*, Ithaca 1971.
39 David Garrioch, *Neighbourhood and Community in Paris, 1740–1790*, Cambridge 1986, 54.
40 Jeremy Boulton, *Neighbourhood and Society: A London Suburb in the Seventeenth Century*, Cambridge 1987, 217.
41 Ian W. Archer, *The Pursuit of Stability: Social Relations in Elizabethan London*, Cambridge 1991, 59–61, 92–3.
42 The argument, a convincing one, is that of Eberhard Isenmann, 'Norms and values in the European city', in Blickle (ed.), *Resistance, Representation*, part IV, 190–5.
43 Cf. Holger T. Gräf, 'Small towns in early modern Germany: the case of Hesse 1500–1800', in Clark, *Small Towns*, 204.
44 Philippe Ariès, *Centuries of Childhood*, London 1972.
45 Michael Anderson, 'The relevance of family history', in C. Harris (ed.), *The Sociology of the Family*, Keele 1979, 50.
46 Cf. Ralph A. Houlbrooke, *The English Family 1450–1700*, London 1984, ch. 3; J.-L. Flandrin, *Families in Former Times: Kinship, Household and Sexuality*, Cambridge 1979, ch. 1.
47 See David Cressy, 'Kinship and kin interaction in early modern England', *Past and Present*, 113, 1986.

48 Cf. John W. Shaffer, *Family and Farm: Agrarian Change and Household Organization in the Loire Valley 1500–1900*, Albany 1982, 19.
49 L. K. Berkner, 'The use and misuse of census data for the historical analysis of family structure', *Journal of Interdisciplinary History*, 5, 4, 1975.
50 Cited in Christopher R. Friedrichs, *The Early Modern City*, London 1995, 40.
51 Houlbrooke, *The English Family*, 71.
52 Houlbrooke, *The English Family*, 76.
53 C. Klapisch-Zuber, *Women, Family and Ritual in Renaissance Italy*, 1985, 193.
54 For Hohenlohe, Thomas Robisheaux, *Rural Society and the Search for Order in Early Modern Germany*, Oxford 1989, 117; for Catalonia, Henry Kamen, *The Phoenix and the Flame: Catalonia and the Counter-Reformation*, New Haven 1993, 277.
55 Robisheaux, *Rural Society*, 108.
56 R. B. Outhwaite, *Clandestine Marriage in England, 1500–1850*, London 1995.
57 David Cressy, *Birth, Marriage and Death: Ritual, Religion and the Life-cycle in Tudor and Stuart England*, Oxford 1997, 277–80.
58 A. Th. Van Deursen, *Plain Lives in a Golden Age: Popular Culture, Religion and Society in Seventeenth-century Holland*, Cambridge 1991, 94.
59 Quoted Flandrin, *Families in Former Times*, 100.
60 T. H. Hollingsworth, 'The demography of the British peerage' (suppl. to *Population Studies*, XVIII, 2, 1965).
61 B. Bennassar, *Valladolid au Siècle d'Or*, Paris 1977, 195.
62 Cited in J. Mathorez, *Les Etrangers en France sous l'Ancien Régime*, 2 vols, Paris 1919–21, I.
63 J. Hajnal, 'Two kinds of preindustrial household formation systems', in R. Wall (ed.), *Family Forms in Historic Europe*, London 1983.
64 Frank McArdle, *Altopascio: A Study in Tuscan Rural Society 1587–1784*, Cambridge 1978.
65 Mainz, in Friedrichs, *City*, 121.
66 A. Simon Tarrés, 'La familia catalana en el Antiguo Régimen', in *La Familia en la España Mediterránea (Siglos XV–XIX)*, Barcelona 1979, 79.
67 Louis Henry, *Anciennes Familles Genevoises: Etude Démographique, XVIe–XX Siècle*, Paris 1956.
68 Cited in Flandrin, *Families in Former Times*, 115.
69 A. Sharlin, 'Natural decrease in early modern cities: a reconsideration', *Past and Present*, 79, 1978.
70 Quoted in H. Bergues, *La Prévention des Naissances dans la Famille: Ses Origines dans les Temps Modernes*, Paris 1960.
71 Jan de Vries, *European Urbanization 1500–1800*, London 1984.
72 Mary J. Dobson, *Contours of Death and Disease in Early Modern England*, Cambridge 1997.
73 Cf. Charles Creighton, *A History of Epidemics in Britain*, 2 vols, Cambridge 1891–4, I, 533.
74 E. Woehlkens, *Pest und Ruhr im 16. und 17. Jahrhundert*, Hanover 1954, 82.
75 J. N. Biraben, *Les Hommes et la Peste en France et dans les Pays Européens et Méditerranéens*, 2 vols, Paris 1975.
76 Friedrich Prinzing, *Epidemics Resulting from Wars*, Oxford 1916, 29–33, 72–4.
77 L. Clarkson, *Death, Disease and Famine in Pre-industrial England*, London 1975.
78 Cf. the essays in Peter Clark (ed.), *The European Crisis of the 1590s*, London 1985.
79 Anne-Marie Piuz, 'Alimentation populaire et sous-alimentation au XVIIe siècle: le cas de Genève', *Schweizerische Zeitschrift für Geschichte*, 18, 1968, I.
80 J. M. Pérez García, *Un Modelo de Sociedad Rural de Antiguo Régimen en la Galicia Costera: La Península del Salnés*, Santiago 1979, 174.
81 Cf. Braudel, *Capitalism and Material Life*, 87–9.

82 E. Scholliers, *Loonarbeid en Honger: De Levensstandaard in de Xve en XVIe Eeuw te Antwerpen*, Antwerp 1960, 278.
83 Cited in *Social History*, 19, 1, 1994, 105.
84 A. Feillet, *La Misère au Temps de la Fronde et Saint Vincent de Paul*, Paris 1862, 127.
85 J. M. Moriceau, in *Annales de Démographie Historique*, 1980.
86 G. Franz, *Der Dreissigjährige Krieg und das Deutsche Volk*, Stuttgart 1961, 8.
87 H. Kamen, *Spain in the Later Seventeenth Century 1665–1700*, London 1980, 57–8.
88 Christopher R. Friedrichs, *Urban Society in an Age of War: Nördlingen, 1580–1720*, Princeton 1979.

2 LEISURE, WORK AND MOVEMENT

1 A survey in David Vassberg, *The Village and the Outside World in Golden Age Castile*, Cambridge 1996, ch. 2.
2 David Vassberg, *Land and Society in Golden Age Castile*, Cambridge 1984, 186–7.
3 Helen Nader, *Liberty in Absolutist Spain: The Habsburg Sale of Towns 1516–1700*, Baltimore 1990, 1, is of the opinion that in Castile 'there was no distinction between urban and rural'.
4 Alfred W. Crosby, *The Measure of Reality: Quantification and Western Society, 1250–1600*, New York 1997.
5 E. P. Thompson, 'Time, work-discipline and industrial capitalism', *Past and Present*, 38, 1967, 49–50.
6 Keith Thomas, 'Work and leisure in pre-industrial society', *Past and Present*, 29, 1964, 61.
7 Kamen, *Phoenix*, 198.
8 Cf. Peter Burke, 'The invention of leisure in early modern Europe', *Past and Present*, 146, 1995, 139.
9 Cited by Thomas, 'Work and leisure in pre-industrial society', 54 n21.
10 What Victor Turner, *The Ritual Process*, London 1969, calls 'liminality'.
11 René Nelli, *Le Languedoc et le Comté de Foix: Le Roussillon*, Paris 1958, 271.
12 J.-L. Flandrin, 'Mariage tardif et vie sexuelle', *Annales ESC*, 6, 1972.
13 H. Medick, 'Village spinning bees: sexual culture and free time among rural youth in early modern Germany', in Hans Medick and D. W. Sabean, *Interest and Emotion: Essays in the Study of Family and Kinship*, Cambridge 1984.
14 Kamen, *Phoenix*, 304.
15 Kamen, *Phoenix*, 175.
16 Barbara Babcock (ed.), *The Reversible World: Symbolic Inversion in Art and Society*, Ithaca 1978.
17 Mikhail Bakhtin, *Rabelais and His World*, London 1968.
18 Wilhelm Abel, *Agrarkrisen und Agrarkonjunktur*, 3rd edn, Hamburg 1978, 105.
19 E. E. Rich, 'The population of Elizabethan England', *Economic History Review*, 2, 1950.
20 P. Laslett and J. Harrison, 'Clayworth and Cogenhoe', in H. E. Bell and R. L. Ollard (eds), *Historical Essays 1600–1750, Presented to David Ogg*, London 1963.
21 Deursen, *Plain Lives*, 32.
22 M. Kitch, 'Population movement and migration in pre-industrial rural England', in Brian Short (ed.), *The English Rural Community: Image and Analysis*, Cambridge 1992.
23 Cited in Leslie Page Moch, *Moving Europeans: Migration in Western Europe since 1650*, Indiana 1992, 34.
24 Michael Anderson, *Approaches to the History of the Western Family 1500–1914*, Cambridge 1995, 17.

25 Steve Hochstadt, 'Migration in preindustrial Germany', *Central European History*, 16, 3, 1983, 203–4.
26 Hochstadt, 'Migration', 211.
27 Quoted in Vassberg, *The Village*, 70.
28 Walter Kuhn, *Geschichte der Deutschen Ostsiedlung in der Neuzeit*, vol. I, Cologne 1955.
29 Roger Portal, 'Les Russes en Sibérie au XVIIe siècle', *Revue d'Histoire Moderne et Contemporaine*, V, 1958.
30 Nicholas Canny, 'English migration into and across the Atlantic', in Canny (ed.), *Europeans on the Move: Studies on European Migration, 1500–1800*, Oxford 1994, 62. Somewhat lower figures are offered by T. C. Smout, 'Scots as emigrants in Europe', in *Le Migrazioni in Europa sec. XIII–XVIII*, Istituto F. Datini, Florence 1994.
31 *Historia General de la Emigración Española a Iberoamérica*, 2 vols, Madrid 1992, I, 42–50.
32 Jean Delumeau, *Vie Economique et Sociale de Rome dans la Seconde Moitié du XVIe Siècle*, 2 vols, Paris 1957–9, I, ch. 4.
33 H. Schilling, 'Confessional migration', *Le Migrazioni*, 175.
34 Andrew Pettegree, 'Protestant migration during the early modern period', *Le Migrazioni*, 447.
35 R. Mandrou, 'Les Protestants français réfugiés à Genève après la St Barthélemy', *Revue Suisse d'Histoire*, 16, 1966.
36 Cf. Jacques Dupâquier, 'Macro-migrations en Europe (XVIe–XVIIIe siècles)', *Le Migrazioni*, 65–90.
37 W. Bodmer, *Der Einfluss der Refugianten-Einwanderung von 1550–1700 auf die Schweizerische Wirtschaft*, Zürich 1946.
38 J.-F. Dubost, *La France italienne, XVIe–XVIIe Siècle*, Paris 1997.
39 J. G. van Dillen, *Bronnen tot de Geschiedenis van het Bedrijfsleven en het Gildewezen van Amsterdam 1512–1632*, 2 vols, The Hague 1929–33, vol. I.
40 G. Witzel, 'Gewerbegeschichtliche Studien zur Niederländischen Einwanderung in Deutschland', *Westdeutsche Zeitschrift für Geschichte und Kunst*, 29, 1910, 117–82, 419–51.
41 T. C. Smout, 'Scottish emigration', in N. Canny, *Europeans on the Move*, 80–4.
42 A. S. Green, *The Making of Ireland and its Undoing 1200–1600*, London 1908, 440.
43 Eduard Winter, *Die Tschechische und Slowakische Emigration in Deutschland im 17. und 18. Jahrhundert*, Berlin 1955.
44 Hochstadt, 'Migration', 201.
45 Fred A. Norwood, *The Reformation Refugees as an Economic Force*, Chicago 1942.
46 H. Schilling, 'Innovation through migration: the settlements of Calvinistic Netherlanders in 16th and 17th century central and western Europe', *Histoire Sociale – Social History*, 16, 1983; Pettegree, 'Protestant migration', 451.
47 Gerhard Fischer, *Aus Zwei Jahrhunderten Leipziger Handelsgeschichte 1470–1650*, Leipzig 1929.

3 COMMUNITIES OF BELIEF

1 Kamen, *Phoenix*, 82.
2 The ground covered here is also surveyed, magisterially and from a different viewpoint, by R. W. Scribner, *Popular Culture and Popular Movements in Reformation Germany*, London 1987.
3 Cf. Euan Cameron, 'For reasoned faith or embattled creed? Religion for the people in early modern Europe', *Transactions of the Royal Historical Society*, 6th series, 8, 1998.
4 See Kamen, *Phoenix*, ch. 1; and Ronald Hutton, *The Rise and Fall of Merry England: The Ritual Year 1400–1700*, Oxford 1994.
5 Hutton, *Rise and Fall*, 37.

6 Jean Delumeau, *Rassurer et Protéger: Le Sentiment de Sécurité dans l'Occident d'Autrefois*, Paris 1989.
7 Magda Mirabet, 'Pregàries públiques', *Ier Congrés d'Història Moderna de Catalunya*, 2 vols, Barcelona 1984, II, 487–93.
8 J. Le Goff, *The Birth of Purgatory*, London 1984.
9 Blickle, *Communal Reformation*, 25.
10 Keith Thomas, *Religion and the Decline of Magic*, Harmondsworth 1973.
11 Cf. Richard L. Kagan, *Lucrecia's Dreams: Politics and Prophecy in Sixteenth-century Spain*, Berkeley 1990.
12 A fine short discussion is Geoffrey Parker, 'Success and failure during the first century of the Reformation', *Past and Present*, 136, 1992.
13 Cf. Nicholas Griffiths, 'Popular religious scepticism and idiosyncrasy in post-Tridentine Cuenca', in L. Twomey (ed.), *Faith and Fanaticism: Religious Fervour in Early Modern Spain*, Aldershot 1997.
14 J. F. Harrington and H. W. Smith, 'Confessionalization, community and state building in Germany, 1555–1870', *Journal of Modern History*, 69, 1, 1997.
15 John Addy, *Sin and Society in the Seventeenth Century*, London 1989, 106.
16 C. Scott Dixon, *The Reformation and Rural Society: The Parishes of Brandenburg-Ansbach-Kulmbach, 1528–1603*, Cambridge 1996, 111, 122, 172.
17 Cf. Hutton, *Rise and Fall*, 126–43.
18 Some examples in Po-Chia Hsia, *Social Discipline in the Reformation: Central Europe 1550–1750*, London and New York 1989, 124–9.
19 Good summary in Po-Chia Hsia, *Social Discipline in the Reformation*.
20 Etienne François, as cited by Harrington and Smith, 'Confessionalisation', 89.
21 Joachim Whaley, *Religious Toleration and Social Change in Hamburg 1529–1819*, Cambridge 1985.
22 Marc R. Foster, *The Counter Reformation in the Villages: Religion and Reform in the Bishopric of Speyer 1560–1720*, Ithaca 1992, 200, 246.
23 Kamen, *Phoenix*, 433.
24 On the persecution of hermits in Spain, Alain Saint-Saëns, *Valets de Dieu, Suppôts du Diable*, New Orleans 1999.
25 Mack Walker, *The Salzburg Transaction: Expulsion and Redemption in Eighteenth-century Germany*, Ithaca 1992.
26 Joachim Whaley, 'A tolerant society? Religious toleration in the Holy Roman Empire after 1648', in Grell and Scribner (eds), *Tolerance and Intolerance in the European Reformation*, 50.
27 C. Marazzini, *Storia della Lingua Italiana: Il Secolo Cinquecento e il Seicento*, Bologna 1993, 93.
28 Louis Châtellier, *La Religion des Pauvres: Les Sources du Christianisme Moderne XVIe–XIXe Siècles*, Paris 1993, 74–88.
29 This was the argument of Robert Muchembled, *Culture Populaire et Culture des Elites dans la France Moderne (XVe–XVIIIe Siècles)*, Paris 1978.
30 P. P. Delgado Alemany and J. Serra i Barceló, 'La reglamentació del Carnaval', *Espai i Temps d'Oci*, Palma 1993, 341–6.
31 W. David Myers, *'Poor, Sinning Folk': Confessions and Conscience in Counter-Reformation Germany*, Ithaca 1996.
32 J.-F. Soulet, *Traditions et Réformes Religieuses dans les Pyrénées Centrales au XVIIe Siècle*, Pau 1974, 246.
33 Alain Lottin, *Lille, Citadelle de la Contre-Reforme? (1598–1668)*, Dunkirk 1984, 228–31.
34 H. R. Schmidt, *Dorf und Religion: Reformierte Sittenzucht in Berner Landgemeinden der Frühen Neuzeit*, Stuttgart 1995.
35 Po-Chia Hsia, *Social Discipline in the Reformation*, 134.

36 Ronald Hutton, 'The English Reformation and the evidence of folklore', *Past and Present*, 148, 1995, 110–11.
37 W. Monter, 'Heresy executions in Reformation Europe, 1520–1565', in Grell and Scribner (eds), *Tolerance and Intolerance in the European Reformation*, 63.
38 A. Macfarlane, *Witchcraft in Tudor and Stuart England*, London 1970, 25.
39 Carlo Ginzburg, *The Night Battles: Witchcraft and Agrarian Cults in the 16th and 17th Centuries*, Baltimore 1983.
40 Cf. W. Behringer, 'Witchcraft studies in Austria, Germany and Switzerland', in J. Barry, M. Hester and G. Roberts (eds), *Witchcraft in Early Modern Europe*, Cambridge 1997, 89.
41 The now classic model proposed by Thomas and Macfarlane.
42 P. Boyer and S. Nissenbaum, *Salem Possessed: The Social Origins of Witchcraft*, Cambridge MA 1974.
43 Henningsen, *The Witches' Advocate: Basque Witchcraft and the Spanish Inquisition*, Reno 1980, 301.
44 C. E. Dumont, *Justice Criminelle des Duchés de Lorraine et de Bar*, 2 vols, Nancy 1848, II.
45 L. Duparchy, 'La justice criminelle dans la terre de Saint-Oyend-de-Joux', *Mémoires de la Société d'Emulation du Jura*, 5th series, vol. II, 1891.
46 Henningsen, *The Witches' Advocate*, 25.
47 This is the crucial argument of H. C. Lea.
48 Stuart Clark, *Thinking with Demons: The Idea of Witchcraft in Early Modern Europe*, Oxford 1997, 296–311.
49 Cited in E. Le Roy Ladurie, *Les Paysans de Languedoc*, 2 vols, Paris 1966, I, 411.
50 Cf. Rainer Walz, *Hexenglaube und Magische Kommunikation im Dorf der Frühen Neuzeit*, Paderborn 1993, 422–57.
51 W. Behringer, 'Weather, hunger and fear: origins of the European witch-hunts in climate, society and mentality', *German History*, 13, 1, 1995, 10–11.
52 Behringer, 'Weather', 17.
53 Kamen, *Phoenix*, 243.
54 Henry Kamen, *The Spanish Inquisition: An Historical Revision*, London 1998, 271.
55 Henningsen, *The Witches' Advocate.*
56 Deursen, *Plain Lives*, 252.
57 See the definitive studies by Alfred Soman, collected in *Sorcellerie et Justice Criminelle: Le Parlement de Paris (16e–18e Siècles)*, Aldershot 1992; my reference is to ch. 2, 35.
58 Gábor Klaniczay, *The Uses of Supernatural Power: The Transformation of Popular Religion in Medieval and Early Modern Europe*, Cambridge 1990, 152.

4 THE RULING ELITE

1 A general introduction is M. L. Bush, 'An Anatomy of Nobility', in M. L. Bush (ed.), *Social Orders and Social Classes in Europe since 1500*, New York 1992, ch. 3; and his *Rich Noble, Poor Noble*, Manchester 1988.
2 Claudio Donati, *L'Idea di Nobiltà in Italia: Secoli XIV–XVII*, Bari 1988.
3 Arlette Jouanna, *L'Idée de Race en France au XVIe et au Début du XVIIe Siècle (1498–1614)*, 3 vols, Paris 1976; also André Devyver, *Le Sang Epuré: Les Préjugés de Race chez les Gentilshommes Français de l'Ancien Régime 1560–1720*, Brussels 1973.
4 Cf. A. Fletcher, *Gender, Sex and Subordination in England 1500–1800*, Yale 1995, 126.
5 Cited Felicity Heal, *Hospitality in Early Modern England*, Oxford 1990, 184.
6 J. P. Cooper, *Land, Men and Beliefs: Studies in Early Modern History*, London 1983, 44, 50.
7 Arlette Jouanna, *Le Devoir de Révolte: La Noblesse Française et la Gestation de l'Etat Moderne 1559–1661*, Paris 1989, 42.

8 Cf. R. R. Harding, *Anatomy of a Power Elite: The Provincial Governors of Early Modern France*, New Haven 1979; and Sharon Kettering, *Patrons, Brokers and Clients in Seventeenth-century France*, Oxford 1986.
9 Gunner Lind, 'Clientelism and the power elite', ch. 7 of Reinhard (ed.), *Power Elites and State Building*.
10 Both cases cited in Jouanna, *Devoir de Révolte*, 66, 105.
11 Kristen B. Neuschel, *Word of Honour: Interpreting Noble Culture in Sixteenth-century France*, Ithaca 1989.
12 Jouanna, *Devoir de Révolte*, 66.
13 Kettering, *Patrons, Brokers*, 114.
14 Donna T. Andrew, 'The code of honour and its critics: opposition to duelling in England, 1700–1850', *Social History*, 5, 1980.
15 François Billacois, *The Duel: Its Rise and Fall in Early Modern France*, New Haven 1990, 112.
16 V. G. Kiernan, *The Duel in European History*, Oxford 1989, 155.
17 Lawrence Stone, *The Crisis of the Aristocracy 1558–1641*, abridged edn, Oxford 1967, 129–30.
18 Gregory Hanlon, 'The decline of a provincial military aristocracy: Siena 1560–1740', *Past and Present*, 155, 1997, 107.
19 G. Zeller, 'Une notion de caractère historico-social: la dérogeance', *Cahiers Internationaux de Sociologie*, 22, 1957.
20 Lawrence Stone, 'The nobility in business 1540–1640', *Explorations in Entrepreneurial History*, X, ii, 1957.
21 H. Kellenbenz, 'German aristocratic entrepreneurship: economic activities of the Holstein nobility', *Explorations in Entrepreneurial History*, VI, 1953, 108.
22 Jerome Blum, *Lord and Peasant in Russia*, Princeton 1961, 129.
23 W. Kirchner, 'Entrepreneurial activity in Russian/Western trade relations during the sixteenth century', *Explorations in Entrepreneurial History*, VIII, 1955.
24 G. D'Avenel, 'La fortune de la noblesse sous Louis XIII', *Revue Historique*, 1883.
25 Kamen, *Spain in the Later Seventeenth Century*, 233–4.
26 J. C. Davis, *The Decline of the Venetian Nobility as a Ruling Class*, Baltimore 1962.
27 E. Ladewig Petersen, *The Crisis of the Danish Nobility*, Odense 1967, 7. I am grateful to Prof. Petersen for this article.
28 Hans Rosenberg, 'The rise of the Junkers in Brandenburg-Prussia 1410–1653', *American Historical Review*, XLIX, i–ii, 1943–4.
29 Cf. comments in Jonathan Dewald, *The European Nobility 1400–1800*, Cambridge 1996, 1–14.
30 Cited in Keith Wrightson, *English Society 1580–1680*, London 1982, 26.
31 Cf. A. Maczak, 'The nobility–state relationship', in Reinhard (ed.), *Power Elites and State Building*, 198.
32 S. J. Woolf, 'Studi sulla nobiltà nell epoca dell assolutismo', *Memorie dell Accademia delle Scienze di Torino*, serie 4, no. 5, 1963.
33 Rudolf Braun, 'Staying on top: socio-cultural reproduction of European power elites', in Reinhard (ed.), *Power Elites and State Building*, ch. 12.
34 This is also the conclusion of Felicity Heal and Clive Holmes, *The Gentry in England and Wales 1500–1700*, London 1994, 381.
35 J. B. Wood, 'The decline of the nobility in 16th and early 17th century France: myth or reality?', *Journal of Modern History*, 48, i, March 1976.
36 H. F. K. van Nierop, *The Nobility of Holland: From Knights to Regents, 1500–1650*, Cambridge 1993, 218.
37 L. Stone and F. Stone, *An Open Elite? England 1540–1880*, Harmondsworth 1986.

5 THE MIDDLE ELITE

1 For example, 'middle' elite does not always imply that there was a 'lower' elite.
2 Cf. Eberhard Isenmann, 'Socio-political concepts of honour values and lifestyles', in part IV of Blickle (ed.), *Resistance, Representation*, 201.
3 Cf. the observations on England by D'Cruze in J. Barry and C. Brooks, *The Middling Sort of People: Culture, Society and Politics in England, 1550–1800*, London 1994.
4 Heal and Holmes, *The Gentry in England and Wales*, 11.
5 Heal and Holmes, *The Gentry in England and Wales*, 27.
6 R. Baron, 'La bourgeoisie de Varzy au XVIIe siècle', *Annales de Bourgogne*, XXXVI, 1964.
7 P. Molas, *La Burguesía Mercantil en la España del Antiguo Régimen*, Madrid 1985, 183–7.
8 Gaston Roupnel, *La Ville et la Campagne au XVIIe Siècle*, Paris 1922, 188–228.
9 A. K. Isaacs and M. Prak, in Reinhard (ed.), *Power Elites and State Building*, 223.
10 William M. Reddy, 'The concept of class', in M. L. Bush (ed.), *Social Orders and Social Classes*, 17; this is a discussion based on his *Money and Liberty in Modern Europe: A Critique of Historical Understanding*, New York 1987.
11 Lucien Febvre, *Philippe II et la Franche-Comté*, Paris 1911.
12 Peter Earle, *The Making of the English Middle Class: Business, Society and Family Life in London 1660–1730*, London 1989, 10.
13 Earle, *Making of the English Middle Class*, 290–301, 336.
14 Data from T. K. Rabb, *Enterprise and Empire: Merchant and Gentry Investment in the Expansion of England 1575–1630*, Cambridge MA 1967.
15 H. Soly, 'The betrayal of the 16th-century bourgeoisie: a myth?', *Acta Historiae Neerlandicae*, VIII, 1975.
16 Cf. the discussion in J. K. J. Thomson, *Decline in History: The European Experience*, Cambridge 1998, ch. 6.
17 Paolo Malanima, *I Riccardi di Firenze: Una Famiglia e un Patrimonio nella Toscana dei Medici*, Florence 1977.
18 Rudolf Braun, in Reinhard (ed.), *Power Elites and State Building*, 235.
19 M. A. Fargas, *Família i Poder a Catalunya, 1516–1626*, Lleida 1997.
20 Joanne Ferraro, *Family and Public Life in Brescia 1580–1650*, Cambridge 1993.

6 SOLIDARITIES AND RESISTANCE

1 Deursen, *Plain Lives*, ch. 1.
2 J. A. Maravall, *Estado Moderno y Mentalidad Social*, 2 vols, Madrid 1972, II, 380–2.
3 Cited John Rule, *Albion's People: English Society 1714–1815*, London 1992, 106.
4 Cited in Molas, *Burguesía Mercantil*, 177.
5 Cf. H. Neveux and Eva Österberg, 'Norms and values', part IV of Blickle (ed.), *Resistance, Representation*, 201.
6 Walker, *German Home Towns*, 89.
7 Cited in Friedrichs, *City*, 148.
8 Susan Dwyer Amussen, *An Ordered Society: Gender and Class in Early Modern England*, Oxford 1988, 98–101.
9 R. and T. Wohlfeil, 'Verbildlichungen ständischer Gesellschaft', in Winfried Schulze (ed.), *Ständische Gesellschaft und Sozialer Mobilität*, Munich 1988, 284.
10 H. Neveux and E. Österberg, 'A methodological discourse' in part IV of Blickle (ed.), *Resistance, Representation*, 161.
11 James R. Farr, *Hands of Honor: Artisans and their World in Dijon, 1550–1650*, Ithaca 1988, 177–95.

12 Examples of 1693, cited in H. Kamen, *Crisis and Change in Early Modern Spain*, Aldershot 1993, ch. IX, 685.
13 Blickle (ed.), *Resistance, Representation*, 170–2.
14 Daniel Roche, *The People of Paris: An Essay in Popular Culture in the 18th Century*, New York 1987, 247–68.
15 Thorkild Kjaergaard, *The Danish Revolution 1500–1800: An Ecohistorical Interpretation*, Cambridge 1994, 18, 71.
16 C. Rahn Phillips and W. D. Phillips, *Spain's Golden Fleece*, Baltimore 1997, 253.
17 Eric Kerridge, *The Agricultural Revolution*, London 1967.
18 W. G. Hoskins, *Essays in Leicestershire History*, Liverpool 1950.
19 Eric Kerridge, *Agrarian Problems in the Sixteenth Century and After*, London 1969, 131–3.
20 Cf. N. J. G. Pounds, *An Historical Geography of Europe 1500–1840*, Cambridge 1979, 162.
21 This is the view, based on strictly Marxist premises, of Brenner: see T. Ashton and C. Philpin (eds), *The Brenner Debate: Agrarian Class Structure and Economic Development in Pre-industrial Europe*, Cambridge 1985.
22 Cited in Pounds, *Historical Geography*, 164–5.
23 Blum, *Lord and Peasant*, 254.
24 A. I. Kopanev, 'Nezemledelcheskaya volost v XVI–XVII vv', in *Krestyanstvo i Klassovaya Borba v Feodalnoi Rosscii*, Leningrad 1967, 185
25 J. H. Elliott, 'Revolution and continuity in early modern Europe', *Past and Present*, 42, 1969.
26 Cf. James B. Collins, *Classes, Estates and Order in Early Modern Brittany*, Cambridge 1994, 257.
27 S. Imsen and G. Vogler, 'Forms and character of peasant resistance', in Part I of Blickle (ed.), *Resistance, Representation*, 25.
28 Wolfgang Schmale, *Bäuerliche Widerstand, Gerichte und Rechtsentwicklung in Frankreich*, Frankfurt 1986.
29 S. Imsen and G. Vogler in Blickle (ed.), *Resistance, Representation*, 26.
30 Charles Tilly, 'Food supply and public order', in Tilly (ed.), *The Formation of National States*, 386.
31 R. B. Outhwaite, *Dearth, Public Policy and Social Disturbance in England 1550–1800*, Cambridge 1991, 42.
32 E. P. Thompson, 'The moral economy of the English crowd in the eighteenth century', *Past and Present*, 50, 1971.
33 Cf. J. G. Scott, *The Moral Economy of the Peasant Rebellion and Subsistence in Southeast Asia*, New Haven 1976, 43.
34 René Pillorget, *Les Mouvements Insurrectionels de Provence entre 1596 et 1715*, Paris 1975.
35 Y.-M. Bercé, *Histoire des Croquants: Etude des Soulèvements Populaires au 17e Siècle dans le Sud-ouest de la France*, 2 vols, Geneva 1974.
36 Victor V. Magagna, *Communities of Grain: Rural Rebellion in Comparative Perspective*, Ithaca 1991, 23.
37 See J. Perez, *La Révolution des Comunidades de Castille (1520–1521)*, Bordeaux 1970; J. A. Maravall, *Las Comunidades de Castilla*, Madrid 1979.
38 Peter Blickle, *The Revolution of 1525*, Baltimore 1981; H. U. Wehler, *Der Deutsche Bauernkrieg 1524–26*, Göttingen 1975.
39 The classic survey is E. Le Roy Ladurie, *Carnival: A People's Uprising at Romans 1579–80*, London 1980.
40 Rosario Villari, *La Rivolta Antispagnola a Napoli: Le Origini (1585–1647)*, Bari 1967.
41 Clark (ed.), *The European Crisis of the 1590s*.
42 Bercé, *Histoire des Croquants*.
43 G. Grüll, *Bauer, Herr und Landesfurst*, Linz 1963.

44 J.-A. De Thou, *Histoire Universelle*, 11 vols, Paris 1742, book 114.
45 I. T. Smirnov, *Vosstanie Bolotnikova 1606–1607 (The Bolotnikov Uprising 1606–1607)*, Leningrad 1951.
46 Albin Czerny, *Bilder aus der Zeit der Bauernunruhen in Oberösterreich*, Linz 1876.
47 H. N. Brailsford, *The Levellers and the English Revolution*, London 1961.
48 Denis Mack Smith, *A History of Sicily*, 2 vols, London 1968, I, ch. 21.
49 M. Schipa, 'La così detta rivoluzione di Masaniello', *Archivio Storico per le Province Napoletane*, new series, vol. II, 1916; A. d'Ambrosio, *Masaniello: Rivoluzione e Controrivoluzione nel Reame di Napoli (1647–1648)*, Milan 1962.
50 A. Domínguez Ortiz, *Alteraciones Andaluzas*, Madrid 1973.
51 S. A. Westrich, *The Osmée of Bordeaux*, Baltimore 1972.
52 P. Smirnov, *Posadskie Lyudi i ikh Klassovaya Borba do Serediny XVII Veka (Townspeople and their Class Struggle in the mid-17th Century)*, 2 vols, Moscow 1947–8.
53 L. Loewenson, 'The Moscow rising of 1648', *Slavonic and East European Review*, 27, 1948–9.
54 H. Wahlen and E. Jaggi, *Der Schweizerische Bauernkrieg, 1653*, Bern 1952. The latest study is by Andreas Suter, *Der Schweizerische Bauernkrieg von 1653*, Tübingen 1997.
55 Paul Avrich, *Russian Rebels 1600–1800*, London 1972.
56 Y. Garlan and C. Nières, *Les Révoltes Bretonnes de 1675*, Paris 1975.
57 A. Simon i Tarrés, 'Catalunya en el siglo XVII: La revuelta campesina y popular de 1640', *Estudi General (Girona)*, I, i, 1981.
58 H. Kamen, *Spain in the Later Seventeenth Century 1665–1700*, London 1980, 179.
59 Cited in Pedro L. Lorenzo Cadarso, *Los Conflictos Populares en Castilla (Siglos XVI–XVII)*, Madrid 1996, 180.
60 Bercé, *Histoire des Croquants*, II, 665.
61 Grüll, *Bauer, Herr und Landesfürst.*
62 P. Smirnov, *Pravitelstvo B. I. Morozova i Vosstanie v Moskve 1648g (The Government of B. Morozov and the 1648 Moscow Rising)*, Tashkent 1929.
63 R. Villari, 'Masaniello: contemporary and recent interpretations', *Past and Present*, 108, 1985, 120, criticises scholars who view social revolt as symbolic.
64 C. Hill, *The World Turned Upside Down: Radical Ideas During the English Revolution*, London 1972.
65 E. F. Gay, 'The Midland Revolt and the inquisitions of depopulation of 1607', *Transactions of the Royal Historical Society*, XVIII, 1904.
66 Yu. Bromley, 'Vosstanie khorvatskikh i slovenskikh krestyan 1573g' ('The uprising of the Croat and Slovene peasants in 1573'), *Uchenie Zapiski Instituta Slavyanovedeniya*, vol. 11, 1955.
67 W. Steinitz, *Deutsche Volkslieder Demokratischen Charakters aus Sechs Jahrhunderten*, vol. I, Berlin 1954, 68.
68 *Calendar of State Papers, Domestic*, vol. IV (1595–7), 345.

7 GENDER ROLES

1 Cf. Martin King Whyte, *The Status of Women in Preindustrial Societies*, Princeton 1978, 167–73.
2 Amussen, *An Ordered Society*, 3.
3 J. A. Maravall, *La Literatura Picaresca desde la Historia Social (Siglos XVI y XVII)*, Madrid 1986, 656–57.
4 I. Maclean, *Woman Triumphant: Feminism in French Literature 1610–52*, Oxford 1977.
5 Fletcher, *Gender, Sex and Subordination*, 27.
6 Maravall, *La Literatura Picaresca*, 695.
7 Cf. Deursen, *Plain Lives*, 83.

8 Joy Wiltenburg, *Disorderly Women and Female Power in the Street Literature of Early Modern England and Germany*, Charlottesville 1992.
9 Cf. Marjorie K. McIntosh, *Controlling Misbehaviour in England 1370–1600*, Cambridge 1998, 74.
10 Martine Segalen, *Love and Power in the Peasant Family*, Oxford 1983, 9.
11 Kamen, *Phoenix*, 297, 330.
12 Cf. Olwen Hufton, *The Prospect Before Her: A History of Women in Western Europe, vol. I: 1500–1800*, London 1997, 145.
13 Pérez García, *Un Modelo de Sociedad Rural*, 119.
14 Friedrichs, *Urban Society in an Age of War*, 69–70.
15 Joel F. Harrington, *Reordering Marriage and Society in Reformation Germany*, Cambridge 1995.
16 Alain Lottin (ed.), *La Désunion du Couple sous l'Ancien Régime: L'Exemple du Nord*, Paris 1975, 114.
17 Kamen, *Phoenix*, 310.
18 Lyndal Roper, *The Holy Household*, Oxford 1989, ch. 4; Robisheaux, *Rural Society*, 105–15.
19 Kamen, *Phoenix*, 108.
20 P. Ariès, 'The indissoluble marriage', in Philippe Ariès and André Bejin, *Western Sexuality*, Oxford 1985.
21 Cf. David Sabean, *Property, Production and Family in Neckarhausen 1700–1870*, Cambridge 1990, ch. 4.
22 Flandrin, *Families in Former Times*, 138.
23 Houlbrooke, *English Family*, 76–8.
24 Flandrin, *Families in Former Times*, 172.
25 Lawrence Stone, *Uncertain Unions and Broken Lives*, Oxford 1995.
26 Ferraro, *Family and Public Life*, 125.
27 Amy L. Erickson, *Women and Property in Early Modern England*, London 1995.
28 Houlbrooke, *English Family*, 209.
29 Quoted Vassberg, *The Village*, 88.
30 Cf. Merry E. Wiesner, *Women and Gender in Early Modern Europe*, Cambridge 1993, 86 onwards.
31 Deursen, *Plain Lives*, 8.
32 Vassberg, *The Village*, 90.
33 Hufton, *The Prospect*, 77.
34 Moch, *Moving Europeans*, 46.
35 Cited by Margret Wensky, in *La Donna nell'Economia secc. XIII–XVIII*, Florence 1990, 140.
36 A. Karpinski, 'Feminization of retail trade in Polish towns', in *La Donna nell'Economia*, 283–92.
37 Maria Bogucka, 'Women and economic life in the Polish cities during the 16th–17th centuries', in *La Donna nell'Economia*, 191.
38 Martha C. Howell, 'Women, the family economy and the structures of market production in cities of northern Europe', in Barbara Hanawalt (ed.), *Women and Work in Preindustrial Europe*, Bloomington 1986, 200.
39 E. Berriot-Salvadore, *Les Femmes dans la Société Française de la Renaissance*, Geneva 1990, 502, 514.
40 Earle, *Making of the English Middle Class*, 170.
41 Joan Thirsk, in Mary Prior (ed.), *Women in English Society 1500–1800*, London 1985, 13.
42 B. A. Holderness, 'Women in agriculture: England 1600–1800', in *La Donna nell'Economia*, 261–74.

43 Cited in Kamen, *Phoenix*, 334.
44 Fletcher, *Gender, Sex and Subordination*, 230–2.
45 Flandrin, *Families in Former Times*, 217.
46 R. A. Houston, *The Population History of Britain and Ireland 1500–1750*, Cambridge 1992, 46.
47 Hufton, *The Prospect*, 185.
48 David Harley, 'Provincial midwives in England: Lancashire and Cheshire 1660–1760', in Hilary Marland (ed.), *The Art of Midwifery: Early Modern Midwives in Europe*, New York 1993, 32.
49 Stephen Wilson, 'The myth of motherhood a myth: the historical view of European child-bearing', *Social History*, 9, 2, 1984, 188.
50 A good selection in Linda Pollock, *Forgotten Children: Parent-child Relations from 1500 to 1900*, Cambridge 1983. She has consulted 496 accounts for her conclusions.
51 Diane Willen, 'Women and religion in early modern England', in Sherrin Marshall (ed.), *Women in Reformation and Counter-Reformation Europe*, Bloomington 1989.
52 Kamen, *Phoenix*, 324.
53 Cited by M. Rowlands, 'Recusant women 1560–1640', in Prior (ed.), *Women in English Society*.
54 Ronald Knox, *Enthusiasm*, Oxford 1950, 162.
55 Cited Hufton, *The Prospect*, 414.
56 Cited Hufton, *The Prospect*, 416.
57 Kamen, *Phoenix*, 332.
58 Cited in Carolyn C. Lougee, *Le Paradis des Femmes: Women, Salons and Social Stratification in 17th-century France*, Princeton 1976.
59 R. Thompson, *Women in Stuart England and America: A Comparative Study*, London 1974.
60 Frances Yates, *Astrea: The Imperial Theme in the Sixteenth Century*, London 1975, part II.
61 Cf. Fletcher, *Gender, Sex and Subordination*, 80.
62 Merry Wiesner, *Women and Gender*, ch. 8, appears to assume that the power structure in Europe considered female rule unnatural.
63 N. Z. Davis, 'City women and religious change', in Davis, *Society and Culture in Early Modern France*, Cambridge 1987, ch. 3.
64 Cf. Berriot-Salvadore, *Les Femmes dans la Société*, 540.
65 Cited Antoine Adam, *Grandeur and Illusion: French Literature and Society 1600–1715*, London 1972, 69.
66 F. Dabhoiwala, 'The construction of honour, reputation and status in late 17th- and early 18th-century England', *Transactions of the Royal Historical Society*, VI, 6, 1996, 210–12.
67 Kamen, *Phoenix*, 307.
68 Houlbrooke, *English Family*, 116.
69 Bernard Capp, 'The double standard revisited', *Past and Present*, 162, 1999.
70 Cf. Elizabeth Foyster, 'Male honour, social control and wife beating in late Stuart England', *Transactions of the Royal Historical Society*, VI, 6, 1996.
71 A. Fletcher, 'Men's dilemma: the future of patriarchy in England 1560–1660', *Transactions of the Royal Historical Society*, VI, 4, 1994.
72 P. S. Seaver, *Wallington's World: A Puritan Artisan in Seventeenth-century London*, London 1985.
73 Fletcher, *Gender, Sex and Subordination*, 104.
74 Cf. Y.-M. Bercé, *Revolt and Revolution in Early Modern Europe*, Manchester 1987, 107–9.
75 D. Underdown, *Revel, Riot and Rebellion: Popular Politics and Culture in England 1603–60*, Oxford 1985.

76 Catherine Killerby, 'The enforcement of Italian sumptuary law, 1200–1500', in T. Dean and K. Lowe (eds), *Crime, Society and the Law in Renaissance Italy*, Cambridge 1994, 115.
77 Cf. Hufton, *The Prospect*, 269–76.
78 Clark, *Thinking with Demons*, 110.
79 Kamen, *Phoenix*, 241–2.
80 Lyndal Roper, 'Witchcraft and fantasy in early modern Germany', in Barry, Hester and Roberts (eds), *Witchcraft*, 211.

8 SOCIAL DISCIPLINE AND MARGINALITY

1 McIntosh, *Controlling Misbehaviour in England*, 71.
2 Heal, *Hospitality in Early Modern England*, 3.
3 Heal, *Hospitality in Early Modern England*, 367–72.
4 Yves Castan, *Honnêteté et Relations Sociales en Languedoc (1715–1780)*, Paris 1974, 22–8.
5 J.-P. Gutton, 'Confraternities, curés and communities', in K. von Greyerz (ed.), *Religion and Society in Early Modern Europe 1500–1800*, London 1984, 51–4.
6 Martin Ingram, 'Ridings, rough music and the "reform of popular culture" in early modern England', *Past and Present*, 105, 1984.
7 André Burguière, 'The charivari and religious repression in France during the Ancien Régime', in R. Wheaton and T. Hareven (eds), *Family and Sexuality in French History*, Philadelphia 1980.
8 For a case in a German Lutheran parish, Robisheaux, *Rural Society*, 118–19.
9 Jeffrey R. Watt, *The Making of Modern Marriage: Matrimonial Control and the Rise of Sentiment in Neuchâtel, 1550–1800*, Ithaca 1992, 51.
10 M. F. Graham, *The Uses of Reform: 'Godly Discipline' and Popular Behaviour in Scotland, 1560–1610*, Brill 1996.
11 Eva Österberg and Dag Lindström, *Crime and Social Control in Medieval and Early Modern Swedish Towns*, Uppsala 1988, 54, 138.
12 Cf. Kamen, *Phoenix*, 189–94.
13 Deursen, *Plain Lives*, 86–7.
14 Cited in Christopher Hill, *Society and Puritanism in Pre-revolutionary England*, London 1966, 225.
15 The view that there was a 'construction of a new authoritarian moral order', argued in James R. Farr, *Authority and Sexuality in Early Modern Burgundy (1550–1730)*, Oxford 1995, 8, is unacceptable.
16 Edward Shorter, *The Making of the Modern Family*, London 1977, 132.
17 Cf. Robert Jütte, *Poverty and Deviance in Early Modern Europe*, Cambridge 1994, 46ff.
18 Cited in Friedrichs, *City*, 226.
19 Archer, *The Pursuit of Stability*, 153.
20 Juan Luis Morales, *El Niño en la Cultura Española*, 4 vols, Madrid 1960, I, 91ff.
21 Frank Aydelotte, *Elizabethan Rogues and Vagabonds*, Oxford 1913, 55.
22 Yves Durand, *Cahiers de Doléances des Paroisses du Bailliage de Troyes pour les Etats Généraux de 1614*, Paris 1966.
23 Linda Martz, *Poverty and Welfare in Habsburg Spain: The Example of Toledo*, Cambridge 1983.
24 Ernst Schubert, 'Die Ausgrenzung des fahrenden Volkes', in Schulze (ed.), *Ständische Gesellschaft*, 113–64.
25 Brian Pullan, *Rich and Poor in Renaissance Venice: The Social Institutions of a Catholic State, to 1620*, Oxford 1971.
26 E. M. Leonard, *The Early History of English Poor Relief*, Cambridge 1900.
27 Michel Foucault, *Discipline and Punish: The Birth of the Prison*, London 1977, 141.

28 Cited in E. Chill, 'Religion and mendicity in 17th-century France', *International Review of Social History*, VII, 1962.
29 W. K. Jordan, *The Charities of London 1480–1660*, London 1960.
30 *Storia di Milano, Vol. XI: Il Declino Spagnolo (1630–1706)*, Milan 1958, 362.
31 Maureen Flynn, *Sacred Charity: Confraternities and Social Welfare in Spain, 1400–1700*, London 1989, 71–6.
32 W. Callahan, *La Santa y Real Hermandad del Refugio y Piedad de Madrid 1618–1832*, Madrid 1980.
33 Erik von Kraemer, *Le Type du Faux Mendiant dans les Littératures Romanes*, Helsinki 1944.
34 Alexandre Vexliard, *Introduction à la Sociologie du Vagabondage*, Paris 1956.
35 J.-P. Clébert, *The Gypsies*, London 1963.
36 An excellent survey in J. A. Sharpe, 'The history of crime in late medieval and early modern England: a review of the field', *Social History*, 7, ii, May 1982.
37 J. A. Sharpe, *Crime in Early Modern England 1550–1750*, London 1999, 7.
38 Cited in Friedrichs, *City*, 233.
39 M. Greenshields, *An Economy of Violence in Early Modern France: Crime and Justice in the Haute Auvergne 1587–1664*, Philadelphia 1994, 68.
40 J. M. Beattie, 'The pattern of crime in England 1660–1800', *Past and Present*, 62, 1974, 86–7.
41 Y.-M. Bercé, 'De la criminalité aux troubles sociaux: la noblesse rurale du Sud-Ouest de la France sous Louis XIII', *Annales du Midi*, 76, 1, 1964.
42 Cf. Trevor Dean, 'Criminal justice in mid fifteenth-century Bologna', in T. Dean and K. Lowe, *Crime, Society and the Law in Renaissance Italy*, Cambridge 1994, 17.
43 J. A. Sharpe, 'Enforcing the law in the 17th-century English village', in V. A. C. Gattrell, B. Lenman and G. Parker (eds), *Crime and the Law: The Social History of Crime in Western Europe since 1500*, London 1980.
44 Cf. Alfred Soman, 'Deviance and criminal justice in western Europe, 1300–1800: an essay in structure', in Soman, *Sorcellerie et Justice*, ch. 4, 13.
45 B. Lenman and G. Parker, 'The state, the community and the criminal law in early modern Europe', in Gattrell, Lenman and Parker (eds), *Crime and the Law*, 15.
46 T. A. Mantecón, *Conflictividad y Disciplinamiento Social en la Cantabria Rural del Antiguo Régimen*, Santander 1997.
47 J. S. Cockburn (ed.), *Crime in England 1550–1800*, London 1977, 55.
48 Kamen, *Spain in the Later Seventeenth Century*, 168–9.
49 Comment by Thomas V. Cohen in *Sixteenth Century Journal*, XXVII (1996), reviewing P. Blastenbrei, *Kriminalität in Rom 1560–1585*, Tübingen 1995.
50 Delumeau, *Vie Economique et Sociale de Rome*, II, ch. 1.
51 Xavier Torres, *Nyerros i Cadells: Bàndols i Bandolerisme a la Catalunya Moderna (1590–1640)*, Barcelona 1993.
52 Cited in J. Deleito y Piñuela, *La Mala Vida en la España de Felipe IV*, Madrid 1951.
53 Denise Eeckaute, 'Les brigands en Russie du XVIIe au XIXe siècle: mythe et réalité', *Revue d'Histoire Moderne et Contemporaine*, 12, 1965.
54 W. Monter, 'Heresy executions in Reformation Europe, 1520–65', in Grell and Scribner (eds), *Tolerance and Intolerance in the European Reformation*, 50.
55 Kamen, *Spanish Inquisition*, 205.
56 Cf. Alfred Soman, 'Press, pulpit and censorship in France before Richelieu', *Proceedings, American Philosophical Society*, 120, 1976, 443.
57 Kamen, *Spanish Inquisition*, 260–2.
58 Richard van Dülmen, *Theatre of Horror: Crime and Punishment in Early Modern Germany*, Cambridge 1990.
59 Peter Spierenburg, *The Spectacle of Suffering: Executions and the Evolution of Repression*, Cambridge 1984.

60 Cited in Friedrichs, *City*, 254.
61 J. Sumption, *Pilgrimage: An Image of Medieval Religion*, London 1975, 99.
62 Both cited in Charles Verlinden, *L'Esclavage dans l'Europe Médiévale, Vol. I: Péninsule Ibérique – France*, Bruges 1955.
63 Ridolfo Livi, *La Schiavità Domestica nei Tempi di Mezzo e nei Moderni*, Padua 1928.
64 J. M. Pelorson, 'Reflexions sur le traitement juridique de la folie', in A. Redondo, *Les Problèmes de l'Exclusion en Espagne (XVI–XVIIe Siècles)*, Paris 1983.
65 Martine Bigeard, *La Folie et les Fous Littéraires en Espagne 1500–1650*, Paris 1972.
66 H. C. Erik Midelfort, 'Sin, melancholy, obsession: insanity and culture in 16th-century Germany', in Steven Kaplan (ed.), *Understanding Popular Culture*, Berlin 1984.
67 C. Lis and H. Soly, *Disordered Lives: Eighteenth-Century Families and their Unruly Relatives*, Cambridge 1996.

9 MODERNISATION AND THE INDIVIDUAL

1 Blickle, *The Revolution of 1525*.
2 A. Macfarlane, *The Origins of English Individualism*, Oxford 1978.
3 Cited by Vittor Ivo Comparato, 'A case of modern individualism', in Janet Coleman (ed.), *The Individual in Political Theory and Practice*, Oxford 1996, 153.
4 Lawrence Stone, *The Family, Sex and Marriage in England 1500–1800*, London 1977, 1979, 151.
5 'The early modern period did not see a growth of individualism': Cressy, *Birth, Marriage and Death*, 10.
6 Anderson, 'The relevance of family history', 58–68.
7 A term conceived by Norbert Elias.
8 Michael Zell, 'Suicide in Pre-industrial England', *Social History*, 11, 3, 1986.
9 Michael MacDonald, *Sleepless Souls: Suicide in Early Modern England*, Oxford 1990.
10 Cited in MacDonald, *Sleepless Souls*, 197.
11 Data in Po-Chia Hsia, *Social Discipline in the Reformation*, 163–6, from M. Schär, *Seelennöte der Untertanen: Selbstmord, Melancholie und Religion im Alten Zürick*, Zürich 1985.
12 Cited in Linda Pollock, 'Living on the stage of the world: the concept of privacy among the elite of early modern England', in Adrian Wilson (ed.), *Rethinking Social History: English Society 1570–1920 and its Interpretation*, Manchester 1993.
13 Cf. Garrioch, *Neighbourhood*, 54.
14 Lucien Febvre, *Le Problème de l'Incroyance au XVIe Siècle: La Religion de Rabelais*, Paris 1942.
15 R. Pintard, *Le Libertinage Erudit dans la Première Moitié du XVIIe Siècle*, 2 vols, Paris 1943.
16 R. H. Popkin, *The History of Scepticism from Erasmus to Descartes*, Assen 1964.
17 Frances Yates, *Giordano Bruno and the Hermetic Tradition*, London 1964, ch. 10.
18 Frances Yates, *The Rosicrucian Enlightenment*, London 1972.
19 David Wootton, 'New histories of atheism', in Michael Hunter and David Wootton, *Atheism from the Reformation to the Enlightenment*, Oxford 1992.
20 Cited in Kamen, *Phoenix*, ch. 1, ch. 12.
21 Carlo Ginzburg, *The Cheese and the Worms: The Cosmos of a 16th-century Miller*, Baltimore 1980.
22 J. Tazbir, *A State Without Stakes*, New York 1973, 35.
23 H. Kamen, 'Toleration and the Law in the West 1500–1700', *Ratio Juris*, 10, 1, 1997, 38.
24 Head, *Early Modern Democracy*, 237.
25 John Sommerville, *The Secularization of Early Modern England*, Oxford 1992.
26 An excellent guide is Houston, *Literacy in Early Modern Europe*.
27 Cited Kamen, *Spain in the Later Seventeenth Century*, 311.
28 Houston, *Literacy*, ch. 6.

29 M.-C. Rodríguez and B. Bennassar, 'Signatures et niveau culturel', *Caravelle*, 31, 1978.
30 J. P. Le Flem, on Segovia, in *De l'Alphabétisation aux Circuits du Livre en Espagne, XVI–XIXe Siècles*, Paris 1987.
31 Richard Kagan, *Students and Society in Early Modern Spain*, Baltimore 1974, 213.
32 John Gascoigne, 'A reappraisal of the role of the universities in the Scientific Revolution', in David Lindberg and Robert Westman (eds), *Reappraisals of the Scientific Revolution*, Cambridge 1990.
33 Cf. Hilde de Ridder-Symoens, 'Training and professionalisation', in Reinhard (ed.), *Power Elites and State Building*, 156–72.
34 Cited in Joan Simon, *Education and Society in Tudor England*, Cambridge 1966.
35 Cited in K. Charlton, *Education in Renaissance England*, London 1965.
36 Quoted Charlton, *Education in Renaissance England.*
37 Otto Brunner, *Neue Wege der Sozialgeschichte*, Göttingen 1956.
38 S. Stelling-Michaud (ed.), *Le Livre du Recteur de l'Académie de Genève (1559–1878)*, Geneva 1959.
39 H. Schneppen, *Niederländische Universitäten und Deutsches Geistesleben*, Münster 1960.
40 Cited in Ralph Houlbrooke (ed.), *English Family Life 1576–1716: An Anthology from Diaries*, Oxford 1988, 3.
41 This, at least, is the argument of Jonathan Dewald, *Aristocratic Experience and the Origins of Modern Culture: France 1570–1715*, Berkeley 1993.
42 Cf. James S. Amelang, 'The mental world of Jeroni Pujades', in R. Kagan and G. Parker (eds), *Spain, Europe and the Atlantic World*, Cambridge 1995. The text of the diary is *Dietari de Jeroni Pujades*, ed. J. M. Casas Homs, 4 vols, Barcelona 1975–6.
43 James Amelang, *The Flight of Icarus: Artisan Autobiography in Early Modern Europe*, Stanford 1998, 123.
44 Amelang, *Icarus*, 239–40.
45 Kamen, *Phoenix*, 129–31.
46 E. A. Beller, *Propaganda in Germany during the Thirty Years War*, Princeton 1940.
47 Christian Jouhaud, 'Propagande et action au temps de la Fronde', in *Culture et Idéologie dans la Genèse de l'Etat Moderne*, Rome 1985, 337–52.
48 M. N. Grand-Mesnil, *Mazarin, la Fronde et la Presse 1647–1649*, Paris 1967.
49 Po-Chia Hsia, *Social Discipline in the Reformation*, 94–9, 107–9.
50 Houston, *Literacy*, 232.
51 Kamen, *The Spanish Inquisition*, 114.
52 J. A. Downie, *Robert Harley and the Press: Propaganda and Public Opinion in the Age of Swift and Defoe*, Cambridge 1979.
53 F. E. and F. P. Manuel, *Utopian Thought in the Western World*, Oxford 1979.
54 L. Firpo, *Lo Stato Ideale della Controriforma*, Bari 1957.
55 M. Mörner, *The Political and Economic Activities of the Jesuits in the Plata Region*, Stockholm 1953.
56 M. Yardeni, *Utopie et Révolte sous Louis XIV*, Paris 1980.

10 THE ABSOLUTE STATE

1 Heal and Holmes, *The Gentry in England and Wales*, 117.
2 Alain Boureau, 'Etat moderne et attribution symbolique: emblèmes et devises dans l'Europe des XVIe et XVIIe siècles', in *Culture et Idéologie dans la Genèse de l'Etat Moderne*, Rome 1985, 155–78.
3 Gérard Sabatier, 'Versailles, un imaginaire politique', in *Culture et Idéologie dans la Genèse de l'Etat Moderne*, 295–324.
4 I. A. A. Thompson, 'Absolutism, legalism and the law in Castile 1500–1700', in R. G. Asch and H. Duchhardt (eds), *Der Absolutismus – ein Mythos? Strukturwandel Monarchischer Herrschaft in West- und Mitteleuropa (c.1550–1700)*, Cologne 1996, 220.

SELECT BIBLIOGRAPHY

These entries are intended to supplement those in the notes, although some are cited there too. Items marked with an asterisk contain a recent bibliography covering all Europe.

1 IDENTITIES AND HORIZONS

Identity and community

Fernand Braudel, *The Mediterranean and the Mediterranean World in the Age of Philip II*, 2 vols, London 1972–3.

G. Cabourdin, *Terre et Hommes en Lorraine 1550–1635*, 2 vols, Paris 1977.

C. Cipolla, *Clocks and Culture 1300–1700*, London 1967.

'Famiglia e Comunita', *Quaderni Storici*, 33, Sept–Dec 1976.

Christopher Friedrichs, *The Early Modern City 1450–1750*, London 1995.*

R. Gascon, 'Immigration et croissance au XVIe siècle: l'exemple de Lyon (1529–1563)', *Annales*, XXV, 1970.

Pierre Goubert, *Beauvais et le Beauvaisis de 1600 à 1730*, 2 vols, Paris 1960.

——*The Ancien Regime*, London 1973.

J. P. Gutton, *La Sociabilité Villageoise dans l'Ancienne France: Solidarités et Voisinages du XVIe au XVIIe Siècle*, Paris 1979.

J. Pitt-Rivers, *The People of the Sierra*, Chicago 1971.

David Vassberg, *The Village and the Outside World in Golden Age Castile*, Cambridge 1996.*

Population and the family

Michael Anderson, *Approaches to the History of the Western Family, 1500–1914*, Cambridge 1995.*

A. Croix, *La Bretagne aux XVIe et XVIIe Siècles*, 2 vols, Paris 1980.

Pierre Deyon, *Amiens, Capitale Provinciale*, Paris 1967.

Dix-septième, 'Le XVIIe siècle et la famille', *XVIIe Siècle*, nos 102–3, 1974.

J. L. Flandrin, 'Repression and change in the sexual life of young people', *Journal of Family History*, 2, 1977.

M. W. Flinn, *The European Demographic System 1500–1820*, London 1981.*

D. V. Glass and D. E. C. Eversley (eds), *Population in History*, London 1965.

D. Grigg, *Population Growth and Agrarian Change*, Cambridge 1980.

P. Goubert, 'Family and province: a contribution to our knowledge of family structure in early modern France', *Journal of Family History*, 2, 1977.

R. A. Houston, *The Population History of Britain and Ireland 1500–1750*, Cambridge 1992.*

P. Laslett (ed.), *Household and Family in Past Time*, Cambridge 1972.

R. Burr Litchfield, 'Demographic characteristics of Florentine patrician families', *Journal of Economic History*, 29, 2, 1969.

A. Macfarlane, *The Origins of English Individualism: The Family, Property and Social Transition*, Oxford 1978.

L. de Mause (ed.), *The History of Childhood*, New York 1974.

H. Medick, 'The proto-industrial family economy', *Social History*, 3, 1976.

R. Mols, *Introduction à la Démographie Historique des Villes d'Europe du XIVe au XVIIe Siècle*, 3 vols, Louvain 1955.

L. Stone, *The Family, Sex and Marriage in England 1500–1800*, London 1977.

R. Wheaton, 'Family and kinship in western Europe: the problem of the Joint Family Household', *Journal of Interdisciplinary History*, 5, 4, 1975.

E. A. Wrigley, *Population and History*, London 1969.

E. A. Wrigley and R. S. Schofield, *The Population History of England 1541–1871: A Reconstruction*, London 1981.

Population checks

W. Abel, *Massenarmut und Hungerkrisen im Vorindustriellen Europa*, Hamburg 1974.

A. B. Appleby, *Famine in Tudor and Stuart England*, Stanford 1978.

P. Ariès, *The Hour of Our Death*, London 1981.

B. Bennassar, *Recherches sur les Grands Epidémies dans le Nord de l'Espagne à la Fin du XVIe Siècle*, Paris 1969.

H. Bergues *et al.*, *La Prévention des Naissances dans la Famille*, Paris 1960.

P. Chaunu, *La Mort à Paris, XVIe, XVIIe et XVIIIe Siècles*, Paris 1978.

R. Finlay, *Population and Metropolis: The Demography of London 1580–1640*, Cambridge 1981.

I. Gieysztorowa, 'Guerre et régression en Masovie aux XVIe et XVIIe siècles', *Annales*, 13, 1958.

J. Jacquart, *La Crise Rurale en Ile de France 1550–1670*, Paris 1974.

H. Kamen, 'The social and economic consequences of the Thirty Years War', *Past and Present*, 39, 1968.

E. Keyser, 'Neue deutsche Forschungen über die Geschichte der Pest', *Vierteljahrschrift für Sozial- und Wirtschaftsgeschichte*, 44, 1957.

E. Le Roy Ladurie, *Times of Feast, Times of Famine: A History of Climate since the Year 1000*, London 1972.

F. Lebrun, *Les Hommes et la Mort en Anjou aux XVIIe et XVIIIe Siècles*, Paris 1971.

F. Lebrun, 'Les crises démographiques en France aux XVIIe et XVIIIe siècles', *Annales*, 35, 1980.

G. Parker, 'War and Economic Change: The Economic Costs of the "Dutch Revolt"', in *Spain and the Netherlands 1559–1659*, London 1979.

V. Pérez Moreda, *Las Crisis de Mortalidad en la España Interior, Siglos XVI–XIX*, Madrid 1980.

O. and P. Ranum (eds), *Popular Attitudes towards Birth Control in Pre-industrial England and France*, New York 1972.

P. Slack, 'The disappearance of plague: an alternative view', *Economic History Review*, 34, 1981.

E. Thoen, 'Warfare and the countryside: social and economic aspects of the military destruction in Flanders', *Acta Historica Neerlandica*, 13, 1980.

J. Walter and K. Wrightson, 'Dearth and the social order in early modern England', *Past and Present*, 71, 1976.

C. Webster (ed.), *Health, Medicine and Mortality in the Sixteenth Century*, Cambridge 1979.*

E. A. Wrigley, 'Family limitation in pre-industrial England', *Economic History Review*, 19, 1, 1966.

2 LEISURE, WORK AND MOVEMENT

W. Brulez, 'De diaspora der Antwerpse kooplui op het einde van de 16e eeuw', *Bijdragen voor de Geschiedenis der Nederlanden*, 15, 4, 1960.

P. Clark, 'The migrant in Kentish towns 1580–1640', in P. Clark and P. Slack, *Crisis and Order in English Towns 1500–1700*, London 1972.

A. Paul, 'Les réfugiés Huguenots et Wallons dans le Palatinat du Rhin du XVIe siècle à la Révolution', *Revue Historique*, 157, 1928.

R. van Roosbroeck, *Emigranten: Nederlandse Vluchtlingen in Duitsland (1500–1600)*, Louvain 1968.

W. Sombart, *Der moderne Kapitalismus*, 3 vols in 5 tomes, Munich/Leipzig 1916–27.

L. Stone and A. Everitt, 'Social mobility in England 1500–1700', *Past and Present*, 33, 1966.

3 COMMUNITIES OF BELIEF

J. Bossy, 'The Counter Reformation and the people of Catholic Europe', *Past and Present*, 47, 1970.

Y.-M. Bercé, *Fête et Révolte: Des Mentalités Populaires du XVIe au XVIIIe Siècle*, Paris 1976.

P. Burke, *Popular Culture in Early Modern Europe*, London 1978.*

S. Clark, 'French historians and early modern popular culture', *Past and Present*, 100, 1983.

J. Delumeau, *Catholicism Between Luther and Voltaire*, London 1977.

——*Le Péché et la Peur: La Culpabilisation en Occident, XIIIe–XVIIIe Siècles*, Paris 1983.

C. Ginzburg, *The Cheese and the Worms: The Cosmos of a Sixteenth-century Miller*, London 1980.

Henry Kamen, *The Spanish Inquisition: An Historical Revision*, London 1998.

Keith Luria, *Territories of Grace: Cultural Change in the Seventeenth-century Diocese of Grenoble*, Berkeley 1991.

R. Po-Chia Hsia, *Social Discipline in the Reformation: Central Europe 1550–1750*, London 1989.*

R. Sauzet, *Contre-Réforme et Réforme Catholique en Bas Languedoc: Le Diocèse de Nîmes au XVIIe Siècle*, Brussels 1979.

G. Strauss, 'Success and failure in the German Reformation', *Past and Present*, 67, 1975.

Witchcraft

S. Anglo (ed.), *The Damned Art: Essays in the Literature of Witchcraft*, London 1977.

J. Barry, M. Hester and G. Roberts (eds), *Witchcraft in Early Modern Europe*, Cambridge 1997.

K. Baschwitz, *Hexen und Hexenprozesse*, Munich 1963.

W. Behringer, *Hexen Verfolgung in Bayern: Volksmagie, Glaubenseifer und Staatsräson in der Frühen Neuzeit*, Munich 1987.*

G. Bonomo, *Caccia alle Streghe*, Palermo 1959.

E. Delcambre, *Le Concept de la Sorcellerie dans le Duché de Lorraine au XVIe et XVIIe Siècles*, 3 vols, Nancy 1949–51.

M.-S. Dupont-Bouchat, W. Frijhoff and R. Muchembled, *Prophètes et Sorciers dans les Pays Bas, XVIe–XVIIIe Siècle*, Paris 1978.

R. A. Horsley, 'Who were the witches? The social roles of the accused in the European witch trials', *Journal of Interdisciplinary History*, 9, 4, 1979.

L. Kittredge, *Witchcraft in Old and New England*, New York 1956.

Brian P. Levack, *The Witch-hunt in Early Modern Europe*, 2nd edn, London 1994.*

R. Mandrou, *Magistrats et Sorciers en France au XVIIe Siècle*, Paris 1968.

H. C. Erik Midelfort, *Witchhunting in South-western Germany (1562–1684): The Social and Intellectual Foundations*, Stanford 1972.

W. Monter, *Witchcraft in France and Switzerland: The Borderlands during the Reformation*, Ithaca 1976.

A. Soman, 'The Parlement of Paris and the Great Witch-Hunt (1565–1640)', *Sixteenth Century Journal*, 9, 1978.

R. Zguta, 'Witchcraft trials in seventeenth-century Russia', *American Historical Review*, 82, 1977.

4 THE RULING ELITE

K. Agren, 'Rise and decline of an aristocracy', *Scandinavian Journal of History*, 1, 1–2, 1976.

G. d'Avenel, *La Noblesse Française sous Richelieu*, Paris 1901.

G. Baker, 'Nobilità in declino: il caso di Siena sotto i Medici e gli Asburgo-Lorena', *Rivista Storica Italiana*, 84, 2, 1972.

M. Berengo, *Nobili e Mercanti nella Lucca del Cinquecento*, Turin 1965.

F. Bluche, 'The social origins of the secretaries of state under Louis XIV, 1661–1715', in R. Hatton (ed.), *Louis XIV and Absolutism*, London 1976.

O. Brunner, *Adeliges Landleben und Europäischer Geist*, Salzburg 1949.

——*Neue Wege der Sozialgeschichte*, Göttingen 1956.

Jonathan Dewald, *The European Nobility 1400–1800*, Cambridge 1996.*

A. Domínguez Ortiz, *La Sociedad Española en el Siglo XVII*, Madrid 1963.

W. Dworzaczek, 'La mobilité sociale de la noblesse Polonaise aux XVIe et XVIIe siècles', *Acta Poloniae Historica*, 36, 1977.

M.-C. Gerbet, *La Noblesse dans le Royaume de Castille: Etude sur ses Structures Sociales en Estrémadure de 1454 à 1516*, Paris 1979.

E. F. Guarini (ed.), *Potere e Società negli Stati Regionali Italiani del '500 e '600*, Bologna 1978.

Arlette Jouanna, *Le Devoir de Révolte: La Noblesse Française et la Gestation de l'Etat Moderne 1559–1661*, Paris 1989.*

J. Kowecki, 'Les transformations de la structure sociale en Pologne au XVIIe siècle: la noblesse et la bourgeoisie', *Acta Poloniae Historica*, 26, 1972.

J. P. Labatut, *Les Noblesses Européennes de la Fin du XVe à la Fin du XVIII Siècle*, Paris 1978.*

R. Mazzei, *La Società Lucchese del Seicento*, Lucca 1977.

R. Mousnier, *The Institutions of France under the Absolute Monarchy 1598–1789*, Chicago 1979.

Thomas Munck, *Seventeenth-century Europe 1598–1700*, London 1990.*

Wolfgang Reinhard (ed.), *Power Elites and State Building*, Oxford 1996.*

H. Rosenberg, 'The rise of the Junkers in Brandenburg-Prussia 1410–1653', *American Historical Review*, 49, 1–2, 1943–4.

L. Stone, *The Crisis of the Aristocracy 1558–1641*, Oxford 1965.

P. de Vaissière, *Gentilshommes Campagnards de l'Ancienne France*, Paris 1903.

S. J. Woolf, 'Economic problems of the nobility in the early modern period: the example of Piedmont', *Economic History Review*, 17, 2, 1964.

A. Wyczanski, *Studia nad Folwarkiem Szlacheckim w Polsce w Latach 1500–1580 (Studies on the Noble Estates in Poland 1500–1580)*, Warsaw 1960.

G. Zeller, 'Une notion de caractère historico-social: la dérogeance', *Cahiers Internationaux de Sociologie*, 22, 1957.

G. Zenobi, *Ceti e Potere nella Marca Pontificia. Formazione e Organizzazione della Piccola Nobiltà fra '500 e '700*, Bologna 1976.

5 THE MIDDLE ELITE

J. Amelang, *Honored Citizens of Barcelona: Patrician Culture and Class Relations, 1490–1714*, Princeton 1986.

F. Angiolini and P. Malanima, 'Problemi della mobilità sociale a Firenze tra la metà del cinquecento e i primi decenni del seicento', *Società e Storia*, 4, 1979.

G. Barni, 'Mutamenti di ideali sociali del secolo XVI al secolo XVIII: giuristi, nobiltà, mercatura', *Rivista Internazionale di Filosofia del Diritto*, 1957.

R. Baron, 'La bourgeoisie de Varzy au XVIIe siècle', *Annales de Bourgogne*, 36, 1964.

S. Berner, 'The Florentine patriciate in the transition from republic to principato, 1530–1609', *Studies in Medieval and Renaissance History*, 1972.

P. Burke, *Venice and Amsterdam: A Study of Seventeenth-century Elites*, London 1974.

P. Bushkovich, *The Merchants of Moscow, 1580–1650*, Cambridge 1980.

B. Caizzi, *Il Comasco Sotto il Dominio Spagnolo*, Como 1955.

Peter Clark, *English Provincial Society from the Reformation to the Revolution: Religion, Politics and Society in Kent 1500–1640*, London 1977.

J. T. Cliffe, *The Yorkshire Gentry from the Reformation to the Civil War*, London 1969.

J. Dewald, *The Formation of a Provincial Nobility: The Magistrates of the Parlement of Rouen, 1490–1610*, London 1980.

H. van Dijk and D. J. Roorda, 'Social mobility under the regents of the Republic', *Acta Historica Neerlandica*, 9, 1976.

J. Estèbe, 'La bourgeoisie marchande et la terre à Toulouse au XVIe siècle', *Annales du Midi*, 76, 1964.

C. H. George, 'The making of the English bourgeoisie, 1500–1750', *Science and Society*, 35, 4, 1971.

R. B. Grassby, 'Social status and commercial enterprise under Louis XIV', *Economic History Review*, 13, 1, 1960.

R. Hellie, 'The stratification of Muscovite society: the townsmen', *Russian History*, 5, 2, 1978.

J. Kaufmann-Rochard, *Origines d'une Bourgeoisie Russe, XVIe et XVIIe Siècles*, Paris 1969.

H. P. Liebel, 'The bourgeoisie in southwestern Germany, 1500–1789: a rising class?', *International Review of Social History*, 10, 1965.

F. Mauro, 'La bourgeoisie Portugaise au XVIIe siècle', *XVII Siècle*, 1958.

P. Molas, *La Burguesía Mercantil en la España del Antiguo Régimen*, Madrid 1985.*

R. Mousnier, *La Vénalité des Offices sous Henri IV et Louis XIII*, Rouen 1946.

R. Mousnier, 'L'opposition politique bourgeoise à la fin du XVIe siècle et au début du XVIIe siècle', *Revue Historique*, 212, 1955.

D. J. Roorda, 'The ruling classes in Holland in the 17th century', in J. Bromley and E. Kossmann (eds), *Britain and the Netherlands*, vol. 2, Groningen 1962.

Winfried Schulze (ed.), *Ständische Gesellschaft und Soziale Mobilität*, Munich 1988.

L. Stone, 'Social mobility in England, 1500–1700', *Past and Present*, 33, 1966.

K. W. Swart, *Sale of Offices in the Seventeenth Century*, The Hague 1949.

H. R. Trevor-Roper, 'The gentry', *Economic History Review*, supplement, 1953.

M. Venard, *Bourgeois et Paysans au XVIIe Siècle*, Paris 1958.

Keith Wrightson, *English Society 1580–1680*, London 1982.

6 SOLIDARITIES AND RESISTANCE

W. Abel, *Agricultural Fluctuations in Europe from the Thirteenth to the Twentieth Centuries*, London 1980.

K. Blaschke, 'Das Bauernlegen in Sachsen', *Vierteljahrschrift für Sozial- und Wirtschaftsgeschichte*, 42, 1955.

Peter Blickle (ed.), *Resistance, Representation and Community*, Oxford 1997.*

G. Delille, *Croissance d'une Société Rurale: Montesarchio et la Vallée Caudine aux XVIIe et XVIIIe Siècles*, Naples 1973.

G. Duby and A. Wallon (eds), *Histoire de la France Rurale, vol. 2: L'Age Classique des Paysans, 1340–1789*, Paris 1975.

C. d'Eszlary, 'La situation des serfs en Hongrie de 1514 à 1848', *Revue d'Histoire Economique et Sociale*, 4, 1960.

G. Franz (ed.), *Bauernschaft und Bauerstand 1500–1970*, Limburg 1975.

C. J. Fuchs, *Der Untergang des Bauernstandes und das Aufkornmen der Gutsherrschaften in Neuvorpommern und Rügen*, Strasbourg 1888.

P. Goubert, *La Vie Quotidienne des Paysans Français au XVIIe Siècle*, Paris 1982.

W. G. Hoskins, *The Midland Peasant*, London 1957.

W. Kula, *An Economic Theory of the Feudal System: Towards a Model of the Polish Economy 1500–1800*, London 1976.

E. Le Roy Ladurie, *The Peasants of Languedoc* (abbreviated edn), Chicago 1974.

A. Lepre, *Feudi e Masserie: Problemi della Società Meridionale nel '600 nel '700*, Naples 1973.

F. Lütge, *Geschichte der deutschen Agrarverfassung vom Frühen Mittelalter bis zum 19. Jahrhundert*, Stuttgart 1963.

F. McArdle, *Altopascio: A Study in Tuscan Rural Society, 1587–1784*, Cambridge 1978.

L. Makkai, 'Neo-serfdom: its origin and nature in east central Europe', *Slavic Review*, 34, June 1975.

A. Mika, 'Feudalni velkostatek v jiznich Cechach, XIV–XVII stol. (The great feudal estates in southern Bohemia)', *Historicky Sbornik*, 1, 1973.

T. Munck, 'The economic and social position of peasant freeholders in late seventeenth-century Denmark', *Scandinavian Economic History Review*, 25, 2, 1977.

Zs. Pach, *Die Ungarische Agrarentwicklung im 16–17 Jahrhundert*, Budapest 1964.

N. J. G. Pounds, *An Historical Geography of Europe, 1500–1840*, Cambridge 1979.*

P. Raveau, *L'Agriculture et les Classes Paysannes dans le Haut Poitou au XVIe Siècle*, Paris 1926.

D. Saalfeld, *Bauernwirtschaft und Gutsbetrieb in der Vorindustriellen Zeit*, Stuttgart 1960.

N. Salomon, *La Campagne de Nouvelle Castille à la Fin du XVIe Siècle*, Paris 1964.

T. Shanin, 'The nature and logic of the peasant economy', *Journal of Peasant Studies*, 1, 1973.

S. O. Shmidt, 'Kizucheniyu agrarnoy istorii Rossii XVI veka (Research into the agrarian history of sixteenth-century Russia)', *Voprosi Istorii*, 5, 1968.

S. D. Skazkin, 'Osnovnie problemi tak nazivaemogo vtorogo isdaniya krepostnichestva v sredney i vostochnnoy Evrope (Basic problems of the 'second serfdom' in central and eastern Europe)', *Voprosi Istorii*, 2, 1958.

B. H. Slicher van Bath, *The Agrarian History of Western Europe AD 500–1850*, London 1963.*

R. E. F. Smith, *The Enserfment of the Russian Peasantry*, Cambridge 1968.

M. Spufford, *Contrasting Communities: English Villagers in the Sixteenth and Seventeenth Centuries*, Cambridge 1974.

R. H. Tawney, *The Agrarian Problem in the Sixteenth Century*, London 1912.

J. Topolski, 'The manorial serf economy in central and eastern Europe in the 16th and 17th centuries', *Agricultural History*, 48, 3, 1974.

D. E. Vassberg, *Land and Society in Golden Age Castile*, Cambridge 1984.

J. de Vries, *The Dutch Rural Economy in the Golden Age, 1500–1700*, New Haven 1974.

H. U. Wachter, *Ostpreussische Domänenvorwerke im 16. und 17. Jahrhundert*, Würzburg 1958.

H. van der Wee and E. van Cauwenherghe (eds), *Productivity of Land and Agricultural Innovation in the Low Countries (1250–1800)*, Louvain 1978.

K. Wrightson, 'Aspects of social differentiation in rural England, *c.* 1580–1660', *Journal of Peasant Studies*, 5, 1977.

K. Wrightson and D. Levine, *Poverty and Piety in an English Village: Terling 1525–1700*, London 1979.

Resistance

P. Barbier and F. Vernillat, *Histoire de France par les Chansons*, 8 vols, Paris 1956.

Y.-M. Bercé, *Croquants et Nu-Pieds: Les Soulèvements Paysans en France du XVIe au XIXe Siècle*, Paris 1974.

Y.-M. Bercé, *Revolt and Revolution in Early Modern Europe*, Manchester 1987.*

K. V. Chistov, *Russkie Narodnie Sotsialno-utopicheskie Legendy XVII–XIXvv (Popular Socio-utopian Legends of 17th–19th Century Russia)*, Moscow 1967.

P. Clark, 'Popular protest and disturbance in Kent 1558–1640', *Economic History Review*, 29, 1976.

C. S. L. Davies, 'Peasant revolt in France and England: a comparison', *Agricultural History Review*, 21, 2, 1973.

P. Goubert, *The French Peasantry in the Seventeenth Century*, Cambridge 1986.

R. Mousnier, *Peasant Uprisings in 17th Century France, Russia and China*, London 1971.

B. Porshnev, *Les Soulèvements Populaires en France 1613–1648*, Paris 1963.

W. Schulze, *Bäuerliche Widerstand und Feudale Herrschaft in der Frühen Neuzeit*, Stuttgart 1980.

——(ed.), *Europäische Bauernrevolten der Frühen Neuzeit*, Frankfurt 1982.

——(ed.), *Aufstände, Revolten, Prozesse*, Stuttgart 1983.

B. Sharp, *In Contempt of all Authority; Rural Artisans and Riot in the West of England, 1586–1660*, Berkeley 1980.

7 GENDER ROLES

Jean Brink, A. P. Coudert and M. C. Horowitz (eds), *The Politics of Gender in Early Modern Europe*, vol. XII, Sixteenth Century Essays and Studies, Kirksville 1989.

N. Z. Davis, *Society and Culture in Early Modern France*, Cambridge 1987.

N. Z. Davis and A. Farge (eds), *A History of Women in the West, III: Renaissance and Enlightenment Paradoxes*, Cambridge MA 1993.*

Anthony Fletcher, *Gender, Sex and Subordination in England 1500–1800*, Yale 1995.

L. Frey, M. Frey and J. Schneider, *Women in Western European History: A Select Bibliography from Antiquity to the French Revolution*, Brighton 1982, supplement 1986.*

Wendy Gibson, *Women in Seventeenth-century France*, London 1989.

J. Goody, *The Development of the Family and Marriage in Europe*, Cambridge 1983.

J. Goody, J. Thirsk and E. P. Thompson (eds), *Family and Inheritance: Rural Society in Western Europe, 1200–1800*, Cambridge 1976.

Olwen Hufton, *The Prospect Before Her: A History of Women in Western Europe, vol. I: 1500–1800*, London 1997.*

H. Medick and D. Sabean (eds), *Interest and Emotion: Essays on the Study of Family and Kinship*, Cambridge 1984.

M. Mitterauer and R. Sieder, *The European Family: Patriarchy and Partnership from the Middle Ages to the Present*, Chicago 1982.

T. Max Safley, *Let No Man Put Asunder: The Control of Marriage in the German Southwest*, Kirksville 1984.

R. Wheaton and T. K. Hareven (eds), *Family and Sexuality in French History*, Philadelphia 1980.

Merry E. Wiesner, *Women and Gender in Early Modern Europe*, Cambridge 1993.*

8 SOCIAL DISCIPLINE AND MARGINALITY

Wilhelm Abel, *Massenarmut und Hungerkrisen im Vorindustriellen Europa*, Hamburg 1974.

J. L. Alonso Hernández, *El Lenguaje de los Maleantes Españoles de los Siglos XVI y XVII: La Germanía*, Salamanca 1979.

A. L. Beier, 'Vagrants and the social order in Elizabethan England', *Past and Present*, 64, 1974.

—— 'Social problems in Elizabethan London', *Journal of Interdisciplinary History*, 9, 2, 1978.

B. Bennassar, 'Economie et société à Ségovie au milieu du XVIe siècle', *Anuario de Historia Económica y Social*, 2, 1, 1968.

P. Bonenfant, *Le Problème du Paupérisme en Belgique à la Fin de l'Ancien Régime*, Brussels 1934.

P. Camporesi (ed.), *Il Libro dei Vagabondi*, Turin 1973.

P. Clark and P. Slack, *Crisis and Order in English Towns 1500–1700*, London 1972.

D. B. Davis, *The Problem of Slavery in Western Culture*, Ithaca 1966.

P. Deyon, 'A propos du paupérisme au milieu du XVIIe siècle', *Annales*, 1967.

A. Domínguez Ortiz, 'La esclavitud en Castilla durante la edad moderna', *Estudios de Historia Social de España*, 2, 1952.

C. C. Fairchilds, *Poverty and Charity in Aix-en-Provence, 1640–1789*, Baltimore 1976.

B. Geremek, 'La popolazione marginale tra il medioevo e l'era moderna', *Studi Storici*, 9, 3–4, 1968.

—— 'Criminalité, vagabondage, paupérisme: la marginalité à l'aube des temps modernes', *Revue d'Histoire Moderne et Contemporaine*, 21, 1974.

J. P. Gutton, *La Société et les Pauvres: L'Exemple de la Généralité de Lyon, 1564–1789*, Paris 1971.

——*La Société et les Pauvres en Europe (XVIe–XVIIIe Siècles)*, Paris 1974.*

R. Hellie, *Slavery in Russia, 1450–1725*, Chicago 1982.

O. Hufton, *The Poor of Eighteenth-Century France 1750–1789*, Oxford 1974.

M. Jiménez Salas, *Historia de la Asistencia Social en España en la Edad Moderna*, Madrid 1958.

W. K. Jordan, *Philanthropy in England 1480–1660*, London 1959.

Robert Jütte, *Poverty and Deviance in Early Modern Europe*, Cambridge 1994.*

H. Kamen, 'Public authority and popular crime: banditry in Valencia 1660–1714', *Journal of European Economic History*, 3, 1974.

J. L. H. Keep, 'Bandits and the law in Muscovy', *Slavonic and East European Review*, 35, 1956–7.

W. Kuhn, *Geschichte der Deutsche Ostsiedlung in der Neuzeit*, vol. I, Cologne 1955.

B. Leblon, *Les Gitans d'Espagne: Recherches sur les Divers Aspects du Problème Gitan du XVe au XVIIIe Siècle*, 3 vols, Montpellier 1976.

E. M. Leonard, *The Early History of English Poor Relief*, Cambridge 1900.

C. Lis and H. Soly, *Poverty and Capitalism in Pre-industrial Europe*, London 1979.*

R. Mitchison and L. Leneman, *Sexuality and Social Control: Scotland 1660–1780*, Oxford 1989.

Kathryn Norberg, *Rich and Poor in Grenoble 1600–1814*, Berkeley 1985.

C. Paultre, *La Repression de la Mendicité et du Vagabondage en France sous l'Ancien Régime*, Paris 1906.

I. Pinchbeck and M. Hewitt, *Children in English Society, vol. I: From Tudor Times to the Eighteenth Century*, London 1969.

B. Pullan, 'Catholics and the poor in early modern Europe', *Transactions of the Royal Historical Society*, 26, 1976.

J. Samaha, *Law and Order in Historical Perspective: The Case of Elizabethan Essex*, London 1974.

A. C. and C. M. Saunders, *A Social History of Black Slaves and Freedmen in Portugal 1441–1555*, Cambridge 1982.

P. Slack, 'Vagrants and vagrancy in England, 1598–1664', *Economic History Review*, 27, 1974.

C. Verlinden, *L'Esclavage dans l'Europe Mediévale, vol. I: Péninsule Ibérique/France*, Bruges 1955.

L. P. Wandel, *Always Among Us: Images of the Poor in Zwingli's Zurich*, Cambridge 1990.

9 MODERNISATION AND THE INDIVIDUAL

M. L. Berneri, *Journey through Utopia*, London 1950.

J.-R. Charbonnel, *La Pensée Italienne au XVIe Siècle et le Courant Libertin*, Paris 1919.

R. Chartier, D. Julia and M. M. Compere, *L'Education en France du XVIe au XVIIIe Siècle*, Paris 1976.

M. Chrisman, 'From polemic to propaganda: the development of mass persuasion in the late sixteenth century', *Archiv für Reformationsgeschichte*, 73, 1982.

D. Cressy, *Literacy and the Social Order: Reading and Writing in Tudor and Stuart England*, Cambridge 1980.

E. L. Eisenstein, *The Printing Press as an Agent of Change*, 2 vols, Cambridge 1979.

J. Frank, *The Beginnings of the English Newspaper 1620–60*, Cambridge MA 1961.

H. F. Kearney, *Scholars and Gentlemen: Universities and Society in Pre-industrial Britain, 1500–1700*, London 1970.

J. Klaits, *Printed Propaganda under Louis XIV: Absolute Monarchy and Public Opinion*, Princeton 1976.

H.-J. Martin, *Livre, Pouvoirs et Société à Paris au XVIIe Siècle (1598–1701)*, 2 vols, Geneva 1969.

R. O'Day, *Education and Society 1500–1800: The Social Foundations of Education in Early Modern Britain*, London 1982.

R. Ruyer, *L'Utopie et les Utopies*, Paris 1950.

K. Schottenloher, *Bücher Bewegten die Welt*, 2 vols, Stuttgart 1951–2.

G. Spini, *Ricerca dei Libertini*, Rome 1950.

L. Stone, 'The educational revolution in England 1560–1640', *Past and Present*, 28, 1964.

——(ed.) *The University in Society, vol. I: Oxford and Cambridge from the Fourteenth to the Early Nineteenth Century*, Oxford 1975.

10 THE ABSOLUTE STATE

T. M. Barker, 'Military entrepreneurship and absolutism: Habsburg models', *Journal of European Studies*, 4, 1, 1974.

R. Bonney, 'The French Civil War 1649–53', *European Studies Review*, 8, 1978.

D. C. Coleman (ed.), *Revisions in Mercantilism*, London 1969.

J. P. Cooper, 'Differences between English and continental governments in the early seventeenth century', in J. S. Bromley and E. H. Kossman (eds), *Britain and the Netherlands*, London 1960.

J. Daly, 'The idea of absolute monarchy in seventeenth-century England', *Historical Journal*, 21, 2, 1978.

M. Fulbrook, 'The English Revolution and the revisionist revolt', *Social History*, 7, 3, 1982.

R. Hatton, *Louis XIV and Absolutism*, London 1976.

J. Morrill, *The Revolt of the Provinces: Conservatives and Radicals in the English Civil War 1630–1650*, London 1976.

D. Parker, *The Social Foundations of French Absolutism*, London 1983.

T. K. Rabb, *The Struggle for Stability in Early Modern Europe*, New York 1975.

M. Roberts, 'Queen Christina and the general crisis of the seventeenth century', *Past and Present*, 22, 1962.

H. H. Rowen, 'The revolution that wasn't: the coup d'état of 1650 in Holland', *European Studies Review*, 4, 1974.

INDEX